New Security Challenges Series

General Editor: **Stuart Croft**, Professor of
of Politics and International Studies at the University of Warwick, UK, and
Director of the ESRC's New Security Challenges Programme.

The last decade demonstrated that threats to security vary greatly in their causes
and manifestations, and that they invite interest and demand responses from
the social sciences, civil society and a very broad policy community. In the past,
the avoidance of war was the primary objective, but with the end of the Cold
War the retention of military defence as the centrepiece of the international
security agenda became untenable. There has been, therefore, a significant shift
in emphasis away from traditional approaches to security to a new agenda that
talks of the softer side of security, in terms of human security, economic security
and environmental security. The topical *New Security Challenges series* reflects this
pressing political and research agenda.

Titles include:

Natasha Underhill
COUNTERING GLOBAL TERRORISM AND INSURGENCY
Calculating the Risk of State-Failure in Afghanistan, Pakistan and Iraq

Abdul Haqq Baker
EXTREMISTS IN OUR MIDST
Confronting Terror

Robin Cameron
SUBJECTS OF SECURITY
Domestic Effects of Foreign Policy in the War on Terror

Sharyl Cross, Savo Kentera, R. Craig Nation and Radovan Vukadinovic (*editors*)
SHAPING SOUTH EAST EUROPE'S SECURITY COMMUNITY FOR THE TWENTY-
FIRST CENTURY
Trust, Partnership, Integration

Tom Dyson and Theodore Konstadinides
EUROPEAN DEFENCE COOPERATION IN EU LAW AND IR THEORY

Håkan Edström, Janne Haaland Matlary and Magnus Petersson (*editors*)
NATO: THE POWER OF PARTNERSHIPS

Håkan Edström and Dennis Gyllensporre
POLITICAL ASPIRATIONS AND PERILS OF SECURITY
Unpacking the Military Strategy of the United Nations

Hakan Edström and Dennis Gyllensporre (*editors*)
PURSUING STRATEGY
NATO Operations from the Gulf War to Gaddafi

Hamed El-Said
NEW APPROACHES TO COUNTERING TERRORISM
Designing and Evaluating Counter Radicalization and De-Radicalization Programs

Philip Everts and Pierangelo Isernia
PUBLIC OPINION, TRANSATLANTIC RELATIONS AND THE USE OF FORCE

Adrian Gallagher
GENOCIDE AND ITS THREAT TO CONTEMPORARY INTERNATIONAL ORDER

Kevin Gillan, Jenny Pickerill and Frank Webster
ANTI-WAR ACTIVISM
New Media and Protest in the Information Age

James Gow and Ivan Zverzhanovski
SECURITY, DEMOCRACY AND WAR CRIMES
Security Sector Transformation in Serbia

Toni Haastrup
CHARTING TRANSFORMATION THROUGH SECURITY
Contemporary EU–Africa Relations

Ellen Hallams, Luca Ratti and Ben Zyla (editors)
NATO BEYOND 9/11

Carolin Hilpert
STRATEGIC CULTURAL CHANGE AND THE CHALLENGE FOR SECURITY POLICY
Germany and the Bundeswehr's Deployment to Afghanistan

Christopher Hobbs, Matthew Moran and Daniel Salisbury (editors)
OPEN SOURCE INTELLIGENCE IN THE TWENTY-FIRST CENTURY
New Approaches and Opportunities

Paul Jackson and Peter Albrecht
RECONSTRUCTION SECURITY AFTER CONFLICT
Security Sector Reform in Sierra Leone

Janne Haaland Matlary
EUROPEAN UNION SECURITY DYNAMICS
In the New National Interest

Sebastian Mayer (editor)
NATO's POST–COLD WAR POLITICS
The Changing Provision of Security

Kevork Oskanian
FEAR, WEAKNESS AND POWER IN THE POST-SOVIET SOUTH CAUCASUS
A Theoretical and Empirical Analysis

Michael Pugh, Neil Cooper and Mandy Turner (editors)
WHOSE PEACE?
Critical Perspectives on the Political Economy of Peacebuilding

Nathan Roger
IMAGE WARFARE IN THE WAR ON TERROR

Aglaya Snetkov and Stephen Aris
THE REGIONAL DIMENSIONS TO SECURITY
Other Sides of Afghanistan

Holger Stritzel
SECURITY IN TRANSLATION
Securitization Theory and the Localization of Threat

Ali Tekin and Paul Andrew Williams
GEO-POLITICS OF THE EURO-ASIA ENERGY NEXUS

New Approaches to Countering Terrorism

Designing and Evaluating Counter Radicalization and De-Radicalization Programs

Hamed El-Said

Chair & Professor in International Business and Political Economy, Manchester Metropolitan University, UK

First published 2015 by
PALGRAVE MACMILLAN

Palgrave Macmillan in the UK is an imprint of Macmillan Publishers Limited, registered in England, company number 785998, of Houndmills, Basingstoke, Hampshire RG21 6XS.

Palgrave Macmillan in the US is a division of St Martin's Press LLC, 175 Fifth Avenue, New York, NY 10010.

Palgrave Macmillan is the global academic imprint of the above companies and has companies and representatives throughout the world.

Palgrave® and Macmillan® are registered trademarks in the United States, the United Kingdom, Europe and other countries.

ISBN: 978–1–137–44996–2 hardback
ISBN: 978–1–137–48002–6 paperback

This book is printed on paper suitable for recycling and made from fully managed and sustained forest sources. Logging, pulping and manufacturing processes are expected to conform to the environmental regulations of the country of origin.

A catalogue record for this book is available from the British Library.

A catalog record for this book is available from the Library of Congress.

Contents

List of Illustrations   vi

1   Introduction   1
2   Counter-de-Rad: Setting the Framework   13
3   Radicalization in a Western Context: The Case of Australia   53
4   Counter Radicalization and De-radicalization in
    Western Democracies: The Case of Australia   76
5   Mauritania: From Toleration to Violent Islam   96
6   Singapore: Crisis of Identity, Shared Values and
    Religious Rehabilitation   138
7   Sudan: De-radicalization and Counter Radicalization in a
    Radicalizing Environment   174
8   From Militarization to Democratization:
    The Transformation of Turkey's Counter Terrorism
    Strategy (CTS)   218
9   Concluding Remarks   254

Notes   265

Bibliography   280

Index   295

List of Illustrations

Box

2.1 A selection of the more commonly identified elements
of IFCVE   48

Figures

7.1 Military operations carried out by participants   215
7.2 Age group of participants in the Sudanese
de-radicalization program   216
7.3 The educational level of participants in the
Sudanese de-radicalization program   216
7.4 The level of radicalization and contribution to jihadi
activities of the participants   217

Table

7.1 Classification of individuals according to groups,
ideology, area of operations and targets   217

1
Introduction

Rehabilitating radicals

Organized terrorism remains a major threat facing many communities of the world. Despite the fact that more than a decade has passed since 9/11, which instigated a long and ongoing first-world 'war on terror', there are no signs that terrorism is receding. On the contrary, the most recent developments not only suggest that terrorism remains a large problem, but that it will be so for some time to come. For example, Christopher Stevens, the former American Ambassador in Libya, along with three other American diplomats, was brutally assassinated in September 2012 by a radical Libyan salafist group, some of whom were allegedly disengaged under a de-radicalization program initiated and supervised personally by Saif Dine al-Islam. In Arab countries that have recently experienced a regime change as a result of the outbreak of the Arab Spring almost two years ago (Libya, Tunisia, Yemen and Egypt), this has been associated with the rise of radical salafist movements in these countries. The outbreak of fighting in Syria has apparently attracted thousands of Ansar radical fighters (an offspring of al-Qaeda) to the country who are now dominating the core fighting units of the so-called 'Free Syrian Army'. The war in Syria has also attracted several hundred Muslim citizens living in Western democratic states, such as Australia. After ten years of occupation and the loss of its once powerful regime, Iraq is witnessing a constant increase in violence. In Afghanistan, the 'war on terror' shows no signs of waning, with the Taliban fighters demonstrating strong determination not only to oust NATO forces from their country, but also to restore their lost political power at any price. They continue to provide logistical, financial and operational support to their Pakistani Taliban partner, which

1

has destabilized and divided Pakistan itself, through the paralysis of its political and economic systems, and cost the country more than $20 billion in economic losses and more than 35,000 human lives. In Western Africa, extreme right and fundamentalist salafist movements are also on the rise, encouraged by the weakness and corruptibility of Western African states and their absent developmental capacities which bred and continue to breed massive inequities, considerable unemployment and unsustainable poverty. In Somalia, the al-Shabab radical group remains influential and threatening both to the stability of the country and the region as a whole. Pirates continue to use Somali territory as a safe haven to threaten international maritime trade. In Nigeria, new militant Islamist groups have emerged, such as the Boko Haram and Ansaru Islam, which are considered today the most 'formidable threat' to the interests of the United States and other Western states in the region (Chothia, 2013. On salafism in the Arab world, see Zelin, 2013; Trager, 2013). The recent launching of military operations by the French government in Mali is a testimony to the rising influence of the fundamentalist-right salafist movements in Western Africa.

The above-cited events and developments will have far-reaching regional and global ramifications, although the full extent of these implications is difficult to predict at the present time. The immediate regional implication of the French military operations in Mali, for example, was the attacks against Algeria's main gas field in January 2013 and the ensuing hostage crisis that claimed the lives of more than 80 individuals, including several Westerners, in a dawn raid in retaliation for France's intervention in Mali and the Algerian government's support for that intervention. While the jury decides the full implications of the aforementioned recent developments, one thing is clear: terrorism's days are not numbered and the death of Osama Bin Laden, the former leader of al-Qaeda, has not ushered in a new era of peace and stability, one in which the threat from terrorism no longer exists.

On the other hand, there is a growing consensus among observers of all political stripes that the fight against radicalism and its offspring, violent extremism, has been mismanaged and mishandled. Even long before the 9/11 attacks of 2001 against the twin towers of the World Trade Center in lower Manhattan and the Pentagon, many scholars and academics were already criticizing the prevailing kinetic approach to countering the phenomenon of terrorism, referred to hereafter as Violent Extremism (VEm). Those critics have long called for a broader and more balanced approach, one which will rely more on, and incorporate larger aspects of, 'soft' or 'smart' policies as an integral part of the counterterrorism tool kit used by state officials, security enforcement, practitioners and wider communities involved in countering VEm (Schmidt, 2000; Angell and Gunaratna, 2011). As the 'war on terror' dragged on longer than expected, voices against the prevailing kinetic response to VEm grew louder, sharper and broader. The fiercest attack from a high-ranking Western official came from the former British Foreign Minister, David Miliband. In 2009, Mr Miliband publicly stated that we were 'wrong' in our approach to the phenomenon of VEm and that the notion of a 'war on terror' has not only delayed the fight against terrorism, but has also 'caused more harm than good'.

Criticism of a kinetic approach to countering VEm has also come from the Afghani leader, Hamid Karzai, who sturdily and unremittingly disparaged increased reliance on drone attacks by the United States, which killed many innocent people in Afghanistan and elsewhere, as a key counterterrorism tactic. He also criticized the alleged US torture of Afghani detainees, and, in March 2013, called upon the US government 'to put in Afghan control...the Bagram Jail, 50 kilometres north of Kabul...within days' (*The Nation*, 2013). In Yemen, drone attacks have not only killed a large number of innocent bystanders, but have also undermined the informal approach to countering radicalization which the Yemeni government began implementing after 2008. This approach relied heavily on mediation between state officials and their relatives and family members in al-Qaeda to convince the latter to repent (El-Said and Harrigan, 2012). Following the end of the military operations launched by the Pakistani armed forces in late 2007 to tackle militants in the Swat Valley region, the Pakistani armed forces launched an ambitious de-radicalization and counter-radicalization program there. This included a population census to list the names of all inhabitants of the Valley, encouraging community and tribal leaders to play a bigger role in countering violent ideology and activism in the area, and providing some educational and health facilities to the inhabitants of the region. The program also included special debates and a religious rehabilitation program for the hundreds of youths radicalized and recruited by the Pakistani Taliban and arrested by the Pakistani armed forces during and after the military operations in the Valley. As in Yemen, 'The program was destroyed by the American drone attacks, which demolished the confidence we built with the inhabitants of the Valley who now believe that we were conspiring with the Americans against them'.[1]

In other words, the kinetic response served to undermine the 'public perceptions of government' and its ability not only to address the threat properly and appropriately, but also to secure its citizens (CGCC, 2012). It neither inspired confidence in the ability of the state to undermine the threat nor stemmed the support for violent extremists. A kinetic approach, which included the invasion of two Muslim states (Afghanistan and Iraq) and drone attacks against another half-dozen were seen as unjust and thereby damaging to social cohesion and social harmony. They also delayed resorting to alternative approaches and paid little attention to the 'the process of radicalisation' (ICSR, 2010, p.8), treated terrorism as an event rather than a process, and as such ignored conditions conducive to radicalization and extremism that lead to terrorism. Equally important, the kinetic approach neglected the fact that this wave of terrorism differs from its predecessors in many ways, including in its brutality, complexity, suddenness and ideology. With regard to the latter, despite the fact that religion is not the essence, the current wave of VEm derives a great deal of its justification for violence from a misunderstood and narrowly applied religious scripture, a fact that makes it politically incompetent and religiously illegitimate (El-Said, 2013).

It is for all of the above reasons that the war on terror has become 'wrong', 'inappropriate' and 'caused more harm than good'. Treating radicalization as a process requires a completely different approach, one where the overriding objective is to win the 'hearts and minds' of communities most vulnerable to radicalization and VEm. This approach should both understand and refute the ideology of VEm to successfully deal with conditions conducive to radicalization and extremism that lead to terrorism. As the Rand Corporation (2006, p.1132) argued, what is really needed is 'Waging the War of Ideas', not 'the war on terror' to defeat radicalization and VEm.

Increased public and official dissatisfaction with purely kinetic approaches to VEm has been associated with, and has perhaps led to, the emergence of 'new and innovative approaches to counter-terrorism' (Horgan and Braddock, 2010, p.1). These 'new and innovative approaches', to be sure, first emerged and were implemented in some Muslim-majority states, particularly in countries like Egypt, Yemen, Indonesia and Saudi Arabia, before migrating to countries like Malaysia and Singapore (El-Said and Harrigan, 2012). More recently, some Western democratic states have also flirted with these 'innovative approaches' and attempted to implement some or a large proportion of them. Examples include the United Kingdom, the Netherlands, Germany, Belgium, Norway and Australia. British, European, American and Australian officials flocked to Riyadh, Yemen, Jakarta and Kuala Lumpur to study these programs and learn about their effectiveness. They have also invited officials from those countries to their capitals to educate their own officials about counter-radicalization and de-radicalization (Counter-de-Rad) programs and verify their potential applicability in and adaptability to Western contexts. As Vidino and Brandon (2012, p.1) noted: 'Since the mid-2000s, several European countries have developed comprehensive counter-radicalization strategies seeking to de-radicalize or disengage committed militants and, with even greater intensity, prevent the radicalization of new ones'. Within this context, the United Kingdom, the Netherlands, Norway and Denmark have carried out 'the most extensive counter-radicalization initiatives' (Ibid).

Goals and objectives of the book

Despite their popularity and increasing fame, Counter-de-Rad programs remain largely 'under-researched' (Bhui, Hicks, Lashley and Jones, 2012, p.2), 'not fully understood' (Bhui, Dinos and Jones, 2012, p.2) and 'the exception worldwide... not the norm' (Angell and Gunaratana, 2011, p.448). Horgan and Braddock (2010, p.267) are in agreement: 'despite their popularity, data surrounding even the most basic of facts about these programs remains limited'.

Several Counter-de-Rad programs have been extensively studied over the past few years. El-Said and Harrigan (2012), for example, have studied such programs in eight Muslim-majority states: Algeria, Bangladesh, Egypt, Malaysia, Morocco, Jordan, Saudi Arabia and Yemen. Horgan and Braddock (2010) have also, very briefly, studied some of same programs, particularly in Saudi Arabia and Yemen, as well as in Northern Ireland, Colombia and Indonesia. Omar Ashour (2009) focused on two countries' de-radicalization processes: Algeria and Egypt. Finally, Lorenzo Vidino and James Brandon (2012) have also very recently studied counter-radicalization programs in four European countries: the United Kingdom, Norway, Denmark and the Netherlands. Apart from several duplications and overlapping in terms of programs studied, the total number of studied Counter-de-Rad programs so far remains small, no more than 14 or 15 out of at least 35 or 40 programs that have been implemented or are currently being implemented worldwide (El-Said and Barrett, 2011).

Apart from El-Said and Harrigan's work (2012), most of the above-mentioned studies sought to describe the key components of Counter-de-Rad programs (Vidino and Brandon, 2012), factors behind the de-radicalization of large violent extremist (VEt) organizations (Ashour, 2009), or to investigate 'critical issues surrounding assessment of their effectiveness and outcomes' (Horgan and Braddock, 2010, p.1). None, with the exception of El-Said and Harrigan (2012), really looked at the process of radicalization itself, why and how individuals are recruited from populations vulnerable to VEm, and why most recruited individuals, particularly in Western contexts, come from certain groups or communities. Other studies, like Sageman (2008) and Krueger and Maleckova (2002), for example, took an individual approach, profiling the demographics of individual terrorists or suicide bombers and generalizing from their work that 'poverty does not cause terrorism'. Here, too, the process of radicalization has been neglected and we were told little about the population from whence those individuals came, were recruited and radicalized. As Bhui, Dinos and Jones (2012, p.1) noted: 'Studies of terrorism have focused on those identified as engaged with terrorist organisations or convicted of terrorism crimes, with little attention given to populations that are vulnerable to recruitment to terrorist action.'

Finally, no study has so far developed any form of framework through which Counter-de-Rad programs can be studied, understood and even effectively designed and implemented. Angell and Gunaratana (2011, p.348) rightly argued that 'there has been very little effort to examine the concepts, processes, and outcomes of terrorist rehabilitation', let alone to develop a framework to facilitate their comprehension and implementation. Horgan and Braddock (2010, p.269) concur; studies of terrorism, they concluded, lack 'a framework for guiding the development of future such initiatives that draw lessons from existing programs (effective or otherwise)'.

This book fills an important gap in the literature. It analyses and evaluates Counter-de-Rad programs in six United Nations Member States in a way that follows up and builds on our earlier work in 2012 (El-Said and Harrigan), or Volume I of this larger project. It differs from Volume I in many ways too.

First, while Volume I focused completely on (eight) Muslim-majority states. This Volume (II) is more diversified. It integrates and analyses Counter-de-Rad programs in both Muslim-majority and Muslim-minority states. Four Muslim-majority states (Mauritania, Sudan, Turkey and Pakistan) and two Muslim-minority states (Australia and Singapore) are discussed and analysed in this volume. Second, we treat VEm as a process, rather than as an event. 'No one is born an extremist or terrorist' (Angell and Gunaratna, 2011, p.365). Harris-Hogan (2012, p.5) of the Global Terrorism Research Centre at Monash University in Melbourne concurs:

> Radicalisation is a process in which individuals develop, adopt and embrace political attitudes and modes of behaviour which diverge

substantially from those of any or all of the established and legitimate political, social, economic, cultural, and religious values, attitudes, institutions and behaviours which exist in a given society.

Treating radicalization as a process suggests that this process is reversible. Its reversal requires a good understanding of the conditions conducive to radicalization in each context. Only through such understanding will the establishment of an effective and context-specific Counter-de-Rad program be possible. This is how 'perhaps we can decrease the numbers of those drawn to that lifestyle' and intelligently and proactively rehabilitate those who have already become violent extremists (Angell and Gunaratna, 2011, p.365). Therefore, and rather than simply describing key elements of Counter-de-Rad programs, this volume analyses conditions conducive to radicalization and VEm in each country case study. The inclusion of Australia and Singapore along with Muslim-majority states in this volume provides a unique opportunity to compare and contrast Counter-de-Rad programs in two completely different contexts. Analysing the radicalization process in Muslim-minority states will have relevance to Western countries in general, as it will shed light on factors that can radicalize members of minority groups in such countries. It will also shed some light on the kind of challenges Western democracies and Christian-majority states can face when attempting to implement Counter-de-Rad programs. Neither the latter nor the former issues have been 'fully understood' or received the attention they deserve (Bhui, Dinos and Jones, 2012, p.1).

Finally, we develop in this volume, for the first time, a solid framework that can guide policymakers, security agencies and practitioners in building their capacity and directing their future efforts in developing effective Counter-de-Rad programs. Such a framework is derived mainly from our analysis of the 14-country case study presented in volume I and II of this project. We draw on, and analyse, lessons from the existing literature on counter-radicalization. We must first define the main terminologies and concepts that will be used repeatedly in this book.

Definitions and terminologies

The abstract and general use of vocabulary and terminology in terrorism studies and literature has been provocative, and at times intimidating. For example, concepts such as radicalization, extremism and terrorism are extensively used in the literature to refer to violence carried out by groups and individuals belonging only to the Islamic faith. In fact, these terms have become synonymous with something called 'Islamic violence', as if the Islamic faith itself encourages violence and terrorism. Worse, such connotations and terminologies have confirmed stereotypes prevalent particularly among 'Many Americans and Europeans [who] see Islam as a religion of violence, especially toward those who do not share the faith...this lens distorts the past, constrains our present, and endangers our future' (Karabell, 2007, p.5).

Historically speaking, the relationship between Muslims and non-Muslims was not constantly characterized by violence, as some would like us to believe. The Islamic empire itself prospered precisely because it protected and coexisted with other monolithic and non-monolithic religions. For example, the Islamic Caliph Harun al-Rashid (of the Abbasid empire which lasted for more than 600 years starting around the middle of the 8th century) insisted on translating and building upon the knowledge of such Greek philosophers as Aristotle and Plato. He also wanted 'to see how their ideas met opposing theologians, and he invited scholars and preachers of other faiths to his court. Jews, Christians, Buddhists, and Muslims engaged in spiritual and spirited jousts, and each tradition was enriched by knowledge of the others' (Karabell, 2007, p.4). His sons after him, particularly al-Mantasour, followed their father's footsteps and continued to protect knowledge imported and translated from other religions, the pursuit of social justice, the recognition of identities, respect for diversity, and maintenance of social cohesion. Minorities of other religions were always treated as 'People of the Book' and cousins of Muslims (ibid). Even today, Muslims are latecomers to the world of terrorism, as we know it. Groups and individuals belonging to all other faiths, cultures and traditions have resorted to violence long before a minority of groups and individuals belonging to the Islamic faith did. As Angell and Gunaratna (2011, pp.351–2) wrote: 'we have witnessed terrorism stemming from the propaganda of deviant versions of Hinduism, Judaism, Christianity, Buddhism, Sikhism, and others'. However, 'There is known history and forgotten history, history that supports our sense of the present and history that suggests other pathways' (Karabell, 2007, p.3). Which version of history we choose is up to us.

Even among Muslims, violence is a 'minority pursuit' (Jarvis, 2009, p.5). The overwhelming majority of Muslims around the world reject violence. In fact, the overwhelming majority of those affected by violence and terrorism, including most victims of fatalities and injuries, are Muslim and from Muslim countries, not Christian, Jewish or any other religion, culture or states. We have to bear this fact in mind when we talk about VEm or terrorism. Radicalization and VEm, in other words, are not confined to individuals and groups belonging to the Islamic faith.

Nor is terrorism confined to non-state groups and individuals. States can and have committed terrorist acts throughout history and continue to do so. This book, however, is not about radicalization and VEm committed by groups and individuals belonging to other faiths or cultures. Nor is it about terrorism committed by states. This is not because the former or the latter are not important or do not happen. They are important and they happen all the time. Rather, the focus on radicalization and VEm committed by non-state actors, right-wing fundamentalist groups and individuals belonging to the Islamic faith stems from the fact that after 9/11 this type of radicalization and VEm became more commonplace. It is also seen by both most Muslim and non-Muslim states as the main threat facing them (El-Said and Barrett, 2011; El-Said and Harrigan, 2012).

Finally, we do not treat radicalization per se as an illicit or illegal act. Treating such a phenomenon as illegal creates ethical dilemmas. Most Western democratic states do not treat radicalization as illegal. In fact, countries like the United States glorify their radicals. As Peter Nuemann (2011, p.26) wrote: 'Not only is being a radical no crime in America, the very idea of radicalism has positive connotations in a nation whose founding principles were seen as radical, even revolutionary, at the time.' Only when radicalization crosses the line and becomes violent do we treat it as illegal and criminal.

At least five concepts will be used repeatedly throughout the chapters of this book. These are: radicalization, VEm, disengagement, counter-radicalization and de-radicalization. Radicalization is defined in this book as a process whereby groups or individuals undergo a psychological transformation that leads them to depart from tradition and increase their advocacy to an extreme political, social or religious ideology. VEm includes not only radicalization, but also 'Participation in politically [or religiously] motivated violence or threat of violence, especially against civilians', including prisoners, hostages, public, private or religious property, 'with the intent to instill widespread fear' and cause extensive damage (Bhui, Hicks, Lahley and Jones, 2012, p.2). This is a standard and accepted definition of VEm or terrorism in the literature and its adoption here does not raise much opposition. It is also consistent with Islam and the teachings of the Prophet Muhammad, who used to instruct his soldiers before every battle:

> Do not kill any child, any woman, or any elderly or sick person. ... Do not practice treachery or mutilation. Do not uproot or burn palms

or cut down fruitful trees. ... Do not kill the monks in monasteries, and do not kill those sitting in places of worship. ... Do not destroy the villages and towns, do not spoil the cultivated fields and gardens, and do not slaughter the cattle. ... Do not wish for an encounter with the enemy. Pray to God to grant you security, but when you (are forced to) encounter them, exercise patience. The Prophet (peace be upon him) had also issued clear instructions for good treatment of prisoners of war. (*Arab News*, 2011)

Counter-radicalization refers to a package of policies and measures designed and implemented by a country to prevent youth or most vulnerable groups and communities from becoming radicalized in their home country. Instead of targeting terrorists, which is the focus of the counterterrorism policy, counter-radicalization targets communities instead that are themselves targeted by violent extremists for recruitment, sympathy or any form of support. The overarching aim is to increase and create resilient communities to VEt ideology and activism. The kind of actions a counter-radicalization package could include is 'unlimited', depending on the culture, norms and innovativeness and capacity of national and local actors, and involves multichannels and various parties, including, in particular, grass roots and civil society (Neumann, 20011, p.7). This may include educational and political reforms and campaigns, messaging, capacity building, outreach to civil society and various communities, and use of role models (ibid.).

De-radicalization, on the other hand, refers to a package of policies and measures designed and implemented by authorities in order to normalize and convince groups and individuals who have already become radicalized or violent extremists to repent and disengage from violence. The process can include a cognitive change (change in ideology and attitudes), simple disengagement (behavioral change to abandon violence while remaining radical), or both. De-radicalization is seen as more enduring, resilient and immune from recidivism. Measures that could also be included in a typical de-radicalization program are also unlimited, including various measures and involving various parties and multichannels. Examples of most known de-radicalization policies include religious rehabilitation, education, vocational training, social training, family programs, physical programs and post-care or release programs to facilitate the reintegration of released detainees (El-Said and Harrigan, 2012).

De-radicalization, moreover, can be either collective or individual. The latter aims at de-radicalizing individuals even if their number is very large (Saudi Arabia, Indonesia, Malaysia). Collective de-radicalization refers more to de-radicalization that occurs among an entire group or organization. De-radicalization, either individual or collective, can also be a governmental top-down process (Saudi Arabia and Yemen) or spontaneously occurring, a kind of bottom-up process (Egypt's Islamic Group and Jihad Organization). It can also occur inside prisons (as most cases are) or outside prisons. The most well-known example of de-radicalization taking place outside prison walls is Algeria's Islamic Salvation Army, most of whose members were de-radicalized in the 'mountains' (Ashour, 2009).

The main feature of counter-radicalization and de-radicalization programs is their reliance on 'soft' or 'smart' non-coercive policies, the aim of which is to 'win hearts and minds' of groups, individuals and communities most vulnerable to VEt recruitment and acts.

The research methodology of the book

Another distinguishing feature of the book is the approach used to analyse and understand the phenomenon of VEm, the process of radicalization and policies of Counter de-Rad programs. First, the book relies on the available literature on terrorism and security studies. This includes not only academic writings, but also journalistic and media outlets, including interviews with and opinions of leaders and commanders of radical movements, state officials and community leaders and members. The book then takes a comparative, mainly qualitative, research approach, contrasting and comparing the radicalization process, policies implemented, challenges faced and outcomes in six countries: Australia, Mauritania, Pakistan, Singapore, Sudan and Turkey. Regional variation, cultural diversity and different political systems in countries compared and contrasted enriches the analysis and provides a unique opportunity to better understand the factors behind radicalization of certain groups and individuals in different environments. It also provides another unique opportunity to better understand and identify factors that lead to success or failure of Counter-de-Rad programs in different political, social and economic settings.

While the number of countries studied in this volume is relatively small, the project remains larger than most available inventory of Counter de-Rad programs, with the exception of El-Said and Harrigan (2012) and the ICSR's 2010 prisons' study. The latter study, however, was much narrower in scope, focusing only on the radicalization process inside detention centers in 15 different countries. Even with six countries, our approach still overcomes 'the problems of a small N case selection' and is 'particularly attractive when searching regions, countries and/or movements that suffer from a lack of reliable aggregate data' (Ashour, 2009, p.17). Indeed, some of the Counter-de-Rad programs studied in some of the countries in this volume, such as Mauritania, Sudan and Turkey, have never, as far as we know, been studied before. The lack of data on some countries/programs has been filled by a 10–14 day field trip that the author spent in each country studied, where state officials, security and intelligence officers, members of the civil society and communities, and former members of VEt groups who repented after attending de-radicalization programs implemented by the government of the country where they reside, were met. This enriched the book and facilitated a better understanding of the process of radicalization in various countries, as well as factors that lead to success or failure of Counter-de-Rad programs in various environments and contexts, by relying on firsthand observations and opinions of the many stakeholders, decision-makers and victims of terrorist environments.

The book proceeds as follows. Chapter 2 sets a new framework that facilitates and guides state officials' attempts in constructing effective and successful Counter-de-Rad programs. Chapters 3 to 8 present our six country case studies and compare and contrast their Counter-de-Rad efforts, factors contributing to radicalization and extremism that lead to VEm in each country, and shed some light on the effectiveness and challenges faced by each country while trying to implement Counter-de-Rad programs. The final chapter summarizes and concludes with some further remarks.

2
Counter-de-Rad: Setting the Framework

Introduction

The self-evident failure of the propagandist 'war on terror', which garnered an unprecedented kinetic global response, has led to a 'renewed interest in how and why terrorism ends' (Horgan and Braddock, 2010, 267). This renewed interest in the question of what leads an individual or group to leave terrorism has been encouraged and motivated by the emergence and/or implementation of some innovative approaches, mostly by and in Muslim-majority states. These approaches carry different names and terminologies but are generally known in the West, for lack of better terminology, as counter radicalization and de-radicalization programs (Counter-de-Rad).

According to a 2010 study by the New York–based think tank, the International Peace Institute (IPI, p. 1), 'deradicalization programs... have been deemed more successful than military approaches and less likely to foment a new generation of violent extremists'. In his work on Saudi Arabia, the late Carnegie scholar Christopher Boucek (2008) reached similar conclusions. Petrus Golose, while analysing the Indonesian de-radicalization program for the *Jakarta Post* in 2009, concluded that 'deradicalization programs are the best measures to eradicate terrorism and radicalism, as these programs will touch the issues to their deepest roots'. The author has recently carried out the largest and most comprehensive inventory of such programs in Muslim-majority states (El-Said and Harrigan, 2013). This work has shown that 'soft' measures implemented under the rubric of Counter-de-Rad programs have indeed yielded more benefits than purely kinetic approaches in countering radicalization and VEm, particularly in reducing the rates of terrorist incidences, recidivism among released prisoners and

13

have achieved other unintended but no less significant benefits and spillovers. Such outcomes have convinced many Western democratic states in Western Europe, North America and elsewhere to implement some aspects or major parts of Counter-de-Rad programs in their own countries. These include Canada, Australia, the United Kingdom, the Netherlands, Norway and Denmark, for example, with the latter four countries carrying out 'the most extensive counter radicalization initiatives' in Western Europe (Vidino and Brandon, 2012, p. 1).

Why have such policies proved to be more effective in countering VEm than purely kinetic approaches? What do they consist of? When do such programs succeed and when do they fail? These are the main questions that this chapter attempts to answer. It seeks to establish a comprehensive framework, for the first time, that will enable state officials, security officers, practitioners and other parties involved in countering VEm by guiding them in their future development of such initiatives. We do so by drawing lessons from existing programs, both effective and ineffective, implemented by several United Nations Member States over the past two decades or so in different regions of the world and under different environments.

The chapter proceeds as follows. The next section briefly surveys the literature on environments where Counter-de-Rad programs have been implemented or attempted and either failed or succeeded. Section two develops a Counter-de-Rad framework based on macro factors such as environment. That is, factors related to the general environment (international, national and local) that can affect the implementation of Counter-de-Rad programs either positively or negatively. Section 3 focuses on the micro-elements, which are the components of a successful or effective Counter-de-Rad program. Section 4 puts the framework together by amalgamating macro and micro factors in one structure or model. The final section summarizes the main points in the chapter.

Conditions conducive to the success/failure of counter-de-rad programs

In the late 1990s, two of the largest former Violent Extremist (VEt) organizations declared a ceasefire, their intention being to disengage from VEm and reintegrate into their society and families. These were the Egyptian Islamic Jihad (IJ) and the al-Jihad Organization (JO). Leaders of IJ and JO went further, writing more than 25 volumes arguing for non-violence, admitting that they had made mistakes and declaring a ceasefire. This despite the fact that the de-radicalization of

IJ was completed in less than two years (July 1997–March 1999), while the de-radicalization of JO 'took about a decade to be completed (July 1997–April 2007)' (Ashour, 2009, p. 102).

During the 1990s the Algerian Islamic Salvation Army (ISA), the self-appointed armed wing of the Islamic Salvation Front, also followed suit and declared a unilateral ceasefire around 1997. To date, the IJ, JO and ISA have maintained their repentance, have not reneged on their disengagement agreement and have not carried out any VEt acts since their de-radicalization/disengagement (see Ashour, 2009; El-Said, 2013a).

The Egyptian and Algerian de-radicalization/disengagement declarations were followed by several other individual and group disengagements in various parts of the Arab world. In Yemen, for example, a de-radicalization program initiated by the former Yemeni President Ali Saleh managed to de-radicalize/disengage hundreds of former Yemeni militants. 'Nearly 400 prisoners [who] attended al-Hitar's classes repented and were released' between 2002–2005 (Peraino, 2009). Between 2003 and 2007 '1,500 Qaeda members [were] freed after counseling' in Saudi Arabia, and after they 'promise[d] to refrain from jihad' (Lake, 2007). In Indonesia, modeling the Saudi efforts, a de-radicalization program, initiated by the authorities around 2004, managed to persuade about two dozen members of Jemaah Islamiah to repent and cooperate with the police. Kurlantzick (2008) described the Indonesian de-radicalization program in the following words:

> *Today, Indonesia has become a far different kind of example. Even as terrorism continues to grow more common in nations from Pakistan to Algeria, Indonesia is heading in the opposite direction, destroying its internal terrorist networks and winning the broader public battle against radicalism. And it has done so not only by cracking heads but by using a softer, innovative plan that employs former jihadists to wean radicals away from terror. ... Indonesia's successes are striking. ... The deradicalization program already has delivered.*

In Libya, finally, the former Libyan Islamic Fighting Group (LIFG) also declared its disengagement/de-radicalization around 2008 under a program supervised personally by Saif al Dine Al-Islam, the son of the former late Libyan ruler, Muammar al-Gaddafi. As Sami Al Saadi, the former ideologue of the LIFG who authored the LIFG's anti-democracy manifesto ('The Choice Is Theirs') and whom the Taliban leader Mullah Omar once called the 'Sheikh of the Arabs' stated after entering the first

Libyan elections in the post-Gaddafi period: 'our future is certainly better than our present and our past' (Ashour, 2012). Sami has also found a political party, Al Umma Al Wasat, and he and his former colleagues in the LIFG have accepted democracy, political pluralism and the state as the main arena for political competition instead of violence.

The above-described disengagement/de-radicalization processes and programs are but a few examples of successful processes and programs that managed to transform groups and direct individuals onto pathways out of VEm. There are many other initiatives which have also had many successes but are less well known and studied, such as in Turkey, Mauritania and Sudan, as the following chapters of this book will demonstrate. What leads to successful de-radicalization/disengagement processes/programs? To be more precise, under what conditions do such programs/processes prove either more or less successful?

The circumstances and conditions under which the de-radicalization/disengagement of former jihadists occurred vary. For example, the rise of the ISA in Algeria coincided with the weakening and even the collapse of the state in the late 1980s and early 1990s, particularly following the cancellation by the Algerian army of the 1992 elections in which Islamist factions were set to win. This not only led to the dismantling of the Algerian state wholesale, but also to the eruption of a long and bloody 'dirty war' that, according to President Bouteflika, claimed the lives of more than 100,000 Algerians and cost more than $20 billion in economic and financial losses (El-Said, 2013a). As long as the fighting remained in favour of the ISA between 1992–5, de-radicalization and disengagement proved difficult to achieve, despite several attempts by the Algerian state to achieve reconciliation. Only after the military balance shifted in favour of the Algerian state did de-radicalization of the ISA leadership and commanders become possible (Ashour, 2009; El-Said, 2013b).

In Egypt, on the other hand, the state has always been strong, at least until the outbreak of the Arab Spring in early 2010. While the rise of the IJ occurred under the presence of a strong repressive state, the de-radicalization and disengagement of the leadership and commanders of the IJ and JO also occurred under the same conditions. In fact, it was the realization by the top leadership of the IJ and JO that a war against the state cannot be won that played a key factor in bringing about these spontaneous and internal de-radicalization processes. Ironically, these processes occurred under the undemocratic and repressive regime of the former Egyptian ruler, Hosni Mubarak.

In Yemen, the Ali Salih regime initiated a de-radicalization program in 2002 when the Yemeni state was still relatively strong. It lasted until

2005 after which the de-radicalization program collapsed. This coincided with the weakening of the Yemeni state following the outbreak of fighting with the Houthi tribes and increased divisions and radicalization of the Yemeni society as a result of the 2003 American invasion and occupation of Iraq, as well as increased corruption and inequalities in Yemen itself. Since then, al-Qaeda in the Arabian Peninsula has turned Yemen into its headquarters (El-Said, 2013b). The failure or the falling of the Somali state following the departure of American forces from the country has had similar effects and led to the emergence of a VEt, salafist group, al-Shabab. The latter continues to represent a major threat to the stability of both Somalia and the region alike. Similarly, in Pakistan and Afghanistan, the weakening and gradual erosion of state power destroyed social cohesion, led to civil wars, undermined the countries' political and social stability, and boosted the emergence of various VEt fundamentalist groups. Similar examples of failing or falling states associated with the emergence of extremist groups and movements abound. Syria (Ansaru Islam), Nigeria (Boko Haram), Kashmir (LoK) and Chechnya (Chechen Separatist) are but a few examples. The point here is that weak states attract radicalism and extremism that lead to terrorism.

Hypothesis No 1: Failed or falling states face a higher threat from VEm than strong states. When faced with the risk of VEm, strong states are also better equipped and prepared to deal with it.

Macro economic and political factors: development and terrorism

The link between the economic status of groups and individuals and terrorism is a very contentious one. 'There is no consensus except beyond the agreement that absolute poverty does not drive terrorism' (Zammit, 2010, p. 1). This 'agreement' is based on a very limited number of studies that relied mainly on the profile of individual terrorists. The most popular two studies in this regard are Krueger and Maleckova's 2003 study and Sageman's 2010 study. The former looked at the links between terrorism on the one hand and poverty and level of education on the other by analysing the individual profile of Hezbollah fighters and Israeli Jewish settlers who attacked Palestinians in the West Bank in the early 1980s. They concluded that 'Although our results are tentative and exploratory, they suggest that neither poverty nor education has a direct, causal impact on terrorism' (Krueger and Maleckova, 2003, p. 119). Sageman, on the other hand, reaches a similar conclusion by analysing the profile of the most dangerous 500 or so terrorists in the world. But such results remain tentative and exploratory indeed, as the numbers involved are too small to reach any definitive conclusion regarding the link between terrorism and poverty and education. More importantly, such studies have neglected the conditions of the population from where such individuals are drawn. As Bhui et al. (2012b, p. 1) argued, 'Studies of terrorism have focused on those identified as engaged with terrorist organizations or convicted of terrorist crimes, with little attention given to populations that are vulnerable to recruitment to terrorist action.' Some observers, like Jessica Stern for example, have cautioned against attempts to focus on individual profiling and 'to demonstrate the role of socioeconomic factors on terrorism writ large'. She called for more attention to be paid to 'particular groups in a particular place under particular conditions at a particular time' (all quotations from GTReC, 2014, p. 6). In fact, there is considerable new evidence which suggests that not only do violent extremists come from economically and educationally disadvantaged groups, but also socio-economic disadvantages can contribute tremendously to the radicalization process. As the chapter on Australia shows, most Australian neo-jihadists emerged from one community: the Australian Sunni Lebanese community, namely, Lebanese Muslims, who suffer considerable socio-economic disadvantages when compared to the main population. Sageman (2010) found that Muslim communities in Europe are also characterized by similar socio-economic disadvantages, although he argued that this is not the case with regard to Muslims in America who tend to be better educated than the national average and more economically secure.

With regard to individual VEts, most Australian neo-jihadists are also characterized by very low economic, educational and employment status. This is not dissimilar to the socio-economic characteristics of individual neo-jihadists in both Europe and America. This led researchers at the Global Terrorism Research Centre of Monash University to argue that 'there is considerable evidence that disadvantages contribute to the process' of radicalization (GTReC, 2014, p. 8). Bhui et al. (2012a and 2012b) also suggested that socio-economic disadvantages lead to social exclusion, social and political immobility, and can encourage VEm as an expression of socio-economic grievances.

Hypothesis No. 2: States with strong developmental capacity are less vulnerable to VEm, and, when faced with the phenomenon, are more capable of dealing with it.

The prison environment matters for both inside and outside prison walls

The issue of prison radicalization has become one of the most important concerns for prison officers. There is a strong belief among state security officials that prisons can, and in some cases have, become schools for radicalization and recruitment of other inmates into VEt movements and acts (Brandon, 2009; Hamm, 2007; Curran 2006). Much of the concern for, and literature on, prison radicalization is derived mainly from European nationalists and terrorists groups, such as the Basque Euskad Ta Askatasuna (ETA) which in the past fought against the Franco government and now battles for Basque autonomy with Spain's democratic government, and the Provisional Irish Republican Army (PIRA) which waged a sustained campaign against the British government to achieve a united Ireland. Both of these organizations maintained their integrated command structures and a high degree of group cohesion inside the prison setting, a fact which facilitated 'the use of prisons as means of recruiting new members into terrorist organizations while providing advanced training for existing ones' (Cuthbertson, 2004, p. 15).

The issue of radicalization of inmates by Islamic radical prisoners, however, is largely not understood, under-researched and perhaps exaggerated (Hamm, 2007). Despite the fact that prisons are places of vulnerabilities, the claim that radical Muslims have been able to turn prisons into schools and universities for radicalization and recruitment purposes is 'based on untested assumptions about inmate behaviour and the dynamics of prison radicalization' (Veldhuis and Kessels, 2013, p. 2). Yet much of the current discourse and literature about prisons and radicalization is negative. The current consensus, which lacks empirically tested assumptions, is that 'prisons matter' because 'they are places of vulnerability in which radicalisation takes place' (ICSR, 2010, p. 1). Not surprisingly, the safety of prison environments and preventing detention centres from becoming schools and universities for radicalization and recruitment have become a priority for security officials throughout the world, at the expense of reforms that benefit the prisoners and community.

We approach this issue, however, from a different angle. We argue here that prisons do indeed matter and safety is important. But what is equally important is the rehabilitation and reintegration of inmates back into their societies after their release, rather than just simply detaining them and preventing them from radicalizing and recruiting others. This process is important not only because of its impact on detainees, but also on family members, relatives, friends and communities of the detained individuals. This, as we will see in later sections, requires well-designed and targeted educational, vocational, religious, therapeutic and social programs to rehabilitate prisoners and prepare them for post-release integration.

Why is it important to design effective de-radicalization/rehabilitation and reintegration programs for VEt prisoners? First, a well-designed and implemented de-radicalization program will not only help disengage and de-radicalize inmates, but will also ensure against prison radicalization in general. Second, reintegration is important because most detained individuals will have to be released at some point and will have to go back to the society and communities from whence they came. According to Angell and Gunaratna (2011, p. 348), 'there are over 100,000 convicted and suspected terrorists languishing in penitentiary and detention centers from Europe to the Middle East and Asia. Although there are vocational and educational programs to rehabilitate criminals, there are very few initiatives to rehabilitate terrorists'. A well-designed and executed rehabilitation and reintegration program will go a long way towards reducing the recidivism rate among released prisoners and therefore ensuring better safety of citizens by reducing the risks that would otherwise be involved in releasing unprepared, unqualified, ill-equipped and un-deradicalized/disengaged individuals back into society.

More important is the impact of a well-designed and implemented rehabilitation and reintegration program on the community of the detained individuals. Mistreating detainees, failing to win their cooperation and trust or to provide fair trials for them, proving unhelpful in the facilitation of visits by families and friends to the detention centre, and failing to win the hearts and minds of family members, relatives and friends of the detainees could end up fomenting a new generation of violent extremists seeking revenge on the state, state officials and other members of society (IPI, 2010, p. 1). The failure to combine counter radicalization with an effective de-radicalization program antagonized the families and relatives of detained members of the Moroccan jihadi Islamyeh movement (as they are called by the Moroccan authorities), and undermined their collaboration with, and trust in, the prison authorities. A father of one of the Moroccan detainees recently called upon the authorities to 'reconsider themselves...before it is too late', warning authorities that 'our sons who live in this electrocuting environment are time bombs who will one day explode' (El-Said, 2013c, p. 185). A few months later, on 15 April 2011, a terrorist attack on a tourist café in Marrakesh claimed the lives of 15 innocent individuals (ibid., p. 187). The case of Australia (next chapter) highlights how social influences (family and friends) and lack of an effective de-radicalization program can impact the radicalization process both inside and outside detention centres. The benefits of prison de-radicalization therefore extend beyond the prison walls. As Porges and Stern (2010) argued:

> *Deradicalization efforts must therefore be considered important not just for their effect on detainees but also for their secondary benefits beyond the walls of detention facilities. Saudi Arabia's rehabilitation program, for example, contributes to broader counter radicalization efforts by facilitating government contact with those who are vulnerable to radicalization and recruitment, including detainees' friends and families.*

In one of their recent Intel Briefs, The Soufan Group (2013) concurs: through de-radicalization, 'countries have demonstrably reduced the vulnerability of individuals and communities by focusing on rehabilitation for violent extremists and their families'. It is ironic that most Western democracies 'tend to ignore' and 'dismiss Terrorist Rehabilitation' the Brief added, whose effective implementation leads to 'Community Resilience'. Ignoring de-radicalization and rehabilitation of VEt detainees can have far-reaching consequences, not only for national counter-VEt strategies, but also for the foreign interests of a country as well. America's neglect, for example, of de-radicalization and rehabilitation of VEts led to 'toxic effects on the geostrategic level – represents a clear and present danger to both the effectiveness of American soft power influence and the security of US personnel and facilities overseas' (all quotations from The Soufan Group, 2013).

Moreover, many countries (both Muslim majority and minority) are content with separating radical and violent extremist prisoners from other inmates and even from one another. Separation alone is an insufficient prison policy whose psychological impact on detainees is yet to be assessed. It is more likely to lead to further radicalization of inmates. As Veldhuis and Kessels (2013, p. 2) wrote: 'Similarly, it is hotly debated whether preventing the spread of extremism among prisoners is served best by segregating or dispersing extremist inmates...' While the psychological impact of segregation is yet to be determined, its impact on community members, including relatives and friends, has already proven to be 'toxic'.

Hypothesis No. 3: Prisons matter. Lack of de-radicalization and rehabilitation is likely to undermine *counter radic*alization measures by reducing collaboration and trust between communities and state authorities, leading to toxic relations between the two, undermining the perception of the state and antagonizing and fomenting a new generation of jihadists.

Civil society is an important source of soft power

No state or one party has all the resources required to counter VEm and refute violent ideology. This is certainly a major problem in Western democracies, where the state is ill-equipped and ill-advised to comment on or intervene in religious matters. The tradition of separating church from politics and the evolution of purely secular states in Western democracies undermines their ability to intervene in religious matters pertaining to the Islamic faith.

Civil society is a key source of soft power because it mediates between state and society, is seen as more neutral and credible, and also because it possesses extra resources which the state lacks. The latter includes the ability of community leaders and members to comprehend more clearly how their elements, including radicals and VEts, think and behave. They are also better at building extensive and intensive networks that reach the most recalcitrant groups and individuals in their country. Members of civil society and communities therefore can act and behave in a more acceptable manner to all societal members than the state, and enjoy more credibility and legitimacy. This makes them better suited to spot and expose any extraordinary behaviour in society when it happens. Empowering communities to *counter radic*alization and VEm will also enable them to deal with such phenomena more effectively. Civil society, due to its 'ubiquitous nature', is more capable of dealing with the threat than the state (The Soufan Group, 2013). Countries with rigorous and dynamic communities and civil society, like Singapore for example, have proved more successful in both designing and implementing Counter-de-Rad programs than countries with weak and non-dynamic civil society (El-Said and Harrigan, 2013).

It is not the sheer presence of a dynamic and rigorous civil society and community that matters most, but rather the ability of the state to build and maintain trustful relationships with its communities. It is self-evident, for example, that the United Kingdom's efforts to counter radicalization and extremism in British society have not proved fully successful. Their effectiveness has been 'hampered by the fact that many British Muslims view [prevent policies] with resentment and suspicion' (BBC News, 2011). In other European countries where 'Prevent and other counter radicalization programs [have been] implemented', their efficacy has also been undermined by the fact that they 'have often been accused of unfairly targeting Muslims, treating Muslims as 'suspect communities' and security threats rather than as ordinary citizens (Vidino, 2010, p. 9). In fact, most Muslim communities perceive programs such as Prevent as nothing more than a cover up for 'spying' on Muslims, leading a British Muslim community activist to call them 'the biggest spying program in Britain in modern times and an affront to civil liberties' (ibid.; Dodd, 2009). In America, Muslim complaints about counterterrorism and counterterrorism-related policies are among the most frequently cited 'grievances' of Muslim Americans. There is a perception that Muslims, based on their names and/or physical appearance, are singled out for searches and questioning at airports and by local law enforcement, and that mosques and Islamic community centres are under blanket surveillance by security agencies (Vidino, 2010, p. 8). In Australia, finally, counter radicalization has also been hampered by 'increased distrust between Sydney's Lebanese community and the police, as well as the wider community' (GTReC, 2014, p. 7).

> Hypothesis No. 4a: Countries with dynamic and rigorous civil societies are less exposed to the threat of VEm, and when faced with VEt threats are better able to deal with it.
> Hypothesis No. 4b: Countries that have strong and trustful relationships with the members of their civil society and community are better able to counter the threat of radicalization and VEm.

The role of the global environment

The role of the global environment has received little attention in the terrorism literature for obvious political reasons: the West has not been keen to discuss the 'root causes' of terrorism and considered it 'politically incorrect, since it gives the impression of condoning terrorism as a legitimate tool for redressing grievances' (Coolsaet and Struye de Swielande, 2008, p. 150). During this author's sabbatical at the United Nations in 2008, where he was invited to lead the research team of the then Working Group on Radicalization and Extremism that Lead to Terrorism, there was a strong opposition from some powerful Western states for the inclusion of 'root causes' of terrorism in the discussion of the phenomenon. They insisted that the discussion should only centre around the question of pathways out of VEm, in particular on the question of what leads an individual or group to repent and leave terrorism behind. The upshot was a simple report, produced by a large project (costing more than $300,000), which simply described the components of soft Counter-de-Rad programs.[1] With so much funding available for studies and subjects that were particularly close to the heart of Western democracies, terrorism became a 'cottage industry' (Turner, 2010, p. 541) seeking the 'terrorism industry' (Lentini, 2008, p. 135). This led to an overemphasis on the 'flip-side – those who decide to leave terrorist and extremist organizations' or the 'drop outs' (Jacobson, 2010, p. 13). The issue of root causes, or conditions conducive to VEm, as the European Union and the United Nations decided to call it (El-Said and Barrett, 2011), did not receive the attention they deserve. Certainly the subject of 'state terrorism' and policies, and their impact on radicalizing individuals and groups, including in particular Muslim young people after 9/11, has received the least attention. As Peter Sproat (1997, p. 3) wrote:

> *It has been noted that the literature on state terrorism, like that on terrorism generally, suffers from a lack of work on the definition of the term … it is difficult to think of any author who has methodically applied a definition to the actions of a particular actor in order to assess whether each constitutes an act of terrorism.*

The end result has been the neglect of not only the subject of state terrorism, but also the link between the international global environment, state actions and terrorism.

Despite the little attention paid to this issue, some daring authors still managed to venture into its waters and to draw our attention to the significance and effects of the policies of the state on the radicalization process. For example, Sageman (2010, p. viii) argued that the 2001 and 2003 invasions of Afghanistan and Iraq caused a 'moral outrage' among Muslims that their religion was under attack from the West, which caused, among other factors, some 'Muslim youth [to] become radicalized'. In his seminal work (*Dying to Win*, 2005), Pape argued that 'foreign occupation is the root cause of suicide terrorism'. Pape derived his findings from analyzing data on 315 suicide attacks from 1980 to 2003. His main finding was that the 'common thread linking 95 per cent of all suicide attacks around the world is not religion or ideology, but rather a clear, strategic, political objective. They are organized campaigns to compel a modern democracy, principally the United States, to withdraw military forces from a group's perceived homeland' (all quotations from Attran, 2006, p. 129).

The subject of aerial bombardment, or drone attacks, by US troops in Afghanistan, Pakistan, Somalia, Yemen and elsewhere has only belatedly begun to receive some of the attention it deserves from the media. While prevalent during the Bush administration, reliance on drone attacks as a key element in the US's counterterrorism strategy increased dramatically under Obama. Although less risky than moving soldiers to the battlefield, the collateral damage that drone attacks can (and have) caused, including the killing of a large number of innocent bystanders, has ended up radicalizing a large number of relatives, friends and tribe members of the deceased individuals (El-Said, 2013b). Criticism of drone attacks has recently been voiced by various sources, in and outside the military establishment. Apart from being illegal, as they violate the sovereignty of other states, drone attacks have 'contributed to a perception of American arrogance' and have been 'generating recruits for Al Qaeda'. Drone attacks, moreover, have divided societies and undermined social cohesion in such countries as Yemen and Pakistan by giving 'the perception ... that the U.S. is colluding with the Yemeni [and Pakistani] government[s] in a covert war against the[ir own] ... people'. As such, drone attacks have undermined the US's 'long term interest in the goal of ... stable' countries like Yemen and Pakistan with 'a functional political system and economy' (all quotations from Worth, Mazzetti and Shane, 2013).

While addressing the historical relationship between strategic bombing and terrorism in his book *Strategic Terror*, Beau Grosscup (2006) shows how, from the beginning of the aviation age, military planners have consciously targeted civilians and civilian areas in order to inflict psychological damage on their opponents. He argues that strategic bombing, which includes drone attacks in today's lexicon, is despicable, 'immoral and illegal like terrorism ... that it should be labeled as terrorism' (quoted in Lentini, 2008, p. 138).

Even before 9/11, the collective damage caused by state actions led Maruna, Wilson and Claridge (1996, p. 47) to 'propose a model by which acts of state violence may be adjudged to be state terrorism'. Igor Primoratz (2002) went further to argue that state violence is of a higher level of immorality because states are bound by legal conventions (also see Lentini, 2008, p. 135). Finally, Pedahzur (2006) provided an explanation for why individuals and groups turn to terrorism, one that demystifies and discredits the notion that most terrorists, particularly suicide terrorists, engage in acts of violence for financial reasons. Those who do engage in terrorism for financial reasons, the argument continues, often pull out before the act occurs. While acknowledging that other factors, such as rapid transitions in their lives, play a role, the loss of loved ones in violent conflict with perceived enemies, humiliation and the desire for revenge all play significant roles in influencing a minority of people to engage in acts of political violence, including suicide terrorism (in Lentini, 2008, p. 135). Examples include the loss of loved ones (fathers, mothers, brothers, sisters, relatives or close friends) by state actions in places like Palestine, Iraq, Pakistan, Afghanistan and Somalia (El-Said and Harrigan, 2013).

While the global environment (particularly states' actions and foreign policies) has an impact on radicalizing individuals elsewhere, it also has a strong impact on the success/failure of Counter-de-Rad programs. As demonstrated elsewhere (El-Said, 2013a and 2013c), drone attacks have undermined the Yemeni government's informal de-radicalization program initiated after 2008 to convince al-Qaeda members in the country to repent and disengage from violet actions. They have also undermined confidence and trust in the government of the former Yemeni ruler, Ali Saleh, which was seen as colluding with the US government against its own people (also see Worth et al., 2013). The same impact was also noted in Pakistan following the end of military operations by the Pakistani armed forces in the Swat Valley in 2009 (El-Said, 2013a).

> Hypothesis No. 5: The global environment has an important impact on the success/failure of Counter-de-Rad programs. Negative external factors (occupation, drone attacks, perceived bias of Western states' policies towards Israel, killing of innocent friends or relatives by foreign powers, etc.) can undermine efforts to effectively design Counter-de-Rad programs.

Micro-components of successful Counter-de-Rad programs

A good understanding of the macro-environmental conditions conducive to successful reforms is necessary but doesn't answer the key question of what are the components or elements that constitute successful and 'smart' Counter-de-Rad programs. There is no universal panacea. The various legal, political, social and cultural systems suggest that what works in one place might not work elsewhere, and that some components may require modifications and adaptations in order to be implemented elsewhere. Transplantation is not advisable. What we describe here is a combination of practices/measures that have been implemented and proven successful in certain environments, particularly in Muslim-majority states, although we do not exclude lessons derived from Muslim-minority states in efforts to identify best practice. In fact, with some adaptations, some of these policies have also proved successful in some Muslim-minority states such as Singapore and Australia. Timing also seems to be an important factor. Some practices were attempted and failed in earlier periods or in different contexts but succeeded later on. In addition to the timing of Counter-de-Rad programs, practices that proved most effective were those that derived from and were consistent with national culture, norms and values. We can identify several practices/measures that appear to constitute what Golose referred to as successful counter radicalization and 'deradicalization' or counter radicalization and 'Deradicalization [that] works' (quoted in El-Said, 2013a, p. 11).

First, religious rehabilitation

There seems to be a general agreement among observers that, while other components are also important, a religious rehabilitation/dialogue program is perhaps the most indispensable. There is logic behind this line of thinking. Most VEts rely on misinterpreted and misunderstood religious excerpts to justify their violent actions. Also, evidence shows that most VEts have weak or no rigorous religious knowledge, which makes them vulnerable to the propaganda of radical preachers. Religious rehabilitation is therefore necessary to delegitimize the actions of terrorists and refute their theoretical and ideological justifications. Finally, the Islamic faith prohibits suicide. Nobody therefore is willing to commit an act of VEm which includes suicide without some kind of a *fatwa* or religious justification. Hence the significance of the religious rehabilitation program.

Saudi Arabia has the best-known and most endurable and well-funded de-radicalization program, which includes a strong religious rehabilitation component (Boucek, 2008). There the Saudi detainees debate and discuss with competent scholars, in individual and group formats, such issues as jihad, the relationship between Muslim and non-Muslim (both states and individuals), international treaties and other subjects that are often used by terrorists to justify their actions. Such efforts intensify during the last six months of the detainees' terms, where they are transferred to a 'halfway house program to ease release into society and programs to reintegration' (Boucek, 2008, p. 17).

It is not only in Saudi Arabia, but also in almost every program studied in volumes I and II of this project that a religious rehabilitation program is included.

Debate and advice, religious or otherwise, is deeply embedded in the Islamic faith and culture. Muslims attribute the genesis of debate to the beginning of humanity, particularly between Allah and his angels, back to the time when the creator decided to establish the kingdom of earth and mankind to inherit and represent him on it. The Holy Quran describes this debate in some detail in *Surat Al-Baqarah*, Part I, Aayah 30:

> *And (remember) when your Lord said to the angels: 'verily, I am going to place (mankind) generations after generations on earth'. They said: 'will you place therein those who will make mischief therein and shed blood, – while we glorify you with praises and thanks and sanctify you'. He (Allah) said: 'I know that which you do not know'.*

Religious debate and advice later took on a different form, one between the creator and his messengers, on the one hand, and the creator and mankind on the other. For example, Allah constantly reminded Prophet Muhammad that he was simply a Prophet of God, a messenger and that his job did not include fighting or killing anybody who did not believe in him or in his message. *Surat Al-Ahqaf* (part 26:9) provides one example of such advice from Allah to Prophet Muhammad, when the Lord advised the Prophet to constantly remind his people that:

> *I am not a new thing among the Messengers (of Allah, i.e. I am not the first Messenger) nor do I know what will be done with me or with you. I only follow that which is revealed to me, and I am but a plain Warner.*

Religious debate and advice were then formalized into state policy during the 600-year enduring Abbasid Empire, especially under the greatest of all its caliphs, Harun al-Rashid, who established the empire and made Baghdad its headquarters and home. As Zachary Karabell (2007, p. 4) wrote:

> *On countless evenings, the court [of Harun] was transformed into an arena for theological debate. Muslim men of learning, schooled in sharia, the law derived from the Quran, offered their wisdom and drew on the philosophical tradition of the ancient Greeks. The works of Aristotle and Plato were translated into Arabic and used not only to enrich Islam but to create new science and new philosophy. And the caliph was not content simply to take the word of his learned men. He wanted to see how their ideas met opposing theologies, and he invited scholars and preachers of other faiths to his court. Jews, Christian, Buddhists, engaged in spiritual and spirited jousts, and each tradition was enriched by knowledge of others.*

There lies a lesson in history, especially for many Westerners who view Islam as a religion of violence, and Easterners who view Westerners as non-believers, imperialists and crusaders. The golden days of collaboration between the two have become part of the forgotten history.

Debate and religious rehabilitation can, have been and should be extended to beyond the prison walls. In Victoria (Australia), for example, the Victoria Islamic Council, in collaboration with the Victoria police and federal government, extended a general debate and discussion program (known as Lecture and Open Discussion Forum – LoD), originally initiated in Victoria's high-security prison in 2010 as part of a religious rehabilitation program, to mosques. A monthly LoD is now being held in mosques located in hotspot areas by the Islamic Council of Victoria. It targets released prisoners (particularly those at medium-to-high-risk of recidivism), vulnerable young people and voluntary participants (whoever wants to attend from the public). The main subjects discussed and debated include core Islamic teachings and practices, the protection of life, conflict resolution in Islam, Islamic views on citizenship, belonging and cultural identity, and the universal Concept of Islam (see the chapter on Australia in this volume). In Singapore, members of the Islamic Religious Council in Singapore (MUIS) and the Religious Rehabilitation Program (RRP), a group of voluntary Muslim scholars from the Muslim community, began organizing public forums, talks and seminars in mosques and Islamic centres in 2006. The main objective of such seminars and public forums is to 'portray Islam in its unblemished form and to demonstrate what it means to be Muslims in this challenging and ever-changing world…to promote a greater understanding of the true teachings of Islam and Muslims in Singapore' (Harmony Centre, 2010, p. 1 and 2).

In Mauritania, the government, particularly after the fall of the Ould Taya's regime in 2005, reactivated religious discussion and debate in mosques through revitalizing the traditional role of imams during the Friday sermons and after the evening prayers. In addition to reviving the traditional role of imams, the Mauritanian government also empowered the traditional role of the old madrasa or *mahdir*. The *mahdir* is an old educational institution run by a scholar or *faqeh* who would establish a *mahdir* in his vicinity or in a close-by area to provide education to the youth in his neighbourhood either free of charge or in return for a small payment. Although its roots are traced back to the fifth Islamic century, the *mahadir* (plural of *mahdir*) have been encouraged to play a greater role in countering radical ideology in the country in the neighbourhoods where they operate. During daily teaching lessons or *halaqat dirasiyah* (study circles) with the students, the *fageh* now discusses the danger of radical ideology with his pupils and debates with them such issues as the genesis and role of fundamentalism and moderation in Islamic *fegh (jurisprudence)*. As the chapter on Mauritania in this volume demonstrates, 'the *Mahdir* today represent one of the main counteractors of violent and fundamentalist ideologies in Mauritania'.[2]

Mauritania has also recently begun relying more on civil society organizations, like the *AlMoustakbal* Association (MKA), to counter VEm in the country. Composed of prominent members of society (both religious and political), the MKA has set itself the complex task of dealing with Mauritania's main social, political and economic problems. To achieve this, the MKA has introduced four major programs, some of which deal directly with countering radicalization and VEt ideology in Mauritania. These include four key programs: *dawa* (missionary) program, cultural program, educational program and the religious program. Such programs focus on some of the most recalcitrant regions of the country where the state has little reach and they are organized mainly in the offices of the MKA in various regions of Mauritania. The cultural and educational programs are also held in places inhabited by the youth, such as universities, schools, Quranic schools and *mahadir*. As the head of the MKA told me, 'rather than expect the youth to come to us, we go to them instead' (personal interview, Nouakchott, August 2011).

Sudan, finally, counters VEt ideology in society by concentrating work in areas or regions that fester and incubate VEt thoughts and activism. Such efforts are coordinated with two key semi-autonomous institutions: *Muntada al-Nahda wal-tawasl al-Hadari* (the Renaissance and Continuation of Civilizations Forum) and International Centre for *Dawa* Studies (ICDS). Both institutions run weekly and monthly workshops, seminars, lectures, educational weeks, missionary programs and public forums that openly discuss and debate the dangerous consequences of VEm, sharia law, jihad, and the role of the Islamic ruler and Islamic state. Such activities are often organized and held in mosques but also in universities, accommodation halls, public halls and areas and institutions in regions deemed as incubators of radical thought. The ICDS and *Muntada al-Nahda* use and rely on competent and credible scholars, scientists, professors and ulama from society, particularly from various universities and educational centres in Sudan. Judges, retired or still working, are also invited to contribute to the activities of the *Muntada* and ICDS, since many extremists believe that the laws of the state are not based on sharia. Judges are deemed best positioned to refute such claims.

Obviously, effective religious rehabilitation programs require the presence of a sufficient number of competent, knowledgeable, moderate and highly respected scholars and ulama. This is no easy task, especially in Western countries. One of the main challenges the Australian authorities faced, and continues to face, in their efforts to introduce a religious rehabilitation program, has been the lack of 'reliable and disciplined imams' which 'proved to be a major challenge' for Australian authorities (personal interview with Dr Llardi, Melbourne, November 2012). The ability to identify competent and 'learned men' willing to collaborate with the state is also a major 'challenge common to most European countries' (Vidino and Brandon, 2012, p. 2). Even in many Muslim majority states, such a challenge is enormous. In Yemen, for example, most Yemeni ulama refused to take part in the dialogue committee which the former Yemini President Ali Saleh created in 2002 in order to debate the Yemeni detained radicals. In Malaysia, some detainees turned out to be more knowledgeable than scholars in certain areas. In Jordan, the incarcerated radicals refused even to talk to, eat with, or pray behind scholars chosen by the government (El-Said and Harrigan, 2013).

Second, education and vocational training

Like debate and advice, education and knowledge also have a privileged status in the Islamic faith and culture. The Quran repeatedly emphasized the role of science and knowledge, and elevated those with knowledge to a higher status. In fact, the very first Surat of the Quran (Al-A'alaq, p. 1–5) urged the Prophet and his followers to learn how to read and become knowledgeable:

> *Recite in the name of your Lord who created – Created man from a clinging substance. Recite, and your Lord is the most Generous – Who taught by the pen – Taught man that which he knew not.*

Surat Az-Zumer (p. 9) blatantly favoured individuals with knowledge over those without: 'Say, are those who know equal to those who do not know? Only they will remember [who are] people of understanding'. Surat Al-Mujadaleh (p. 11) was even more transparent in encouraging Muslims to learn and acquire knowledge, and openly elevated those with knowledge above those without: 'Allah will raise those who have believed among you and those who were given knowledge, by degrees'.

In the history of Islam, only the knowledgeable, credible and competent scholars, ulama and scientists were allowed to teach and deliver sermons in religious, formal institutions and public places. Detained non-Muslim combatants were not sent to Gitmo-like centres: they were asked to teach ten Muslim men in return for their freedom. The learned and knowledgeable, whether Muslim or otherwise, were also favoured by the Muslim Caliph for their knowledge, and brought closer to the Caliph's company. The Muslim Caliph himself always sought to become knowledgeable enough to acquire credibility among his followers and was always keen to deliver the Friday sermons at mosque. Not surprisingly, the imams always acquired a special place among Muslims wherever they were. This remains the case even today (Karabell, 2007; *Arab News*, 2011).

Therefore, knowledge was encouraged and sought as a way of recognizing the power and presence of the creator, as well as the 'right path'. This has direct relevance to today's phenomenon of VEm. As mentioned earlier, most jihadists have little or no rigourous knowledge of the Islamic faith, a fact that makes them vulnerable to the VEt ideology and activism. Enhancing their religious knowledge and understanding helps immunize them against such violent ideologies. It is precisely for this reason that in most countries facing the threat of VEm, both Muslim-majority and Muslim-minority, 'Education [has been]…identified…as the most critical element in reducing the appeal of violent extremism…education was also seen as important in helping develop and sustain the level of critical reasoning and analytical skills that can strengthen resilience against violent extremists' ideology and suasion' (Tahiri, 2013, p. 17).

But education, moreover, and vocational training are absolutely key to social and economic mobility. How can released individuals, who are not educated and trained, find jobs in the labour market, a source of income to prevent her/him from joining VEt organizations for financial gain, and ease their way back into society and their families? Not only do most detained VEts have insufficient levels of education, but they also have no pension, savings or other source of income. Detainees with insufficient levels of education, skills and training demanded by the local market face increased difficulties in finding jobs and reintegrating. 'Education is everything', a high-ranking Saudi official involved in the country's de-radicalization program once told me (personal interview with Dr. Abdurrahman al-Hadlaq, Riyadh, August, 2009). 'Education is everything' because educated violent extremist detainees can respond better to the religious and educational components of de-radicalization, they can refute the misinterpreted violent ideology and activism, and can reintegrate themselves into society more comfortably.

Ironically, while educational and vocational rehabilitation of other criminals and detainees is a common thing, it is the exception rather than the rule with regard to VEt detainees. The most known efforts here are also by Saudi Arabia. The late Carnegie scholar, Boucek (2008, p. 20), described these policies succinctly:

> *In April 2007, the newspaper al-Jazirah reported that Prince Muhammad ordered the introduction of educational training outside prison for released detainees, repentant prisoners, and Guantánamo returnees. And recently, the Advisory Committee began working with local chambers of commerce and other certification organizations to establish training courses for program participants. Under this scheme, detainees would be able to learn skills and earn qualifications while in the rehabilitation program that would qualify them for better, more substantive, employment upon their release than they previously had. The government hopes that this training, when paired with government start-up funds, will empower released detainees to start their own businesses, such as travel agencies, automotive garages, and professional support offices.*

Saudi Arabia went even further to carry out 'education reforms ... throughout the country, province by province ... to educate students about the dangers of terrorism and aim to promote nationalism' (ibid, p. 9). Outside Saudi Arabia there are few known educational and vocational training programs effectively designed and tailored to the needs of VEt detainees. Educational and vocational programs for VEt detainees remain the exception, not the rule, despite their significance. In fact, stigmatization and labelling present in many countries complicated further the reintegration of released Muslim detainees. Media and official discrimination and even attacks not only offended Muslim communities, but also led to biases in labour markets against Muslims in general and released detainees in particular. In most Western democracies, de-radicalization, rehabilitation and education of VEt detainees were neglected because Western democracies decided to lock the detainees up for a very long time in detention centres or deport them back to their countries of origin (ICSR, 2010). This is a very dangerous policy to follow, one that can come back to haunt Western democracies, as the failure of the Yemeni de-radicalization program after 2005 demonstrated.

Psychological rehabilitation

The available empirical evidence suggests that most VEts are rational human beings who do not suffer from any psychological or psychiatric disease (El-Said and Barrett, 2011; Sageman, 2010; Bhui et al., 2012a and 2012b). However, the field of psychology must still be an integral part of any de-radicalization program for at least two reasons: first, because the discipline of psychology is largely concerned with human behaviour, it can help us better understand how VEts think and what motivates them to behave in the way they do; also, because the discipline of psychology is constructed both socially and culturally, the field also helps us study and better understand how the sociocultural factors inform the process of radicalization, the impact of grievances (real and perceived) on the human mind, and the role of cognition, emotions, personalities and interpersonal relationships, issues which are important for the development of appropriate and tailor-made programs. Second, while VEts do not suffer from psychological or psychiatric diseases, a large number have a strong personal factor. In fact, it is not enough to have an enabling environment for individuals to turn to VEm. This still requires a personal factor. As Coolsaet and Struye de Swielande (2008, p. 157) argued, a 'common characteristic of all forms of radicalization is that it takes place at the intersection of a personal history and that enabling environment'. The personal factor varies from the mundane to the major (such as losing a job, a friend or a family member). It is the personal factor that translates the enabling environment into action because the enabling environment works best 'when it resonates more with...personal experiences, which in turn gives strength to the [violent] ideology from indisputable biographical evidence' (Sageman, 2010, p. 99).

In Saudi Arabia, most detained VEts have a history of personal and individual factors, such as lack of parental attention caused by the widespread nature of the polygamy system. This also causes other problems related to inheritance, financial settlements, jealousy, arranged marriages, and family and interpersonal relationships (El-Said and Harrigan, 2013). In Australia, most neo-jihadists come from families with widespread strong domestic violence and a large number of siblings, thus causing similar effects to those observed in Saudi Arabia (see chapter on Australia in this volume). Moreover, arrest and detention can cause 'anger and frustration', making the detainees 'weary from their lifestyles and imprisonment' and concerned regarding the impact of their arrest on their family members and children (DeAngelis, 2009). Many also have fractured self-esteem or self-worth which makes them insular and unresponsive to many prison initiatives. Detainees with psychological and physical problems might require different types of treatment, especially if they suffer from lack of self-esteem and confidence. This status might undermine their absorptive and collaborative capacity. There is a need therefore to identify and classify detainees according to their psychological and physical status. This suggests that they will require 'emotional' and psychological support by a professional team to pacify their fears and concerns, and restore their self-esteem and worth (DeAngelis, 2009). The field of psychology helps in explaining the mind and brain of the individual in the context of real life.

The most known psychological programs are found in Singapore, Saudi Arabia and Australia. In Singapore, the psychological program aims at studying the psychological reasoning behind joining Jamma' Islamiah (JI), as well as the psychological conditions of the detainee in general. Sessions between professional psychologists from the IDS and the detainees are designed to take place on an almost daily basis as part of a larger, well-structured daily de-radicalization program. It seeks to identify whether the detainees suffer from any psychological condition, as well as detecting any psychological factors that may have led the detainees to join JI. Psychologists also seek to assure the detainee about the future of his children and immediate family and help him restore self-esteem and self-worth. They also provide appropriate counseling sessions not only to detect but also to take out and neutralize violent ideology (see chapter on Singapore in this volume).

The Saudi psychological program involves not only a constant assessment of the psychological condition of the beneficiaries, but also their training in positive thinking, handling psychological pressure, discerning signs of psychological abnormality, building and boosting self-confidence and overcoming anxiety. The main premise of the Saudi psychological program is that:

> *Nobody is born a terrorist. Terrorism is a process. Our program works according to this principle. We have not noticed any major psychological disorders among the beneficiaries. They may suffer from stress, even from mild depression or maladjustment but there has not even been one case of major psychological disorder. We try therefore to help them control their emotions by teaching them self-management. (personal interviews with staff at the Care Centre, Riyadh, August, 2009. Also quoted in El-Said and Harrigan, 2013, p. 214)*

Social rehabilitation program

Detainees come from different social and economic backgrounds. While some are more financially solvent, others suffer from deprivation. In many cases the main breadwinner of the family is detained, thus jeopardizing the family's livelihood and economic and social mobility. For example, most neo-jihadists and their families in Australia experience substantial economic disadvantages. In fact, Sunni Muslims of Lebanese descent in Australia, who account for 60 per cent of neo-jihadists in the country, are over-represented at the bottom end of employment as labourers and under-represented at the top end. Their employment level also remains significantly lower than the Australian average. The economic disadvantages experienced by Lebanese Australian Muslims also manifest themselves in low educational achievement, a feature which they share with their Muslim counterparts in Europe (GTReC, 2014, p. 6; Sageman, 2010). Sudan and Mauritania are among the poorest countries in the world per capita. Unemployment rates exceed 30 per cent in each country (at least), with more than 68 per cent of all Mauritanians living below the international poverty line of $2 per day, while 85 per cent of the rural population in Sudan are estimated to be living in extreme poverty (IFAD, 2002, p. 1). Under such circumstances, weak developmental capacity of the state itself becomes a radicalizing factor. Detaining the breadwinner of the family without protecting their economic, educational and social needs will alienate them, turn them against the state and society and guarantee the emergence of future generations of VEts. In particular, the needs of the detainees' children for education, health, food and shelter must not be undermined as a result of detaining the breadwinner. The statement 'if we don't reach family members the terrorists will' is repeatedly heard from officials in Riyadh, Sanaa, Singapore and Kuala Lumpur. Detainees' anger and frustration can and should be diffused 'by showing authentic concern for their families, through means such as funding their children's education or offering professional training for their wives' (DeAngelis, 2009).

While Saudi Arabia provided the most formal, comprehensive, generous and financially sustained social program, Singapore and Turkey relied more on community, charity and societal organizations to meet the social and economic needs of the detainees and their families, thus saving public money. In Singapore, MUIS created a special fund for the needs of the detainees and their families funded from charities paid by the Singapore Muslim community. In Turkey, regional funds, largely from charity and zakat money, are used to provide social welfare to the poor and the needy, including the families and children of the detainees. In Australia, a trained community member teaches detained individuals just before their release about existing public and societal institutions that provide social welfare to the poor and needy, guides them how to apply to such organizations and where to find them, and helps them with filling the necessary application forms.

Family rehabilitation program

There is a strong case to be made for mentoring and involving family members in de-radicalization efforts. The most important case here, especially with regard to Muslim VEts, is the role of the family. Most prisoners return to their families within their societies after release, and the family becomes the most important conduit for reintegration or recidivism. When asked about the most important factor that facilitated their reintegration into society, most Kuwaiti returnees from Guantánamo Bay (around nine) said that it was their family. When asked about the most important help they received during their reintegration process and after their return from Guantánamo Bay, they also ranked assistance and help from the family as the most significant factor facilitating normalization and reintegration.[3]

That family and social networks can play a key role in radicalizing individuals is now hardly contested. That the family can also play a de-radicalizing role, convincing their sons and family members to stay away from or abandon VEt groups and activism, has not gone unnoticed but received much less attention than it deserves. In Australia, for example, the impact of family connections has not always been 'negative...there are also clear cases of family members persuading individuals away from extremism' (Harris-Hogan, 2012, p. 2). Under what conditions families and social networks become radicalizing or de-radicalizing in the first place deserves more attention. The literature however is replete with examples of both released detainees returning to a radicalizing or de-radicalizing social and family network, with the latter encouraging disengagement and resilience and the former encouraging recidivism (El-Said and Harrigan, 2013). This is one of the main reasons why families also require mentoring and rehabilitation, mainly to make sure that released individuals do not return to a radicalizing family network, that families will support the goals and objectives of the de-radicalization program, and that they will contribute to the resilience of the individual and by extension to the resilience of the community.

There is another intertwined and related reason why families should be more directly involved in the de-radicalization program itself to convince their children and relatives to repent. Families and the collective structure remain important in most Muslim societies and communities, even when living in a Muslim-minority state. The influence of family members, therefore, particularly the elderly over the young members, remains as influential as it has been for hundreds of years. The role of parents in Islamic families and societies specifically is paramount from all perspectives, including religious, traditional and cultural perspectives. Nobody wants to see their sons dying or joining a VEt act or group and most parents would be receptive to efforts and policies that would keep their sons out of harm's way. This is especially the case with Muslim families living in Western countries, who migrated in search of better economic, social and political conditions and a brighter future for both themselves and their children. This is precisely why the London 7/7 bombers and the Australian neo-jihadists captured in the 2005 Pendennis and 2009 Neath operations never informed their parents about their intentions, knowing very well that their parents would oppose their actions and thoughts. Involving families in the de-radicalization efforts will facilitate disengagement, speed up detachment from VEt ideology and lead to a more sustainable and resilient repentance.

Many families, however, are unaware of the reasons and conditions that lead their sons to embrace VEt ideology. They are neither aware of the psychological and mental changes their sons underwent as a result of the radicalization process, nor how to respond to such a phenomenon. There is a need therefore to train and mentor families to enable them to deal with their 'new sons' correctly, ensuring that the environment to which detainees return to will not lead to re-radicalization and recidivism. Involving families can also lead to winning their support for the de-radicalization efforts, an important strategy given the significance of social milieu in terrorism and social and family networks.

Most secular, Western democracies remain silent on the role of families in the de-radicalization process. As one high-ranking Australian official told me: 'we do not encourage' a strong role for families in the de-radicalization process 'because we don't want to be seen as interfering in family affairs' (personal interview with Goulburn High Security Prison authorities, November 2012). Neither in Turkey nor in Sudan or Mauritania have families been made an integral part of the de-radicalization process, as is the case in Saudi Arabia, for example. The role of the families of the detained JI members and ROs in Singapore is confined to keeping them (families) informed about the conditions of their incarcerated sons/relatives and also facilitating family visits to incarceration centres. The role of families in Singapore, however, is also not as prominent and integrated as it is in the case of Saudi Arabia, which has the best-known social and family programs.

Improvisation/Discretionary program

Counter-de-Rad as a program and process is evolutionary and continuously evolving and developing. There is a need for constant evaluation, upgrading and development. The new and emerging requirements of detainees and parole officers need to be taken into consideration, as well as the general prison and external environment where they are being implemented. For example, Saudi officials suggested the need for a history program because many detainees seemed 'ignorant' of historical events, particularly concerning the life of the prophet who they wrongly believe spent most of it in jihad.[4] In their mind, the history of Islam is a constant struggle – wars and rivalry with the West. Saudi officials also felt that many detainees have difficulty in expressing themselves verbally and so suggested using art as therapy. The result was two new programs in history and art. They also made physical education and sport an integral part of the de-radicalization process, encouraging scholars and security officers to join detainees in playing soccer or volleyball. It is a well-established fact that healthier individuals (including detainees) are more productive. Healthier and happier detainees, due in part to a healthy lifestyle and exercising within a cordial environment, can result in them also being more cooperative and receptive to information and advice from scholars and mentors.

Another important area here is training. In most cases training will be required for everybody involved in Counter-de-Rad programs, including scholars, sport instructors, security and parole officers and others. As Angell and Gunaratna noted in 2011, training is a 'collective' process that should exclude nobody. The Turkish government has created the best, most comprehensive Counter-de-Rad–tailored training programs among all countries studied in volumes I and II. Diplomas and Masters degrees were set specifically to meet the needs of the Counter-de-Rad efforts, and human rights, another key area in countering VEm, has been instituted and formalized by state laws and special training program. Sudan, Mauritania – even Australia – none has been able to introduce an effective training program for state officials involved in countering VEm, including in particular parole officers and those who deal with detainees on a daily basis. The Australian incarceration officials, however, have recently introduced a program to train imams, as finding competent, credible and law-compliant imams proved to be a challenge. Yet most Australian officials openly admit that 'we have no training in Islamic radicalization and we have no idea about the process of radicalization, signs of radicalization and what to consider as a radicalizing behaviour or normal religious practice' (personal interview, Goulburn High Security Prison, November 2012). Indonesia decided to 'use former militants who are now law-abiding citizens to convince former terrorists that violence against civilians compromises the image of Islam' (DeAngelis, 2009, p. 60)-an approach that has also recently been tried in Saudi Arabia (El-Said, 2013a).

Post-care/release program

The post-release environment can be rather problematic for the released detainees and their families and communities. As argued earlier, a large number of released detainees lack education, training, savings, jobs, pensions or rich families upon which they can rely for support after release. On the contrary, some even have a large number of family dependents. Social pressure, stigmatization and state regulations can sometimes prevent released extremists from finding jobs or working in certain sectors. In Australia, for example, media bias fostered 'a perceived negative link between Islam, violence, and extremism' and that led to stigmatization and labelling of the Muslim community in Australia in general (Tahiri, 2013, p. 4). This made it more difficult for Muslim community members to integrate fully into Australian society and led to social exclusion that facilitated radicalization among many young Australian Muslims. Muslim women in particular face numerous difficulties as a result of Muslim stigmatization and labelling, particularly when seeking employment. Such an environment, without assistance, provides a recipe for recidivism. Indeed, lack of such support caused a large number of Yemeni detainees to return to al-Qaeda after they were discharged from prison in 2005. The Saudi government goes further to help released detainees in finding new jobs by enrolling them in and subsidizing their education. It also helps them establish new businesses and even facilitates the marriage process for the single ones, paying for all costs involved, including accommodation, furniture and transportation. The government also provides a monthly stipend of 2,000–5,000 Saudi riyals ($400–$1,000) for almost one year, or until they manage to stand on their own feet without government support. Most 'psychologists' now agree that a post-release program to 'address the reality that detainees often re-enter societies that may rekindle their radical beliefs' is necessary (DeAngelis, 2009). In addition to the above, such a program can include: extending the debate and religious rehabilitation program for a few more (2–3) years after the release of the former vulnerable prisoners; inviting former militants who are now law-abiding citizens to continue to advise released detainees; facilitating their education, finding new jobs or returning to their old jobs; micro-finance to assist in establishing new businesses; facilitating families to support released members; empowering civil society, community and NGOs to assist in the reintegration process; and other measures that can increase the reintegration and employability of those hardest to reach and employ (ex-offenders) by increasing their skills, training and confidence. Such efforts can also include training for CV writing/application forms, how to disclose past offences to a prospective employer, work ethic (what makes a good employee), how to seek out job vacancies, work trials/voluntary work, general training and mock interviews/real interviews.

The main tenets of the international framework for countering violent extremism (IFCVE)

The principal tenets upon which our framework for international and national Counter-de-Rad programs is predicated are that the level of threat of VEm and the ability to counter the threat of VEm depend on a myriad of both macro and micro factors. The former is concerned with international and national environments, while the latter is concerned with the kind of policies and components employed to counter the threat under certain environments. In other words, the success of Counter-de-Rad programs will depend on certain conditions being satisfied. Four major conditions/components make up our International Framework for CVE. These include the following:

1. The extent to which a country has specific macro advantages. Not all Muslim-majority or Muslim-minority states face the threat of VEm or face the threat to the same extent. Some Muslim-majority states, like Malaysia, for example, faced and continue to face very little VEt threat. This is partly a function of certain characteristics that the country possesses, including the political capacity and developmental capacity of the state. The former includes the ability of the state to defend itself, its borders, society, property and to provide security. The latter, as defined by Lubeck (1998) includes the ability of the state to manage relatively high growth rates, create employment

opportunities, restrain corruption, reduce inequality and manage relations with its minorities. The available empirical evidence derived from outside the terrorism literature is supportive of these arguments. For example, the economic and international business literature, known to be more rigorous, expansive and data-oriented than the terrorism literature, has long argued that 'Terrorists tend to emerge from areas characterized by poverty, low economic development, and ungoverned spaces' (JIBS, 2010, p. 833. See also Innes, 2007; Li and Schaub, 2004; Stern, 2010; Suder, 2004b). The major international business journal (JIBS) goes further to find a strong link between the weak political and developmental capacities of the state, arguing that 'Poverty and underdevelopment often characterizes regions in which governments fail to address basic needs, such as ensuring adequate infrastructure or the rule of law, and therefore are either unwilling or unable to expel terrorists from their borders'. (JIBS, 2010, p. 833)

It is important to remember here that a strong state does not necessarily mean a repressive state, or a state that relies on 'repression', as some have argued (Ashour, 2009, p. 14.). The extensive political literature has demonstrated that repression leads to strong opposition, riots, terrorism and political instability (see Pape, 2005; Attran, 2006). Revolutions, terrorism and political instability that engulfed several former repressive Arab regimes (Libya, Yemen and Syria) provide clear examples. In fact, most terrorists belonging to the Islamic faith either emerged from undemocratic countries (the Arab world) or were migrants living in Western democracies with memories of repressive regimes still fresh in their minds, either directly (in the case of first-generation migrants) or indirectly (second- and third-generation migrants) (Bhui et al., 2012a and 2012b).

There is a consensus today that points to the role of human rights and real democracies as more successful in creating politically and developmentally strong states. The overwhelming majority of participants in a recent survey in Australia, which included members of various Muslim and non-Muslim communities, stated that democracies are more 'capable of responding ... to diversity of view point and orientation ... the best available political system for guaranteeing highly valued rights such as freedom of speech, movement, political beliefs and the right to practice one's religion without discrimination or persecution'. These values were particularly important 'to those participants who hailed from countries or regions where such rights and freedoms were curtailed or absent', including specifically the Muslim regions (Tahiri, 2013, p. 12). The United Nations thus warned against undermining human rights while fighting terrorism, while other observers, like Hoffman (2004, p. 932), criticized the 'war on terror' for 'undermin[ing] the international human rights framework so painstakingly built since World War II'. In the Arab world in particular, from whence all of the 9/11 bombers emerged and the region which experienced more terrorism in terms of incidents and fatalities than any other region of the world, the United Nations Arab Human Development Report condemned the Arab state for terrorizing its own people, turning itself 'into a threat to human security' of its own citizens, and repressing freedoms of speech, choice, expression and political participation (UN, 2009, p. 4).

The macro component of our framework of location-specific advantages goes beyond the political and developmental capacities of the state to include the role of civil society and prison policies. Certainly, democratically strong states with strong developmental capacity enjoy more dynamic and rigorous civil society (UN, 2009). However, the issue here is not the presence or absence of dynamic and rigorous society, but rather the quality of the relationship between communities and state officials, especially policy–community relationships. There is no question that most Western societies enjoy a strong and dynamic civil society. Yet such a relationship, especially between the state and some of its ethnic minorities, is characterized by distrust and suspicion. The UK's Prevent strategy, for example, has been unpopular and less effective than was believed would be the case before its introduction. 'Its effectiveness [has been]...hampered by the fact that many British Muslims view it with resentment and suspicion. It is seen as embodying their government's unequal approach to violence emanating from their communities compared to others' (BBC News, 2011). In Australia, a recent survey showed 'sharp distinctions emerged between government and community perspective on the efficacy and integrity...of counter-terrorist operations' and police in general (Tahiri, 2013, p. 16). The way counterterrorism operation programs and policies have been implemented in Western democracies has frequently targeted Muslims, stigmatizing and labelling them 'suspect communities, as security threats rather than as fully-fledged citizens', thus undermining their collaboration with the state and creating distrust and suspicion on both sides of the relationship (Kundnani and Patel, 2011).

Nor are capturing, disrupting and detaining VEt detainees for long periods of time to be regarded as sufficient policy programs. Such policies are more likely to lead to further radicalization of some of the inmates, members of their families and social network. The aim of such disruption and detention should be to rehabilitate and prepare detainees for reintegration into society and diffuse detainees' anger and frustration by showing authentic concern for their families through means such as funding their children's education or offering professional training for their wives. This aspect also capitalizes on the fact that detainees are weary from their lifestyles and imprisonment (DeAngelis, 2009). This means that well-designed and implemented rehabilitation and reintegration programs that also incorporate not only religious aspects, but also more secular and intellectual aspects such as education, vocational training, social and family programs, as well as measures to boost self-esteem, self-worth, health and personal skills of detainees represent 'the best measures to raise the costs of terrorism and eradicate VEm, as these measures will touch the issues at their deepest roots.

2. Assuming the above-mentioned conditions (which are more or less internal to the environment of the country) are satisfied, the external environment also needs to be taken into consideration. For example, the situation in Palestine and the lack of peace there has admittedly assisted in the radicalization process of many young Muslim youths around the world. The occupation of Afghanistan and Iraq has led to moral outrage among Muslims that their religion and some of their countries were under attack from the West. Many countries obviously have little control over the external environment, particularly over some of the perceived radicalizing policies of Western countries. However, some influence can still be exerted as in the case of Saudi Arabia, for example. On the eve of commencing the Kingdom's internationally touted de-radicalization program, King Abdullah gradually distanced himself from the United States, openly criticized American policy in the region, particularly the perceived American unconditional and biased support towards Israel, which he held responsible for the collapse of peace talks between the Arabs and Israelis. He even went further to issue an 'extraordinary warning to Washington... threatening a reconsideration of bilateral relations' (El-Said and Harrigan, 2013, p. 205). A similar argument can be made in Malaysia, when the former Malaysian Prime Minister, Mahathir Mohammad, also distanced himself from the United States and Israel following the occupation of Iraq in 2003, which coincided with Malaysia's introduction of its own de-radicalization program (Asia Times, 2003).

3. Given the configuration of the macro (internal and external environment) factors in our framework, and assuming that those conditions are favourable to countering VEm, the next step is to determine what kind of policies and programs can best counter the phenomenon of VEm, refute violent ideology and prevent the kind of radicalization and extremism that lead to terrorism. Here debate, whether inside or outside the prison walls, must be an important component of any CVE program. Debate can take several forms, some theological and some political. Whether the former or the latter, debate is a key element in the process of Counter-de-Rad. Lyons (2009, p. 64) pointed to the prominent role which debate and discussion assumed in the political discourse under the Abbasid caliphates in the following words 'other than face to face, how else could a learned man meet his colleagues and collect and debate their ideas'? Such debate can, and has, taken a religious form in some countries, like Saudi Arabia, for example, or Mauritania and Sudan. In others, like Malaysia, it has taken more of a political form. However, in most countries, including Saudi Arabia, religious rehabilitation has been, and should also be, extended to include other intellectual and skill-building programs, such as education, vocational training, social programs, family programs, physical education programs and post-care-release programs. The aim of these programs is not just, important though it is, to rehabilitate and prepare detainees to join their society and family after release. It is vital also to defuse detainees' anger and frustration by showing authentic concern and care for their families, prevent recidivism, win the support of society and families, improve state–society–community relations and thus prevent the emergence and fomentation of a new generation of VEts.

In fact, programs that include debates, education, social, physical and other aspects should also be extended to society. Communities of various backgrounds should be empowered to play a larger role in debating and taking care of their members. Terrorism is not a Muslim problem. It is a process caused by various intertwined international, national and personal factors. Empowering communities to play a larger role in Counter-de-Rad programs can do much to enhance state–community relations, build trust and a resilient and immune society. Failing to win the hearts and minds of communities and community leaders will create distrust, suspicion and deprive a country of the 'benefits' of collaboration with community, which include information generation, exposition of VEt acts and ideology and deprivation of VEt groups and individuals of vital societal support and resources, and provision of effective solutions.

4. Assessment and evaluation of Counter-de-Rad programs remains the weakest link in the entire process. The 'difficulty to fully assess their impact' is widely recognized (Vidino and Brandon, 2012, p. 2). As the CGCC (Romaniuk and Fink, 2012, p. 9) argued:

> *Despite the massive investment of resources in this field, few states and multilateral organizations have elaborated robust and succinct methodologies to evaluate the counterterrorism measures per se. Likewise, the academic literature on the effectiveness of counterterrorism generally remains in its infancy.*

Vidino and Brandon (2012, p. 2) are in agreement:

> *Authorities have also struggled to establish clear metrics to assess the effectiveness of their programs. While methods of verifying the success of deradicalization and disengagement measures are relatively easier to find, general preventive measures are extremely difficult to empirically assess.*

It is important, however, to build in assessment and evaluation when developing Counter-de-Rad programs to allow for improvement, adjustment and to ensure that policies are fed the correct information about the effectiveness of their counterterrorism strategies. The unanswered question remains what metrics to include in such assessment.

Policymakers are advised to include as many matrices as possible, including the rate of recidivism. While an imperfect assessment tool, recidivism rates remain an important proxy for the effectiveness of deradicalization programs in the short and medium term. It is an easy measure to use, provides good information on the period required before some individuals return to VEt life and bestows an important indicator on how radicalizing or resilient the environment which the released detainees return to actually is. While other factors, such as increased repressive powers of the state's security agencies, improvement in surveillance techniques and constant monitoring of individuals will reduce the motive to return to the VEt path, some individuals will still return to VEm as soon as they get the opportunity to do so. Hence monitoring the recidivism rate will assist in building a set of data over time that is significant for understanding certain patterns and trends, as well as testing the pro-release environment.

Relying on recidivism rates alone, however, is incomplete and misleading. There is a need to ensure that not only disengagement but also de-radicalization occurs among both released individuals and vulnerable community members. This metric is far more difficult than measuring recidivism rate and requires longer time spans perhaps. Some psychologists, nevertheless, have embarked on such an exercise. A good example here is the National Consortium for the Study of Terrorism and Responses to Terrorism (START), led by social psychologist Arie Kruglanski, PhD, co-director of START. Kruglanski and his team at START are developing a new assessment instrument that relies more on gauging 'attitude change in those who have undergone such programs, including gauging implicit attitude change that more accurately reads their true feelings than simply what they claim is the case' (DeAngelis, 2009). This is a very promising approach, although it is still at its early phase of development. Approaches that seek to gauge attitudes to change would complement short-term efforts that rely on recidivism rate and provide a clearer distinction between disengagement and de-radicalization. The downside of such an approach is that it takes time to measure attitude and cognitive changes, and requires time, resources and a skilled team of researchers. But this might be necessary to acquire the relevant information, enhance our understanding of both radicalization and de-radicalization processes and develop effective policies.

It is also important to gauge views and opinions of various communities. As Coolsaet and Struye de Swielande (2008, p. 161) stated, 'surveys often offer fascinating reading. They bring us as close as one can get to gauging the mood of the...citizenry' (p. 161). Equally important is that gauging the views and opinions of various communities, helps to avoid 'one big problem with terrorism policy altogether...that it tends to interpret things from our perspective, based on what makes sense to us....That's not really the issue: The issue is what makes sense to people on the ground' (DeAngelis, 2009). There is a need therefore to pay more attention to the populations that are vulnerable to recruitment to terrorist action instead of the current approach in terrorism studies and policy which focuses more on those identified as engaged in terrorism organizations or convicted of terrorism crime (Bhui et al., 2012b, p. 1). This approach will provide important indications for the radicalization level in society, and will also lead to the development of accurate radicalization signs based on those that understand the radicalization process best: community members.

At the end of the day, terrorism ceases to be a threat when VEts are no longer able to radicalize and recruit, and when vulnerable members of communities are more resilient to their calls. This will be partly based on the level of trust among various communities on the one hand, and state officials, state institutions and state policies on the other. Approaches and metrics that seek to measure the level of trust among various communities and state institutions and personnel can provide important insights into the degree of collaboration of community members with state security, lead to the development of accurate signs of radicalization, and better understand the degree and type of grievances that can lead to radicalization and extremism that lead to terrorism.

Box 2.1 sets out a selection of the more commonly identified elements of IFCVE. Some of these can best explain the initial act or presence of VEm in one place and not in another (weak political capacity, weak developmental capacity, lack of prison policies, torture, external environment, etc.). Others are more valuable in terms of explaining not only the conditions conducive to radicalization and VEm, but also to the success/failure of counterterrorism strategy in general. They can and should be developed further to include the specific roles of various actors that can support the process of Counter-de-Rad programs and sequential acts or outcomes of such programs.

Box 2.1   A selection of the more commonly identified elements of IFCVE

A. Macro National Factors

I.   Political capacity (ability to defend and secure borders, citizens, property and businesses.)
II. Developmental capacity: ability to manage growth rate, create jobs, restrain corruption, reduce inequities and manage relations with minorities.
III. Prison environment that is characterized by safety, security, sufficient space and advanced structure and is not conducive to radicalization and recruitment.
IV. Strong and dynamic civil society that enjoys good and trustful relations with state officials.

B. External Environment

Presence/absence of international/regional radicalizing environment (aligning a country's policies with a foreign power that is perceived as unfriendly or biased, occupation, war, civil war, attacks on civilians, drone attacks, etc.); relations with neighbouring countries.

C. Micro Components of a Successful Program

I.   Religious rehabilitation.
II. Educational rehabilitation.
III. Vocational training.

IV. Family rehabilitation.
V. Physical rehabilitation.
VI. Post-care-release reintegrating.
VII. Activation and empowering the role of societies.

D. Assessment and Evaluation

I.   The role of the state; presence/lack of political will; facilitation or program design and implementation; provision of needed financial and human resources; dissemination of information on challenges and best practices to different regions and parties; promoting and facilitating of research; feedback of state officials, including detention parole officials and those involved in community policing.
II. Response of detainees to prison programs: their respect for the rules of the game, participation, collaboration, complaints, feedback and so forth.
III. Recidivism rates.
IV. Violations and other offences.
V.   Cognitive versus behavioural changes.
VI. The response of society to Counter-de-Rad programs: information provided to state officials; role-playing in bridging cultural gaps; collaboration in financial resources available; human resources.

Conclusion

This chapter sought to develop a general framework that would guide policymakers in their attempts to develop and implement effective Counter-de-Rad programs. It is worth reiterating that there is no silver bullet and that one –size –does –not –fit all. Also, because of the wide variety of the cultural, economic, legal and social conditions where Counter-de-Rad programs can and have been implemented, it is essential that efforts to design successful programs are conducted on a case-by-case basis, based first and foremost on a good understanding of the conditions conducive for radicalization and extremism in each place.

The international framework to counter VEm developed in this chapter is general, flexible, expansive and adjustable. The generalized predictions of the framework are straightforward and derived from the experiences (successful or otherwise) of countries that sought to implement Counter-de-Rad programs, both Muslim-minority and Muslim-majority states. At any given moment of time, the level of radicalization and VEm in a country is a function of at least five factors: the political capacity of the state; the developmental capacity of the state; the type of prison environment in place and policies implemented inside prison walls; the rigour and dynamism of civil society and the level of trust between various communities and state institutions and personnel; and the strength of the effect of external radicalizing factors influencing a country. Changes in the level of radicalization in a country can also be explained by changes in one or more of the factors cited above.

Assuming that the above conditions are present or satisfied and a country requires a program to counter the emergence of or re-emerging radicalization and VEt trends, the next step is to determine what kind of policies are most suitable and fit the kind of external and internal configuration a country faces, taking into consideration its culture, norms and legal structure. Such policies include religious rehabilitation, educational and vocational rehabilitation, social rehabilitation, family rehabilitation and involvement, physical rehabilitation, art, history and political rehabilitation, as well as a post-release program to ease the transition of released detainees back into society. Building assessment tools and matrices into such programs from the very beginning is imperative in order to monitor performance, change in attitudes and ideas, response of groups and individuals most vulnerable to VEm, check effectiveness and improve performance.

The IFCVE is flexible in the sense that not only can it be applied to all countries, but it is also suggested that it can be extended to all forms of VEm, whether by groups or individuals belonging to the Islamic or other faiths. It suggests that all forms of VEm can be explained by reference to the above conditions, and that all can be dealt with by employing similar, although not necessarily identical, policies. For example, weak developmental capacity of a state may suggest that a Western developed state might have mismanaged relations with certain ethnic groups, a fact that might lead to more attention being paid to ethnic minorities. Weak political capacity may not necessarily mean a weak military, but rather a state that relies too heavily on repression against its ethnic minorities. The important role of society also applies to both strong and weak states, given the fact that what matters most is not the sheer presence of a rigorous civil society but rather the quality and type of relations that exist between members of civil society and state institutions and personnel. Similarly, the external environment can be a cause and an effect at the same time, with both strong and weak states affected by and affecting the external environment simultaneously.

With regard to the component of Counter-de-Rad programs, these can also be applicable to all countries, with some modifications and adjustment. For example, there is no reason why religious rehabilitation cannot be carried out in a Western context, particularly by competent and credible community members of the detained individuals or most vulnerable groups in society. If the detained individuals are more secular in nature, such as the Tamil Tigers in Sri Lanka, for example, a spiritual or secular debate program will be more desirable. The main thing is to debate, particularly the issues that matter most to the targeted groups and individuals by competent and credible scholars. There is also no reason why a social program that is funded by the community of the detainees and most vulnerable groups in society cannot be established to provide social welfare to the families of the detainees. Educational and vocational rehabilitation has always been part and parcel of any prison system. There is no reason why it cannot be extended to those charged with or convicted of VEm. Programs that facilitate and ease transformation of ex-convicts back into society have existed for decades. It makes sense to extend them to those convicted of and charged with VEt offences.

The configuration of factors and components are not fixed or static either. These can change all the time to take into consideration new developments, new contingencies, and the latest developments in sciences and opinions. For example, more radicalizing/de-radicalizing factors pertaining to national or external environments can be added if they arise at some point. By the same token, more components and policies can be added in order to take into account the specificities of each country and conditions conducive to radicalization and extremism in each place. Assessment tools and matrices can be developed and added in the same way all the time.

States can also use the IFCVE to improve and strengthen certain sectors in their efforts to prevent and counter radicalization and extremism within their borders. They can rely on the IFCVE, for example, to identify weaknesses in their political or developmental capacities, improve their understanding of conditions conducive to VEm, including political repression/weakness, high unemployment, corruption, inequalities, discrimination, mistrust, prison policy or external factors. States can also use such information to develop effective policies to improve on and tackle the root causes of VEm within their borders.

The IFCVE also has international implications for developmental agencies, regional organizations and other funders. Such organizations and institutions can link their aid and other policies to improving certain sectors in third countries facing the threat of VEm, or where there is concern of exporting radicalization and VEt ideologies. For example, the European Union can use its financial power to promote democracy and human rights in the Middle East, as it did in Eastern Europe. It can also link its assistance to improving the developmental capacity of the region's states. The same applies to the United States and other rich Western states and institutions.

Nothing we propose here is completely new or unprecedented. Programs to rehabilitate and reintegrate other convicts existed for decades, along with policies and measures to fight crime in society. The problem is that we decided not to extend them to a special category of detainees and members of certain ethnic minorities in our society, namely Muslims. This has led to stigmatization and labelling resulting in discrimination that has undermined trust between Muslim ethnic communities on the one hand and the Western democratic state, its institutions and personnel, on the other, not to mention between the Muslim community and other communities within the same society. The time has come to unravel and undo the damage we have inflicted upon ourselves.

3

Radicalization in a Western Context: The Case of Australia

Introduction

Before the end of the 20th century, violent extremism (VEm), or terrorism as we know it today, was virtually non-existent in Australia. This is despite the fact that Australia, in the mid-1970s, opened its doors to immigrants from Muslim states and developed a sizeable Muslim community by the end of the century. Its open-door migrant policy was associated with a policy of multiculturalism, which aimed at facilitating the integration of minorities into Australian society and maintaining social harmony. This was to be achieved by protecting the culture of all individuals living in Australia, guaranteeing social justice and equality of opportunities for all, and effective development and utilization of skills and talents of all Australians (The Australian Government, 2013). Initially multiculturalism bred, or was concomitant with, peace at the societal level, free from the kind of political violence that plagued many Western counterparts in Europe and North America. Some commentators went as far as arguing that Australia produced 'great[er] settler immigrant societies... more successful immigrant societies than those of Europe in the modern era... [and] that our settlement practices are superior to that of Europe' (Sheridan, 2011). At the official level, VEm did not figure among the number of potential non-military threats to Australia listed in the 1997 Foreign and Trade Policy White Paper. Not surprisingly, 'Australia's peak intelligence analysis agency, Office of National Assessments, did not employ a single analyst dedicated full time to the threat of terrorism' at the turn of the century (Harris-Hogan, 2012a).

All of this was to change at the beginning of the 21st century. Australia's geographic and strategic remoteness from the main theatres of instability (Afghanistan, Algeria, Iraq, Lebanon, Palestine, Somalia and so on) seemed to no longer be able to provide immunity against VEm to the country's society and citizens. International events like 9/11 and the 2002 Bali bombing, which killed more than 200 Australians, were followed by 'home-grown' events that led to the arrest of several 'neo-jihadists' in 2005 and 2009 in operations code-named Pendennis and Neath, respectively. 'Operation Pendennis (2004–5)' was described as 'Australia's largest counter-terrorism investigation' (Lentini, 2010, p. 8). It also included 'The largest number of arrests...when 13 people in Melbourne and nine in Sydney were arrested in a coordinated effort by ASIO, Australian Federal Police and the NSW and Victorian police services' (Zammit, 2010, p. 2). Operation Neath, on the other hand, led to the arrest of five people based in Melbourne after being 'accused of planning an attack on Holsworthy Barracks in Sydney' (Zammit, 2010, p. 2). In addition, Australian embassies in Iraq, Jakarta and Phnom Penh were targeted by VEts. The continued police operations and raids (in 2010 and the second half of 2012, for example) are 'a testament' to the persistent threat of VEm which the country continues to face (Harris-Hogan, 2012b, p. 4).

These developments have massively divided Australian society. For some observers, the rise of VEm in Australia was taken as 'evidence that multiculturalism – after a promising start – has failed' (Henderson, 2012). For others, the 'problem lied [sic] with Islam' itself (Sheridan, 2011). The main problem with the latter argument is its poor explanatory power, particularly its failure to explain why the majority of Australian Muslims did not embrace violent ideology. It also fails to explain why and how some grass-root Muslim movements emerged to fight and counter VEm and activism. More importantly, few have truly questioned or investigated the changes that occurred in the local, national and international 'environment[s]' that Australia underwent and which have been responsible for the embracing of VEm by a small group of Muslim Australians over the past decade and a half (Harris-Hogan, 2012a p. 25).

This chapter seeks to address 'some of these lacunae' (Lentini, 2010, p. 9) by looking at conditions that conduced radicalization and extremism that led to VEm in Australia, at the local, national and international levels. Australia is a very interesting case to study, first because the government of Julie Gillard supported a large project with Monash University, The Monash Radicalization Project, to generate new understanding of the radicalization process in Australia and to 'facilitate better understanding of counter-terrorism policy-making and practice'.

The project has generated a great deal of information and data on the radicalization process in Australia, socio-economic characteristics of Australian 'neo-jihadists' and their social network. Most of this information has been drawn from court documents and transcripts derived from electronic bugging devices and wiretaps (telephone intercepts and listening devices) by the Australian police, which they used to penetrate, disrupt and capture Australian neo-jihadists in 2005 and 2009, and which were made public after the end of the court trials. This process has addressed a significant 'knowledge gap and enhanc[ed] our knowledge on how terrorists think' (Lentini, 2010, p. 8). Second, being a Western, Muslim-minority state facing the threat of VEm, Australia provides a fertile research ground to study conditions conducive to radicalization and extremism that leads to terrorism in a Western, democratic context. This has important implications for other Western, democratic nations facing a similar threat. Finally, while the process of radicalization has been investigated rather extensively by Australian scholars, particularly scholars at Monash University, this analysis remains one-sided, 'from an Australian Perspective' (Zammit, 2012). It would be useful to study the same process from the point of view of a more neutral, external perspective.

The chapter proceeds as follows. The second section analyses the evolution of Australia's multicultural approach since the early and mid-1970s. Section 3 discusses the developments that led to the official but unrecognized abandonment of Australian multiculturalism by the conservative government of John Howard in the late 1990s and early years of this decade. Section 4 sheds light on the socio-economic characteristics of 'neo-jihadists' in Australia and analyses the socio-economic environment that produced conditions conducive to radicalization and extremism in the country. The fifth section concludes with some further remarks.

Immigration policy: assimilation, integration, multiculturalism and back to integration

Australia is no stranger to immigrants. Arabs and Muslims (including Lebanese, Somalis and Syrians) and Asians (Chinese, Filipinos, Koreans and Vietnamese) have long sought better social and economic conditions in Australia. As the Australian government stated: 'Cultural and linguistic diversity was a feature of life for the first Australians, well before European settlement' (Department of Immigration & Citizenship, 2013). Political factors have also affected Australia's immigration policies. For example, Australia aligned its foreign policy very closely with the United States during the Vietnam War (1971–5) and supported the South against the communist North. The defeat of the South at the end of the war created a 'refugee crisis among southerners. As a result, the Australian government[1] stepped in to facilitate the immigration of a large number of southern Vietnamese into the country. The demographics of the immigrant community underwent further transformation in the mid-1970s when the Liberal Party, led by Malcolm Fraser, came to power following the dismissal of the Whitlam Labour government in 1975. Although Arab migration to Australia has a long history, Fraser's Liberal government, following the outbreak of civil war in Lebanon in the mid-1970s, provided Muslim refugees of Lebanese origin with special privileges to settle in Australia under what was then called the 'Lebanon Concession' (Henderson, 2012).

The 'come-one, come-all admissions policy for … refugees from the Lebanon conflicts' led to tens of thousands of Lebanese migrating to Australia, benefiting from the 'Lebanese Concession Act' (Sheridan, 2011). The arrival of Lebanese immigrants contributed to further diversifying the Australian immigrant communities and society. It also drew attention to the differentiated needs of the new Australian society. The government policy therefore shifted from its earlier emphasis on 'assimilation' and 'integration', enacted following the end of the Second World War in 1945 and oscillating since then between assimilation and integration in order 'to manage the post-war immigration and displaced persons' towards 'multiculturalism' (Koleth, 2010, p. 4).The key objective of Australian multiculturalism of the 1970s was to facilitate integration of immigrants, and it reflected the government's response to the new priorities and challenges facing an increasingly more diversified Australian society.

The Australian government defines multiculturalism as 'simply a term which describes the cultural and ethnic diversity of contemporary Australia … [and is a] necessary response to the reality of Australia's cultural diversity. As a public policy, multiculturalism encompasses government measures designed to respond to that diversity' (Department of Immigration & Citizenship, 2013). The main goals of Australian multiculturalism is the pursuit of social justice,[2] the recognition of identities and appreciation of diversity,[3] the integration of migrants, nation-building, and attempts to achieve and maintain social cohesion (Koleth, 2010, p. 3; Department of Immigration and Citizenship, 2013, 1 & 15).[4]

Multiculturalism was also associated with a number of strings attached. These included the following:

• multicultural policies are based upon the premise that all Australians should have an overriding and unifying commitment to Australia, to its interests and future first and foremost;
• multicultural policies require all Australians to accept the basic structures and principles of Australian society – the Constitution and the rule of law, tolerance and equality, Parliamentary democracy, freedom of speech and religion, English as the national language and equality of the sexes; and
• multicultural policies impose obligations as well as conferring rights: the right to express one's own culture and beliefs involves a reciprocal responsibility to accept the right of others to express their views and values (Department of Immigration and Citizenship, 2013. See also Koleth, 2010).

'Police and community programs' were also an important element of Australia's multiculturalism and in turn, 'have been successful at building social cohesion' and trust between Muslim community leaders and Australian security apparatuses. Multiculturalism and community programs also enabled Muslims to 'harmonise their Australian and Muslim identities' (all quotations from Harris-Hogan, 2012b, p. 3).

For almost two decades, multiculturalism has been associated with peace, stability and a high level of social harmony and cohesion. Not only have 'most Muslims settled well in Australia' (Henderson, 2012), but 'Government and other services established under multicultural policies have played a significant role in facilitating the settlement of immigrants, and many elements of the service infrastructure have endured ... ' (Koleth, 2010, p. 3). Australians prided themselves on creating 'settlement practices ... superior to that of Europe' and other Western countries, and for creating 'a welcoming diversity within Australia' (Sheridan, 2011).

Within a short period, some Australian cities – like Sydney in particular – have come to constitute some of the most diversified and multicultural cities in the world. For example, despite the very small number of Muslims in Australia in general (not exceeding 1.5–2.0 per cent of the total population, or between 400,000–500,000), 58 per cent of Sydney's population in 2007 comprised first- or second-generation immigrants from most corners of the globe. Most of Sydney's immigrant minorities, particularly new arrivals, live in southwestern and western Sydney

(Collins et al., 2007, p. 2). A survey of young people from minority back-grounds between the ages of 14–17 living in western and southwestern Sydney conducted in 2007 and funded by the Australian Department of Immigration and Citizenship, found that they, the young people, 'generally feel good about living in Australia. Two in three young people reported to often feeling good about living in Australia. ... Only a small percentage (5.6 per cent) reported that they rarely or never felt good about living in Australia' (ibid., p. 4). The study concluded that: 'This is a very significant finding, providing evidence that despite the alarmist predictions of anti-immigrant and anti-multiculturalism crit-ics, Australia's multicultural society works in a cohesive, inclusive way for most youth of minority backgrounds most of the time' (ibid., p. 4).[5]

It is the nature of immigrant communities, however, that some indi-viduals do better than others – some succeed as entrepreneurs while others as labourers, some focus more on education and others on less education-oriented activities, and some are more prone and susceptible to criminal/illegal activities than others. The background of the immi-grants, including their culture, financial resources available, initial level of human capital, and the social and political environments where they reside influence their activities, employment opportunities, social mobility, perception of their new societies and every aspect of their lives. As later sections will reflect, the available empirical evidence sug-gests that second-generation immigrants, of all backgrounds, are more susceptible to violence, crime and illegal activities than their fathers and forefathers.

Evidently, illegal activities and crime rate, including drug-related crimes, social, domestic and ethnic violence, and 'boy street gangs' began increasing in areas inhabited by ethnic minorities (Harris-Hogan, 2012b, p. 11. See also Zammit, 2010). Many of these activi-ties were solely blamed on Muslims in general and on Lebanese Sunni Muslims in particular (Collins et al., 2000). Relations between Muslims in general and Lebanese Muslims in particular, on the one hand, and Australians, on the other, reached new levels of tension in 1988 when 'two crimes occurred in Sydney's south-western suburbs and were blamed on Lebanese gangs – the murder of 14-year-old schoolboy Edward Lee and the drive-by shoot-up of the Lakemba Police Station' (Collins et al., 2000, p. 1).

Immediately the Australian press started portraying Muslims, specifi-cally Lebanese Muslims, in very offensive and derogatory terms. They were held responsible for the increase in all illegal activities, including crimes and drug-related delinquencies, and later VEm. They were no longer portrayed as true Australians, rather as aliens to Australian values and traditions. Islam itself came under attack and was held responsible for Muslims 'committing much violent crime...in Australia' (Sheridan, 2011).

While some individuals from Arab and Muslim ethnic minorities and backgrounds might have participated in, and committed crimes, such activities are not confined to individuals of an Islamic background. As a report by the South Wales Police (2006) investigating the infamous 2005 'Cronula Riots' concluded:

> Crime trends and police interaction with persons of interest did not identify any significant trend for involvement by people of Middle Eastern background in local incidents. Research also indicated that the majority of crime in the local area command is committed by people who live in the Sutherland Shire. ... The review also established that historically there have been incidents of public disorder...that did not involve ethnic tension, but were brought about by the atmosphere of an occasion and excessive consumption of alcohol...recording practices within the COPS program can produce inflated statistics. Examples of these recording practices found include: Double recording. Situations occurred where two police powers were utilised during one interaction, e.g. a person was searched and given a 'Move-On' direction at the same time. These were recorded as two separate involvements on COPS; thereby a single ethnic descriptor is recorded twice.

The upshot, however, of the two 1988 crimes and media response to them and other similar events has been the increased and heightened tensions between the two communities, marking the beginning of a series of ethnic riots and violence in Australia, the weakening of community policing and relations, as well as the trust that once prevailed between Australian Muslim communities and the police and security apparatuses of the country. Worse, many interpreted these events as 'evidence that multiculturalism – after a promising start – has failed' (Henderson, 2012). As a result of all of this, 'In the 1990s and beyond, Australia moved away from multiculturalism' (Sheridan, 2011) and again 'towards integration' (Koleth, 2010, 15). The strongest sign of this shift came after the 1999 NSW election, when the government of Premier Bob Carr announced that it would change the name of its Ethnic Affairs Ministry to the Citizenship Ministry and abolish the state government–run Ethnic Affairs Commission (EAC), replacing it with the Community

Relations Commission instead (Boland, 2000). This was seen as a key moment in Australian policy towards migrants, a confirmation of the failure and abandonment of multiculturalism.

Howard playing the race card and changing foreign policy

The abandonment of multiculturalism was slowly replaced by a return to a reintegration approach. This was based on the vision of a 'new Australia' by Prime Minister John Howard who established the first coalition government in 13 years following the March 1996 elections. The centrepiece of the 1996 and more so of the 2001 election campaigns was not only the leadership of John Howard, but also the assertion that 'We will decide who comes to this country and under what circumstances' (*Australian Politics*, 2001).

The new Australian government's hold on power was marked by important changes in the country's foreign policy. For example, when violence broke out in East Timor following an overwhelming vote for independence from Indonesia on 30 August 1999, the Howard government supported the breakaway of the island from Muslim-majority rule of the Indonesian government. It also led international efforts towards East Timor's independence by sending an Australian contingent of 2,500 troops to lead a United Nations peacekeeping team there. Not all Muslims interpreted Howard's East Timor intervention positively. For many, it was interpreted as a conspiracy to divide the largest Muslim-majority state in the world.

Not surprisingly, the first global terrorist plot that occurred in Australia came in 2000, less than one year after Australia's intervention in East Timor in 1999. The Indonesian Jemaah Islamiyah (JI) and al-Qaeda (AQ) recruited and directed a British immigrant, Jack Roche,[6] to bomb the Israeli embassy in Canberra, the Israeli consulate in Sydney and to murder a prominent Jewish businessman in Melbourne (Zammit 2010; 2012). The plot was foiled by the arrest of Roche who pleaded guilty to the charges and was given a four-year sentence.

Internally, two key issues that were perhaps responsible for his 2001 third-term electoral victory dominated Howard's premiership: immigration and terrorism. Restrictions against immigrants, especially immigration of Muslims to Australia, were tightened drastically and noticeably. In order to secure another victory in the 2001 elections, and to 'deflect public attention from domestic problems in health, aged care and education', Howard 'played the race card in an election campaign by focusing on the threat of asylum seekers' (Schrato and Webb, 2003, p. 91). The

Australian government's insistence, under premier John Howard, on 'We decide who comes to this country and under what circumstances' turned into an embarrassing international fiasco when, in late August 2001, a boat full of mostly distressed Muslim refugees fleeing repressive regimes in Afghanistan and the Middle East, were refused entry into Australian waters. When the boat began sinking along with its refugees, it was a Norwegian cargo ship, the *Tampa*, that intervened to rescue the refugees from drowning in the Indian Ocean. When the rescued boat eventually crossed into Australian waters, its refugees were taken to security holding camps in the Pacific while their eligibility for political asylum was assessed (*Australian Politics*, 2001; Schrato and Webb, 2003).[7] As one commentator noted, the *Tampa* was no mere incident in the life of the government. It slowed and reversed multiculturalism:

> Howard saw multiculturalism as a project for demeaning the achieve-ments of the British settlers and turning Australia into a nation of tribes. He believed that during the Hawke and Keating years, in the cause of Asian integration, Australia's ties with the West and the US had been dangerously diluted. As he put it, time and time again, he did not believe Australia had to choose between its history and its geography. (Manne, 2006, p. 2)

A few days following the *Tampa* fiasco, al-Qaeda terrorists flew hijacked United States airliners into the twin towers of the World Trade Center in lower Manhattan, and into the Pentagon, the US Defense Department headquarters in Washington. A fourth airliner crashed before nearing its apparent target, the White House. The death toll reached almost 3,000 with financial costs exceeding $20 billion. When the then American President, George W. Bush, announced the 'War on Terror' and signaled his intentions to attack Afghanistan (and then Iraq), Prime Minister John Howard, who happened to be in Washington when the attacks occurred, invoked the ANZUS Treaty[8] for the first time in 50 years to declare that 'In America's hour of need Australia would not stand idly by' (Manne, 2006, p. 4). He lent unconditional support to the world's first 'War on Terror' financially, politically and even physically and logis-tically. Australia sent troops both to Afghanistan and Iraq to support America-led wars on these countries. As Manne (2006, p. 4) wrote:

> According to the US National Security Advisor, Condoleezza Rice, Australia clamoured, as it turned out successfully, to be invited to participate in the invasion force. ... From that moment until the

present day, during the war on Afghanistan and then the invasion and occupation of Iraq, Australia would prove itself to be, in company with the UK, the most impeccably faithful ally of the US in the War on Terror. In the words of the Book of Ruth, 'wherever America would go, so would we'.

At the same time, and determined to win an upcoming election at any cost, Prime Minister John Howard attacked the Islamic faith, and characterized the Islamic 'Taliban regime in Afghanistan as barbaric and an enemy of civilisation, while simultaneously demonising a boatload of Afghanis who sailed into Australian waters to claim refugee status' (Schrato and Webb, 2003, p. 15).

Within a week of the 9/11 attacks, mosques were attacked not only in the United States, but also in Australia. Many Australians indiscriminately viewed Muslims as the main culprits. Prime Minister John Howard's foreign policy, moreover, also led him to publicly and blatantly increase his praise for and support to the State of Israel, particularly after the peace talks collapsed in the Middle East after 2000. John Howard 'was widely regarded in Australia as a good friend of Israel by the community when he was prime minister' (*The Australian Jewish News*, 2011). In one of his visits to the State of Israel, he publicly attacked the Muslim and Arab states for not being more sympathetic and understanding to the democracy of the Israeli state:

> In an area of the world where people are demanding democracy for the first time, Israel stands as an oasis of freedom and democracy. ... It is difficult for me to understand why certain countries don't appreciate this fact. (ibid.)

Even after he lost the elections in 2007, John Howard continued to pressure the Australian government to maintain its support to Israel.

One of the most devastating effects of John Howard's policies and stands was its impact on the media. The government's image of Muslims and Islam, its foreign policy stands and an 'alternative vision of Australia's future' began gradually to inform the press and the media. We often worry about the 'narrative of the terrorists' but pay little attention to how our own narrative affects the communities from which the terrorists draw their support and sympathy. After 9/11, the Australian state-supported and sympathetic media and press intensified the publication of material containing derogatory statements against Islam and Muslims, demonizing both Islam and Muslims. Articles carrying such titles as 'Muslim Religion Is Not So Soft', 'Civilised World Is Threatened' and 'Can Liberty Survive a Clash of Cultures?' became commonplace in many Australian daily newspapers. Derogatory and demeaning material became even more common following the publication of the demonizing cartoons of the Prophet Muhammad, first in Denmark before spreading to other Western democracies. As Kabir (2006, p. 3) stated: 'opinion columns consistently criticised Islam and upheld superior Western secular values'.

Kabir carried out an interesting study in 2006 on the treatment of Muslims by the Australian media and how it handled the debate on Islam, including the debate on the cartoons of the Prophet Muhammad. He concluded that 'in the name of free speech', the Australian press 'reinforce[d] negative perceptions of Muslims through images, cartoons and headlines' and ended in 'a form of attack' on Australian Muslims. Instead of taking at least a neutral position, the Australian media has also increased its 'bias' against Arabs and in favour of Israel (Kabir, 2006, p. 5), a very sensitive issue for most Muslims around the world (El-Said and Harrigan, 2012).

The late Edward Said (1997), even long before the 9/11 attacks took place, once wrote that the national media is often informed by the opinions and views of national politicians. Images published do not necessarily reflect accurate accounts. Their significance, rather, is in reflecting the power of the people behind their influence (also see Kabir, 2006). Esposito (2010) went further to argue that the problem with the media 'portraying Islam and Muslims as fundamentally different contributes to a popular culture' in which all Muslims are seen as 'potential enemies' and that 'become[s] embedded' in people's minds and hearts. Such a phenomenon, Esposito continues, diverts attention from the fact that the 'primary drivers of violence and terrorism are political grievances – not religion and culture'. Such a context not only leads to the development of an 'intolerant, irrational fear and hatred of Muslims', but it also undermines the search for 'positive solutions' by creating 'an identity-based conflict' which justifies hatred as a result of believing in an 'irresolvable identity-based conflict', a clash of civilizations, or Christianity versus Islam (Esposito, 2010). In Australia, certainly, Islam became synonymous with terrorism and religious hysteria. This is reflected in the writings of Australian journalists like Sheridan (2011), who has been most vocal and expressive in this line of argument:

> Does Islam itself have a role in these problems? The answer is complex and nuanced but it must be a qualified, and deeply reluctant,

yes. This is the only explanation consistent with the fact other immigrant communities, which may have experienced difficult circumstances in the first generation, don't display the same characteristics in the second generation ... young men of Islamic background experience failure and alienation, they are much more readily prone to entrepreneurs of identity who offer them purpose through the jihadi ideology, which has a large overlap with what they hear at the mosque and what they see on Arabic TV. This is simply not true for Buddhists or Confucians or Sikhs or Jews or Christians, and to pretend so, to make all religions seem equal, is to simply deny reality.[9]

The upshot of this media hysteria is that Muslims became objects, rather than subjects, of policy and this in turn leads to 'secondary traumatization'.

While analyzing the impact of the media, including satellite television, press, the Internet and other modern communications on the process of radicalization of Muslims, Spechard and Khapta (2006) found that 'secondary traumatization' developed through viewing downloaded footage of certain traumatic images from different parts of the world, such as from Palestine, Iraq, or Chechnya. Spechard and Khapta's work suggested that globalization and revolution in telecommunication technology can lead to the radicalization of Muslim youth even in other parts of the world. They found 'secondary traumatization' to be present among many al-Qaeda–affiliated groups and individuals in Chechnya, the Moroccans responsible for the 2003 attack in Casablanca, and particularly significant in radicalizing alienated Muslims in Europe. The available empirical evidence suggests that the Australian government's policies under John Howard's premiership, and the media hysteria that was informed by these policies might also have had a similar effect on some of Australia's Muslims. Indeed, Muslims interviewed by Kabir (2006, p. 5) confirm that, as a result of media bias, they were labelled, stigmatized, and 'vilified in society as terrorists' and criminals, an issue that we will return to in the following section.

It is against such a background that the terrorist plots that occurred in Australia, and other places, after 2000 should be understood. In 2002, members of the terrorist JI network detonated explosive devices in a nightclub in Bali, killing more than 200 innocent Australians in the Indonesian resort. In 2003, Sydney resident Faheem Khalid Lodhi, who had trained with Laskar e-Toiba (LeT), was charged and later convicted of conspiring to prepare a terrorist attack. The links with international terrorist organizations, such as AQ and LeT, suggest that such organizations had listed Australia as one of their legitimate targets. Between 2001 and 2003, Osama bin Laden and Dr. Ayman al-Zawahiri made six separate statements citing Australia as a potential target due to its military involvements in East Timor, Iraq and Afghanistan (Harris-Hogan, 2012a and 2012b).

While the above-mentioned plots and attacks were directed, controlled, funded and guided by external international terror organizations, the picture changed after 2003. After that year, 'home-grown' terrorism became the norm, while 'imported terrorism' the exception. As Harris-Hogan (2012a) argued, the early plots (up to 2003):

> appear to have been brainstormed, funded and to some extent controlled overseas, although both attempted to recruit members from within the Australian community. From 2004 onwards Australia has faced jihadist plots which have been largely home-grown. Peter Varghese, former Director of the Australian Office of National Assessments stated in May 2006: The greatest terrorist threat now comes from a large, diverse and fluid network of Islamist groups and individuals more often inspired by Al Qaeda than directed by it.

Support for these arguments came between late 2005 and early 2006, when the Australian security forces made the largest number of arrests in Melbourne and Sydney in a joint investigation between federal and state police services and ASIO in an operation code-named Operation Pendennis. Eighteen men were convicted under terrorism legislation. Operation Pendennis[10] was followed by Operation Neath in 2009, the second largest operation in Australia, when five men based in Melbourne were arrested and accused of planning a suicide attack on Holsworthy army barracks in Sydney. Out of the five men arrested, three were convicted (Harris-Hogan, 2012a and 2012b; Zammit 2010, 2012; Lentini, 2010). So far a total of 38 individuals have been charged with terrorist-related crimes, 23 of whom have been convicted under threat to national security/Commonwealth Anti-terrorism legislation (2003–5).[11] Thirty-seven of the 38 charged individuals are Australian citizens, 21 of whom are Australian-born.[12]

In addition to being 'home-grown', the involvement of Lebanese descendants in Australian jihadist networks has been an important feature of VEt networks in the country. Of the 38 prosecuted, at least 20 have been of Sunni Lebanese birth or descent. This includes the majority of those charged with involvement in terrorist plots on Australian soil, and half of those charged with terrorism offences not related to a specific plot. 'The predominant involvement of Lebanese origin individuals in Australian jihadist networks is itself a significant factor that requires explanation' (GTReC, 2014, p. 2). What is it about Australian Lebanese Sunni Muslims that makes them more prone to VEm? What other factors, in addition to the international and national factors ('war on terror', invasion of Afghanistan and Iraq, and Howard's anti-immigration policies), can explain the significant Lebanese involvement in VEm networks in Australia? The answer to these questions is the main goal of the next section.

The Lebanese link: national, local and personal factors

That the international environment played a key role in radicalizing several Australian Muslims is hardly controversial. Relying on wired and monitored telephone conversations emerging from the court of the convicted 33 Australian neo-jihadists Monash University leading scholar, Peter Lentini (2010, p. 4) wrote:

> The evidence presented here has been successful in identifying that the *jema'ah* members, particularly the leader, felt that it was necessary to engage in violence in this country because they believed that Australia violated a non-aggression treaty between the state and the Muslims residing in the country as citizens and permanent residents by participating in wars in Afghanistan and Iraq. Their understanding is that Australia's participation in these wars violated what they considered to be a treaty with Muslims, which prohibits Muslims from engaging in violence against the state in which they reside or which provides them safety... beyond Muslims' feelings of outrage against these military campaigns and sympathy with their co-religionists enduring violence in those countries, which other terrorists such as the 7/7 Bombers expressed in relation to their attacks in London in July 2005.

Also, anger towards the policies of the Prime Minister, John Howard, and his 'new vision of Australia' were blatantly expressed too. One of the individuals arrested in the 2005–6 Pendennis Operation, 'even while his phone was tapped and he was recorded saying: "I will kill John Howard". That call was made on August 27, 2005. Howard was prime minister and the young man under surveillance...' (Brown, Feneley and Maley, 2010).

Yet the threat of terrorism remains small in Australia when compared to other Western countries, such as the United Kingdom, the United

States and France. Neither the radicalizing international environment nor John Howard's government's anti-immigrant policies alone explain why only a small number of Australian Muslims decided to take matters into their own hands and attempt to commit violent extremist acts. This is an important question given the fact that most Muslim Australians have been and remain 'peaceful' (Harris-Hogan, 2012a) and 'have settled well in Australia. The notable exception involves some of the Muslim Lebanese ...' (Henderson, 2012). Most 'local Muslim leaders', moreover, 'condemn violence' (Zwartz, 2012) and therefore there is no evidence of large-scale indoctrination or madrasa-type indoctrination to brainwash individuals to commit violence in the country. In fact, members of the Pendennis and Neath operations sought religious advice and fatwa from Al-Shabab in Somalia because they could not find anybody qualified enough among themselves, or even a willing Muslim scholar in Australia to provide them with a religious order or justification to commit violence in Australia. Al-Shabab, on the other hand, refused to sanctify their violent actions in Australia and remained focused on their own Somali context (Lentini, 2010; Zammit, 2012; Harris-Hogan, 2012a and 2012b). The fact that terrorism shifted inwards after 2003 and became 'home-grown' suggests that certain factors, internal to Australia itself, might have also shaped and influenced what is now officially recognized as the 'radicalisation process of Muslims within [the Australian] Diaspora communities' (Harris-Hogan, 2012b, p. 4). These include economic and educational disadvantages, as well as social and personal factors. Shedding some light on these internal factors will go a long way towards enhancing our understanding of the radicalization process of minorities in Muslim-minority Western states.

The Australian Muslim population remains relatively small, no more than 450,000–500,000 or just under 2 per cent of the total population. While Lebanese Australian Muslims make up 60 per cent of all individuals charged with jihadist activity in the country, they constitute only 20 per cent of all Muslims living in Australia; almost 70,000 descendant Lebanese live in Australia (GTReC, 2014, p. 3). Clearly the share of Muslim Lebanese involved in VEm is unusually high and this warrants an explanation.

What do we know about the Muslim Australians convicted of terrorism-related charges? Researchers at the Global Terrorism Research Centre (CTReC) of Monash University in Melbourne have amassed a large amount of data on the demographic characteristics of these individuals and provided a comprehensive analysis for their socio-economic characteristics. We draw here on their work.

Violent extremism is officially called 'neo-jihadism in Australia', while violent extremists themselves are called 'neo-jihadists' (Harris-Hogan, 2012b, p. 2). Neo-jihadists, on the other hand, prefer to refer to themselves as *'Jama'a'* (Group) (Lentini, 2010 and 2011).

Australian neo-jihadists, like their counterparts elsewhere, are young, averaging 27 years old, although their age range varies from 18 to 48. Unlike those arrested in other Western countries, however, most Australian neo-jihadists are married with children: 77 per cent of the 33 convicted individuals were married at the time of their conviction and 60 per cent of them had children.[13] Another variance between convicted Muslim Australians and their counterparts in the United Kingdom and United States, for instance, is that Australian neo-jihadists are highly uneducated. Sixty-two per cent of Australian neo-jihadists did not complete secondary school. The majority had completed an apprenticeship or TAFE course only. Only one out of 33 neo-jihadists has a university degree. These ratios are much lower than averages for Australian Muslims in general. Twenty per cent of all Australian Muslims have attained a university degree, compared to only one per cent neo-jihadists. Their economic status is also low, unlike the economic status of home-grown American or British neo-jihadists, for example. Twenty-eight per cent of Australian neo-jihadists have been classified as unskilled labourers, while 59 per cent are skilled labourers who acquired their skills from learning a profession in the labour market or from their family business rather than through formal education per se. It goes without saying therefore that hardly any neo-jihadists have rigorous religious education; the majority have little formal knowledge of Islam. We have shown elsewhere how the lack of deep religious knowledge makes individuals more vulnerable to the narrative of radical ideologues and social networks because they lack the religious understanding and knowledge necessary to counter these narratives (El-Said and Harrigan, 2013). A small, unspecified number of Australian neo-jihadists were unemployed. Finally, only 10 per cent of Australian neo-jihadists are converts.[14] This ratio is also consistent with the number of Muslim converts in Australia in general and it is difficult therefore to argue that converts are more prone to radicalization and VEt acts or are more dangerous than other VEts, at least in the case of Australia (Zammit, 2010, p. 7; 2012).

What do the above characteristics tell us about the Australian neo-jihadists or about the factors that determine membership in neo-jihadist networks in Australia? The obvious and oversimplified answer to this important question is that uneducated, unskilled individuals married with children who are of Sunni Muslim Lebanese origin or descent are more likely to join neo-jihadist networks in the country. Yet this does not answer the question of why only such a small number of Muslim Australians join a neo-jihadist network while the majority, a large number of whom enjoy similar characteristics, do not. Clearly, much more information is needed in order to allow us to reach a more rigorous understanding with regard to the true triggers of radicalization among Lebanese Sunni Muslims in Australia, both at a community and a personal level.

Most neo-jihadist networks and activities (almost 95 per cent) in Australia are based in Sydney and Melbourne.[15] Most Australian Muslims also live in these two cities, with the majority of Lebanese communities in Sydney living in 'Lakemba and surrounding areas such as Punchbowl [which] had a large Lebanese Muslim population, many of whom had come when Malcolm Fraser... instituted a come-one, come-all admissions policy for... refugees from the Lebanon conflicts of the 80s' (Sheridan, 2011). In other words, most of the neo-jihadists in Australia did not come from the old Arab/Muslim immigrant community, but rather from the post-1976 Lebanese immigrant refugee community. Given the young age of the Australian neo-jihadists, it becomes clear that it was not those who migrated in the 1970s who figured in the neo-jihadist networks or activities. 'Replicating the European experience that the second generation had more trouble than the first, it was the sons of some of these immigrants who figured heavily in [Australian neo-jihadist] activities' (ibid.).

Being refugees themselves, the Australian Lebanese Sunni community in general had insufficient time, like the older Lebanese/Christian Australian community, for example, to settle down properly and build strong social capital and wealth.[16] Lacking a high level of education did not help either: social and political mobility were hampered by educational and economic disadvantages. As one observer noted:

Lebanese-Australians do experience substantial economic disadvantage as they are overrepresented at the bottom end of employment, as labourers and related, and underrepresented at the top end. While the second generation is 50% more likely to be in professional employment than the first their employment level remains significantly lower than the Australian average. This disadvantage experienced by Lebanese-Australian Muslims also manifests itself in low educational achievement. (GTReC, 2014, p. 6)

It is from this economically and educationally disadvantaged community that most neo-jihadists emerged in Australia. As we showed earlier, and as argued by Henderson (2012), 'quite a lot of them [neo-jihadists] have very low employment and a huge lack of education'. The situation of Muslim Australians, in that sense, is similar to the situation of their counterparts in Europe, who are also equally disadvantaged economically, educationally and in the labour market (Sageman, 2010). It should also come as no surprise that most neo-jihadists in Australia, and elsewhere, came from the second and third, rather than the first generation of immigrants. While the first generation of immigrants came to Australia and other Western countries by their own choice, their sons and grandsons were born there. Unlike their fathers, therefore, the second- and third-generation immigrants do not see themselves as immigrants or 'guests'. They rather see themselves as true Australians and are therefore more likely to react to real or perceived grievances or discriminations. They are less likely to accept any form of discrimination against themselves or their community. As a father painfully questioning his son's motivation behind joining an Australian neo-jihadist network asked:

'Why my son, have you joined them? They are nothing but trouble.' The son said 'I want to go to heaven'. The father replied 'this is heaven (Australia) I already brought you to heaven'. (personal interview with a high-ranking Australian police officer, Sydney, November 2012)

Other differences between the first, second and third generations of immigrants are also important in understanding the personal factor that often triggers VEm. For example, 'domestic violence is also very high among the current Muslim Australian community, although most of it goes unreported and undocumented' (personal interview with a Muslim community member, Sydney, November 2012). Many also come from large and extended families, with several siblings. This creates problems of attention and other matters related to inheritance and material issues with members of the same family. Such factors have been found to be common among a large number of Saudi jihadists[17] (El-Said and Barrett, 2012a). It is safe to argue that the 'personal' factor is a necessary factor not only for joining a jihadist network, but also to perpetuate a VEt act (El-Said and Barrett, 2011). Even in other crimes the personal factor remains important. In February of last year (2013), 'A former Los Angeles cop with military training vowed war against other men in blue Thursday, leaving one officer dead days after he allegedly killed two other people to begin a wave of retribution for being fired' (Vercammen et al., 2013).

Second- and third-generation Muslim immigrants also grew up in a completely different environment from the one of their fathers and members of their community. Most grew up in Australia, went to Australian schools,[18] learned about Australian values and the political system, but might also have experienced first-hand stereotyping of their community and discrimination. They heard fairy-tale stories about their original countries told to them by their parents. Satellite TV channels provide another source of information and various images, both good and bad, about their original homelands. They are eager for information and knowledge about many aspects of their life, including their religion, heritage, who they are and who they should be. Having been born or raised in Australia, most don't speak or understand proper Arabic. They turn to the mosque for information but the imam there delivers his sermons in Arabic, a language they mostly don't understand. Many, lacking good job opportunities, a prosperous life and the right social and human capital, develop nostalgia, and a cultural and identity crisis. All these factors combine to create vulnerabilities facilitated by the realities of a Western individualistic society, one that stereotypes, labels and marginalizes immigrants. 'Their needs therefore differ tremendously from the needs of their fathers. They need somebody to educate them properly about where they came from and where they are today, and how to bridge the cultural gaps. These gaps have been filled by some self-appointed radical Salafists who talked to these guys, most of whom left school, have no or very poor jobs and spend the nights roaming with like-minded failures and friends' (personal interview with a Muslim community member, Sydney, November 2012).

By the late 1980s, and following the alleged spread of crime and gang culture in many areas inhabited by Lebanese Muslims, most former Australian residents of these areas left them, leaving Lebanese Muslims living in isolated, marginalized and labelled enclaves (Sheridan, 2011). Socialization between Muslim and Australian communities was undermined, and former social capital, which once both communities relied on to 'get by' and understand each other better, bridge cultural differences, and even to facilitate the integration of most first-generation Muslims in Australia, diminished. Stereotypes emerged instead and the cultural distance between the two communities widened.

The politically charged environment under Howard's premiership made a bad situation worse. Such an environment, as argued earlier, informed the media and led to the repetitive use of derogatory and demeaning language and accusations by the press. The end result has not only been to offend Muslim Lebanese Australians, it has also contributed to further radicalization of some individuals through labelling, marginalization and stigmatization of the Muslim community. Editorial and opinion columns criticizing Muslims and Islam and upholding superior Western secular values remain common in Australian media even today. A quotation from a recent article written by Sheridan (2011).

A survey of Muslims in Australia showed that most Muslims 'believe that, as a result of media bias, they are vilified in society as "terrorists", and discriminated against in the workplace' (Kabir, 2006, 5). Figures derived from the Australian Bureau of Statistics support Muslims' claims of discrimination in the workplace. For example, in 1996 the unemployment rate for Muslim Australians was 25 per cent, compared to 9 per cent for the national total. Although unemployment was reduced to 18.5 per cent in 2001, compared to 6.8 per cent for the national total, the ratio of underprivileged positions in the labour market remained almost three times higher than for the wider community (ibid.). A Muslim Australian female told me 'as soon as a Muslim woman turns up for a job interview she is immediately rejected the moment the employer sees her hijab' (Sydney, November 2012). Other empirical evidence from the GTReC (2014, p. 7) of Monash University is supportive:

> Lebanese-Australian Muslims have often been stigmatised and marginalised by sections of the public, media and some politicians. The immediately identifiable starting point for this issue would be the 1998 media controversy that emerged over gangs in Sydney. The media response proceeded to implicate the entire Sydney Lebanese community in the activity of criminal gangs. ...

While it is difficult to pinpoint one factor behind the joining and perpetuation of acts of VEm, all of the above-mentioned factors, including the personal, economic, social and educational factors, have served 'as a structural cause that helped radicalise some Lebanese-Australian Muslims' (ibid., 2014, p. 6). Disadvantaged economic and educational conditions of the Muslim community in Australia can also lead many to 'identify with this group's alienation', a fact that facilitates estrangement from one's own society and creates dissatisfaction, disillusionment and grievances that are often exploited by jihadist networks and groups (Henderson, 2012). Economic, social, political and educational disadvantages, in other words, create conditions conducive to radicalization and VEm. The personal provide the 'trigger' (El-Said and Barrett, 2012a; El-Said and Harrigan, 2013).

Under such conditions and circumstances, social and familial networks function as a conduit for radicalization and VEt activism. Scholars at Monash University have diligently and accurately depicted and exposed the role of social and family networks in the process of radicalization in Australia, while acknowledging the presence of other radicalizing factors. As Harris-Hogan (2012b, p. 2) wrote:

> Family connections in particular have played a significant role in the passing of ideology as well as the recruitment and retention of jihadists into the network. While there are many external influences which persuade individuals as to whether or not they should engage in violence, one of the most prominent factors explaining which members have joined the Australian jihadist network is the influence of family and close friendships.

Ironically, the very same family and social networks have also played a key role in preventing further individuals from joining VEt groups and in convincing other members to leave terrorism behind, both in Australia and elsewhere (Bjorgo and Horgan, 2009). As Harris-Hogan (2012b, p. 2) also wrote of the Australian context:

> However, the impact of such connections is not inherently negative and there are also clear cases of family members persuading individuals away from extremism. Though it is impossible to completely extricate the influence of friends and family away from the myriad of other external effects which impact the radicalisation process. ...

It is perhaps because of all of the above-mentioned factors that the available empirical evidence confirms that second- and third-generation immigrants are more prone to problems of psychosis, obsession, phobia and even violence. While working on the UK's immigrant community, for example, Agius (2012, p. 194) observed 'a higher rate' of such problems to be prevalent among 'immigrant populations as compared to the indigenous populations of the UK. Specifically, second-generation immigrants (born in the UK) have been noted to have the highest risk.' This suggests that policies simply based on 'multiculturalism', although necessary, might not be sufficient. Some went as far as calling for professional 'accurate risk assessments ... of violence risk' at an individual level as 'particularly pertinent to the early identification and prevention' of violent tendencies among some individuals (Sand et al., 2012, p. 690).

Concluding remarks

This chapter has analysed the evolution of VEm in Australia and the macro and micro factors that have led to the radicalization of many Muslim Australians since the late 1980s at the international, national, local and personal levels.

The evidence presented in this chapter suggests that radicalization and VEm are more complex phenomena than suggested by the so-called 'conventional wisdom' approaches which currently dominate the literature on radicalization and CVE and which perceive radicalization narrowly as a function of 'ideology, alienation,' political orientation, or 'the internet as the causes of radicalisation (while vehemently rejecting foreign policy as a causal factor in the run-up to the invasion of Iraq and Afghanistan' (Githen-Mazer and Lambart, 2010, 889)). Terrorism in Australia is not a Muslim problem. It is an Australian problem. The change in the international environment since the late 1990s, coupled with changes in Australia's foreign and immigrant policies, has planted the seeds of radicalization in the country. Economic and educational disadvantages, as well as labelling and stigmatizations of some groups and individuals created conditions conducive to radicalization and extremism that led a small number of Muslim Australians to embrace VEm. Repressive responses by the police to ordinary crimes destroyed years of trust and community policing, and undermined the perceptions of the police and the social capital that once linked the Muslim community to authorities and police forces. Domestic violence, social networks and living in 'Muslim enclaves' that stigmatize Muslims and uphold Western values as superior, created the personal trigger factor that resonates among more second – and third-generation immigrants than is the case with the first-generation immigrants, making the former more prone to violence and activism.

In order to be able to better understand the root causes of radicalization in Australia, and other Western societies, there is a need to break away from the conventional wisdom approach that currently dominates the literature on radicalization and VEm, and which reduces the complex problem of VEm to ideology or cultural Islamic difference factors that produce contradictory ethics and values to liberal Western democracies. Such an approach, as Githen-Mazer and Lambart (2010, 891) observed, leads to a 'feedback loop between policy-makers, the media and scholars' that generates extremely counterproductive stigmatization and labelling of Muslim communities, particularly in Western democracies. For more effective policy responses there is a need for a better understanding of conditions conducive to VEm in Western democracies, or, as Sageman (2004, 69) argued, 'identification of variables specific to the creation, maintenance and demise of terrorists'. This requires a departure from the current conventional wisdom that narrowly perceives VEm as simply a function of Islamic ideology and/ or exposure to violent, neo-jihadi philosophy.

4
Counter Radicalization and De-radicalization in Western Democracies: The Case of Australia

Introduction

Following the emergence of some serious Violent Extremist activities and individuals during the first decade of the 21st century (see the previous chapter for more detail), the Australian government promoted modest de-radicalization and counter radicalization procedures. The literature has paid little attention to how the Australian government actually responded to the rise of Violent Extremism (VEm), including the rise of 'home-grown' terrorism in particular. This is not only because these efforts remained nascent, but also because the Australian government felt uncomfortable publicizing them for fear of undermining them. This chapter fills an important gap in the literature by focusing entirely on Australia's response to the emergence of VEm in its territory.

The chapter proceeds as follows. The next section focuses on the evolution of Australia's counterterrorism policies and focuses in particular on how the Australian government's approach to countering terrorism began to slowly change after 2010 to embrace more 'soft' measures. The third section sheds light on the government's de-radicalization approach, while the fourth section studies Australia's counter radicalization policies. The final section attempts to provide a tentative evaluation for Australia's counter radicalization and de-radicalization measures.

Australia's response to the emergence of violent extremism (VEm)

The initial response of the Australian authorities to the emergence of the VEm phenomenon was to rely more on traditional security measures or even repression. This approach, in fact, started in 1998, following the allegations and accusations that implicated the entire Sydney Lebanese community in the activity of criminal gangs, and before the emergence of the first global terror attempt in Australia in 2000. The 'response of the police to the[se] allegations and accusations...was a zero tolerance policing approach' (GTReC, 2014, p. 7). This approach intensified following the introduction of 'anti-terrorism laws' in 2013 which gave police extra powers and was used to prosecute all neo-jihadists (Brown, Feneley and Maley, 2010).

Although few people actually question the involvement of the police in countering terrorism, 'their precise role is unclear and indeed controversial' (Weisburd et al., 2011, p. 81). In most countries, the police traditionally have the primary responsibility of maintaining public safety, by focusing on prevention through visible patrolling and deterrence through the application of criminal law. The 'war on terror' has had a tremendous impact on the role of the police almost everywhere. Australia is no exception. The Australian police became more directly involved in counterterrorism activities, a fact that has changed the nature of policing in the country. Covert intelligence gathering, disrupting neo-jihadist activities, raiding neo-jihadist premises, capturing neo-jihadists and providing court witnesses and supporting evidence have become some of the key tasks of the Australian police. The Australian police, no doubt, have been successful in penetrating jihadist networks, disrupting their plans and capturing them. But this type of 'high policing' might have been at the expense of other important services the Australian police once provided and is expected to provide in a Western democracy. This includes, among other things, building and maintaining relations with communities. Being the face of the state, or the front line that the community sees when something goes wrong, whatever the police do will have important implications for police–community relations. The shift in the role of the Australian police from 'low' to 'high policing' not only changed its character and nature, but also the community's perception of it. As GTReC (2014, p. 7) wrote:

This zero tolerance campaign undermined years of community relations and policing, increased distrust between Sydney's Lebanese community and the police, as well as the wider community. Religious and community leaders who had supported the calls for stronger laws and an increased police presence felt alienated by the response.

Even after the authorities successfully penetrated, disrupted and captured neo-jihadists in the 2005–6 Pendennis Operation, it continued to follow a 'high policing' approach based on more of the same tactics followed before the 2005 Pendennis Operation. The problem with such a 'high policing' approach, even when successful, is that 'high policing differs sharply from the standard practices of normal or low policing because it is less transparent, less accountable and less careful with respect to human rights' (Weisburd et al., 2011, p. 82). Although there is no evidence to claim that the Australian police actually violated human rights, the Muslim community's *perception* of the police in Australia changed dramatically. As one observer, following the Neath Operation in 2009, noted:

> Many Muslims feel under siege this week; that Islam has been prosecuted and its adherents persecuted. Uthman Badar, from the Australian arm of Hizb ut-Tahrir, a group banned in some countries for its extremism, said anti-terrorism laws here had lowered the burden of proof. People were being prosecuted merely for their ideas. Here we have a case where there is no direct evidence, no established intent to kill, and no specific target...many of the extreme views, as mentioned in the sentencing remarks, are basic Islamic views which Muslims generally hold; views like Muslims being obliged to defend themselves and jihad being the way to do this. Criminalising these views is to criminalise criticism of Western foreign policy in Muslim lands, and this is the crux of the matter. The anti-terror laws were designed to silence Muslims through fear and intimidation. (Brown, Feneley and Maley, 2010)

The Pendennis Operation, which led to the arrest of several Australian neo-jihadists, provided a good opportunity for the Australian authorities to learn more about, and improve their understanding of, the process of radicalization in the country, including how jihadist networks form and their motivations. But it also should have provided a good opportunity to launch a de-radicalization program to prevent the emergence of future generations of neo-jihadists and minimize chances for future attacks. Such a program could at least have included a social element to prevent wives, children and families of the captured individuals from suffering and paying a heavy price for something they had no role in or influence over. Instead, the capturing and arrest of individuals

> has caused a lot of suffering – not least for the families of the jailed men. Many had relied on them as the sole breadwinners. After their arrests,

some Centrelink payments and bank accounts were frozen. There were death threats. Eggs were thrown at houses. 'People drive by screaming at us and swearing', the sister-in-law of one of the men said at the time. 'They beep their horn and tell us to go back to our own country.' But she said: 'This is my home.' (Brown, Feneley and Maley, 2010)

As we argued elsewhere, de-radcalization of captured individuals is necessary not only for its impact on the prison environment and detainees themselves, but also the wider society and community (El-Said and Barrett, 2012a). Porges and Stern (2010, p. 1) rightly argued:

Deradicalization efforts must therefore be considered important not just for their effect on detainees but also for their secondary benefits beyond the walls of detention facilities. Saudi Arabia's rehabilitation program, for example, contributes to broader counter-radicalization efforts by facilitating government contact with those who are vulnerable to radicalization and recruitment, including detainees' friends and families.

Lack of de-radicalization in Australia following the Pendennis Operation, not surprisingly, has had the kind of negative consequences which we and others warned about. The Neath Operation, for example, was very much linked to and partly influenced by the way the Pendennis Operation was handled. Zammitt (2012) of Monash University's research team described these links, and the motivations behind the Neath Operation, eloquently:

In this case, the transformation did not occur through overseas instigation or online radicalization, but through the involvement of non-diaspora–based ideological sympathizers, socially linked to an earlier cell, determined on revenge, and restricted from traveling abroad...had strong social links to the cell arrested in Melbourne during the 2005 Operation Pendennis raids. ... In this case, one such factor was the imprisonment of their friends in the cell, led by the self-proclaimed Shaykh Abdul Nacer Benbrika, who was arrested in Operation Pendennis in 2005...in June 2009...the court heard the plotters were partly motivated by revenge for Benbrika's imprisonment.

Harris-Hogan (2012b, p. 6 and p. 7) concurs:

each neojihadist plot that has materialised in Australia has had strong social links to a previous operational cell. Indeed, individuals who have participated in the Australian network frequently had pre-existing ties with members already inside and it is often a key condition for joining.

The defeat of the Liberal–National Party Coalition in the November 1997 elections brought the Labour Party to power, after winning a clear majority in the House of Representatives, 83 of the 150 seats. Not only did Prime Minister John Howard lose the general election and his premiership, but he also lost his seat of Bennelong to Labour. This made Australia's forty-second federal election the second time where a sitting prime minister was voted out of his own seat. The first was the twelfth federal election in 1929. The arrival of Labour in 2007 initially did not usher in a new era of a marked shift in Australia's counterterrorism policies. The first-ever removal of an Australian Prime Minister, Kevin Rudd, from office before completing a full term in 2010 and his replacement by Julia Gillard, Australia's first female Prime Minister, did.

The first task of Gillard's new government in the area of counterterrorism was to commission The GTReC at Monash University to examine multiple factors that lead individuals to become radicalized and conduct terrorist acts in the country. The key objective of the four-year multidisciplinary project, The Monash Radicalization Project, is 'to generate new understandings of radicalisation' process and 'facilitate better understanding of counter-terrorism policy-making and practice', as well as 'identifying potential counter-measures'. The project, which became the most significant and detailed examination of the radicalization process in Australia and by Australian institutions and academics, involves a partnership of Monash University, Victoria Police, the Victorian Department of Premier and Cabinet, Corrections Victoria and the Australian Federal Police.[1] Whether and how to inject 'soft' measures into the counterterrorism tool kit is another key objective the project sought to determine.

Australia's modest de-radicalization efforts

In 2010, Victorian authorities were the first, and so far the only, state to initiate a pilot scheme inside the prison. The scheme remains at its infancy, far from being comprehensive, and currently operates in Victoria (Melbourne) only.[2] It remains a pilot rather than a fully-fledged program, although growing all the time and constantly incorporating new elements. It is designed and implemented in collaboration with various Islamic and multicultural organizations, including in particular the Islamic Council of Victoria (ICV). In this scheme, the ICV, in collaboration with the police and correctional authorities, sends imams into prisons on a weekly basis (once a week) to provide religious support and mentoring to detainees convicted of terrorism-related charges. This also takes the form of 'a lecture series' whereby Muslim scholars chosen by the ICV initiate a series of lectures on several issues pertinent to the detainees' narratives, including on core Islamic teachings and practices, the protection of life and conflict resolution in Islam, Islamic views on citizenship, belonging and cultural identity, and the universal concept of Islam. Six to seven imams are involved in the program. They come to the prison once or twice every week, depending on the status and needs of the detainees, and talk to and debate with the detainees. The ICV was established in 2009–10 following Operation Neath especially for this purpose. The choice of the imams is a cooperative task between the Police and the ICV. The program is designed by the ICV who run the daily affairs of it, while the police authorities simply supervise the operations of the program. The police and members of the ICV meet regularly to discuss progress and other main developments. Religious rehab is mainly on a one-to-one basis. These components constitute Victoria's main religious-ideological part.

Obviously Victoria's religious rehabilitation scheme is far from being the kind of intensive or extensive program seen in countries like Saudi Arabia, for example, which treats religious rehabilitation as a crucial part of the entire de-radicalization process (El-Said and Barrett, 2012a).

Individuals charged with VEt-related charges are also dispersed in small numbers in two or a maximum of three high-security prisons in Victoria and New South Wales (NSW). The Australian authorities believe that partial dispersal and partial concentration with selective and careful socialization is a superior approach to complete dispersal and complete isolation:

> We do not isolate VEt detainees but partially concentrate them. We disperse them in three main high security detention centres. We keep the very radical members in a more high security prison and less radicals in lower security prison. Putting them in high security prison is obviously more costly as it requires more security, monitoring and special arrangements but has more advantages. (Personal interview with Australian counterterrorism officials, Australia, November 2012)

Trial and error has played an important role in Australia's choice of prison system, particularly in opting for a partial dispersal approach.

As a high-ranking officer at the country's main Super Max Correction Centre, Goulburn, in NSW, stated:

> Initially we dispersed them in three different centres. But after 2003 a new government policy emerged and focused on concentrating them together in Goulburn. We did this for two or three reasons. First for consistency reasons, as we felt that it would be better to provide the same treatment to all VEt detainees instead of providing different treatment to different detainees in different centres. Second, we were worried about the possibility of them radicalizing others while in different centres. ... Third, logistically it also proved difficult and costly. In one prison, for example, you can transport all of them to court in one trip instead of three trips taking place from three different detention centres with all the difficulties involved in providing strict road security and other logistical support. We therefore decided to move them to one place in NSW instead, to Goulburn.[3] (Personal interview, NSW, Goulburn, November 2012)

While Victoria initiated a modest religious rehabilitation scheme, no such scheme exists in NSW. When Goulburn was established in 2003, a chaplaincy was already attached to it to provide religious counselling for inmates who need it:

> We do not have a religious rehabilitation programme in Goulburn. But Goulburn was built with a chaplaincy, and since day one of building Goulburn we have been providing religious counselling to all detainees regardless of their religion, whether Jews, Christians, Muslims, Hindus, etc. This continues to be the case today. The imam, for example, comes in once a month and walks around, passing by each cell inhabited by a Muslim inmate. He says hello to the inmates, how are you and keeps on walking unless a detainee asks him for advice or wants to see him for further discussion. Sometimes the inmate can make a request to see the imam in advance. In this case, we arrange for a meeting between the imam and the inmate who made the request in an especially equipped room, which looks like an office and where the detainee is inside a cage in the room alone with the imam in the same room but [the imam] is outside the cage. Most Muslim inmates, however, talk and rely on their leaders a lot for advice and psychological support and don't talk to us much, either about religious or psychological issues. They rely more on their three key leaders, Fahim, who is the number one leader,

and Mohammed Elamo and Jamal. (Personal interview, Goulburn at NSW, November 2012)

Whether Victoria's modest religious-ideological program or NSW's chaplaincy, the challenges faced are similar:

> We have a major problem with the facilitator. We cannot get somebody we can trust to tell us the right thing. We had a Turkish imam but the detainees rejected him because he was from a different sect and we had to let him go. We then had two other imams and we had to let them go too because they were not doing and saying the right things. We are now looking for new imams.[4] (Personal interviews, Goulburn, NSW, November 2012)

Neither Victoria nor NSW have a family program, one which would incorporate the role of families undergoing a de-radicalization process, or even to simply utilize the important role of families in de-radicalizing their detained sons and family members. This despite the fact that the available empirical evidence derived from Australia itself suggests that although some family members and friends have played a radicalizing role, others played a significant de-radicalizing role. The latter has also resulted in reducing the number of neo-jihadists in the country, either by convincing many youths not to join jihadist networks or by persuading many to withdraw from current jihadist networks. In fact, and in the country's highest security incarceration centre, Goulburn, families are only allowed to visit their detained family members once a week, for no more than an hour or two, and are only allowed to come during weekends (Saturday or Sunday). Sometimes, when mitigating circumstances exist

> We allow extended visits for family members. For example, the brother of one of the detainees came to see him from Lebanon and he applied for an extended visit to see him. The detainee himself does not give us a hard time so as a reward we accepted his request, which allowed him to see his brother on Saturdays and Sundays for three weeks in a row. Otherwise, we do not encourage families to visit their detained relatives because we don't want to be seen as interfering in family affairs. We however facilitate such visits whenever families decide to come for a visit. (Personal interview, Goulburn, NSA, November 2012)

This approach is in stark contrast to the Saudi program, for example, which incorporates the families of the detainees and utilizes strong family relations as a mechanism to convince detained individuals to repent. Not only do the Saudi authorities go out of their way to encourage families to visit their detained relatives regularly, but they also cover all costs involved in such visits wherever they come from (El-Said and Barrett, 2012). When Australian Muslim families turn up to visit their detained relatives, moreover, the Australian incarceration authorities, instead of making use of interpretation services, insist that they, the families and their detained relatives, must communicate in English. This reinforces feelings of distrust between families and detained relatives on the one hand, and incarceration authorities on the other. It also fails to build the kind of bonding and cordial atmosphere that proved so important for successful de-radicalization programs in other countries, such as Singapore, Malaysia and Saudi Arabia (El-Said and Harrigan, 2013).

Goulburn high-security prison consists of three main units: 7, 8 and 9. Unit No. 7 is called the main Integration Unit and is the one where detainees are subjected to a comprehensive assessment as soon as they arrive at Goulburn.[5] This period lasts for 14 days, unless the detainee refuses to cooperate. In this case, the assessment period is extended to 28 days. Most VEt detainees cooperate and pass the first 14-day assessment period without causing too much trouble, unlike some other non-Vet–related detainees 'who refuse to cooperate with prison authorities in many cases' (personal interview, Goulburn, NSW, November 2012). The assessment rates the detainees' psychological, physical and mental health, as well as their level of education, age, network of relatives and friends, history of alcohol and drugs and crime. This is a very important step, one that allows the authorities from the very beginning to identify any health-related problems, educational and social disadvantages, drug addiction problems, and even the level of radicalization of each detainee and how each was radicalized. Identifying these issues from the very beginning is a necessary exercise for the successful and effective design of a tailor-made de-radicalization program, one that would take the special needs and requirements of each detainee into account.

Unlike many VEts in other countries, most Australian 'VEt detainees, at least those in Goulburn detention centre, have no previous criminal record, no alcohol history, no drug history and no history of crime. They also demonstrate their best behaviour inside the prison walls. They do not give us a hard time like other detainees' (personal interview, Goulburn, NSW, November 2012).

Goulburn also has a clinic, a nurse available on a daily basis, and a doctor who comes in once a month. If a detainee needs to see a doctor, an appointment can be made through the prison authorities. In the case of an emergency, detainees can be taken to a nearby hospital almost immediately.[6] Most detainees in Goulburn are situated in Units 8 & 9, and are kept in individual cells. Each cell has its own sink, shower and toilet. The cells are adjacent to one another, sharing a common wall, but detainees inside the cells cannot easily communicate with one another. Each two cells share a front and a back day room. Detainees often use the front room to play chess, read, socialize, cook, eat and drink tea or coffee. The back room is often used for exercise. The distribution of detainees in the adjacent cells is not a random exercise. They are classified according to some association. For example, Muslim detainees are close to one another and socialize with one another. Detainees are also allowed to socialize with other, non-Muslim inmates if they want but they have to make a formal request to the prison authorities first in order to do so. As long as security permission is granted and their action does not jeopardize the security of the prison in any way, their request is often met and they can then socialize with any other inmate they choose.

Detainees can only stay in the same cell for a maximum period of 28 days. At the end of the 28 days detainees are shifted to other cells. 'We do this because we do not like to keep them in the same cell for longer periods than 28 days for security reasons. We check each cell completely every 28 days, make sure there is no security breach, and then we shift detainees to other cells' (personal interview, Goulburn, November 2012).

Goulburn has a library, two meeting rooms (for when families come to visit), and three sports fields, one of which is larger and has a natural grass surface. The detainees are only allowed to leave their cells for four hours every day. They spend the remaining 20 hours each day in their solitary cells: 'They are let out for two hours between 9 and 11 every day and are then brought back for lunch. After lunch, they are also allowed to leave their cells for another two hours but by 2:30 they need to go back to their cells and are locked up there for the rest of the day' (personal interviews, Goulburn, NSW, November 2012).

There is no well-designed educational, vocational or even physical program inside the prison.[7] Some like to spend their time reading in the library, some opt to exercise, while others prefer to socialize. Whatever they choose to do, it is voluntary and is not part of a well-structured, disciplined program that often characterizes effective de-radicalization programs. The Goulburn Super Max authorities, furthermore, follow a carrot-and-stick approach with the detainees. Good behaviour, for example, is rewarded through being allowed to socialize with other groups, take more books from the library back to the cell, accept food and other gifts from family and friends, see family and friends regularly during weekends and accept mitigating circumstances whenever they arise. They are also allowed to exercise on the larger field, which has a natural grass surface as opposed to the harder, synthetic ground that characterizes the other two fields inside Goulburn. Bad behaviour, on the other hand, means that all of these benefits are withdrawn.

'Most VEt detainees behave very well inside the prison, much better than all other detainees. They do not give us a hard time. They get on with their lives and religious duties, and just want to do their time and go back to their families and friends' (personal interviews, Goulburn, NSW, November 2012). They are more demanding, however, than other detainees. If they ask for something and don't get it, for example, they file a series of formal complaints, paper after paper, complaint after complaint. They do this even if the matter they are complaining about is trivial and can often be solved internally. As an experienced Australian high-ranking officer in Sydney stated, 'this is their way of expressing resistance to the system. They are in prison and they don't like it and this is their way of expressing rejection for their situation' (personal interview, Sydney, November 2012).

While in prison, VEt detainees also attempt to influence and convert other inmates. This happens in two places inside Goulburn detention centre:[8] first, outside in the fields where exercising occurs. Although no more than two detainees are left alone at any one time, the release of inmates for exercising gives them the opportunity to talk to other inmates from behind the fences and at the corners that link the three exercise fields together. Secondly, attempts to influence other inmates also take place during the night, when the number of security officers is down to a minimum and it is very quiet. During this time, 'radicalization happens through chatting and shouting behind cell walls' (personal interviews, Goulburn, NSW, November 2012).

According to the Goulburn authorities, Muslim detainees there have so far managed to convert six original Australian inmates (both Aboriginal and Anglo-white Australians). For Aboriginal Australians, with no family or friends, conversion offers an opportunity to make new friends and social networks. Conversion also offers an opportunity for some financial gain, as Muslim detainees go as far as supporting converts financially if their economic situation is dire. This is not surprising, given the fact that the Australian authorities do not have a social program in place inside incarceration centres, either in NSW or Victoria, to support the detainees and their families financially, as is the case in Malaysia or Saudi Arabia, for instance. This gap therefore is left for Muslim detainees to fill.

Of the six converts, three oscillate between Islam and their previous status. The other three have become committed Muslims. For example, they changed their names, appearance (grew beards), and behaviour (pray five times a day). For the Australian incarceration authorities, who have ironically received no training in Islam, radicalization, or sensitization to the Islamic culture, conversion is not only a cause for concern, but is also taken as a sign of radicalization:

> Although protection and material factors explain conversion in prison in our opinion, we are very concerned about this phenomenon because we don't know what it means, we are not trained to understand the Islamic culture and we don't know what it means to convert to Islam, but we are very concerned about it. (personal interviews, Goulburn, NSW, November 2012).

Needless to say, 'Religious conversion is not the same as radicalisation' (ICSR, 2010, p. 2). Religious conversion sometimes improves the behaviour of a prisoner. Becoming a religious person sometimes leads to better behaviour as religion can have a calming influence on individuals.

Finally, neither in Victoria nor in NSW does a strong social or post-release program to facilitate the integration of released former detainees exist. What the authorities in both regions have recently done is to provide information to detainees, particularly detainees who are approaching the end of their sentences and will soon be released, about how they can claim unemployment benefits, for example, which state or other agencies can help while looking for jobs, how they can obtain a loan for education or business, and so forth. They also teach them how to start the process of applying for such services and benefits, how to complete the necessary application forms, and which state or other agencies will assist them. This approach is more in line with Western democratic systems and values which treat all citizens as equals and do not distinguish between them based on the offence or crime committed, as some Muslim-majority states do (El-Said and Harrigan, 2013).

Counter radicalization measures

Outside the prison walls, the Australian authorities have recently initiated/supported several new community-based initiatives in an attempt to revive the dented and once-vibrant relations with the Muslim community. The first of these programs is the Community Outreach Program (COR) which started in Sydney around 2007–8. Its origin owes much to a Muslim officer in Melbourne, Sam al-Mugrabi, who noticed around the Pendennis Operation in 2005 that a large number of Muslim children were wandering the streets, school dropouts without jobs, involved in drugs and with no strong family relations. All of these factors, he believed, made them vulnerable to radicalization and extremism that leads to terrorism. After a pilot study in Melbourne in 2005–6, the program was extended to Sydney in 2007–8.

'The program is called COR because we seek to reach out to the community' (personal interview with a social worker, Sydney, November 2012). Liaison Communities (LC), each consisting of three members (a social worker, a psychologist and a police official), have been formed and seek to identify geographical hotspots where youths wander in the streets at night. The identification process initially relied heavily on communications with, and information generated from, schools and Rotary clubs. Later the sources of information expanded to include community leaders, imams of mosques and informal networks of LC members themselves. The high-risk youth, between the ages of 12–16, are the main targets of the COR and the LC. Once identified, youths are approached by a member of the LC, often the social worker. During these encounters, the LC member tries to engage in discussion with the youths over such issues as the importance of education, getting a good job, establishing and maintaining good relations with one's family, succeeding in Australia and becoming a role model. The LC, in other words, seeks to reintegrate Muslim youth into society. As a social worker in one LC stated:

> We target high-risk youth in collaboration with schools, youth centres, Migrant Resource Centres, police, mosques and schools. We go to hotspot areas where Muslims live and where crime is high. We often start our work after 9 p.m., when the youths start gathering at the end of the day and after they finish school and work so not to disturb their education and work. Our target is youths between 12–16 years old. Once identified, we try not to overpower them by sending three LC members. We only send one member to talk to

them, most often me as I come from the same background as them. (Personal interview, Sydney, November 2012).

In Victoria, a similar Lecture and Open Discussion Forum (LoD) was introduced in 2010. The program is a joint collaborative project among the Islamic Council of Victoria, the Victoria Police and the federal government. It targets the former violent extremist detainees who were released from prisons after spending their time. Here, former detainees choose a topic for a scholar who comes from the Islamic Council to lecture on, followed by a discussion with the former detainees. This LoD is held once a month, often in a mosque, and is part of Victoria's violent extremist rehabilitation program. The aim here is to ensure the success of the rehabilitation process inside the prison and reduce the risk of recidivism after release. The main subjects discussed in the LoD are similar to those discussed inside a detention centre: core Islamic teachings and practices, the protection of life and conflict resolution in Islam, Islamic views on citizenship, belonging and cultural identity, and universal concept of Islam.

The NSW's COP tasks have recently (November 2012) been extended not only to reach out to high-risk youth in hotspot areas, but also to study their economic and social needs. Those are then reported back to the relevant authorities. The idea here is not to provide direct social and economic assistance to vulnerable youth, as is the case with the social program in Malaysia or Saudi Arabia, for example. Rather, and consistent with Western democratic systems, to refer them to state agencies that specialize in the provision of such services to the population, like unemployment benefit agencies, recruitment agencies, grant-giving agencies, family support agencies, and so forth.

A Counter Narrative Program has also been introduced by the Muslim community of NSW since 2009. Here, popular Muslim role models, including poets, artists, politicians and scholars are invited from all over the world to address Australian Muslim youths. The aim of this program is to defeat the hardliners and to provide a counter-narrative to the hardliners' arguments in all areas. This program was called for by the imams and mufti of NSW (see endnote 24 for more information on the Islamic Council). Some of the scholars invited include Hamza Yusuf, John Esposito and, more recently (January, 2013), Aftab Malik from the United Kingdom.

Another, more recent initiative is designed to teach 'proper Islam' to Muslim migrant communities from all backgrounds, Lebanese, Iraqis, Syrians, Somalis, and so on. The scheme, known as Youth Forums, takes place mainly in the offices of the Social Community Liaison Group (SCLG) which consists of several storeys and was established to support the community's work in these areas. In this scheme, high-risk youth, also the main target of the project, are invited to attend a Q&A forum conducted in the offices of the SCLA. While there, the youth are taken on a tour to see the facilities of the building. They are then invited for a game of fencing with members of the liaison committees at a nearby shooting range. The scheme, which started in 2011, usually hosts up to ten youths at a time and takes the form of a six-to-eight–week course. It starts with an introduction about Islam and Muslims in Australia, followed by teaching individual respect and self-esteem, breaking stereotypes, team bonding and relationships. During the period of the course, the youths attend from 9 a.m. to –3 p.m. once a week. Muslim role models, such as soccer players, are also invited to talk to the youths and to show them how Muslims can be successful in Australia. Given the fact that most of the youths targeted are of Lebanese descent, 'we bring mostly Lebanese role models that are famous. ... It is all about individual self-respect, breaking stereotypes, team bonding and relationships. We do not seek to change them but rather to challenge their ideas about police, policies of the state and Australian society' (personal interview with a social community worker, Sydney, November 2012).

Another innovative scheme by Australia's Muslim community is the Community Partnership Program. Here the community runs youth camps and events, such as football games, youth leadership programs and counter-narrative debates. The community itself arranges for this while the authorities fund it. All community members, both men and women, and families are invited. This happens almost once every month. An annual festival (Haledon Street Festival), which includes an Iftar celebration, is also arranged during Ramadan by the community and coordinated with the local council. This aims at desensitizing ideas about the police, security and state. In addition to food, skilled performers, Arabic dancers (*dabka*) and singers are some of the main activities included in the festival. The festival is also open to all Australian communities in an attempt to bridge cultural gaps and narrow differences among various ethnic groups.

Finally, an imams' Conference Program was launched in 2010. The program was called for by Australia's most eminent imams, who organize it with the state's Islamic mufti through the Imam Council in the same state.[9] The imams' conference is a mechanism through which Muslim community leaders communicate their demands and exchange views, opinions and information with state officials. The Commissioner at the Federal Police level is usually invited to the Conference. The commissioner has been attending this conference, which concludes with a dinner party, on an annual basis since 2010. Initially the conference and the dinner were organized during the last day of Ramadan, but since 2011 the time changed to the first day of the Muslim Eid due to the very short time between the Iftar dinner and the last Muslim prayer.

Most Australian officials and academics believe that social and family networks played a key role in radicalizing jihadist members and that the Internet played a minor role or its role came at a later stage:

> While the internet plays a role in the radicalisation process, within the Australian neojihadist context this has predominantly occurred only once individuals are connected to the network, or at least engaged in its periphery. Individuals are far more susceptible to recruitment into terrorist networks through close social connections than any form of top-down or 'virtual' recruitment. (Harris-Hogan, 2012b, p. 8)

Zammit (2012, p. 15) concurs: 'The internet does not appear to play a significant role in jihadist radicalization compared to personal attachments to radicalizing agents'. Nevertheless, the Australian authorities have moved recently to utilize the role of the Internet not so much as to provide a religious counter-narrative to the VE ideologues, but rather to inform Muslim communities about rules and regulations of the country, how to become a rule-abiding citizen in a democracy, why participation in foreign conflicts (like in Lebanon and Syria, for example) is illegal, and about what is permissible and what is not in Australia. In other words, the counter-narrative that Australia is developing takes a political, rather than religious or ideological nature.

A special website has been designed by the Australian authorities about how to create a 'resilient community' in Australia (www.resilientcommunities.gov.au). In addition to information about what is legal and illegal, the website provides information about the 'strength of Australia's diversity', how to create a community that is 'resilient' to violent ideology, what the government is doing with community, state and community initiatives, successful Australian Muslim stories, and a series of 'advice to the Australian Muslim youth' often given by credible Muslim scholars.

Evaluation of the Australian efforts

This chapter analysed the evolution of Australia's Counter-de-Rad policies since 2010. The aim of this final section is to provide a preliminary evaluation, based on anecdotal evidence, for the country's 'soft' measures.

Evaluating the impact and effectiveness of any Counter-de-Rad program is not easy. Evaluating the Australian 'soft' measures at this stage is equally difficult for several reasons. First, these measures remain at their infancy and it is too early to evaluate their effectiveness. Longer periods are required before conclusions on effectiveness can be reached. Second, they remain 'measures' or 'processes' and they do not amount to a fully fledged program at this stage. This is particularly the case with measures being implemented inside the detention centres (religious support) which are currently confined to Victoria. Even in Victoria, the religious support process is not extensive and is not supported by other non-religious elements, such as physical, social, vocational, educational and post-care-release programs. Sometimes it is the lack of these non-religious elements that can undermine the effectiveness of the more religiously oriented parts of a program.

The number of released individuals, moreover, is very small, and they remain under constant surveillance. The incentive to violate the terms of their release is therefore very weak. As a result, assessing the recidivism rate, another important evaluation criteria (although inconvenient and not encompassing), is also difficult. As a high-ranking official at Goulburn super-security detention centre commented:

> Only three individuals have so far been discharged from prison, one of whom was completely released and completed his parole period,[10] while the other two are yet to complete their parole period under community compliance programme. So far they have not done anything to revoke their parole period and they have been behaving in a manner that does not bother us. (Personal interview, Goulburn, November 2012)

During parole released individuals are monitored randomly. That is, the police do unexpected visits to their houses to see whether they are still living there and what they are up to. They are allowed to work and resume a normal life but need to report any changes in their place of accommodation, phone numbers, movements, and so forth. Therefore, it is only after former VEt detainees have been fully discharged and completed their full sentences (see endnote 25) that some appraisal of the recidivism rate in Australia can be made. This requires much longer time intervals as well.

Put differently, many key components of a comprehensive Counter-de-Rad program are missing currently in Australia, with most released former detainees remaining under the strong eye of the police. If improvement is noticed, say in the recidivism rate, under these circumstances it is difficult to establish the real cause of it: Is it the strong police monitoring efforts? Growing age of released individuals? Real de-radicalization? Disengagement? Similarly, increased recidivism might be caused by a lack of police training and/or a lack of non-religious education, which are vital components of the program. Establishing the cause of improvement/deterioration in a variable requires longer periods, a more comprehensive program and much more information than we have on the post-release phase.

Anecdotal evidence, however, suggests some improvements have indeed been recorded in many areas. The Australian experience, for example, confirms the significant role of families in facilitating reintegration and reducing the rate of recidivism. As a high-ranking state official in the counterterrorism department in Canberra told me about the three released individuals:

> So far they have been good, although they return to their old social networks after release. All have jobs now and seem well integrated. The father of one of them has a big business so he is working with his father now. Many are married with children, one with six children while another has three. (personal interview, November 2012).

In Australia too, police–community relationships remain the key to overcoming the small risk of VEm from which the country suffers. Most Australian Muslims have indeed settled well in Australia, are peaceful, reject violence, and the minority of individuals who decided to take matters into their own hands do not pose the kind of threat faced by other Western democracies. This is partly due to the fact that most Muslim Australians reject violence, and also partly due to the community–police relations that they enjoyed prior to the 1998 riots. Here there are both encouraging and worrying signs simultaneously. On the one hand, families and community members seem to be playing a more proactive role. As Harris-Hogan (2012b, pp. 10 and 23) noted:

> within the context of the Australian neo-jihadist network the significant influence of close social relationships has also been used to mediate extreme thinking and behaviour. There have been several noteworthy examples of close family members providing

a positive influence and guiding individuals away from the net-work. ... Crucially, there are also instances of families attempting to prevent radicalisation by approaching authorities for assistance.

Such mediation and community prevention and resilience needs to be supported, strengthened, maintained and built on. We feel that it is here where Australia's Achilles' heel lies at the moment: the relationship between police and community. As the analysis throughout this chap-ter has demonstrated, the Muslim community still does not seem to fully trust the authorities and their motivations behind the newly found enthusiasm for 'soft' measures. This requires time, sustained efforts and the introduction of more comprehensive counter radicalization and de-radicalization measures in partnership with various Australian com-munities, not just Muslims. Such measures should be part of a wider integration policy, one that includes all communities and ethnicities, not just Muslims in Australia.

Moreover, Australia's federal system seems to hinder, rather than support, countrywide Counter-de-Rad efforts. 'The Federal constitu-tion provides too much autonomy to states and we as a Federal gov-ernment cannot impose anything on states' (personal interview with a high-ranking Australian official in the counterterrorism department, Canberra, November 2012). This caused the Australian federal govern-ment to become reactive rather than proactive. This need not be the case. The Dutch government, for example, has encouraged a healthy competition between its regions, facilitated the adoption and imple-mentation of Counter-de-Rad polices at national, regional and local levels, supported such a process financially and played a key role in disseminating information and key lessons derived from each region (Vidino and Brandon, 2012).

Playing a similar proactive role will lead to faster adoption, implemen-tation and dissemination of information and best practices in Australia. It will also bring all Australian officials to provide a better evaluation of the real degree of threat of VEm in the country and thus allay the fears of federal officials who seem to be very concerned about the phe-nomenon of VEm. For example, the 2010 Commonwealth Government Counter-Terrorism White Paper 'emphasized the threat posed by a broad movement consisting of Al Qaeda, and groups allied, associated with it, and individuals inspired by it. Completed and ongoing prosecutions demonstrate that there are Australians committed to this movement' (Australian Government, 2013, p. 7–8; Zammit, 2010, p. 1). Similar concerns have been raised more recently when a man was arrested in

September 2012 in Victoria and charged with terrorism-related offences following a series of police raids in Melbourne:

> Australian Federal Police (AFP) charged the man with four counts of making a document likely to facilitate terrorist acts, a police spokesman said on Thursday. ... Police say officers seized a number of items from the properties, including a USB memory stick, computer equipment, registered firearms and fake firearms. (*The Age*, 2012)

Rather than bragging and 'showing off', the Australian police need to communicate more with community leaders, explain to them why an arrest has taken place, the dangers of radicalization, and work closely with them to explain the policies of the state. This is necessary because such arrests (like the one made in September 2012) 'does not mean there is a significant terrorist presence in Australia. Australia has enjoyed a peaceful recent history, relatively free from the threat of political violence' (Harris-Hogan, 2012a).

To sum up the main points in this section, Australia has enjoyed a peaceful recent past and has not experienced anything like the 2005 and 2009 Pendennis and Neath plots since then. There are also strong signs of the Muslim community becoming a mediator, a de-radicalizing factor, more aware of the dangers of radicalization and more proactive in preventing the emergence of VEm. The partial and half-hearted measures adopted/supported by the Australian government might be partly responsible for these achievements. It is high time that such efforts gather pace at the national, regional and local levels. They should also be expanded to include both counter and de-rad policies simultaneously.

5
Mauritania: From Toleration to Violent Islam

Introduction

For a long time Mauritania has been disregarded by the media and international community. The country was hardly mentioned or received much attention in international relations. This is partly due to the limited resources (such as oil) that Mauritania possesses, and partly due to the fact that Mauritania has 'always espoused a more tolerant brand of Islam', spearheaded by historical, religious and social factors that prevented the kind of radical thoughts preached by al-Qaeda and like-minded organizations from finding roots in the country (Choplin, 2008). Even when some Mauritanian individuals joined the Mujahideen against the Soviet invasion of Afghanistan in the 1980s and later joined the al-Qaeda organization, they proved less extremist in their views than many other of their colleagues from different nationalities. The late Abu Hafs Al-Muritani, for instance, an al-Qaeda religious cleric, 'warned Bin Laden not to disobey Mullah Omar and to cease military activity outside Afghanistan', arguing that 'what was necessary at the time was not jihad on a global level but the rebuilding of Afghanistan' (quoted in IICT, 2011, p. 8).

However, a radical shift has taken place in Mauritania over the past few years. Mauritania is today among a few countries where al-Qaeda and like-minded terrorist organizations have raised their profile in a wave of attacks and kidnappings (Prieur, 2011). This brought Mauritania to the fore of international relations as a big 'theater for terrorism...a training and recruitment camp for mujahedeen before sending them to Chechnya, Iraq, Pakistan, and Somalia' (Ould Ibrahim, 2010). As Choplin (2008) put it: 'Mauritania, a previously little known country, suddenly hit the headlines...and has come under sharp focus from the West, and particularly the US who suspect a growth in influence of...extremists'.

The rise of violent radical ideology in Mauritania in recent years comes as a surprise to the international community. Several developments have undermined the historical, social, cultural and political factors that once prevented the spread of, and provided immunity to, society from violent extremist thoughts and ideologies. Such factors seem no longer to be able to provide protection for the Mauritanian state and society from violent ideologies and activism which became widespread since the late 1990s and early 21st century (ICG, 2005). Mauritanians are today 'puzzled at how their country had overnight transformed from a "peaceful country" into a dangerous enemy of the West' (Choplin, 2008).

The rise of radical, violent ideology and activism in Mauritania in recent years, and the government's response to such a phenomenon, has received little attention from both Western and Eastern scholars and observers alike. As Ould Ibrahim (2010) noted while analysing the root causes of radicalism in Mauritania and the government's strategy in countering it:

> There has been no scientific diagnosis for the problem that would lead to a suggested appropriate...working plan in the right time and with the available resources in order to deal with the root causes...of spread of radical political Islam in Mauritania and providing appropriate solutions before a catastrophe takes place...and before the country becomes the dangerous gate for the African Sahel area.

This chapter fills an important gap in the literature by looking, in the next section, at the historical, cultural, social and political factors that prevented the rise of radical, violent ideology and activism in Mauritania until recently. The third section looks at the evolution of the political system since independence in 1960, and analyses the conditions that have recently conduced terrorism in Mauritania, and how the national, and, to a lesser extent, international, environment has changed over the past two decades in a way that radicalized some members of Mauritanian society and led them to commit acts of terror. The fourth section looks at the government's response to the rise of terrorism in the country, including the National Dialogue Conference which was initiated and supervised by the new president, Abdul-Aziz, himself in October 2010 and whose main 'aim was to abolish the phenomenon of terrorism and radicalism' (Al-Sirag, 2010; IICT, 2011). The final section summarizes and concludes the above.

Mauritania: historical background

It is not easy to write about Mauritania. Not only Western, but also few Mauritanian chronicles and scholars 'cared about their history enough to write it down in a respectful book from the beginning of time until now, this despite the large number of big events that took place in this country which require taking care of' and documenting (Ould Sheikhana, 2009, p. 3). The problem is also exacerbated by the fact that Mauritanians themselves disagree on the interpretation of events, and tend to give different accounts for the same incident. This is why, we dare to think, that this chapter, by analysing the historical factors that led to the evolution of a peaceful and non-violent Mauritanian culture and tradition, will make an important contribution to the literature on Mauritania. Further value is added by investigating the recent events that led to a radical change in the Mauritanian environment that caused some Mauritanians to embrace terrorism.

Mauritania,[1] formerly known as the Changuet Country,[2] is vast, poor and largely underdeveloped. It has a small, largely scattered population and porous borders. Its land stretches over 1,000,000 square kilometres, and its borders extend over 5,000 kilometres. Because of its geographic location between North and West Africa, and point of connection between western and eastern former African French colonies, Mauritania is often referred to as *Bawabat al-Sahel*[3] (The Sahel Gate).[4] In addition to iron ore, fishing is the country's main export thanks to Mauritania's 756 kilometre stretch on the Atlantic Ocean, and 850 kilometre stretch on the Senegal River. Mauritania's total population did not exceed 3.291 million in 2009, with a very low population geographic density of 2.5 people for each square metre, (World Bank, 2011a; Ould Ibrahim, 2010).

Mauritania's strategic geographical location[5] attracted several empires, power centres, groups and immigrants throughout history. This included the Roman Empire, the al-Maraboutoun Empire, the al-Hassaneya Empire and finally the French colonial authorities between 1889 and 1960. Despite the harsh desert conditions, the Sahel area nevertheless remained historically a route for trade and people between North and West Africa. Political stability provided by various empires, particularly by the Maraboutoun and al-Hassaneya empires, led to prosperity of trade and commerce. Stability and economic prosperity attracted, in turn, a large number of immigrants, including a large number of merchants, scholars and tribes from neighbouring countries in the north and south of the Sahel. Ould al-Salim (2010, p. 6) argues that the people of the Sahara, from the 2nd Islamic *hijri* century (8th Christian century) and until at least the 6th Islamic *hijri* century (12th Christian century) consisted of various and very different peoples. West, East and Central Sahara was inhabited by Arab and Amzegh (Berbers) mixed with African blood.[6] The southern part of the eastern Sahara was also inhabited by black people from the Toboo, belonging to such tribes as Zaghawa, Tedah and Darzah.[7] The Berbers played an important role in linking and building networks and relations between North and West Africa on the one hand, and West and East Africa on the other.

Historians divide Mauritania's history into four key phases (Ould al-Salim, 1997, 2008 and 2010; Ould Muhammad, 1999). First is the Old History phase, before the 7th century. This phase was characterized by the introduction of the cart by the Garamants, which was pulled by bulls and horses and seen as a revolution in the country's history. The Old History phase ended around the 7th century, coinciding with the Islamic opening, and paved the way for the second phase, Middle History, often referred to as the Senhaji Age, in reference to the Senhaji tribes which dominated the region in this period (see endnote 39). This phase experienced the birth of one of the most important Islamic empires in the history of the region, the Maraboutoun Empire,[8] starting roughly from the beginning of the 7th century until it collapsed completely in 1591. The third phase, the Modern History, is usually referred to as the Al-Hassaneya era, which saw the complete control of the Arab Bani Hassan tribes over the country between 1591 and 1778, the spread of the Arabic language as the dominant language of the country and culminating in a civil war between Arab and Berber tribes that paved the way for the final phase, namely, the Contemporary Phase, between 1889 and 1960. This latter phase was characterized by European (French) colonization of Mauritania.

Islam initially spread in the Sahel via trade and hajj (pilgrimage) around the 5th and 6th Centuries. However it was not before the Maraboutoun Empire was fully consolidated in the region that Islam became widespread and the dominant religion. The Maraboutoun initially started as a Salafist movement before becoming a full empire. The Maraboutoun were unhappy with corruption, dilution and distortion of Islamic principles that prevailed in North and Western African societies and the spread of *albeda'* (innovation), alternative interpretations and atheist practices, and idol worshipping in some societies. They were relentlessly uncompromising, followed a pure Salafi route (the path of the Prophet Muhammad, caliphs and his and their companions). They were rejectionist, rejecting all alternative interpretations of the Quran and Hadith:

> The Maraboutoun were strict salafists who solved their differences with their opposition by the sword and arrow, and they neither entered into a debate nor negotiations. They opposed fun and innovation and moved through strict salafi paths and killed whoever refused to follow their principles. They destroyed music instruments and fun ... and idol worshippers (Ould al-Salim, 2010, p. 3).

The Maraboutoun, whose name is derived from the Qur'an in reference to the discipline and determination of the true believers, followed a strict Islamic Maliki school. They also succeeded in imposing the Maliki principles on regional tribes. The imposition of Maliki schools was facilitated by both the simplicity and straightforwardness of the Maliki school itself and the unsophisticated nature and intellectuality of tribes, which meant a lack of ability to engage in deep and disciplined theological alternatives. Like Ibn Saud and Ibn Wahaab in Saudi Arabia, the Maraboutoun was an extension of a tribal system, which they subjected to a religious order, Islamic Maliki school (Ould al-Salim, 2008 and 2010; Ould Muhammad, 1999).

One of the striking features that characterized all of the above-mentioned four phases of Mauritanian history is a political 'vacuum', or lack of central authority, turning Mauritania into what Ould Ibrahim (2010) called a 'vacuum area'. Despite the importance of its geographical location, none of the powers that trespassed in the country throughout its history opted to invest in creating a powerful central state in Mauritania. Administratively, Mauritania was run by, and in most cases belonged to, a powerful central authority in North Africa from whence the Maraboutoun and their empire originated. Even while under the French authorities, Mauritania was turned into a civilian region in 1904, before it was later tied to the rest of the Western African French colonies in 1920 (ibid.). Since then, Mauritania was administratively tied to Senegal, until the 1956 French *loi-cadre*, which gave the 'countries behind the Sea', including Mauritania, 'the right to establish an executive system with limited powers to run their local affairs' (Ould Sheikhana 2009, p. 9). The *loi-cadre* gave Mauritania nominal independence, turned it into an independent region from Senegal and led to the establishment of the first Mauritanian government in 1957, then headed by a French ruler, Muragh, and deputized by Mukhtar Ould Dada who went on to become the country's first president after full political independence was gained in 1960.

This does not mean, however, that Mauritanian society lived a 'chaotic life' without rules, regulations, organization or collective action. As the Mauritanian historian, Ould al-Salim (2010, p. 38) wrote, despite the lack of a strong central state, 'The Mauritanian society was organized and was not living a chaotic and unregulated life, as the colonial orientalists claimed'. Several social classes emerged thanks to the melting pot of Mauritanian society, as well as the harsh conditions of the Sahel area that interceded to forge cooperation, coordination and collaboration. These included, in terms of their social influence and importance, the following, respectively: the Arab political elite (which represents the majority of the population today);[9] *al-Zawaya*;[10] *al-Lahmah* group, sometimes referred to as *Iznakah*;[11] *al-Sunaa*';[12] *al-zafafoon*;[13] al-*Harateen*[14] and the slaves, who migrated or were brought to Mauritania via trade a long time ago[15] (Ould al-Salim, 2008, p. 13).

A strict division of labour emerged among Mauritanian social classes, each with its own social function and responsibilities, as alluded to above. Such divisions and responsibilities, ironically, emerged within a context of absent powerful central authority. In fact, it was this political vacuum that led 'to the emergence of a [dynamic] civil society organisation', led mainly by a class of scholars (*al-Zawaya*) that 'legitimized political leaders and slavery...and secured religious legitimacy for commercial contracts' (Ould al-Salim, 2010, p. 149. Also see Ould al-Salim, 2008; Ould Muhammad, 1999). One of the most significant manifestations of this dynamic civil society was *Jamaat al-Hal Wal Aqid* (The Groups of Solution and Decision).

Jamaat al-Hal Wal Agid (JHA) emerged in almost every city and community in Mauritania, and especially in the centre of the country, around fertile and coastal areas, and main cities where trade prospered. They were responsible for organizing every aspect of life in these communities, including collection action, protecting and managing public goods, fighting societal corruption, organizing hajj (pilgrimage), overseeing education and health systems, *imammah* and religious teaching, building and renovating mosques, managing the judiciary system and solving people's problems, collecting taxes and taking care of the poor, needy, and widows and orphans. They were led mostly by a group of scholars, usually referred to as *al-Zawaya* (or students), which became the second-most important class in the social hierarchy, after the political leaders' class.

The *al-Zawaya* were, and continue to be, made up of various tribal elements versed in religious and judicial matters. They derived their legitimacy from their religious and theological knowledge, their role as imams and judges at the same time, and their relative wealth which they accumulated from donations and gifts from politicians and merchants as a result of their status in the society. They also derived their legitimacy from their ability to rule by 'consensus (*le consensus social*)' through agreement reached at community level 'through debates and discussions' (Ould al-Salim, 2010, pp. 154–5. Also see Ould al-Salim 1997 and 2008; Ould Abduallah, 1999).

Both the Maraboutoun and the al-Hassaneya empires, under which umbrella the JHA prospered and gained significance, supported and protected the *al-Zawaya* and *Jamaat*. In return, they (JHA) espoused an apolitical version of Islam, a sort of Sufi version that 'legitimatised political leaders' and de-legitimized violence, revolutionary change and de-radicalized society at large (Ould Abduallah, 1999; Ould al-Salim, 2010). They were responsible for inoculating Mauritanian society against radical ideology and activism, and for keeping radicalization that led to violent extremism out of reach in most corners of Mauritanian society.

Mauritania continued to thrive as a result of its dynamic civil society, led mainly by *al-Zawaya* and JHA. Mauritanians pride themselves that while the 'Arab world was going through intellectual deterioration, Mauritania was experiencing intellectual renaissance' (personal interview with Professor Hamden Ould Tah,[16] Nouakchott, August 2011. Also see Ould Abduallah, 1999; Ould al-Salim, 2008 and 2010). During this period, the sciences did prosper, and Mauritanian scholars managed to deepen debate and discussion about theological and religious issues. They neither challenged the status quo, however, nor deviated from supporting the strict *Salafi-Maliki* school of thought. In other words, while they deepened debate, they failed to extend it to new areas or introduce new alternative interpretations, as their counterparts in Damascus and Cairo did. Their significance, nevertheless, further improved under the Maraboutoun and Al-Hassaneya empires as a result of political stability and the rise of trade and commerce. This led to the introduction of, and increased reliance on, written contracts instead of verbal agreements in commercial transactions, as was the case in earlier periods. Being knowledgeable in religious and judiciary matters, the scholars performed and supervised those contracts, which were based mainly on Islamic principles and rules.

Put differently, *al-Zawaya* and the *Jamaat* represented or played the role of true political leaders, since they assumed theological, judicial, social and economic functions. They were not simply imams or judges in mosques. They interpreted the rules of the game and defended them, fought radicalism and violence and succeeded in keeping them at bay, ruled over disputes and provided binding solutions based on informal societal mechanisms, created consensus and maintained a vibrant and dynamic civil society throughout the country's history (Ould Abduallah, 1999; Ould al-Salim, 2008, 2010).

The Mauritanian civil society remained dynamic and active until the civil war between the Arabs and Berbers in the decades that preceded the French colonization which disrupted it and undermined its social, economic and political institutions. The French colonial authorities deliberately targeted JHA and *al-Zawaya*, and sought to terminate their influence. The French followed a divide and rule policy, isolated scholars, cut and controlled food and other supplies to the entire Mauritanian society and created a split within the scholar community. A political schism emerged among the scholars. Some opposed outright the French occupation of the country and called for jihad, and some feared retribution and hence opted for collaboration. A large number of the former left the country, migrating to such countries as Turkey, Libya, Sudan, Morocco and especially to Saudi Arabia. The latter's leadership provided financial and political incentives to attract Mauritanian and other scholars to fill a gap reflected in a lack of sufficient numbers of religious scholars in a tribal society that itself was brought together through a similar religious movement, Wahhabism, that legitimized political leaders and denounced revolutionary change (El-Said and Harrigan, 2013; Ould al-Salim, 2008, 2010; Ould Abduallah, 1999; Ould Sheikhana, 2009).

As Ould al-Salim wrote (2010, pp. 124, 125, 132, 149), the French occupation divided and:

> led to the migration of a large number of *ulama* and prominent sheikhs...many went to Morocco, Libya, Sudan and Saudi Arabia. ... The departure of the *ulama* represented the most difficult challenge to the colonial authorities and the largest motivation for migration and jihad. A group consisting of 600 individuals, with their families from several prominent tribes...led by Sheik Muhammad al-Ameen Ben Zini al-Qalqami...departed from the eastern part of the country in 1908 passing through the Sahara towards Libya then Jordan then Turkey....Many joined Libyans in their Jihad against Italians...[the migration of the *ulama*] increased in the 1950s as a result of benefits provided by the Saudi government, including the wavering of haj and residency fees and provision of nationalities to Mauritanian scholars. The French occupation sought to wipe out

the significance of the African history and to raise doubts about the African civilization.

Political independence and the challenge of nation building: planting the seeds of violent extremism (VEm)

The challenge of building a newly independent nation, both internal and external, was felt from day one in Mauritania. Externally, the United Nations (UN) refused Mauritania's membership as a result of a veto by the Soviet Union in December 1960. It was not before a political settlement took place later on, in which the Soviet Union agreed to abstain from voting in return for accepting UN membership of Mongolia, that Mauritania joined the international organization (Ould Ibrahim, 2010).

Regionally, most Arab states, under pressure from Morocco which considered Mauritania as an undivided and 'inseparable part of Morocco', refused to recognize Mauritanian independence. Even France, who initially was not in favour of full Mauritanian independence and preferred Mauritania to join the Common Sahara Regional Organization to tie it to its colonies in the west, flirted with the idea of 'merging Mauritania with Morocco. ... Had it not been for the Moroccan position which was supportive of the Algerian revolution, France would not have supported Mauritania's independence' (all quotations from Ould Sheikhana, 2009, pp. 38, 42). It was not until 1973, after Morocco had given up its interests in Mauritania for political and regional factors in the late 1960s, that Mauritania was permitted to join the Arab League.

From early independence, therefore, Mauritania has been the subject of significant external interventions in its affairs. This remains the case today. As Ould Ibrahim (2010) noted, Mauritania:

> has become the country most affected by the changes in the balance of international relations as a result of its strategic geopolitical location ... it continues to search for its identity since independence between an extremely difficult internal national state building process, on the one hand, and extensive search for appropriate formulas to meet the requirements of dealing with the constant concerns of international challenges to interfere in its affairs.

The internal challenges of nation building were no less daunting. Having rejected the old name of the country, the Shinguetti Country, France accepted the new title put forward by the country's political elite, namely, The Islamic Republic of Mauritania (IRM).[17] The name also reflected the political aims of Mauritania's new political elite, particularly those of the country's first president, Mokhtar Ould Daddah, who:

> envisioned the country as a bridge between North Africa and Black Africa. In order to overcome the dual cultural identity and ensure cohesion between the Moors and the 'Black Mauritanians', Islam was brought to the fore. This lent legitimacy to the Mauritanian state and brought together a 100% Muslim nation. (Choplin, 2008)

On 22 March 1959, the country's first Constitution was promulgated. It announced the birth of the Islamic Republic, 'an Islamic Republic notwithstanding of a French Made'[18] (Ould Sheikhana, 2009, p. 52). The new Constitution nevertheless confirmed the Islamic identity of Mauritania and the centrality of Islam to the Mauritanian people.[19] It also provided for political pluralism and parliamentary democracy. This led to the birth of several political parties, including the president's party, *al-Tajamua'* (Regroupment),[20] *al-Nahda* (The Renaissance Party), which became the main opposition party, *al-Itihad al-Watani* (National Union Party), known as black party, and *al-Itihad al-Ishtiraki al-Islami* (the Islamic Socialist Party).

The Mauritanian state, however, was born undemocratic. Even before full independence was declared in 1960, Ould Daddah moved to undermine his opposition and consolidate his power over the executive and the country as a whole. For example, Ould Daddah, a few months before the first National Assembly elections in May 1959 took place, charged the main opposition party, *al-Nahda*, with corruption, banned the party from participation in national elections, declared the party illegal and arrested its top leadership. This trend of harassing and arresting opposition leaders continued throughout Ould Daddah's hold on power until 1978 (US Library of Congress, 1990).

Ould Daddah's fixation on survival and the holding of power led him, in November 1960, to change the political system from a parliamentary one into a 'presidential system'. One year later, on 25 December 1961, Ould Daddah amalgamated and forced the merger of the four main political parties into one: The Mauritanian People's Party (*Parti du peuple Mauritanienne*, or *Hizb al-Sha'ab*). The authority of the National Constituent Assembly was further undermined in 1964 by the firing of opposition members, their replacement with loyal elements and ending financial authority of all members. The latter (weakening financial position of MPs) was carried out through a constitutional amendment which made membership in the Assembly 'voluntary' and free of any financial benefits, such as wages or salaries. Just in case some members contemplated joining the opposition in the future, elected members of the Constituent Assembly (a mini-parliament) were also forced to write a letter of resignation in advance as soon as they were elected to the Assembly. The aim of this policy was to allow the president to fire potential opposition members and to prevent them from opposing his policies (all quotations from Ould Sheikhana, 2009, pp. 82–3 and 112–120. Also see US Library of Congress, 1990, 2011).

Even when the opposition tried to regroup and create a new party in 1964 (the Mauritanian Democratic Front), the government refused to license it. On 12 November 1964, a new constitutional amendment ended political pluralism and constitionalized *Hizb al-Sha'ab*. The new law stated that 'the will of the people can be expressed through the party of the state [*Hizb al-Sha'ab*], which is organized democratically and which the state recognized as coalition of national parties as existed on December 25, 1961, as the only state party'. Constant rigging and irregularities of elections followed through these measures and policies. In 1971, for example, Ould Daddah claimed that he achieved 99 per cent victory in that year's elections (Ould Sheikhana, 2009, pp. 115–7).

The aim of the above-mentioned measures was to subject MPs, politicians and the politics of the country as a whole to the will of the president. In the process, democracy, political pluralism and public freedoms were arrested in the name of the 'requirements of the period'. Ould Daddah himself explained his policies in the following words:

> My short and incomplete experience with the executive authority convinced me of the need for a strong executive authority at the top of the young, maturing national state, which cannot allow itself to go through the instability and lack of coordination which the fourth French Republic suffered from. (Quoted in Ould Sheikhana, 2009, p. 81)

The personal politics of Ould Daddah and the extreme concentration of power in his hands naturally led to divisions inside and outside his political party, splintering and fragmenting Mauritanian politics. Many saw Ould Daddah and the tight network of elites which he surrounded himself with as implementing and serving French interests in the country. Many groups and individuals fled to Morocco and started to organize their opposition to and mobilization against Ould Daddah from there. While most defected opposition groups chose peaceful means, one group in particular, the Hurmah Group (named after their leader Ahmad Ould Hurmah), opted and called for violent and terrorist methods to get their message across (see endnote 53). Supported by Morocco and Mali (they had established bases in the latter), they carried out several attacks against both Mauritanian and French targets inside Mauritania.

The two most significant and well-documented attacks by the Hurmah Group took place in February and March 1962. In the earlier, a foreign construction company was attacked and its tools and instruments, including explosives used by the company in its work as well as small weapons used by its guards, were stolen, leading to long delays in the operations of the company. In the second attack, the *al-Na'mah* operation, the perpetrators opened fire and threw explosives in a military club, killing three French soldiers and injuring ten French and Mauritanian soldiers (US Library of Congress, 1990, 2011; also see Ould Sheikhana, 2009, pp. 92, 96).

The above-mentioned violent acts, which were organized by Mauritanians and included Mauritanian targets at the same time, were the first to take place in the country.[21] The response of the government was very swift. A large number of suspects, sympathizers and even family members of those accused of planning and executing the operation were arrested. The authorities refused to release prisoners until the three main accused individuals in the *al-Na'mah* attack gave themselves up, which they did later in the year.[22]

The regime sought no dialogue, debate or discussion either with the attackers or their sympathizers and family members. This despite the fact that several societal elements called for and interceded to carry out such a dialogue and reconciliation in what they saw as an unprecedented development in Mauritanian society. It was also the case that such violent attacks proved very unpopular among most Mauritanians and political and ideological figures, who strongly condemned such attacks. This led the attackers themselves to ask for amnesty and forgiveness. Despite 'calls for amnesty' by the accused attackers and societal elements alike, however, the three main individuals accused in the *al-Na'mah* operation were tried in a closed military court and sentenced to death. By doing so, Mauritania missed a golden opportunity to pioneer a de-radicalization or counter radicalization program in the region, one which could be used in later years to prevent the emergence of violent extremists or de-radicalize those who would cross the line and become violent activists, as proved to be the case after 2003 (see next sections).

Sentencing them to death instead led most Mauritanians to treat them as martyrs and 'historic heroes' who were sentenced to death for fighting the French colonial authorities (Ould Sheikhana, 2009, p. 209).[23]

Even when several individuals who defected to Morocco in earlier years, including some supporters and sympathizers of the Ahmad Ould Hurmah Group, gave up violence and returned to Mauritania in 1963 to rejoin their families, society and the political process,[24] 'the regime dealt with the returnees' file in a very negative way' and treated the returnees as 'conspirators'. The returnees were arrested and some of their leaders soon died, including Prince Muhammad Ould Ameer on 8 May 1965 in a hospital in Senegal after his health had deteriorated in his cell where conditions were described as harsh and torturous (Ould Sheikhana, 2009, pp. 99–101).

The political, regional[25] and economic crisis[26] brought about by Ould Daddah's personal style of politics destabilized his regime and invited a military coup in 1978. Ould Daddah and his colleagues were arrested and kept in prison until 2 October 1979 when he was secretly sent to France for treatment as his health began to deteriorate while he was incarcerated. Political division, dissension, wrangling and disagreements, as well as continuous worsening of economic conditions characterized the period between 1978 and 1984 and thereafter. This was reflected in several successful and failed military coups, in addition to the 1978 coup, in April 1979 (successful), January 1980 (successful), March 1981 (failed), February 1982 (failed), December 1984 (successful), 2005 (successful) and 2008 (successful). Apart from the March 1981 failed military coup, what distinguishes all these coups is their bloodless nature (US Library of Congress, 1990, 2011; Ould Sheikhana, 2009). All coup leaders, nevertheless, resorted to the same personal and tribal style of politics designed and literally followed by Ould Daddah. The exception is the 2008 coup, which seems to have produced, so far, a genuine democratic process.

The link between terrorism, economics and political repression

The link between economic development, equality and ethnicity, on the one hand, and violent extremism on the other remains a very contentious subject. What is evident, however, is that mishandling economic and social development, including the failure to manage economic development and growth rates, job creation and inequalities, as well as failure to successfully incorporate minorities, can create an environment that is conducive to radicalization and extremism that, in the presence of political repression, can lead to terrorism (El-Said and Barrett, 2011; Harrigan and El-Said, 2011; Coolsaet and Struye de Swielande, 2008; Attran, 2006; Pape, 2003).

Like many other countries in the region, Mauritania emerged from colonization not only poor, but also largely uneducated, underdeveloped and with a poor infrastructure, education and health system. The country's economic and industrial base was also and remains very narrow, based on undifferentiated products and a small number of primary commodities. While in Mauritania, the French colonial authorities not only showed little interest, but also made no major investments in infrastructure or industry, unlike Japanese colonial authorities in Korea and Taiwan, for example, which invested heavily in, and created and bequeathed, a strong industrial base to these countries after independence (Wade, 1990). When the colonial power left in 1960, not only did Mauritania have no strong central authority and bureaucracy, but it also inherited a weak economy and industrial foundation. To make things worse, Mauritanians largely boycotted the small number of schools built or sponsored by the French authorities to educate the progeny of both French officials and Mauritanian elites who collaborated with France. At the time of political independence in 1960, therefore, the overwhelming majority of Mauritanians were poor, illiterate and deprived. Their limited involvement in running their own affairs under the French colonization of Mauritania and the lack of a strong central authority meant that they also lacked the skills necessary to successfully run a modern state.

Most newly independent states, including those which achieved the most rapid level of economic development and industrialization, like South Korea and Taiwan, started their independence by initiating a strong economic and industrial program to accelerate economic development, diversify economic base, build infrastructure and develop their private sector[27] (Wade, 1990). Mauritania's first government under Ould Daddah, however, opted instead for 'austerity measures', higher taxes through the 'unification of the tax system … without discrimination among citizens, and to subject to military conscription all able citizens' (Ould Sheikhana, 2009, p. 44). Ould Daddah's fixation with power and survival also led him to reject much needed French subsidy in order to weaken the financial autonomy of his rivals in the parliament and government.

Lack of investment and state support affected the mostly rural economy which was hit by a long and unprecedented drought in the late

1960s and early 1970s, leading to massive and equally unprecedented rural to urban migration. For example, in 1962 there were only five cities whose population exceeded 5,000. This rose to 16 in 1977. In 1972, Nouakchott's population represented only 7.9 per cent of the total population of Mauritania. In 1977 this rose to 44.9 per cent, from 5,807 to 138,530, a 21.1 per cent annual growth rate. Mauritania also had no cities whose population exceeded 10,000 in 1962. By 1977, the number of cities with 10,000 people rose to seven (Ould Sheikhana, 2009, p. 163).

Unplanned and prepared for rural to urban migration had political, social and economic consequences. It unexpectedly brought more underprivileged classes to areas little prepared for hosting them. A lack of jobs, education and health facilities in a system traditionally dominated by tribal and class divisions politicized many individuals in their newly inhabited areas. The most important economic achievements of Ould Daddah's 18-year reign included the linking of railways with mines in the Izwerat region in 1963, exiting the Franco-African money zone and introducing a national currency (awqeya) and a central bank in 1973, nationalizing Mephrama (Iron and Steel Company) and developing relations with Morocco and Senegal which led to an improvement in trade relations with these countries. Ould Sheikhana (2009, p. 196) eloquently summarized the economic achievements of Ould Daddah's government in the following words:

> This class system, which was supported by the colonial authorities did not experience any development during its first eighteen years since independence. On the contrary, it was consolidated through policies of control and domination and not through opening schools beyond the sons of sheikhs and heads of tribes, as well as by direct support to those leaders... [Ould Daddah]... established the first republican government which reflected in an open way the degree of domination through individuals who came from the same aristocratic and tribal roots, and what strategies produced by this government openly ignored putting in place structural solutions for such problems as slavery and marginalization and poverty and lack of schooling among the *Harateen*. [Those policies] in addition to the drought problem which led to mass migration towards the cities led to the emergence of the *tin* [slum] *neighborhoods*.

Tribalism, corruption, nepotism and internal power struggles sapped the capacity of the state and further undermined its ability to provide even the most basic services to its citizens. No other factor, however, bankrupted the Mauritanian state more than entering an unnecessary war over the Sahara in 1974.

Under pressure from Morocco, Ould Daddah agreed to King Hassan II's demand to divide the Sahara between Mauritania and Morocco. Mauritania thus entered its first war after independence in 1975 against the Saharan Polisario Front. The army was poorly prepared for such an unnecessary war, which officially ended in August 1979 before taking its toll on the Mauritanian economy. The Polisario fighters started targeting Mauritanian economic interests inside Mauritania, such as the railway and foreign technical workers and planted explosives on main trade routes to North and West Africa. The war also disrupted exportation from mines, which declined from 11.6 million in 1974 to 8.4 million in 1977, and was coupled with a large reduction in the international price of iron ore. More importantly, state finances were redirected to serve the war in the Sahara at the expense of urgently needed infrastructure and other productive sectors. The cost of the war rose from 1,200 million ouguiya in 1975 to 1,800 million ouguiya in 1977, or from 30 per cent of the state budget to 60 per cent. The cost of the war was funded mainly by foreign borrowing which in turn rose from US$140 million in 1973 to U$700 million in 1978, reaching US$1billion at the end of the war in 1979. Worse, the war corrupted many army officers and state officials who sought to enrich themselves by expropriating donations from some oil-rich Arab states, such as Saudi Arabia and Kuwait. In 1978, for example, France stopped a military shipment and other supplies to Mauritania which Saudi Arabia had paid for because the French suppliers failed to receive their money. Saudi Arabia also stopped a US$100 million loan to Mauritania at the last minute for reasons related to corruption, and convinced Kuwait to follow suit. The reputation of Mauritania was tarnished, and the result was financial bankruptcy. According to the World Bank (quoted in Ould Sidi Muhammad, PhD dissertation in Baghdad, p. 285), Mauritania, by June 1978, was no longer able to cover one week of imports or even to pay wages and salaries to its bureaucrats and state officials.[28] In short, 'the state treasury was empty' (Ould Sheikhana, 2009, pp. 260–3).

Mismanagement went beyond the economic sphere to include regional and international relations,[29] as well as a failure to manage relations with various Mauritanian minorities and ethnic groups. As the US Library of Congress Case Study on Mauritania (1990) stated: 'The greatest challenge to national unity was [and remains] Mauritania's heterogeneous population'. As stated earlier, mainly peasants who identified with black Africa, both culturally and racially, inhabited the southern regions of Mauritania at the time of independence. Desert nomads identified with the Arab world and inhabited the northern regions (US Library of Congress, 1990). Arab elites had long dominated political systems since the al-Hassaneya Empire, which made the Arabic language the main language in Mauritania. The French authorities, however, sought to replace Arabic with French as the main language of the country, including within the education system. Following independence, Mauritania's new political elite sought to re-Arabize the system. Under pressure from his Arab nationalists, Ould Daddah introduced a new ruling on 30 January 1965 (Law No. 026–65), making the Arabic language compulsory in schools and the education system. This 'educational reform, which replaced French with Arabic on a massive scale, was a resounding failure, as mastery of French remains a key asset for job-seekers. Moreover, the forsaking of the French language cut off young generations from the West and its values' (ICG, 2005, iii). Educational reform was also carried out with little concern for its impact on the country's black ethnic groups who identify more with Africa.

Indeed, educational reform raised concerns of black African Mauritanians, who saw in the replacement of the French with the Arabic language a way to further undermine their African culture, as well as their economic, political and social mobility. Demonstrations expressing opposition to the law by black Mauritanian school students erupted on 4 January and 4 February 1966 in various cities, including Nouakchott, and disrupted the entire educational system. This was followed by a document signed by 19 Mauritanian black leaders, who were all state officials, supporting students in response to a government threat to fire demonstrators if they did not return to their schools immediately. When the students refused to end their demonstrations, the 19 black leaders were fired, arrested and demonstrations repressively put down. Nine demonstrators died and many were injured (Ould Sheikhana, 2009, pp. 120–3).

In addition, Mauritanians of African origin were, and continue to be, underrepresented in the political system. The Mauritanian state always argued that black Mauritanians represent less than a quarter of the total population. This has been reflected in official positions held by their representatives in state, bureaucracy and even the parliament[30] (Choplin, 2008; ICG, 2005). In fact, 'this group of black Maures was essentially a slave class until 1980, when slavery was abolished', following a military coup in 1979 (US Library of Congress, 1990).

It is against the above-mentioned social, economic, political, regional and international developments that the 1978 military coup and subsequent coups should be understood. The 1978 coup brought down the Ould Daddah regime, imprisoned him until the early 1980s and then deported him to France. Since then, ten military coups, both failed and successful, have taken place in Mauritania. In addition to the June 1978 coup, these include the following: 6 April 1979, 4 January 1984, 16 March 1981 (failed), February 1982 (failed), 12 December 1984, 3 August 2005, and the August 2008 coup which brought the current president, Mohamed Ould Abdel Aziz, to power. Despite important developments after the 2005 military coup (see below), the system remained 'endemic[ally] corrupt' (ICG, 2006, ii), tribally based, internally divided and largely mismanaged in terms of economic development and growth rates, employment creation and job opportunities, equity and relations with ethnic groups and minorities (Choplin, 2008; ICG, 2005, 2006; Ould Sheikhana, 2009).

Despite the discovery of oil in recent years, 'forty percent [of Mauritanians] live below the poverty line in a nation that exports fish and iron ore' almost solely (Fertey, 2009). Unofficial sources put the poverty figures at much higher rates. Between 2000 and 2010, Mauritania's GDP PPP[31] grew by a paltry 1.9 per cent (CIA World Factbook, 2010). In June 2011, Mauritanians took to the streets peacefully, protesting against high food prices, lack of job opportunities, declining living standards, bad governance and perceived widespread corruption among state officials. They 'call[ed] for an Egypt-style revolt' and moral regeneration in government (Middle East Online, 2011). This is not the first time Mauritanians rose against their government in recent years. Just a few months before the 2005 military coup, 'bread riots' broke out in 'several towns following the rise of consumer prices [which] pointed to social breakdown' (Choplin, 2008).

There is a consensus inside Mauritania today that, apart from the short-lived and societally condemned Hurmah movement in the early 1960s, a contemporary terrorism movement linked to al-Qaeda only emerged in the country in the second half of the 1990s and gained momentum in the early years of the 21st century (interviews with state officials, ulama and members of civil society organizations, Nouakchott, August, 2011). This period warranted further investigation and that is the aim of the next section.

The rise of Islamic current

On 12 December 1984, Maaouya Ould Sid'Ahmed Taya (the former chief of staff and former prime minister) deposed his president, Mohamed

Khouna Ould Haidalla, while the latter was outside the country attending a French–African summit. Ould Taya was one of the key leaders of the 1978 military coup, which ousted President Ould Daddah in an attempt to forestall government collapse and bankruptcy caused by widespread corruption and the war over Western Sahara against the Polisario Front (1975–9). He was appointed prime minister in March 1981, in the aftermath of a failed military coup against Ould Haidalla, as a reward for his role in thwarting the coup.

While prime minister, Ould Taya convinced President Ould Haidalla to 'implement the Islamic Shariah, meaning … implementing the Shariah law regarding criminal Islamic law and not consolidating the Islamic system in all of its dimensions' (Ould Sheikhana, 2009, pp. 397–8). Several theories were put forward to explain Ould Taya's move to implement sharia law. One was to gain the Islamists' support in ending the slavery law and freeing the blacks, an issue over which Islamists were consulted and lent support to. Another was to undermine the rising popularity of Nasserist and Arab nationalists, especially among students and workers who were becoming more strong and daring in expressing their demands, evidenced by direct confrontation with nationalists in 1981 and frequent demonstrations which they organized in the early 1980s. A final hypothesis, one put by Ould Taya himself, is that introducing Islamic sharia law was the result of widespread corruption among state officials and a 'large wave of crime which hit the length and breadth of the country' which necessitated, according to Ould Taya, a tougher punitive system to undermine corruption and crime (Quoted in Ould Sheikhana, 2009, p. 398). One consequence of introducing sharia law, however, was obviously to strengthen the Islamic current in the country.

The roots of the Islamic current in Mauritania can be traced back to the al-Shabab Movement which played an important role in resisting the French colonization in the 1950s. In 1958, members of the Al-Shabab, taking advantage of the 1958 constitution which provided for parliamentary elections and political plurality, established Hizb Al-Nahda (The Renaissance Party) in August 1958, with the purpose of 'liberating all Chinguite country and mov[ing] it forward to the road of happiness and prosperity until it joined the path of developed countries'. This was to be achieved 'through political resistance', not violence (all quotations from Ould Sheikhana, 2009, p. 47).

Members of Hizb Al-Nahda, despite its general Islamic orientation, came from different backgrounds. It included both seculars and conservatives, civilians and state officials, employed and unemployed. It soon gained large popularity and became the main opposition party, a fact that led to its banning in 1961, as mentioned earlier.

Not permitted to establish a political party, members of the former Hizb al-Nahda established the Islamic Culture Association in 1978, following the coup which ousted President Ould Daddah in that year. Until then, religiosity in general and the religious movement in particular were not particularly strong. Ould Sheikhana (2009) shows how even starting a speech with the usual Islamic introduction (in the name of Allah the Compassionate and the Merciful) would be laughed at in the country. But Islamists benefited tremendously from a 1979 education reform, known as *Khayar al-Sha'b* (the Choice of the People), which gave students the choice between the Arabic system in schools or an Arabic–French system. Although this led, later on, to two different generations of students, it facilitated the spread of Arabic and Islamic cultures in the country. This has also been consolidated through the cultural, social, charity and missionary efforts and programs of the Islamic Culture Association and the *Jema'at al-Da'wa wa 'l-Tabligh*, the most firmly established Islamic institution in Mauritania. Islamists in general, and their ulama in particular, also played a key role in terminating the slavery system in Mauritania in 1980, by providing religious explanations for its termination. Given the significant traditional role of ulama in both Islam and Mauritania, they were consulted over the legitimacy of the slavery system in the country and provided fatwas that delegitimized it (US Library of Congress, 1990; ICG, 2005; Ould Sheikhana, 2009, p. 362).

Through their emphasis on moral regeneration, participation and equity, Islamists also called and pushed for more participatory political and social systems. The termination of the slavery law, for example, was accompanied by the appointment of several Haratines (former slaves) in state positions, such as Abu Baker Ould Massoud who was appointed as a Minister of Construction. Several other Haratines were appointed as advisors and ambassadors. On 11 December 1980, the president, following an emergency meeting, announced his intention to appoint a civilian government to prepare a new constitution and carry a general referendum to lead to a transition period before parliamentary and municipal elections were fully restored. On 19 December 1980 a new constitution to that effect was announced. Such calls for a participatory approach, emphasis on morality and ethics, as well as equity, began to gain Islamists significant popularity in the country[32] (Ould Sheikhana, 2009, p. 399).

Nothing, however, increased the popularity of Islamists more in an environment characterized by massive poverty, inequity and deprivation than their involvement in charity work. Not permitted to have their own political party, Islamists became heavily engaged in charity and social network provisions in the country. As the ICG (2005, iii) wrote:

> Although Islamism's political expression remains constricted, the number of its sympathizers is rapidly growing. It is expanding chiefly in the towns (Nouakchott, Nouadhibou, Rosso and Zouérat) and among groups such as the Haratines (the former slave stratum which currently constitutes most of the urban sub-proletariat) as well as young Mauritanians who emerge from an Arabised educational system without any legitimate qualification and end up adrift on a thoroughly depressed labour market. ... Islamism has also found fertile ground in urban poverty, rejection of the corrupt political class and the abortion of the democratic project. Finally, Islamism prospers thanks to a charitable sector whose funds are mostly of Gulf origin.

It is important to note here that Mauritanian Islamists are not violent extremists. Nor have they ever espoused a violent extremist ideology like the one preached by al-Qaeda and its like-minded organizations.[33] As the ICG (2005, 2006) noted, violent extremist and fundamental ideologies are a recent phenomenon in Mauritania. They had no foothold in the country before the mid-1990s due to a traditionally tolerant socio-religious system and a powerful, antiviolent extremism and activism Islamic movement that curtailed the spread and appeal of extremist ideas. Choplin (2008) concurs:

> Radical Islamism is not new in Mauritania, but terrorism and the sheer scale of violence witnessed in these acts is unprecedented. Although radical trends are on the rise, this should not be confounded with terrorism, which has not taken root in Mauritania.

What then changed that led to the emergence of terrorism in Mauritania in recent years? How did the government deal with it? What factors led to a sudden shift in government policies towards de-radicalization after 2008? The answer to these questions is the main aim of the next sections.

State-manufactured terrorism: from Ould Taya to Ould Abdel Aziz

The preceding analysis shows that the state always had a vague and unclear position towards Islam and Islamists. To confront the rising influence of Nasserites and Arab nationalists in the late 1970s and early 1980s, the leaders of the 1980 military coup, particularly Colonel Haidar Ould Haidalla, sought to further entrench Islam and its practices in the country. For that purpose, sharia law was enacted in 1982. Ould Haidalla's successor, Maouiyya Ould Sid'Ahmed Taya, who took over in 1984, 'maintained the trend, instituting restrictions on, among other things, alcohol' (Choplin, 2008).

An abrupt shift in Ould Taya's position towards Islamists, however, occurred in the late 1980s. As international pressure to democratize Mauritania mounted, Ould Taya calculated that Islamists, given their increasing influence and popularity, would dominate the political system:

> In this new climate, Islamists were prevented from active involvement in politics: in 1991 Taya further eroded their influence by banning the formation of religion-based political parties. Between 1994 and 2005, there were numerous arrests, followed by equally frequent pardons. This was part of a government strategy to harass these groups rather than openly fight them. (Choplin, 2008)

The traditional alliance between the ulama and the state, which kept fundamentalism outside Mauritania for decades, was undermined by Ould Taya's policies. All Islamists, whether moderates or radicals, were indiscriminately harassed, arrested and imprisoned. The threat of fundamentalism was deliberately exaggerated by Ould Taya in order to deny Mauritanians democratic rights, on the one hand, and to gain access to international financial assistance and legitimacy on the other:

> Although the official discourse tends to tie the issue of political stability to the question of Islamism, the reality is far more complex. President Ould Taya's regime is taking advantage of the international context (the struggle against global terrorism) to legitimize its denial of democratic rights, while giving credence to the concept that Islamists are linked to the armed rebels in order to discredit them. (ICG, 2005, p. i)

Mauritanian officials and ulama also give similar accounts:

> Terrorism is a new phenomenon in Mauritania, one that goes back only to the period between 2001–5. This was the *fatrat ihtigan* [period of repression] practiced by the previous regime [of Ould Taya] against moderate Islamists in particular. The regime targeted everything that is Islamic, including political parties, charity work, associations, Quranic schools, teachers, scholars, imams, ulama, and so forth. Injustices led to radicalism, especially among sympathizers of the Islamic movement who themselves were not very religious. The regime wanted to attract financial support from the West by playing the terrorism card. But this led to anger and incubation of fundamentalism. Hence terrorism was a state-fabricated and -made phenomenon in Mauritania. (Personal interview with Salem Ould Boudou, First Advisor in the Ministry of Islamic Affairs, Nouakchott, August, 2011)

It was not surprising therefore that this period, the post-1995 period, witnessed the birth of the first Mauritanian home-grown terrorist movement: *Ansar Allah al-Murabiteen* (AAM), which derived its name from the Quran itself. Ideologically, AAM was very much influenced by the Algerian terrorist group, the Salafi Group for Preaching and Fighting (GSPC), which in 2007 turned into al-Qaeda in the Islamic Land of North Africa (AQMI), after declaring its loyalty to al-Qaeda. AQMI succeeded in planting seeds of jihadism in Mauritania by attracting several disgruntled Mauritanians into its ranks. They provided special logistic and military equipment and encouraged them to open a new front in the country. AAM is believed to be the branch that represents al-Qaeda in Mauritania (Ould Ibrahim, 2010; Al Jazeera Network, 2011b; Choplin, 2008). Both AAM and AQMI launched several attacks that recently radically changed the international image of Mauritania into one associated with global terrorism.

For example, the cancellation of the 10th and 11th Dakar Rally between al-Na'meh City in West Mauritania and Bobo-diolaso in Burkina Faso in 2004 followed a direct threat from al-Zarqawi in 2004 to Mauritanian authorities to stop collaborating with Western powers in the 'war on terror'.[34] Less than a year later, on 4 April 2005, a military unit was attacked in the Lemghayti region, in the northeastern part of Mauritania, almost 150 kilometres from the Mali border. The attack led to the death of 15 soldiers, 17 wounded and 2 missing. On 24 November 2007, four French citizens from the same family were assassinated close to Illak City. On 27 November 2007 a plot killed four Mauritanian soldiers during a surveillance operation planned by al-Qaeda in the north, near Wadan City. In March 2008 a café near the Israeli embassy was attacked in Nouakchott, injuring two individuals. On 6 and 7 April a bloody confrontation took place in the streets of Nouakchott between security forces and terrorists belonging to the al-Qaeda organization. On 9 September 2008, an army unit was trapped in a plot by the terrorists near Toureen City in the north, killing 11 soldiers during Ramadan. Their bodies were desecrated. On 23 June 2009, an American citizen was killed in the capital in an operation that al-Qaeda took responsibility for two days later. In September 2009, the French embassy was targeted by a suicide bomber attack. On 29 November 2009 three Spaniards were kidnapped on the highway and were led to al-Qaeda camps in the north of Mali before they were later released as a result of a complicated international deal with the Spanish government. On 25 August 2010 al-Qaeda sent a car full of explosives to the military headquarters in al-Na'emah City in the east, on the border with Mali, killing one soldier and injuring several others (Ould Ibrahim, 2010; Prieur, 2011; African News24, 2010; CNN News, 2010).

In addition to Mauritania's political, economic and social environments, where the conditions for the rise of violent extremism were ideal, the regional and international environments did not help either. Washington's support for the undemocratic regime of Ould Taya is an example. This led the ICG (2005, p. iii) to warn that:

Western powers also would be well served by revising their analyses and policies. Washington's emphasis on the purely military aspect of its 'war against terrorism' in the Sahel in general[1] and Mauritania in particular risks becoming increasingly indefensible insofar as there is no genuine terrorist movement on the ground and insofar as this policy is being exploited to justify denying political rights to non-violent opposition currents. Instead, the United States should encourage the Mauritanian government to address its socio-economic and cultural challenges, and help it do so.

Washington's wars in Afghanistan and Iraq, as well as the deteriorating situation in Palestine, also added trigger factors:

There was also the international environment which was equally radicalizing, including the invasion of Iraq in 2003 and Afghanistan, and the continuing deterioration of the situation in Palestine, as well as other perceived injustices against Muslims in the world. (Personal interview with Salem Ould Boudou, First Advisor in the Ministry of Islamic Affairs, Nouakchott, August, 2011).

From counter terrorism to de-radicalization

Until a new military coup deposed Ould Taya's regime in 2005, the Mauritanian government relied on repressive practices to deal with its opponents, real and perceived, including all forms of Islamists. Such practices evolved around arresting, imprisoning and harassing Islamists and their sympathizers. Publicly, the government even refused to recognize the existence of the phenomenon (terrorism). Regionally, however, Ould Taya's government not only sought to avoid confrontation with any terrorist groups outside Mauritania, but also resorted to a truce with such groups in order to avoid internal instability and weaken the regime by dragging it into a debilitating war with al-Qaeda and like-minded organizations. Hence:

> Despite the announcement of the presence of the first salafi trend in Mauritania in 1994, successive governments always chose *muhadana* (truce) policy. ... the focus of the political speech has been on the historical factors that prevented growth of radicalization in the country, leading the government to exaggerate the role of historical, social and cultural factors in undermining radicalisation, such as the nature of the tribal system in the country, sufi methods, and tendency of Mauritanians to resists 'imported Islam'. (Ould Ibrahim, 2010)

Indeed, Colonel Ould Taya, as the quotation cited above implied, 'had conducted a secret agreement with AQIM ... approximately a year before the Lemghayti attack [in 2005] (Al Jazeera Network, 2011a, p. 5). The agreement, which was mediated by tribal elders in the north of Mali, called upon AQIM and Mauritanians to avoid confrontation. Two months after AQIM launched its first attack against a Mauritanian military unit in Lemghayti in 2005, Ould Taya lost his position as president through a military coup.

Apart from national and local repression and harassment and regional truce, the only two initiatives which Mauritania joined reflected Ould Taya's desire to take advantage of the international context (the struggle against global terrorism) to legitimize its denial of democratic rights and gain access to international finance. These were the 2002 Pan Sahel Initiative and the 2005 Trans-Sahara Counter Terrorism Initiative

(TSCTI).[35] Both were US-led initiatives, and were part new 'fronts' which the United States opened following the 9/11 2001 attacks in order to 'support the US national security interests in the Global war on Terrorism' (Global Security, 2011). In the context of Africa, this was to be achieved by preventing huge tracts of largely deserted African terrain from becoming a safe haven for terrorist groups.[36] To that end, the initiatives provided funding, equipment and training to ten African and Maghreb countries, including Mauritania (also see Archer and Popovic, 2007; Al Jazeera Network, 2011b).

Both the Pan Sahel and TSCTI initiatives, led and managed by US military forces, were based on hard, military approaches to counterterrorism. They provided no 'soft' measures to counter radicalization in the region.[37] They also ran contradictory to Ould Taya's regional 'truce' policy with al-Qaeda and its affiliates in the region. As a result, Abu Musa'b Al-Zarqai, then the leader of the al-Qaeda branch in Iraq, sent (in 2004) a direct threat to the Mauritanian government to immediately terminate its collaboration with Western powers or face the consequences.

The perception that Ould Taya's policies 'led to a deviation that endangered the country's future' (ICG, 2006, p. ii) led 'one of his closest assistants [Ely Ould Mohamed Vall] to depose him on 3 August 2005. Ould Vall knew very well the danger and implications of Ould Taya's policies and therefore deposed him' (personal interview with Salem Ould Boudou, Nouakchott, August, 2011).

Ely Ould Mohamed Vall, director-general of the Sûreté National, and Mohamed Ould Abdel Aziz, commander of the presidential security battalion, led the junta that seized power in 2005 in Mauritania. The coup leaders responded to the growing unpopularity and declining legitimacy of President Maaouya Ould Taya's regime. They attempted to signify a break with the past by claiming that their coup was intended to 'end the regime's totalitarian practices... and vowed to create favourable conditions for an open and transparent democratic game in which civil society and political actors can freely participate' (ICG, 2006, p. 1).

Fundamental changes in the political climate occurred following the August 2005 military coup. The coup leaders began by opening up the political system, providing freedom of expression to the media and press, as well as to the ulama and scholars. To distance themselves from the repressive policies of Ould Taya, the new regime of Ould Vall also moved closer to civil society by initiating a consultation process with political parties and civil society organizations, and promised a return to legitimate institutions and the introduction of senatorial and presidential elections by March 2007 (ICG, 2005, 2006, p. 1). By March 2007, Ould Vall indeed became the first democratically elected Mauritanian president, although the leaders of the coup committed to excluding themselves from presidential elections in order to restore civilian rule. The junta which led the 2005 coup seemed nevertheless to have indeed embarked on a democratic renewal.

'In this climate of change, the Islamists quickly remerged' (Choplin, 2008). Perhaps the most radical change of policy was towards the Islamists. This was reflected in the return of the Muslim weekend (Friday and Saturday), the construction of a mosque at the presidential palace, and frequent raids and arrests by security forces at bars and restaurants in Nouakchott suspected of selling alcohol. In June of 2007, a large number of individuals accused of being members of Islamist organizations were acquitted for lack of evidence. Among those acquitted was Sidi Ould Sidna, one of those accused of murdering four French tourists. This shift in attitude is further evidenced in the registration of Tawassoul (National Congress for Reform and Development), led by Mohamed Jemil Ould Mansour, a moderate Islamist. Tawassoul today is the largest Islamic party, opposition party, and the fourth largest party in the country. It has five seats in the lower house and three in the upper house, a clear symbol of its legitimacy (Choplin, 2008; personal interviews with officials at AlMoustakbal Association, August 2011).

Ould Vall also openly recognized the presence of the problem of terrorism in Mauritania. Genuine moves to tackle the problem of terrorism began in 2007, following the first presidential elections. In addition to relaxing restrictions against political parties, the regime:

> empowered ulama to counter radical ideology in the mosque and more importantly in media and newspapers. This was followed by the establishment of a Higher Committee in late 2007 and early 2008, consisting of 20 fageh, scholars, ulama, political parties, and other civil society members in addition to seven presidential-committee members. The aim of the committee was to study the root causes of terrorism in Mauritania and offer best solutions. It was the president himself who issued the order to establish the Higher Committee. (Personal interview with Sheikh Ahmed Ould Ahal Daoud, Nouakchott, August 2011)

Despite opening up the political system, improving freedom of expression and creating the Higher Committee, the Ould Vall regime constantly warned that 'the threat [which terrorism] ... represent[s] should not be overestimated' in Mauritania (World Analysis, 2008). But Ould Vall's democratic opening was not able to reduce poverty, inequity and corruption in the country, which remained very high. Worse, Ould Vall's establishment, not unlike its predecessors, was bogged down by internal divisions and power struggles. Rivalry was most intense between the two most powerful men in the country: the president (Ould Vall) and his commander of the presidential security battalion (Ould Abdel Aziz). When the former attempted to remove the latter, Ould Abdel Aziz deposed President Ould Vall and ceased power in August 2008.

To be sure, it was Ould Abdel Aziz who convinced Ould Vall to restore not only parliamentary but also presidential elections, which Ould Vall himself won in 2007 (*The Economist*, 2008). It was not surprising therefore that Ould Abdel Aziz did not undermine the liberal political environment and freedoms introduced earlier by Ould Vall's regime, but he also built on them and further liberalized the political environment. For example, immediately after seizing power, Ould Abdel Aziz promised to hold presidential elections, which he did on 18 September 2009 and won in what was described as a fair and transparent manner. He also continued his predecessor's policy of liberalizing civil society from stifling state restrictions imposed during Ould Taya's 20 years in power, and provided Islamists in particular with further flexibility to counter radical ideology in the mosque and their *hawader* (see below). He was able to quickly regain the confidence of national and foreign investors, as well as the confidence of the international community, particularly the United States and France, the former colonial power, which immediately froze non-humanitarian aid following the August 2008 military coup. Ould Abdel Aziz was also able to restore US counterterrorism cooperation and aid which had also been suspended after the 2008 coup. Even before the August 2008 military coup, 'Mauritania was held up as a fine new democracy for Africa' and the Arab world (*The Economist*, 2008).

Ould Abdel Aziz also revitalized efforts to tackle the problem of terrorism in Mauritania. In his public appearances he 'vowed to tackle terrorism' in the country (Fertey, 2009). Ould Abdel Aziz called for an inclusive dialogue between all political forces and for a national reconciliation process with political parties, Islamists in general and violent extremists in particular. As one source put it, Abdel Aziz 'underscored with satisfaction his absolute availability for the national political dialogue and the consolidation of the reconciliation process' (quoted in ReliefWeb Report, 2009).

The Ministry of Religious Affairs (MRA), under whose umbrella fall a large number of respected Mauritanian scholars and ulama, was empowered by the president to take the lead in efforts to counter radical ideology and to replace the Higher Committee which was created for that purpose by the Ould Vall regime. The first act of the MRA was to organize a scientific workshop (*nadwa*) entitled 'Islam and the Arguments For and Against Moderate and Extremist Views between Theory and Behaviour' on 6 January 2010. All ulama, politicians and individuals of various intellectual backgrounds were invited to the *nadwa*:

> The authorities also expressed their willingness to respect the recommendations of the *nadwa*. One of the most important recommendations of the *nadwa* was to recommend a dialogue with the radical elements in prisons, and the state responded to the wishes of its *ulama*. (Ould Daoud, 2011, p. 1; personal interview with Sheikh Ould Daoud, Nouakchott, August 2011)

The dialogue process started on 15 January 2010 when a Committee of Ulama, made up of the country's 30 most prominent scholars, was established. Only 14 of the 30 ulama, however, were chosen to go to the prison and debate incarcerated individuals, whose number totalled around 60. The rest of the ulama, 16, provided guidance, intellectual and logistical support. The debate occurred over two phases. In the first stage the ulama simply listened to the arguments of the prisoners to try and understand their mentality, logic and way of thinking. In the second phase, the ulama went back to the prison armed with an arsenal of scientific and religious evidence, both empirical and theoretical, to counter the radical arguments of the 'fundamentalists'.

The ulama and scholars started the first meeting by telling the prisoners that:

> We are here for the interests of our religion, country and our youth. We do not want our youth to be wasting their time behind bars and we want them to be productive and to do good deeds instead. This is why we came to talk to you today. (Personal interview with Ould Ameno, Nouackchott, August 2011)

This is very similar to the Saudi approach, in which scholars were careful to distance themselves from the state and emphasize their sovereignty from the regime. The idea here is to gain the confidence of the incarcerated individuals by convincing the prisoners that their efforts are simply motivated by genuine concern for the prisoners themselves, and that they (the scholars) are not state stooges (El-Said and Barrett,

2011). Failing to gain the confidence of the prisoners can jeopardize the entire dialogue program, as the Yemeni experience clearly demonstrates (El-Said and Harrigan, 2013).

The debate focused on four key issues which emerged from the first meeting with the prisoners. These issues are also common in dialogue programs implemented by other Muslim-majority states (El-Said and Harrigan, 2013). Following the first phase:

> We discovered four key points which the debate in prison evolved around: the idea that the ruler is an infidel because he does not rule according to the sharia law and collaborates with the infidel West; the relationship between Muslims and non-Muslims; the true concept of jihad (we explained for them the conditions for, and ethics of, jihad in Islam); and the principle of *al tattaros*, which relates a story when the infidels in the past, fearing the Muslim army crushing them, used captured Muslim hostages as human shields. We explained to them that this was a very contentious subject in Islam, that the Islamic ulama did not agree on it and that it was a face-to-face war with two armies involved in a battlefield, and cannot be therefore compared to the current situation. (Personal interview with Abdullah Ould Ameno, a Salafist scholar and a key member of the team that debated prisoners, Nouakchott, August 2011)

The first phase of the debate (listening to the prisoners) not only allowed the scholars to understand the mentality, line of thinking and background of the prisoners, but also to divide them into three main groups.[38]

> We found three categories of prisoners: the first category is those who went through an internal revision of their own while being in prison and decided to repent even before we talked to them. This category was the easiest to deal with, and their number was no more than 2 or 3 individuals. They were not hard-core and we simply left them aside. The second category was the hesitant group. This group said that we leave the matter to the ulama and that we have nothing to say beyond what the ulama will tell us. The third and final category was the hard-core, unrepentant category. (Personal interview with Sheikh Ould Ameno, Nouakchott, August 2011)

The scholars obviously focused on the second and third categories, whose number totalled 46 (or 47) and 11, respectively. The scholars went into the prison well prepared for the dialogue, with their positions and roles coordinated among themselves and ready for the second phase of the debate. Each scholar was thus asked to focus on his area of expertise and to talk about only one subject that was raised by the prisoners during the first meeting. The dialogue took the shape of a semi-structured, face-to-face discussion, but, more accurately, it took the form of a well-prepared-for lecture by each scholar. Some sessions were recorded and then broadcast on national TV (Ould Daoud, 2011; personal interviews with Ould Daoud, Ould Boudou, Ould Tah and Ould Ameno, Nouakchott, August 2011).

After delivering their talk, the scholars then met individually with each prisoner to allow for a discussion and debate to take place. The sessions lasted for two weeks, with each session led by 3 to 4 scholars.

From the very beginning, however, the 11 most radical individuals were hard to convince and were determined not to repent. Out of the total 60 prisoners and 11 from the hard-core radical group, three refused to join the first meeting and did not enter the room where the discussion was taking place (in the prison mosque's hallway). The remaining eight individuals of the hard-core group which joined the talks proved no less difficult:

> As soon as we sat down, Khadeem al-Samaan, who claims to be the leader of al-Qaeda in Mauritania, stood up and said jihad is proceeding no matter what you say. He was also wearing a T-shirt with an al-Qaeda slogan painted on it to confirm his allegiance to al-Qaeda and his unrepented position. (Personal interview with Ould Ameno, Nouakchott, August 2011)

The scholars then paid special attention to the 11-strong hard-core group and called for another general session with them:

> We asked them to debate with us and tell us their opinions. We then responded to each one of them but we failed to convince them on the status of the ruler, but beat them on the subject of foreigners visiting Muslim states and again failed to convince them on the issue of *al tattaros*. In the end, we failed to convince them and they refused to repent. We did not give up on them. We decided to establish a committee made up of only three individuals, including the eminent Sheikh Muhammed Hassan al-Doaud, the adviser of the president, and Sheikh Muhammad al-Khattar to further debate them and give them more opportunity to rethink what was said. They still refused

to repent. This session lasted for almost 24 hours with breaks in between. Three of them initially said that they repented but then they changed their mind. Some of those 11 individuals were also indicted in the murder of French hostages. (Personal interview with Ould Ameno, Nouakchott, August 2011)

The role of inducements

The available empirical evidence suggests that specific inducements are a vital element for any successful de-radicalization process (Ashour, 2009). Not surprisingly, the debate inside Mauritanian prisons was also accompanied/followed by other, specific and targeted inducements for the repented individuals. For example, almost eight months after the Committee of Ulama completed its debate inside the prison in January 2010, a presidential amnesty released 35 prisoners in September 2010. They were released after the 'debate that was led by Mauritanian scholars and ulama...led to revisions that led tens of them to abandon violent ideology and return to the *wasatiya* line and moderation. Many other prisoners who have accepted these revisions remain in prison' (Assakina, 2011).

Other inducements also included financial support in order to facilitate the process of reintegrating released prisoners back into society and to their families. Mauritanian officials admit that financial assistance was decided as part of the de-radicalization process, but are secretive about the amounts determined for each repentant and released individual. According to Al Jazeera (2011c), the Mauritanian government allocated $11,000 to each released individual.

Mauritania does not have the resources to enact an effective follow-up or after-release program, like Saudi Arabia, for example, either to monitor released individuals, to provide further psychological and religious counselling, or to meet their family or job requirements. Such a program, therefore, an integral part of the much-touted Saudi de-radicalization efforts, has been lacking in Mauritania. The latter, however, relies on the tribal and dense social networks to help released prisoners:

> If anyone needs assistance from somebody in Mauritania they simply go to his house. We are very informal here. Our houses are open to everybody; this includes released prisoners, and we will help them with whatever we can if and when they come to us. (Personal interview with Hamden Ould Tah, Nouakchott, August 2011)

The reintegration process has also been facilitated by the fact that the nature of Mauritanian society and structure did not stigmatize the released prisoners as 'terrorists' as has been the case in Yemen, for example. There, stigmatization undermined the reintegration of released former radicals into society (Birk, 2009). In Mauritania, on the other hand, lack of stigmatization meant that the traditional role of family, tribe and societal networks in providing assistance remained intact and available to draw on by repented radicals.

Unlike the Yemeni and Saudi states, for example, the Mauritanian authorities decided not to interfere in the labour market and provide amnestied individuals with jobs. 'This is because trade in Mauritania is blessed. Most people like to be engaged in trade, following the footsteps of our prophet. This includes in particular the former fundamentalists, due to their strong religious beliefs. We therefore gave them money because many of them wanted to become traders and be engaged in trade activities' (personal interview with Sheikh Ahmed Ould Daoud, Nouakchott, August 2011).

Counter radicalization: the role of civil society

As mentioned earlier, the most significant counter-radicalization measure in Mauritania has been the renewal of the democratic process after 2005. This included the reintroduction of parliamentary and presidential elections, expanding freedoms of expression and legalizing political parties, including Islamist ones. Within this context, the most important, direct and official counter-radicalization measure has been to tacitly encourage imams to play a greater role in countering the spread of radical ideologies in the country through media and their *khutab* (Friday ceremonies), as well as lessons which they usually deliver at mosques, particularly after the evening and morning prayers. This policy has been recently reactivated after the role of imams and Islamists was curtailed for more than 20 years by the Ould Taya regime's policies, and is now a key component of the government's counter-radicalization policy. The government is confidently able to rely on its ulama to counter fundamentalist ideology in the country because they (ulama) continue to genuinely espouse a Sunni, Salafist anti-violent version of Islam that rejects violence as means to achieve ends. They therefore not only denounce violence in their *khutab* and activities, but also call for loyalty to the ruler (personal interview with Sheikh Ould Daoud and Sheikh Ould Ameno, Nouakchott, August 2011).

Encouraging imams to counter violent extremist ideologies dovetails well with a long and well-established tradition in the country. It is consistent with the traditional role played by Mauritanian scholars throughout history which played a significant role in keeping fundamentalism from spreading in Mauritania. The only exception was the period between 1994 and 2005, when the role of imams and Islamists in general was severely undermined and restricted by the Ould Taya regime.

In addition to resuscitating the role of imams, another traditional, Mauritanian-specific institution whose role has also been revived in countering radical ideology after 2005 is the *mahadir* (plural). The *mahdar* (singular) is an old institution in Mauritania. Its roots are traced back to the fifth Islamic century, in particular to the era of the Murabiteen Empire. The *mahadir* were originally launched by Mauritanian scholars and *fugaha* to fill a gap in the country represented by a lack of public education resulting from the absence of a central authority. A *faqeh* would establish a *mahdar* in his vicinity or in a nearby area to provide education to the youth in his neighbourhood free of charge. The *fugaha*, who enjoyed a prestigious position in society due to their religious knowledge and their role (through *Jamaat alhal walagaad*) as consensus-makers, judges and imams, would fund their *mahdar* from their own resources. This included donations which they received from merchants, political leaders and other societal elements in recognition of their knowledge and role in society. Although attending the *mahadir* was voluntary, the *mahadir*, due to the lack of alterative educational institutions and their spread in almost every city and village in old Mauritania, attracted a large number of Mauritanians. They taught religious studies, Arabic, poetry, history, and even mathematics and algebra. They soon became Mauritania's main schools, universities and educational centres. They were responsible for graduating a large number of Mauritanian *fugaha* and scholars who played an important role in the country's history. More importantly, the *mahadir* embraced a tolerant, Sunni version of Islam that historically had been held responsible for creating a peaceful Mauritanian society that placed high emphasis on tolerance, moderation and peace. They were also responsible for 'protecting the new generations from western influences and cultural weakening and support the position of the Arabic language' (Ould Sheikhana, 2009, p. 323).

Although they were weakened by the French colonial authorities and migration of a large number of Mauritanian *fugah* during the first six decades of the 20th century, the *mahadir* started to regain their position in the 1970s as a result of both external and internal factors. Externally, there was the spread of Islamism in the region, including the Muslim Brotherhood branches outside Egypt, the jihad in Afghanistan and the 1979 Iranian revolution. Internally, there was the spread of secular ideologies and movements, including Nasserism, Marxism and other imported ideologies. All of these factors led to the 'stirring of Islamic sentiments' in Mauritania. Not only did the state under President Mukhtar not oppose Islamists, it also supported them and reactivated their *mahadir* to counter Nasserists and Marxist trends in Mauritania:

> President Mukhtar always gave consideration to the word of the imams.... The president once stated that 'I demand from the Imams to play their role in this era in which religion has become an individual matter'. (All quotations from Ould Sheikhana, 2009, p. 194)

Following the ousting of Ould Taya's regime in 2005, the *mahadir* have quickly regained their position in society as disseminators of knowledge, tolerance and a moderate version of the Sunni-Sufi model of Islam in Mauritania. 'The *mahadir* today represent the main counterers of violent and fundamentalist ideologies in Mauritania', stated Ould Daoud, who runs one of the main *mahdar* in Nouakchott (personal interview, Nouakchott, August 2011). As in the old days, the *mahadir* focuses on language, religion, science, poetry and mathematics. What makes the *mahadir* influential is their perceived sovereignty from the state, both financial and administrative. As Ould Daoud elaborated:

> The *mahadir* continue to function exactly as they did historically; they are voluntary and the *fugaha* which run them do not get paid by the state for anything. They sponsor the activities of their *mahadir* from their own resources, and sometimes, when the resources of the *fageh* is limited and those of the students better off, the students pay towards their accommodation. It is seen as a religious duty on behalf of the *fageh* to provide education. The problem with some *fugaha* now is that if they see a radical among their students they dismiss him out of their *mahdar*. I disagree with this approach. Instead, I spend more time talking to him instead of leaving him vulnerable to the terrorist groups and individuals until I convince him of my views. (Personal interview, Nouakchott, August 2011)

Another important civil society organization that has been playing a significant role in countering radical ideology in Mauritania in recent years is the *AlMoustakbal* Association (MA). MA was established only in 2008 by a group of ulama who are closely linked to the main Islamic party, al-Tawasoul. 'The creation of the MA aimed at restoring the right place of ulama in the Mauritanian society', which, according to the

Secretary General of the Association, Ould Sidi, 'was lost as a result of twenty years of repressive policies under the Ould Taya regime'. In 2008, members of the MA, which today amount to around 700, met in order to determine the main duties and responsibilities of the association and how it can best face what members perceived as the 'four most urgent challenges' facing Mauritania at the current time. These challenges were identified as the following: Christian missionaries that are trying to 'Christianize' Mauritanian society; radicalization and extremism that lead to terrorism; social stability threatened by the heterogeneity of the Mauritanian society; and ignorance, illiteracy and primitiveness (personal interview with Muhammad Ould Sidi, former Minister of Higher Education and Secretary General of the *AlMoustakbal* Association, Nouakchott, August 2011).

These are obviously intertwined and overlapping challenges. MA has set itself the complex task of dealing with them. To achieve this, MA has introduced four major programs, some of which deal directly with countering radical, violent ideology in Mauritania: *dawa* (missionary) program, cultural program, educational program and the religious program.

The missionary program is implemented through regular workshops and *halgat* (religious circulars) organized by the association. 'Rather than coming to us, we go to the youth.' MA has an office in every region of the country (25 offices in total). Every week there is a *halaqa* or a lecture delivered by the ulama of the association, that is, four lectures a month or 48 lectures annually. Although the ulama lecture on various issues, 'terrorism, tolerance and the true interpretation of Islam are key subjects in our lectures' (all quotations are from a personal interview with Muhammad Ould Sidi, Nouakchott, August 2011).

The cultural program, second, focuses on the places of the youth, such as universities, schools, Quranic schools and *mahadir*. During holidays, workshops (*dawrat*) are regularly organized by the association in these institutions for students. During these *dawrat*, several subjects are discussed, including the rights of the parents, ruler's duties and responsibilities, *takfir* (excommunication), jihad and how to pray. 'We seek to promote the Islamic model in all of these daily activities, including in economic, media, and national unity activities, as well as in daily mores and ethics' (ibid.).

Finally, the educational and religious programs. MA, through its ulama, owns around 40 *mahdar*, mostly in rural areas where formal education is lacking. Religious education receives extra efforts through additional classes in theology delivered at the *mahadir*. This approach is also extended to the formal educational sector. MA currently collaborates with some private schools, currently only three, but the hope is to expand this number in the near future. In addition to the formal national curriculum, additional religious material is delivered by the ulama of the association in these private schools. The additional material is based on delivering the 'true interpretation of Islam, tolerance and moderation. We also focus on teaching students how to pray, separation between men and women, Islamic ethics, self-reliance and Islamic mores and ethics. Our volunteer ulama go to these three schools and deliver the material and coordinate work with the management of these schools, which are happy to collaborate with us' (ibid.).

Mauritania has not been able to either use the Internet or devise an effective Internet strategy to counter the spread of radical ideology in the country. Nor has it been able to exploit the Internet to de-radicalize those who have already been radicalized and/or committed violent acts. The limited technical and physical capabilities of the Mauritanian state, as well as limited human capital resources, meant that al-Qaeda and its offspring in the region, AQIM, has been more able to use the Internet to radicalize and recruit Mauritanian youth:

> In Mauritania, and after 50 years of independence, the Ministry of Defense's Internet website until now remains empty of any information that could at least provide a minimum amount of information to introduce the main task of this key ministry, or to keep a contact with the outside world. ... [Mauritania] suffers from absence or weakness of logistical and technological abilities such as satellite capabilities and monitoring and intelligence systems, dataset networks, bugging systems, information analytical systems etc. (Ould Ibrahim, 2010)

Mauritania, however, has relied more on its limited number of radio and TV channels to counter fundamentalist ideas in the country. As part of Ould Abdul Aziz's strategy to empower Mauritanian ulama to play a greater role in countering radical fundamentalist ideology in the country, the ulama were encouraged to establish a radio station (in early 2011) especially for the purpose of interpreting the Quran and sharia the 'right way'. They were also empowered to use the main TV channel to broadcast, on a weekly basis, programs that provide a moderate and tolerant version of Islam. The former members of the Higher Committee, which the Ould Vall regime created in 2007 to diagnose the root cause of terrorism in Mauritania and to provide solutions to the phenomenon, now rotate and coordinate among themselves to provide religious programs that are commensurate with the state version of Islam. Such programs are broadcast live twice a week in a two-hour session platform. During broadcasting (on radio and TV), questions are received openly from the public, which the ulama provide answers to in a way that reflects their non-violent beliefs, peaceful ideology and loyalty to the ruler (personal interviews with Ould Daoud and Ould Boudou, Nouakchott, August 2011).

Along with the above-mentioned 'soft' counter-radicalization and de-radicalization measures at the national level, the Ould Abdul Aziz regime, ironically, has also increasingly relied on 'hard' and traditional security approaches as an additional counterterrorism measure. This has been particularly the case at the regional level. In fact, Ould Abdel Aziz has replaced Ould Vall's 'truce' policy with one that relies more on 'pre-emptive attacks' (Ould Ibrahim, 2010; WorldAnalysis, 2011). Since Ould Abdel Aziz came to power in 2008, for example, al-Qaeda positions in neighbouring Mali have been attacked several times by the Mauritanian army. Such attacks, which took place in October 2010 and June and October 2011, have been described by the Mauritanian authorities as 'preventative air strikes in order to destroy the enemy' and prevent it from 'preparing to launch an attack on Mauritania from Mali' (Reuters, 2011).

The effectiveness of Mauritanian 'soft' measures: some concluding remarks

The emergence of a radical, violent extremist ideology in Mauritania in recent years contradicts the old Murabiteen tradition which, until the mid-1990s, pre-emptively undercut the growth of fundamentalist thought and activism. The Mauritanian environment, however, either national (economic, political, social) or external has changed dramatically to warrant such a radical shift. Nationally, economic failure, social injustices, corruption and, most importantly, political repression before 2005 provided the fodder that nurtured the kind of radicalization and extremism that led to terrorism. This was coupled with an external radicalizing environment, including the occupation of Afghanistan in 2001 and Iraq in 2003, and the deterioration of the situation in Palestine. To this should be added the political leadership's, particularly Ould Taya's, abuse of the 'global war on terror' to justify repressive policies through alliances with the West, especially the United States and France. These internal and external factors created perfect conditions for the emergence of the first contemporary Mauritanian violent extremist movement, namely, *Ansar Allah al-Murabiteen.*

Since 2005 Mauritania has been engaged in implementing wide-ranging counter-de-rad measures to curb the spread of violent extremist ideologies and activism in the country. This included democratic renewals, enlarging freedom of expression and thought, and allowing Islamists to establish a political party and to join the political process. Mauritania has also empowered its Islamists, imams, ulama and civil society in general to resume their traditional role of rebutting radical-militant ideology and activism in the country.

To that effect, the new Mauritanian regime under Ould Abdul Aziz launched a dialogue process with radical prisoners in early 2010. The process included dialogue with 60 prisoners. Among the prisoners are a few hard-core individuals who committed acts of violence, kidnapping and/or murder. They also include sympathizers who were simply 'offering shelter... providing food to the kidnappers... and suspected of having given logistical assistance' (African News24, 2010). Some served in foreign countries, while others never left Mauritania. Most, according to Mauritanian officials, lack deep religious education, have a low level of education and are mostly young, with the exception of their speaker who is in his mid-40s. The dialogue process also included selected inducements for the repented individuals, ranging from amnesty to all repentants, to economic and financial assistance.

In terms of participation, almost 82 per cent (49) of prisoners participated in the dialogue process. Only 11 (18 per cent) refused to take part in the discussion and 58–61 per cent (35 or 37) repented, denounced violence and were released as a result through an amnesty in October 2010. In terms of recidivism, out of the 35–37 released, 'The president, Muhammad weld Abdul-Aziz, stated that at least one of the graduates returned to al-Qaeda in the Islamic Maghreb' (Assakina, 2011).

Mauritanian officials and scholars interviewed assess the de-radicalization process as a success, since 'out of the 37 released prisoners only one returned to violence. He was very radical from the very beginning and it was obvious that debate was not going to work with him' (personal interview with Sheikh Ould Daoud and Ould Boudou, Nouakchott, August 2011).

Such statements and evaluations need to be taken cautiously. The fact remains that the most radical elements (11 individuals or 18 per cent of the total) refused even to participate in the dialogue process.[39] This may suggest that the Mauritanian de-radicalization process had, at best, succeeded with 'soft', rather than 'hard-core' fundamentalists. This could be partly attributed to the fact that the process itself was short, lasting for no more than two weeks in general. This is unlike the Saudi dialogue program which usually not only lasts for years, with the *naseha* (advice) available for the incarcerated individuals whenever they need it, but also intensifies during the last six months before the graduates are released. During this period, the graduates are in fact transferred to a purpose-built rehabilitation centre, where a special program is designed to facilitate their reintegration into society and their families. Hardcore radicals, in other words, might require a more medium- to long-term program before its fruits become visible. The short-term nature of the Mauritanian de-radicalization process, unfortunately, deprived us of the opportunity to reach any definitive conclusion regarding the impact of the dialogue process on most radical elements of the group.

The external (outside prison) environment might also have played a role in undermining the de-radicalization process in Mauritania and the ability of Mauritanian ulama and scholars to convince most radical elements to repent inside the incarceration facility. For example, despite democratic renewals and provisions of new freedoms after 2005, 'soldiers' or the army 'never went away' and they continued to hold a tight grip on the country's politics (*The Economist*, 2008). In fact, power remains concentrated in the hands of a few tribal groupings, of which Ould Abdel Aziz's tribe is one. Ould Abdel Aziz and some of his 'colleagues are pillars of the old power structure' and have thus chosen to 'turn the page rather than, examine it, redress past injustices and shed light on the practices of the previous regime'. The fact that Ould Abdel Aziz and the former regime which he ousted, the Ould Vall's, belonged to the same former privileged tribal group raises questions on the junta's intention to change Mauritanian clientelist structure, tackle corruption, and improve equities and distribution of wealth in the country (all quotations from Emirates News24/7, 2011). This fuelled political tension in recent years. Following the outbreak of the Arab Spring in early January 2011, thousands of Mauritanians also took to the streets, demanding genuine reforms, including political reforms that would reduce the grip of the junta over politics and eliminate corruption and discrimination, as well as economic reform capable of creating new jobs, reducing poverty and improving living standards. The repeated 'bread' and other riots in Mauritanian cities since 2004 (intensified in 2011) suggest that Mauritanians are disillusioned with their much-touted democratic transition. Riots in several Mauritanian cities simultaneously also point to a social breakdown propelled by falling standards of living, a rise in poverty and inequities, and rampant and widespread corruption among state officials. It is these political and 'social conditions [that] led to a growth of sympathy for extremist views' and that exploit 'moral [d]egeneration in government' to attract sympathizers from among the poor citizens where such messages and views 'resonate' most (Choplin, 2008).

Mauritania, moreover, has also initiated a regional war against al-Qaeda in the Sahel. Despite its meagre resources and its own economic, social and political challenges, Mauritania under Ould Abdel Aziz 'has been the only country in the Maghreb and West Africa to go beyond its borders to confront al-Qaeda operatives' (Al Jazeera Network, 2011a, p. 3). This not only raises questions about the nature and objectives of this conflict and its political and military costs, but has led some Mauritanian intellectuals to question whether Mauritania has really 'put in place a comprehensive [Counter-de-Rad] strategy...to take this responsibility as a priority for the existence of the Mauritanian state, its continuity and stability...' (Ould Ibrahim, 2010).

Not surprisingly, not only al-Qaeda and AQIM, but also many Mauritanian officials and civil society entities have 'accused Mauritanian President Mohamed Ould Abdel Aziz of fighting a proxy war on behalf of France'. They urged him to learn from the past when Mauritania was enmeshed in a war with the Polisario in the Sahel between 1975 and 1978 to placate Morocco with dire human, political and economic consequences. They called upon their president (Ould Abdel Aziz) to 'save [Mauritania] from a war which is not theirs' (all quotations from WorldAnalysis, 2011). It is also perhaps not coincidental that one of the areas in which the Mauritanian ulama and scholars failed to beat the radicals over during their dialogue process in prison in January 2010 was 'the status of the ruler', as demonstrated earlier. The point here is that what happens inside prison cannot be isolated from the external environment, national and international. Other policies and conditions, external to the prison environment itself, can have an impact on the dialogue process, a conclusion supported by our work elsewhere (El-Said and Harrigan, 2013).

To sum up, the reconciliation process, which Ould Abdel Aziz has initiated since he came to power in August 2008 resembles the country's Counter-de-Rad efforts: incomplete and partial. Mauritanian Counter-de-Rad efforts, for example, remain devoid of a strong and fully integrated communications pillar (particularly the Internet) to identify and act to weaken and pre-empt the message of the violent extremists. Nor are there any post-release policies to facilitate reintegration into society. In fact, 'after one year of their release, former al-Qaeda prisoners complained about their poor conditions ... [and] criticized the Mauritanian authorities for slowness in reintegrating them into society and public life, and not fulfilling their promises of securing for them funds and projects that would allow them to restore their lives after years of pursuit and imprisonments' (Assakina, 2011). To claim success, Counter-de-Rad policies must not only prevent violent extremists from recruiting new members and expanding their reach nationally and internationally, but must also succeed in nudging those who have already been radicalized onto a different path. Only if such policies dissuade vulnerable groups and individuals from turning to violence or actively support those that formerly have, success can be claimed. It is too early to claim success in Mauritania.

6
Singapore: Crisis of Identity, Shared Values And Religious Rehabilitation

Introduction

Despite its impressive economic development, Singapore has not been immune against the threat of violent extremism (VEm). In January 2001 and August 2002 respectively, 13 and 21 members of Jemaah Islamiyah (JI), the most dangerous, militant and al-Qaeda-affiliated regional group, were arrested. The 34 JI members were arrested under the Internal Security Act (ISA) introduced by the imperial power (United Kingdom) to deal with the Communist threat. They were charged with an attempt to carry out a series of terrorist attacks against several local installations and foreign targets in Singapore, including water supplies, a train station and vessels belonging to the American navy in Singapore.[1] The 2001 and 2002 arrests 'exposed the most serious direct threat posed by any terrorist organisation to Singapore's security since the days of the Communist Party of Malaya' (Bin Kader, 2007, 2009). The Singaporean government responded to the threat of VEm by introducing what has been described as 'one of the most advanced' and 'successfully initiated' 'Religious Rehabilitation Programmes' in East Asia (Jerard, 2009, p. 95).

As alluded to above, this is not the first time Singapore has faced the threat of VEm. Immediately before and after independence in 1959 and throughout the 1960s the country had to wrestle with VEt threat coming from Communists/Marxists. As Deputy Prime Minister and Home Affairs Minister, Mr Wong Seng stated in a speech delivered on 21 June 2005 during the opening of a five-day seminar on the role of community in countering VEm in Singapore:

> We learnt this the hard way. Our society was not always as peaceful. We remember the 21 July 1964 as a dark day for us when we saw

death and bloodshed due to racial riots. We therefore commemorate this day every year as racial harmony.

The strategies which the Singaporean government has developed 'to battle [Islamic] radicalisation has been governed by a framework instituted since independence and which has evolved in response to the changing times and circumstances of its strategic environment'. The chief objective of these strategies is to 'not allow a repeat of the bloody racial riots of the 1960s as a result of external events and conflicts' (both quotations from Ju-Li, 2009, pp. 69, 70).

Little is known about the Singaporean strategies to counter the rise of radicalization and VEm by JI. The two most important publications in this regard are a collection of speeches and articles by Singaporean officials and academics published by the Singaporean Muslim nongovernmental organization, Taman Bacaan, and compiled by Abdul Halim Bin Kader in 2007 and 2009, respectively. As such, they provide a 'Singapore[an] Perspective' which lacks critical and external evaluation for such a historically complex phenomenon (Bin Kader, 2007; also see Bin Kader, 2009).

This chapter fills an important gap in the literature by analysing the Singaporean government's strategies to counter the recent rise of Islamic Violent Extremism (IVEm) after the year 2000. Although the focus is on the post-2000 Countering Violent Extremist (CVEt) strategies, the chapter also analyses the evolution of VEm and internal threats to Singapore since its independence in 1959. This historical analysis stems from our belief that history matters, not only in terms of how states respond to internal and external challenges, but also to how certain historical events can be causally linked to current episodes of VEm.

Singapore is an ideal case study for the examination of the management of economic development and counter radicalization and de-radicalization (Counter-de-Rad) in a socially diversified and religiously and racially harmonized society (Clammer, 1998). Singapore is not only a multiracial, multi-religious society, but it is also a Muslim-minority state, unlike most other countries studied both in volumes I and II of this project (El-Said and Harrigan, 2013). As such, Singapore provides important lessons to other diversified and particularly Muslim-minority states, both inside and outside Asia, specifically including countries in the Western hemisphere. The chapter argues that Singapore's strategies to counter IVEm are characterized by contradictions, not dissimilar to the kind of contradictions characterized by the country's attempts to forge a 'Singaporean identity' from the day of its independence.

The evolution of the Singaporean state: racial tension, chaos and insecurity

Although it lacks credible natural resources, Singapore is today classified as a Newly Industrializing Country (NIC) and one of the four Asian Tigers. Indeed, since independence Singapore has achieved impressive economic development and sustainable growth rates. Singapore is surrounded by predominantly Muslim states (Malaysia, Indonesia and Brunei), although its mixed and multiracial/multi-religious society is not only the reverse of its Muslim-majority neighbours, it also lacks the homogeneity of other Asian states, such as Vietnam and Thailand (Ju-Li, 2009, pp. 69–70). Singapore had a total population of around five million in 2012, 74.2 per cent, 13.4 per cent and 9.2 per cent of which are Chinese, Muslim-Malays and Indians, respectively.

The demise of the British Empire, the outbreak of World War II, and occupation by Japan disrupted the stability of Singapore. After Japan's surrender in 1945, Singapore was returned to British rule (The British Military Administration) and an uncertain future until 1963. Its leaders felt that Singapore could neither survive by itself nor that Britain would agree to a fully independent Singaporean state. They therefore joined the Federation of Malaya, Sabah and Sarawak to form Malaysia in 1963. Although Singapore was given full independence by the British imperial power in 1963, the Federation with Malaysia proved problematic, distrustful and characterized by mutual suspicion. Malaysia, on the one hand, was not only suspicious of the ethnic Chinese majority of Singapore, but also feared the loss of economic gravity to Singapore. Malaysia thus sought to dominate the Federation economically and politically, and sought to promote a pro-Malay society. Singapore, on the other hand, hoped for a society with equal representation and sought Malaysia's support to terminate its own Communist insurgency (see below). The failure to reach an acceptable agreement with a suitable political formula led the Malaysian Parliament in 1965 to unanimously vote to expel Singapore from the Federation (Cahyadi et al., 2004). This led to the birth of the Republic of Singapore.

The rise and fall of the Communist threat and racial strife

As shown in the analysis cited above, Singapore's political and social evolution had been marked by serious challenges. This was not only caused by the country's geopolitical location, surrounded by hostile and overwhelmingly Muslim-majority states, but also the lack of resources, including land and water, as well as an immigrant society whose loyalty seemed confused and dispersed. The situation was further complicated by the emergence of the Communist insurgency, which first sprang up under, and in opposition to, the presence and policies of the British colonial power and did not dissipate before the early 1970s. It was not surprising therefore that 'a perceived absence of shared values has long concerned Singapore's rulers' (Nichol and Sim, 2007, p. 18). How did the Singaporean officials seek to overcome the problem of multi-ethnicity and perceived absence of shared values? The answer to this question requires a good understanding of the kind of threats which the Singaporean state faced immediately before and after both self and full independence in 1959 and 1965 respectively, particularly the twin threat of Communist insurgency and racial tension that continues to haunt the Singaporean state until the present day.

As many observers of Singaporean politics have noted, the 1940s, 1950s and at least the first half of the 1960s, were marked by instability and insecurity, stemming from both internal and external threats to the country. The former included chiefly the mounting Communist insurgency and social and racial riots and strife. The latter comprised hostilities from such neighbours as Malaysia and Indonesia[2] (Porter, 1998; Goh, 2008; Cahyadi et al., 2004).

Communism has a long history in Singapore. Its roots are traced back to the early 20th century among Chinese workers who officially initiated its activities around the year 1925. It gained popularity for its anti-colonial policies and campaigns to improve the living conditions of workers. Initially, the demands of the Communists evolved around economic factors. They sought higher wages and salaries for workers, as well as better housing conditions and living standards. Later, particularly in the 1940s through to the mid-1960s, they sought not only to end colonization, but also to replace the Singaporean state with a Communist regime controlled or dominated by China. The prestige of the Communist movement was further enhanced as a result of its anti-Japanese campaign between 1942 and 1945. By the end of the Second World War, the Communist movement emerged as 'the most powerful organized force save probably the British Military Administration (BMA)' (Goh, 2008).

At first the Communists focused on mobilization, recruitment and consolidation. They penetrated the workers and trade unions and called for peaceful demonstrations to demand higher wages and better living conditions and standards. After the Japanese Imperial Army surrounded Singapore following their defeat in the Second World War in 1945, they also resorted to the political system, establishing their own political party (MCP) in order to lobby for the interests of the workers through Parliament. However, the

> Communist policies and course of actions changed during the 1940s and 1950s in light of the different circumstances. It transformed from a passive role in politics by continuing the pre-war policy of building a united-front movement as a preliminary to directly attacking the colonial political system in the 1940s, to an active one by mobilizing masses to strikes and riots, and [more] involvement in politics in the 1950s. (Goh, 2008)

Several factors led to a process of radicalization among many members of the Communist movement in the 1940s, 1950s and even 1960s. First, not only did the Communists feel that their 'passive' methods failed to convince the BMA to yield to their economic demands, but they also fiercely opposed BMA's policies which aimed at preserving and promoting British economic interests in Southeast Asia. For the Communists, the BMA's policies were discriminatory against the Chinese, not only aimed at preserving the colonial power's economic and political interests, but also intended to use the key position of Malaya to safeguard and advance its strategic operations in the region. In addition, the BMA relied on, and provided more employment and educational opportunities for the English-educated than for the Chinese-educated. The handful of English-education schools and institutions thus received the bulk of state spending (more than 90 per cent) at the expense of Chinese education. In fact, under the BMA the Chinese community was left to fend for themselves in many aspects of life, including, in particular, education, which traditionally has a special place in the Chinese Confucian culture. The Chinese immigrants thus used their own resources and pooled capital to build their own schools and educational institutions. Many textbooks and teachers came from a supportive and sympathetic approach to China, particularly after the rise of the Communist regime in China in 1947. But a system that favoured English-speaking individuals meant that non-English-speaking educated Chinese lacked opportunities for social and political mobilization. They became fodder for the Communist propaganda. In addition to workers, the Communists successfully penetrated schools and educational institutions. Their supporters came overwhelmingly from workers and educated students and teachers. They used the educational system to spread their anti-colonial and state messages and to indoctrinate their followers with their anti-colonial and anti-state violent ideology. This process was facilitated by an absence of any state monitoring and surveillance of the educational system (Goh, 2008; Europe-Solidaire, 2012; US Library of Congress, 2012a; *New York Times*, 1990; ThinkQuest, 2012).

Discontent built up not only because of low pay, poor living conditions and discriminatory educational and employment systems, but also reached a climax in 1954, following the introduction by the BMA of part-time military service for all males aged 18 to 20. The Chinese community felt that the National Service system aimed at excluding them because a large number of Chinese students were over 20 years of age, since they missed several years of schooling during their anti-colonial struggle and activities. The year 1954, like the year 1947, was known as the 'Year of Strikes', since so many strikes took place in these two particular years, many of which turned into bloody riots with several people losing their lives.[3] Communist leaders were held responsible for what came to be known as the 1954 National Service Riots, Chinese Middle Schools Riots and Hock Lee Bus Riots[4] in Singapore (ThinkQuest, 2012). The situation was so serious that the army was called in to quell the riots, which soon turned into bloody violence. Thirteen people died and more than 100 were injured (Goh, 2008).

In addition to using every opportunity to stir feelings against the colonial and Singaporean authorities, calling for demonstrations and riots to disrupt the economy as much as possible, and using the educational system to indoctrinate students and teachers with a radical anti-state ideology, 'The communists wrote articles in the Chinese newspapers to stir up the feelings of the people by blaming the government for all the hardships they faced' (Goh, 2008). The Communists also resorted to terrorist activities, such as 'intimidat[ing] and liquidat[ing] witnesses who gave evidence in court' against their members, as well as burning and damaging public and private buildings, vehicles and property (Porter, 1998). Communist leaders, students, labour unions and teachers began working together 'to cause disruptions to vital public services. One key area they focused on was the transportation of Singapore. It was the core of the economy, and their goal was to create an economic standstill in their attempt to undermine local authority' (Goh, 2008).

Demonstrations and riots were also caused by interethnic strife and class struggle. The relationship between the Chinese majority and minorities in Singapore was marked by distrust and suspicion. Just like the Chinese majority was concerned about the 'Malayanization' of Singapore, the minorities became also concerned about the 'Chinaization' of Singapore. The colonial power policies and politics also further encouraged societal, ethnic and class polarization and divisions to facilitate their grip over the country. The 1960s therefore were accompanied and characterized by 'racial and religious riots in Indonesia, Malaysia and Singapore...' (Chia, 2011, p. 387). Each community lived in a world apart from the other communities culturally, politically and socially. Some communities even felt ostracized and lived in enclaves, distancing themselves physically, culturally and psychologically from other communities.

Crisis of identity and the forging of a Singaporean identity

As a result of the Communist insurgency and 'serious racial riots' and ethnic and religious strife experienced in the 1960s, the Singaporean officials 'laid strong foundations for managing racial and religious harmony' (Tong, 2009, p. 17). S. Rajaratnam, Singapore's Second Deputy Minister in 1973 and Minister of Foreign Affairs in 1965 shed some light on the thinking behind, and nature of, the problem confronting Singaporean officials following independence in 1965:

> In a multi-racial, multi-lingual and multi-cultural society like ours, the communal problem... must be and will always remain one of the major problems which, if we do not resolve intelligently, could break our society, especially of an independent Singapore. (S. Rajaratnam,[5] 16 March 1967, quoted in Chin and Vasu, 2007, p. 2.)

From day one of independence, therefore, interracial and inter-religious harmony came to constitute the main concern of Singaporean officialdom, the key policy obsession, the most important element in nation-building, and foundation of Singapore's social cohesion and official policy. The first priority, however, was to deal with the Communist insurgency.

There is little evidence to suggest that the Singaporean state implemented the kind of de-radicalization witnessed in countries like Saudi Arabia, Yemen or Egypt, for example, in its dealings with the Communist insurgency. This despite the fact that the Communists, not unlike Islamist Violent Extremists (IVEts), also sought to distort the image of the state, officials and policies by indoctrinating their pupils and followers with a violent, anti-state ideology similar to the one promoted by al-Qaeda. Instead, the Singaporean government, relying on the Internal Security Act (ISA), a draconian law introduced by the BMA to deal with the Communist insurgency itself, arrested Chinese Communist leaders, closed down several hard-core Communist Chinese schools and expelled hundreds of students for their involvement in Communist activities. Goh (2008) eloquently described the response of the Singaporean state to the Communist insurgency:

> Under Lim Yew Hock, the government took firmer action against the communists as the frequency of the riots increased. ... Lim [w]as tough and flat-footed in the way he dealt with the communists ... Lim wished to demonstrate to the British his commitment to fight the growing power of Communism in Singapore. The Lim Yew Hock government arrested 219 persons in October 1956 including Lim Chin Siong and Fong Swee Suan. As a result, the communists were no longer a violent threat by 1960.

In fact, the Communist threat remained strong throughout the 1960s, and it was not before 1970 that it subsided. As Porter (1998) noted:

> [On] February 2, 1963 ... the Singapore government, headed by a then more youthful Lee Kwan Yew, carried out the arrest of about 100 political activists fearful of a communist insurgency ... [they] wanted to fight for a fair, just independence from Britain.

Several Singaporeans were also radicalized in the early 1960s by the Vietnam War,[6] lack of proper democratic process in the country and expulsion of Singapore from the Federation of Malaya in 1965, the process which many Communist Singaporeans felt was not legitimate. As a former Communist leader stated:

> The People's Action Party (PAP) suddenly announced Singapore's split from the Malaya Federation in 1965. The separation was never discussed in parliament. There was no referendum. We protested and asked for a convening of parliament. (Quoted in Porter, 1998.)

Aggressive policies implemented by the Singaporean government in the 1960s to deal with the Communist threat lacked a dialogue program to de-radicalize incarcerated radical Communists. They also lacked a specific welfare program to look after the families of the incarcerated individuals while their breadwinners remained in prison, or the kind of human rights and proper treatment that characterized either, for example, the Saudi government's de-radicalization efforts after 2003 or the policies of the Singaporean government itself in its attempt to de-radicalize JI members after 2001 (see below). In fact, many Communist leaders spent long years, some more than 20 years, 'in solitary confinement' and their life after release was 'spent under severe restrictions': they still needed written approval to make public statements, address public meetings or take part in any political activity at home or overseas which 'Of course, if applied for, this would have been automatically refused'. Many could neither make contact with any political activists or former political detainees, nor could they belong to any organization or 'even a chess club'; they 'were not allowed to see their families either' and were placed 'under detention or ROs [Restriction Orders]'. This was especially the case for those incarcerated individuals who 'refus[ed] to renounce violence' (all quotations from Porter, 1998).

To cope with its survival as a newly formed state, and in order to deal with the challenges which surrounded its formation, including in particular the problem of ethnic and religious strife, the Singaporean government adopted 'Since independence...an "ideology of pragmatism"', which 'entailed the embrace of economic goals, with an emphasis on employment and infrastructure' (Hill and Lian, 1995, p. 2). Such pragmatism was said to be a means to an end, 'the mechanism through which citizens were made to identify with the economic successes of the state' (ibid., p. 189. Also see Shan-Loong, 1999). Nichol and Sim (2007, p. 18) concur:

> A perceived absence of shared values has long concerned Singapore's rulers. ... From independence in 1965 Singapore adopted an ideology of pragmatism, of economic development, with a focus on infrastructure, education, training and employment. By the late 1970s most of the nation's economic needs had been met.

There were good reasons why Singaporean officials focused on economics as a mechanism to forge a Singaporean identity. The people of Singapore were badly affected in many ways by the strikes and riots of the 1950s and 1960s. During the two-year Malaya Federation, the Singaporean economy, as a result of the Malaysian Parliament's policies of favouring Malaysia and thus blocking many economic initiatives in Singapore, the latter's economy came to a standstill. Poverty and unemployment rose to unprecedented levels, and most Singaporeans, as mentioned earlier, lived in poor and isolated conditions. Goh (2008) described the situation in Singapore in the 1950s as follows:

> there was chronic overcrowding, poverty, disease and acute unemployment. The Chinese congregated in cubicles or 'black holes' in the

already overcrowded shop houses in the confines of Chinatown ... a report had been done on living standards published in 1954, thereby exposed the unspeakable population density of 50,000 persons per square kilometer in the city area and as many as 100 persons per shop house. On top of that, poverty rates were high to the point of 19.2% of all households lived in absolute poverty. Unemployment and underemployment rates for this period were estimated to be around 10% to 15%.

Over the coming four decades or so Singapore experienced phenomenal economic growth and sustainable development. By the mid-1970s all basic needs of Singaporeans were met, and poverty and unemployment declined to unprecedented levels as described by Cahyadi et al. (2004, p. 2):

> ... over the past few decades, Singapore has achieved astonishing economic achievements. Singapore's annual GDP growth rate from the 1960s to the 1990s has averaged about 8%, more than double of the 3.3% average of the OECD growth rate and more than three times of the US growth rate. ... Currently, Singapore ranks as the top Asian country with the highest standard of living. About 90% of Singaporeans live in proper houses with modern facilities, while the city itself is virtually slum-free. It is also a base of more than 3000 multinational companies from the developed world. All of these achievements have been realized in a country that is no more than 685 sq. km and with no fortunate endowment of any natural resource. How is it possible then for Singapore to attain and maintain such amazing economic growth as it has experienced over the past forty years?

Indeed, the phenomenally exceptional performance of the Singaporean economy, within such a short period of time, has generated tremendous and contentious debates over 'how' it was achieved. Most arguments and explanations evolved around either free market economy or government intervention. Although the debate has not been settled in favour of one side or the other, the argument which receives most votes suggests that the Singaporean government got the balance between the 'market' and 'government intervention right'. As the World Bank (1993, p. 5) stated, the High Performing Asian Economies, including Singapore: 'achieved high growth in getting the basics right. In most of these economies, in one form or another, the government intervened –

systematically and through multiple channels – to foster development, and in some cases the development of specific industries' (quoted in Chia, 2011, p. 385).

Regardless of how high growth rates and sustainable development were achieved, rapid industrialization and Westernization created new problems in Singapore: they were associated with a 'moral crisis' which alarmed the Singaporean officials. 'The chief manifestations of "moral crisis" were alarming increases in the rate of abortions, crime, drug abuse, and other related social problems...brought about by rapid Westernization' (Shan-Loong, 1999). Singaporean officials were concerned that, within the context of rapid industrialization, widespread use of new forms of technology and an English-dominated educational system, that the new generation of Singaporeans were becoming too Westernized and individualistic at the expense of family and community. Rapid Westernization, they feared, 'would de-culture Singapore, individualizing the society' (Nichol and Sim, 2007, p. 19). To contain the 'evils of westernization', the Singaporean government launched a Moral Education Programme based on Asian Values in 1979, with the government promoting bilingualism and the use of mother tongue in order to '[blend] the best of the East and of the West'. The Asian Values Programme was buttressed by another Religious Knowledge Programme, which became a compulsory subject for all upper secondary students in 1984. The introduction of the Religious Knowledge Programme 'was due to the belief that religious studies help to "reinforce" the teaching of moral values' (all quotations from Shan-Loong, 1999. Also see Nichol and Sim, 2007; Hill and Lian, 1995).

Neither the Moral Education nor the Religious Education Programmes solved Singapore's 'moral crisis'. Not only did the concerns over the individualization of Singaporean society and declining morality remain genuine, but Singapore was now facing new problems, ones that were related to religious fever and the rise of Christian evangelist fundamentalism.

By the mid-1980s, the Singaporean government was compelled to rethink its Religious Knowledge Programme. One of the key factors behind this revision was the arrest of 16 individuals in 1987 under the ISA on charges of a 'Marxist conspiracy' to overthrow the PAP government and establish a Communist state instead. A report published in 1988, however, concluded that, although the arrestees might have been influenced by Marxism or socialism, it is more likely that they were religious extremists. Indeed, the 'Report highlighted the phenomenal growth of Christianity, which was especially so amongst the Protestant evangelical charismatic groups'. It also suggested that the Religious Knowledge Programme, introduced by the government itself, 'had some part to play in the heightened religious climate, particularly amongst the Christians and Buddhists' (all quotations from Chia, 2011, p. 395). As a result, the government scrapped the Religious Knowledge Programme and replaced it with the Maintenance of Religious Harmony Act in 1988. 'The Act sought to secularise the civil society and turn religion into a personal, rather than a public matter. ... It was hoped that a secularised, "civil religion" would "serve as a source of shared national values" (Shan-Loong, 1999). It was around this time too that the term 'National Shared Values' was becoming popular among the Singaporean official circle. In 1990, the Moral Educational Programme was also scrapped and the Shared Values Programme (SVP) was put in its place (Shan-Loong, 1999. Also see Chia, 2011; Nichol and Sim, 2007).

The failure of shared values and the rise of Islamist fundamentalism

In 1991, the Singaporean government published what it called a 'White Paper' in which it formally and officially incorporated and adopted the Shared Values Programme. It also explained the reasons for, and the rationale behind adopting the program (Singaporean Government, 1991). Given the traditional importance of the educational system in the Chinese Confucian culture, the Singaporean educational system, particularly the social studies, have been seen as the main instrument of nation-building, a vehicle for instilling, inculcating and indoctrinating Singaporeans through National Education with messages of the PAP government, of which six were seen to be of special significance to create a Singaporean identity, or 'Singaporean Singapore': a sense of belonging and patriotism, racial and religious harmony, a meritocracy without corruption, economic opportunity, efficiency and prosperity, and developing a secure, confident, forward-looking, cohesive citizenry (Nichol and Sim, 2007, p. 1). A group of prominent Singaporean (mostly Chinese) scholars and religious leaders rewrote the entire social studies and National Education Programme to be taught as a compulsory subject at all primary and secondary schools. All schools in Singapore were also brought under the direct supervision and control of the Ministry of Education, and 'no special schools for any one race other than the handful of madrasas whose annual intake of students is capped at 400' were allowed (Tong, 2007, p. 17).

In addition, the government also announced a Racial Harmony Day (RHD), celebrated every year on 21 July, the day the racial riots broke out in 1964. The aim of RHD, first celebrated in 1997, is to remind all Singaporeans of the fragile nature of racial harmony, that racial harmony should be taken seriously and that it should not be taken for granted by any citizen. In the words of the Ministry of Education (2011), the aim of the RHD is to 'promote inter-racial understanding among our students and is an important part of our national education'. This was also accompanied by Community Development Councils (CDCs), formed in 1997 to promote social cohesion and strengthen community bonding in the various districts. The CDCs organize activities in their districts, which include family outings, sports carnivals, job fairs and cultural performances for residents to interact and bond together (ibid.). Even Public Housing Policy has been used, since the early 1980s, to support government policy of promoting social cohesion and ethnic integration. For example, public policies set maximum proportions for various ethnic groups in each Housing and Development Board (HDB) block and neighbourhood. The aim of this policy is 'To prevent the formation of racial enclaves and promote ethnic integration'. This also meant that 'The HDB will not approve the sale of a new or re-sale flat to a particular ethnic group if it would lead to that ethnic group's limits being exceeded' (all quotations in Chew, 2009).

The Singaporean Shared Value Programme (SVP) has generated a great deal of controversy, especially with regard to the intentions of the state behind its introduction and ability of the program itself to achieve its objectives, including in particular the goal of creating values shared by all Singaporeans. Shan-Loong (1999) criticized the program for being 'top-down' and 'contradictory':

> national identity and nationhood are not principles that can be 'mandated and managed from the top'. Instead, the nation is an 'imagined reality' that transcends institutions such as government and civil society. Consequently, the citizen creates the nation. It is in this vein that the Shared Values cannot achieve ideological consensus – that their very existence contradicts the cultivation of a national identity.

Others criticized the program for being no more than a vehicle to reaffirm the People's Action Party government's grip over society and the political system, a 'vehicle to shape and coordinate' all aspects of life of the Singaporeans, expressing concern not only 'about the level of indoctrination and top-down processes' involved in the SVP, but its contradictory nature which is reflected in the 'absence in the curriculum of the opportunities to develop the skills of critical thought considered crucial to active citizenship' (Nichol and Sim, 2007, pp. 19–20). The PAP government was also criticized not only for over-relying on top-down policing to sustain racial harmony and inter-ethnic peace, but also argued that, in the long run, promoting civic education and active citizenship would be far better for national identity and cohesion (Nichol and Sim, 2007, p. 19; Shan-Loong, 1999).

The impact of the SVP has been no less controversial. Indeed, within three years of introducing the White Paper in 1991, concerns were already raised over the health of the family as a central institution in Singaporean society, and the continued declining morality of society. Increasing nonchalance over sexual morals and marriage, as well as rising disputes between men and women, and between parents and children were key manifestations of the continued declining morality of Singaporean society (Shan-Loong, 1999). The situation became so dire that Lim Boon Heng, the Minister Without Portfolio, warned against a societal 'breakdown of the family' (Lim, 1994). A good indication on the failure of the SVP came in 1995, when the Singaporean government launched the Family Values Programme to strengthen the role of the family in Singaporean society, and to 'address the inadequacy of the Shared Values in upholding the family' (Shan-Loong, 1999).

Perhaps the most alarming and relevant issue for the purpose of this chapter is the impact of the SVP on minorities in Singapore, including in particular on the Muslim community, a subject that has received little attention thus far. Surveys and polls provide important insights into the minds of various groups and individuals and how they perceive, interpret and/or react to a particular policy or subject. They provide an importunate method therefore to gauge the opinion of minorities in Singapore. Two surveys (George, 2000; Nichol and Sim, 2007) aim specifically at gauging the opinions of minorities in Singapore with regard to the SVP. They are considered as the most comprehensive and important studies in this area of research and have thus been cited frequently in the literature. Some quotations from these surveys are worth mentioning.

Chia (2011, pp. 382–3) argues that at the heart of the issue of forging and articulating a Singaporean identity through the role of citizenship/moral education/shared values was the promotion of the 'Asian Values' concept alongside, or synonymous with, the 'Confucius culture' which became popular in the Singaporean political discourse in the 1980s and 1990s. This stemmed from the belief that only an Asian values framework, based on the Confucian culture and ethics 'as reflected in government leadership, competitive education, a disciplined workforce, principles of equality and self-reliance, and self-cultivation, provides a necessary background and powerful motivating force for the rise of East Asia', including Singapore, and would enable the state to govern society (Berger and Hsiao, 1988, p. 7). Even the aborted Religious Knowledge Program which the Singaporean government promoted in the late 1970s and early 1980s was based on, and aimed at, promoting Confucian ethics and 'Asian Values via the vehicle of Religious Knowledge, which was therefore unsuccessful', as reflected by its abandonment in the mid-1980s (Chia, 2011, p. 395).

There was no question that the minorities in Singapore raised their concerns over the state's SVP and policies. One of the chief reasons behind this concern was the fact that the program itself was badly communicated by the Singaporean government, raising the fears of many members of the ethnic minorities of a process of 'Asianizing Singapore' (Chia, 2011, p. 389). For many members of the community, the SVP seemed not only a way to entrench the 'pre-independence' underprivileged Chinese majority, but also 'appeared to other racial groups as an attempt to make the country, as a whole, more Chinese' (quoted in Nichol and Sim, 2007, p. 24). This problem has been aggravated by the approach of the Singaporean government, which often discussed ethnic diversity in connection to fears of Malay birth rates, Chinese low birth rates, increased Malay and other immigration into the country, and even Islamic terrorism (ibid., p. 24; George, 2000).

In general, the government attempt to create shared values among all Singaporeans was disdainfully greeted by the Singaporean ethnic minorities. As a Malay teacher whose opinion reflects 'The frequently heard "minority" perspective', stated:

> Every race in the country has a culture that is unique. ... If we are to adopt the model of 'Singaporean Singapore' melting pot, then the uniqueness will disappear. I disagree with the movement of wanting to create a culture common to all Singaporeans. With globalization, Singapore receives people from many parts of the world who have their own unique cultures and I do not think they would want to be included in the 'Singaporean Singapore' melting pot, which means losing their own culturally distinct characteristics. ... (Quoted in Nichol and Sim, 2007, p. 22. Also see George, 2000.)

Even the Public Housing Policy (PHP), which has been in place since 1989 and was sold as a way to increase the integration of the minorities, seems to have been received less positively by the ethnic minorities, and may even have backfired. For many members of the Singaporean ethnic minorities, the PHP was interpreted as an attempt to weaken their ability to galvanize political clout and sought to disperse them and splinter their communities. As such, the PHP failed to increase the integration of the ethnic minorities. As a Malay teacher commented:

> with superior architecture, landscaping and facilities. The dramatic change in housing has resulted in changing race relations in the country. As each household became more insular, and mixed less with their neighbors, knowledge and understanding of other cultures was reduced, as different races had less opportunity to mix and mingle.... In the past, minorities such as the Malays lived as a community, settling in kampongs. However, the public housing scheme...splintered the Malay community in housing estates throughout Singapore. The ethnic quotas were introduced in 1989, on the pretext of preventing the emergence of ethnic enclaves that might harm racial harmony. These measures were undertaken to ensure no ethnic group, especially the minority groups, can gather enough electoral support to push for their agenda. (Quoted in Nichol and Sim, 2007, p. 23.)

All of the above-mentioned concerns and insecurities have been intensified by discriminatory state employment policies (either real or perceived) in some sections of the economy, such as the military and education.

> For example, many interviewees said that nearly all officers and fighter pilots are Chinese...some schools have only Chinese students...some teachers and trainees, mostly from minorities, made comments similar to the following, that...[such policy] 'surfaces a lot of pent-up feelings that many minorities in Singapore feel....' A Chinese teacher was passionate when she asserted that, 'In fact, people of all races express a deep longing for a nation that is more integrated.' (Quoted in Nichol and Sim, 207, p. 24.)

It was within this context and against this background that IVEts emerged as the most dangerous threat to Singapore's social and religious harmony in the early years of the 21st century.

Countering Islamic violent extremism (CIVEm) and de-radicalizing JI members

In the early 21st century, Jemaah Islamiyah (JI) emerged as the most serious threat to Singapore's security and social and religious harmony. According to the Singaporean government, the arrest of 34 JI members in 2001 and 2002, respectively, 'exposed the most serious direct threat posed by any terrorist organization to Singapore's security since the days of the Communist Party of Malaya' (quoted in Bin Kader, 2007, p. 208).

JI is a radicalized splintered faction of Darul Islam (DI), a local Indonesian jihadi group established in 1949 with the aim of creating an Islamic state in Indonesia. Since its creation in the late 1940s, members of DI fought the secular regimes of both Sukarno (1948–62) and Suharto (after 1966). Both leaders (Sukarno and Suharto) pursued and persecuted DI members, leading to the radicalization of several of their followers. In the 1970s, however, Suharto's regime reactivated the DI to protect Indonesia from the Communist threat against the Indonesian–Malaysian border in Borneo. As their influence grew, the Indonesian government arrested, in mid-1977, more than 185 JI members, including the two main leaders of the group, Abu Bakar Ba'asyir and the late Abdullah Sungkar allegedly to prevent them from ruining the 1977 elections. Although the two leaders were not originally DI members, they nevertheless endorsed its goals and were charged as members of DI, calling for disobedience to the secular rule of Suharto and refusing to acknowledge validity of the Constitution. They were tried in 1982 and sentenced to nine years in prison on subversion but their sentences were reduced on appeal to three years and then to ten months. After their release they fled to Malaysia where they established the JI in 1993 (Gunaratna, 2007).

The goals of the JI members were transformed in the 1980s, particularly after several of the group's members participated in jihad against the Russian forces in Afghanistan with the Mujahedeen. Being in Afghanistan not only led JI members to come into contact with, but also to be influenced by, al-Qaeda and its global violent ideology. This caused the JI to be transformed 'into a regional group with a global focus' (Gunaratna, 2007, pp. 57, 72). Their publicly stated goal is to create an Islamic caliphate in the region, by force if necessary. Although originating in Indonesia, JI today has cells in Malaysia, Singapore, the Philippines and even in Australia (Bin Ali, 2007, p. 108).

JI first appeared on the radar in Singapore in 2001, when a small group of its members were arrested by the Singaporean government under the

ISA while they were preparing to launch a series of attacks that targeted mainly Western, particularly American, interests in Singapore. The arrest of the first group, which was poorly communicated by the Singaporean state, might have been responsible for the shift in the JI strategy to target national strategic objectives, as was reflected by the second wave of arrests of JI members in 2002.

The 2001 and 2002 episodes truly alarmed the Singaporean state. First, it threatened to undermine one of the core policies and foundations of the Singaporean state: national religious and social cohesion. As the then Singaporean Prime Minister Tong (2009, p. 15) stated: 'The JI episode could undermine our national cohesion ... [and] threaten our national security ... and also economy'. Second, unlike the Communist threat in the 1950s and 1960s which sought better economic conditions and living standards for themselves and for the Singaporean workers, the new, post-2000 threat differed in the sense that it was imposed by a small group of ethnic minority, namely Muslim Malay. They were neither motivated by economic factors nor coming from uneducated or poor backgrounds who sought to better the economic status of Malay Muslims in Singapore. As Musa (2007, p. 52) noted, it is interesting to know that:

> many of those involved especially the younger operatives do not come from poorer communities ... the same is true for the profile of the JI members arrested in Singapore. They are educated, employed and have families and their own homes.

Third, and more importantly for the subject of this chapter, the planners of the 2001 and 2002 failed attacks belonged to a different ideology, an ideology which the Chinese secular-dominated Singaporean state and society knew little about and were ill-equipped to deal with. Singaporean officials openly admitted that they were not 'qualified' and 'prepared' to deal with an 'entirely new phenomenon' imposed by a group of

> individuals who have been caught up by their misguided identification and attachment to an alien ideology which they have erroneously romanticised as a noble cause ... [for] their way of life ... [and which] constitutes deviant behaviour against the norms of a rational society ... they are armed with gullible mind, a very narrow perspective of Islamic universal values, as well as a very limited and skewed understanding of international politics, international relations and world history. (Bin Kader, 2009, pp. 10, 22, 144)

The then Deputy Prime Minister (Wong Kan Seng, 2009, p. 23) was even more outspoken: 'To debunk the JI's teachings which were falsely grabbed in religion, the Government being secular had no locus standi as it is not an authority of any religious belief'. What happened then, in the 'Singapore perspective' or experience in dealing with this 'entirely new phenomenon', confirms the soundness of one of our key findings on the central determinants of successful Counter-de-Rad programs: the prominence, vivacity, vitality and superiority of the role of the state in such a process (El-Said and Harrigan, 2013). The Singaporean government, indeed, adopted an 'integrated approach' to countering the threat of JI (Bin Ali, 2007, p. 110), one that proved perhaps more comprehensive and integrated than all other case studies we have so far investigated, either in this or the first volume of this project.

The first step taken by the Singaporean government was to acknowledge the existence of the problem, unlike many other governments which tended to initially deny the existence of VEm until it became too serious to neglect. As the former Singaporean Prime Minister (Tong, 2009, p. 16) publicly stated: 'We must acknowledge that there is a terrorist threat in our region and in Singapore, even though the number of people involved in Singapore is only a handful'. One of the early measures then taken by the Singaporean government to protect the country and prevent the occurrence of a terrorist attack was to 'harden the physical security of our borders and key installations, and take several measures' in this regard (Shanmugam, 2009, p. 8). These include the strengthening of intelligence and border controls, including sophisticated screening, use of X-ray machines to scan containers, deployment of sniffer dogs at airports and borders, and naval escort for tankers and other high-value vessels. A new law to prevent dealing with terrorist funding was introduced, in addition to a new biometric passport system introduced in 2005. The Singaporean state also expanded the use of CCTV in public places, and increased protection for key installations, including IT, telecommunications and financial sectors (Bin Ali, 2007, p. 112).

Equally important, the Singaporean government realized from the very beginning that, unlike the situation with the Communist threat in the 1950s and 1960s, that 'a new approach' was needed to win 'as much hearts and minds of the moderate Muslim community' (Jerard, 2009, p. 96) and that it rely solely on security and traditional military strategies:

> Hence, we urgently need a new approach to tackle violent terrorist ideology that seeks to undermine our societal fabric. This approach

must be based on both security measures and community efforts. The aim should be not just to stop people from committing violence but also to challenge the ideology that drives them. We cannot afford to rely only on security forces to guarantee our defence against the terrorist threat. We need the effort of the whole community and the government to do this effectively. (Bin Kader, 2009, p. 12)

The 'entirely new phenomenon' of VEm was then framed in terms of a 'national' problem, not the responsibility of only one particular community: 'putting an end to this threat is a national responsibility. Hence, everyone has to work together and fight against any ideology that breeds intolerance and violence, regardless of race and religion' (quoted in Bin Kader, 2009, p. 13).

Although the phenomenon of VEm was framed in a national perspective, it was the state which took the initiative first, called upon and facilitated the role of community leaders to play a leading part in countering violent ideology and de-radicalizing JI members who had already crossed the line and committed, or attempted to commit, violent extremist acts. Following the foiling of attacks in January 2002, therefore:

As Prime Minister then I was concerned that revelation of Singaporean Muslim involvement in the JI could affect the confidence and attitude of our non-Muslims towards our Muslims. Together with key members of the Cabinet, I held several dialogue sessions with leaders from various communities and religions to explain why the government had made the JI arrests. We stressed that they were not targeted against Muslims. We also urged upon non-Muslims to reach to Muslims, and for the Muslim community to integrate more with the other communities. (Tong, 2007, p. 18)

Being 'secular' with no 'locus standi' or religious authority, Singaporean officials acknowledged that countering VEm and de-radicalizing JI members could only be done 'by Islamic scholars and teachers'. The Muslim community, on the other hand, responded positively and immediately to the PM's and his officials' initiative to take a key role in countering VEt ideology in Singapore. The arrest of JI members in 2001 and 2002, with the revelation that they were prepared to kill innocent Singaporean civilians, 'caused fear and panic' that the JI episode could arouse 'anger and retaliation against Muslim community...that some Singaporeans might overreact and start looking at the entire Muslim community with suspicion'. The main impact would be felt in the workplace, especially among Muslims looking for employment (all quotations from Tong, 2009, pp. 15–16). In other words, the Muslim community in Singapore, no doubt, also felt threatened that by the JI episode they could be undermined economically and socially, and maybe even lose the rights granted to them by the 1959 Citizenship Law. Equally important, they feared the loss of 'The life of peace, security and prosperity in Singapore that we [Muslims] benefit' and, when compared to Muslims in other societies, 'is a great achievement that we all should be happy with' (Mohamed, 2009, p. 89).

The first step taken by the Muslim community leaders was to condemn JI actions and declare support for government policies. A letter signed by more than 120 Muslim community leaders to this effect was issued and published. Two of the most prominent Muslim religious and community leaders, Ustaz Haji Ali Mohamed, a council member of MUIS[7] and Chairman of Khadijah Mosque, and Ustaz Hj Md Hasbi Hassan, the President of PERGAS (The Singapore Islamic Scholars and Religious Teachers Association), were approached by the Ministry of Home Affairs to assess the JI detainees in mid-2002. After several interviews with detainees, the two leaders concluded that the actions of JI members 'were the results of their misconstrued religious ideology…that the JI had misunderstood different Islamic concepts to suit their political end of establishing a utopian Islamic Caliphate' (Hassan, 2007, p. 151). The two leaders then 'volunteered themselves to form the Religious Rehabilitation Group [RRG]…primarily with the objective of counselling the JI detainees and showering them with rightful, mainstream understanding of these concepts' (ibid.). The former Deputy Prime Minister, Wong Kan Seng (2009, p. 27), summarized the key duties of the RRG to include both rehabilitation and prevention:

> From the Government's perspective, the RRG's primary role is rehabilitation – it exposes our detainees and those on ROs [Restriction Orders], who are infected by terrorist ideology to alternative mainstream Islamic knowledge.…. We see the RRG playing a preventive role as well. It works with the authorities and other groups to organise discussions and seminars that raise awareness against terrorist ideology, and also to drive home the message of peace, tolerance and moderation.

In early 2009, the RRG consisted of 21 members, 16 males and five females. They are all qualified in religious matters and work on a voluntary basis. Today the number of RRG members has risen to around 34. A strong collaborative relationship soon developed between the RRG and Singaporean government. The latter supports and facilitates the work of the former, including, for example, through the organization of regular meetings with RRG members where they are briefed on security and other matters pertinent to detainees. Although qualified in religious matters, many working as teachers themselves, RRG's members are not counsellors. The government thus arranged for counselling and training programs for RRG's members to improve their counselling skills and technique:

> The RRG members are aware of their limited experience in counselling. ... The Government has given tremendous support to the RRG in their efforts to counter radical Islamic ideology ... we have helped to arrange for relevant training for RRG members, for example, in counselling technique, and shared with them insights into terrorism threat. (Seng, 2009, pp. 25, 26)

Some RRG members spent more than seven months undergoing special courses and special training in counselling to improve their counselling skills, capacities and formal qualifications in counselling and psychology before starting the process of rehabilitating and de-radicalizing JI detainees. The establishment of the RRG thus marked the beginning of Singapore's rehabilitation, de-radicalization and preventative processes.

The RRP, which is implemented inside incarceration centres, formally started its counselling activities in 2003 'by producing a manual to assist the religious counselling of individuals who were found to have subscribed to terrorist ideology' (Angell and Gunaratana, 2011, p. 352). The objective of this exercise was to further train, prepare and guide RRG members for religious counselling and to facilitate their work by improving their understanding of radical ideologies, behaviour and how best to counter their narrative through complementary religious texts derived from the Quran, *Tafsir* (exegesis of the Quran), *Hadith* (sayings and deeds of the prophet), *Fiqh* (Islamic jurisprudence) and *Sirah* (prophet's history and stories). A second manual was produced in 2009 to update, incorporate and take into consideration almost seven years of religious counselling (ibid.).

After their detention, JI members spend 30 days under investigation. Religious rehabilitation starts immediately after the end of the 30 days, and consists of three main parts: psychological, religious and social. It is modelled along the lines of the Saudi program. This is not surprising because, when entrusted with the responsibility of de-radicalizing JI detainees, RRG's members began their job by touring some Muslim-majority states, including Saudi Arabia in particular, in order 'to draw lessons from the experience of Muslim communities in these countries and to apply them where relevant to the context of Singaporean Muslim community' (Musa, 2007, p. 35).

Between 2002 and 2007, RRG conducted, in total, more than 500 counselling sessions (Hassan, 2007). The psychological program/sessions aim at studying the psychological reasoning behind joining JI and the psychological condition of the detainee in general. It seeks to identify whether the detainee suffers from any psychological condition, as well as detecting any psychological factors that may have led the detainee to join a VEt group. Specialized psychologists from the IDS then provide appropriate counselling to detect, take out and neutralize violent ideology.

Scholars and psychologists meet detainees on a daily basis, along with prison staff. The detainees, however, do not mingle and socialize with other groups:

> They are kept in single cells because we believe group dynamic is very important in radicalising them and therefore we try to undermine the influence of group dynamic by separating them and keeping them away from the Jamaa's influence or from being subjected to Jamaa's influence. Our approach is based on singular or individual cell-counselling basis with inmates not meeting or talking to one another inside the prison. We try to evaluate the psychological factors of each individual away from the group dynamic. (Personal interview with officials at the ISD, Singapore, 2010)

The Religious Programmes follow the psychological evaluation of the detainees. Religious counselling sessions focus on key areas or subjects, which the detainees seemed to 'misconceive' or lack understanding of. These areas are not uncommon in other de-radicalization programs implemented in countries like Saudi Arabia, Yemen and Egypt, for example (El-Said and Harrigan, 2013). They include the concepts of al-Wala' wal Bara', Jihad, Ummah, Bai'ah (Pledge of Allegiance), and al-Daulah al-Islamiyah; relations of Muslims with non-Muslims; duties of true Muslims in non-Muslim states (personal interviews with officials at the Ministry of Interior, Singapore, April 2010. Also see Mohamed, 2009).

Three groups qualify for counselling by RRG members: the detained JI members, JI members placed under ROs[8] and the families of both (Bin Ali, 2007, p. 114; personal interviews with officials at the Ministry of Interior, Singapore, April 2010). The detainees themselves have been classified into three categories: the minority hard-core radical group; those almost already de-radicalized even before counselling started; and those in between the last two categories, and who represent the majority of the group (ibid.).

Families of the detained JI members and ROs are integrated in the Religious Rehabilitation Program (RRP) by keeping them informed about the conditions of their incarcerated sons/relatives and by allowing family visits to incarceration centres. The role of families in Singapore, however, is not as prominent and integrated as it is in the case of Saudi Arabia, for instance. There the Saudi government strongly encourages the families of the detained individuals not only to visit their sons regularly, but also covers all costs involved in such a process and uses families as an integral part of the program to de-radicalize their family members. In Singapore family visits are less regular, once a week on average, and families are not encouraged to talk to their family members while in incarceration centres, as is the case in Saudi Arabia (El-Said and Harrigan, 2013). One of the reasons for the weaker integration of family members in the RRP is due to the fact that some families might themselves be radicalized and are in need of de-radicalization and religious rehabilitation to debunk their VEt beliefs. Hence, families themselves are counselled by RRG groups, with female scholars playing a key role in counselling female members of the detainees and ROs.

Families, however, are supported in other ways. In addition to religious counselling to correct their misconceived religious opinions and beliefs, families also receive emotional and psychological counselling to comfort them and enable them to cope with the new realities of life and the situation in which they find themselves (including the arrest of a close member of their family).

The aim of the Social Programme is 'to reintegrate detainees into society and families after release. Hence, while in prison, we *provide opportunities for educational advancement*, work and promoting work ethics' (ibid.). For example, detainees are given the opportunity to complete a degree while in prison. They are also provided with job opportunities, where they are paid in the form of a voucher which they can give to their families to buy, for example, food, furniture or whatever they need. Hence they feel that they are useful, contributing to, and supporting their families while in prison. This increases their self-esteem and worthiness, helps them develop positive working habits and makes them feel productive while in prison. This aspect of the program is, of course, voluntary and it is up to the detainees whether they participate or not. Not all accept working or even participating in the counselling program. Many initially refuse to do so but change their minds later on and agree to participate when they see the majority of their colleagues participating. Some, a minority, continue to refuse to participate in the work and counselling programs to the present time.

The Social Programme also provides various financial incentives to the families of the detained JI members. If poor, families receive financial support, especially the spouses and children of the detained JI members and those placed under ROs. If their economic status is very weak and their children require fees for education, these are also paid for, in addition to some subsistence income: 'Apart from the house visits made, educational assistance for the children, upgrading courses were offered to the families to ensure that they are able to cope with the situation emotionally, socially and economically' (Bin Ali, 2007, p. 113). As is the case in most other Muslim-majority states that implemented/ implement similar rehabilitation programs, released detainees are also supported in finding a job or to return to their former jobs if possible (El-Said and Harrigan, 2013).

Interestingly, financial support provided to detainees, their spouses and children costs the Singaporean government nothing. It is all paid for by a 'group of Muslim organisations and a few local mosques [which have] also extended their contributions towards the welfare of the detainees' families' (Bin Ali, 2007, p. 113). The most important Muslim-community institution here is the Interagency-After Care Group (ACG), which was created in 2002 by five Muslim groups: Yayasan MENDAKI, Voluntary Welfare Organization Taman Bacaan, the community self-help group Association of Muslim Professionals, Khadijah Mosque and En Naeem Mosque. The ACG draws its resources mainly from the Central Provident Fund (CPF), a 35-year-old project unique to Singapore. It taps on Muslims to help build mosques in new Housing Board Estates (HBE). The idea to create the CPF came from the then Prime Minister, Lee Kuan Yew, following a meeting in 1975 with Muslim community leaders. Yew suggested using the CPF as a mechanism to deduct contributions from Muslim workers, with the right to opt out. Very few did. Contributions started at 50 cents in 1975, although the fund today gets $1 from Muslims earning less than $2,000 a month, up to $7.50 from those making over $4,000. Muslims, of course, can opt to give more if they wish. The rationale behind creating the CPF was the need of Muslim community members moving into new HDB for new places of worship. The state was unwilling to provide these and there were not enough wealthy patrons existing in the society to respond to this need (Hussain, 2009, pp. 113–4). The CPF today provides the main financial resources required not only to build and maintain mosques in Singapore, but also to support needy Muslim families, widows, orphans and deprived families, as well as being responsible for 'the welfare of the families of the detainees' (Jerard, 2009, p. 101). Angell and Gunaratna (2011, p. 355) comprehensively described the unique approach of the ACG as

a voluntary community effort between different Malay/Muslim agencies and organisations that provides assistance to the families of the detainees, including their wives and children. Within the after-care framework, the unique approach by these agencies and organisations is aimed at supporting the families of the detainees during the transition period. Yaysan Mendaki (YM), Association of Muslim Professionals (AMP), and Taman Bacaan focus on their specialised expertise, consolidate expert areas, and coordinate efforts between different agencies for the benefit of each client. YM covers the educational program and assistance in the form of tuition fee subsidy or program fee waiver that it provides to the families. In addition to coordinating with Taman Bacaan and AMP to help the families, YM also refers such families to relevant agencies and organisations that also might help with financial assistance.

The ISA, a draconian act from the colonial days used to arrest VEts before they committed a terrorist act, has been condemned as 'a damning indictment on the Singapore Government' to hold individuals without a trial and 'when finally releasing [them] issue all those restrictions' (Porter, 1998). However, there is no evidence of torture inside Singaporean incarceration centres as an investigative technique. The Singaporean government seems to have provided decent treatment and conditions for the detained JI members while incarcerated. Although 'there have been calls to do away with Singapore's Internal Security Act (ISA) ... the Singapore government feels that it has been instrumental in uncovering and dismantling a Singapore JI cell in 2001' and also 2002[9] (Bin Ali, 2007, p. 117).

In addition to psychological, religious and social programs (grouped under the rubric of RRP), the RRG has also extended its efforts to preventative, counter-radicalization measures at the societal level in an attempt to prevent Muslim youth from falling prey to the calls of VEt ideologists. It thus sought to mitigate and undermine the impact of radical ideology through developing talks, forums and anti-VEt publications. Singapore's official policy towards the Internet is that 'We cannot shut down all radical websites. ... It will neither be practical nor effective to try to cut off access to radical materials such as blocking radical websites.' Therefore, both the RRG and MUIS have set up websites to challenge the radical call for violence and clarify Islamic precepts that are often misused by radicals to legitimize the call for violence. Forums, discussions and the Internet are also used to reach out to, and engage with, non-Muslims. All of these educative initiatives (counter-ideology websites, forums, discussions and seminars) used to raise awareness against terrorist ideology have become the Muslim communities' 'mainstay to prevent radicalism' (all quotations from Seng, 2009, pp. 28–29).

The websites built by the RRG and MUIS in particular address critical issues of ideology and serve as an effective tool for public education, enabling access to a wide range of scholarly publications, news, articles and media interviews that focus on effective response to extremism (Jerard, 2009, p. 101).

Public forums, talks and seminars are often organized by RRG and MUIS leaders in mosques and Islamic centres. One of the most important Islamic centres in this field is the Harmony Centre (HC), a two-storey centre officially opened on 7 October 2006 by the Prime Minister of Singapore, Lee Hsein Long. More than 200 guests from various faiths, religions and community leaders were invited not only to attend the opening ceremony, which coincided with the Muslim fasting month of Ramadan, but also to attend a dinner, or Iftar, on that day. The HC is a dedicated centre, housed in An-Nahdhah Mosque. Its main objective is to promote greater understanding of Islam and to present the true Islamic way of life in a transparent and honest way to all Singaporeans. In the words of leaders of HC itself, the aims of the centre are to:

> Portray Islam in its unblemished form and to demonstrate what it means to be Muslims in this challenging and ever-changing world ... to promote a greater understanding of the true teachings of Islam and Muslims in Singapore. (An-Nahdhah, 2009)

In addition, the HC also seeks to promote inter-faith dialogue and engagement at all levels of Singaporean society, including leadership, community, grass roots, youth and students. This is done through seminars, workshops, experiential learning journeys and visits to the centre which is open to the public six days a week. The HC has come to symbolize one of the Islamic religious councils in Singapore's (MUIS) efforts to engender a greater understanding of Islam and Muslims among the multiracial population of the country through programs such as mosque open houses, the mosque visits program and collaborative initiatives between mosques and grass roots national as well as social service agencies (Harmony Centre, 2010, pp. 1 and 2).

The HC consists of four main sections. The first shows images of Islam, a showcase that greets people with an array of audios and visuals illustrating the different faces of Islam. The second section, Civilizational Islam, is a sort of a 'walk down memory lane', where visitors delve into the history of renowned Muslim personalities of the past, with their great contributions commemorated and the impact of the changes they made to modern civilizations featured. The third section is called Essence of Islam, and is designed for visitors interested in learning and finding out about the basic principles of Islam with relevant information provided. The final section, Islamic Lifestyle Section, presents items and objects used in the daily lives of Muslims such as prayer mats, religious books and garments for Muslim women such as headscarves. Food and some samples of Islamic art are also displayed to give visitors a feel and understanding of Islam (Harmony Centre, 2010, pp. 3–4).

In addition to organizing exhibitions of Islamic art and culture and free guided tours to visitors, the HC also organizes regular talks, dialogues on such issues as understanding Islam, interfaith issues and relations, and building a cohesive and resilient Singapore family. Tours are free and the centre operates Monday to Friday 9 a.m. –5 p.m. The standard tour of the Harmony Centre takes 1.5–2 hours, including welcome and introduction sessions, Tour Level 1; Tour Level 2, Video Presentation; and a Q & A session at the end of the tour. Each tour could accommodate 80 visitors. The tours deal with questions of life and afterlife, and all aspects of daily living, personal, family, civic and religious duties. Visitors explore the meaning behind Islam and the Islamic way of life, trace the contribution of Islam to the world through its scholars and inventions, and learn the basic tenets of faith in Islam (Harmony Centre, 2010, pp. 5–6).

It is not only the An-Nahdhah Mosque, but also other mosques in Singapore have become active in promoting peaceful messages and social and racial harmony. In fact, MUIS, the main Islamic institute responsible for managing all mosques in Singapore, has transformed the role of mosques in the country into much more than a place for worshipping. It is not uncommon, for example, to find kindergartens, counselling rooms and food stalls on mosque premises in Singapore.

Some mosques, like the Al-Falah Mosque in Orchard Road have a drop-in centre for troubled teens to help reduce delinquency in the Muslim community. Other mosques have organized activities like rock-climbing and the screening of World Cup matches to attract youth. The Mujahidin Mosque in Queenstown has brought together Muslim foreign workers. Its premises offer a training centre to attend classes on Islam and teach English, cooking and IT skills on Sundays, as well as teaching that 'Islam does not condone violence or terror acts' (Hussain, 2009, pp. 114–115).

Finally, MUIS not only manages and maintains all mosques in Singapore, but also recommends most imams preaching in mosques, warns Muslims in Singapore against radical preachers and books, and advises Singaporean Muslim students about places of education abroad (ibid.). Friday sermons are prepared by the Islamic Centre too before being given to all mosques. 'Friday's sermons focus on how to become a better Muslim and are distributed to all mosques. All mosques give the same Friday sermons, which are sometimes delivered in three languages.' The Internal Security Department, which oversees the Counter-de-Rad efforts in the country, monitors all religious sermons. Nobody is intentionally allowed to proselytise and preach anti-integration–harmony slogans, and encouraging violence has also been made illegal in Singapore regardless of one's religion or race (Singapore, April 2010).

Evaluating the impact of Counter-de-Rad efforts in Singapore

Anybody who wants to study the Counter-de-Rad programs is immediately faced with 'critical issues surrounding assessment of their effectiveness' (Horgan and Braddock, 2010, p. 267). The recidivism and incidence rates remain the most commonly used, although not without contention and not without problems.

According to officials at the Internal Security Department (ISD), the total number of individuals detained by security officers between 2001 and April 2010:

> reached 50+, two-thirds of which, or around 40, have already been released. Only around 10 remain in custody. None of those released went back to violence. They have been neutralized both ideologically and behaviourally. We have a 100 per cent success rate. (Personal interview, Singapore, April 2010)

But when the procedures pertinent to the conditions of arrest and release are looked at more closely, a picture of an absolute success becomes less definitive. Relying on the ISA, detainees spend the first 30 days under investigation, during which they are being questioned and investigated by security officers from the ISD. Based on the results of the investigation, a decision is made on whether to release the detainees (as some might prove innocent), detain them or place them under restriction order. Even after their release

All detainees must go under a restriction order first and before they are completely released. Some have been detained since 2001. However, when they are released, most go into, and remain under, RO. There is no specific time for the RO, but while they are under RO they are supposed to report regularly to the security officer, either on a daily, weekly or monthly basis, it depends on the situation of the individual, the charges against him and his degree of cooperation. They are also not allowed to leave the country without a permit, change jobs without a permit, leave their area without a permit, and they are not allowed to join any political activity without a permit. Most remain under RO until today where they are constantly monitored by security officers. A very small number of released individuals have their ROs lifted completely. Eighty to ninety per cent have their ROs still remaining in place, while the big guns are still in prison. (Personal interviews with officials at ISD, Singapore, April 2010)

It would be premature to undoubtedly and unambiguously conclude that the Singaporean de-radicalization program (also known as the RRP) has met with absolute success. Individuals under ROs and constant monitoring by state security personnel have neither the incentive nor the ability and capability to return to their former life of VEm. The chance of slippage and recidivism in this case is very small since the released individual knows very well that he is under constant surveillance from his case officer.

Counter-de-Rad programs can only be judged as absolutely successful if they manage to eliminate not only the incidence of terrorism and recidivism, but also recruitment and radicalization. Even the most moderate Singaporean officials admit that many 'individuals' remain 'easily seduced by the lure of self-radicalisation' (Bin Kader, 2009, p. 9), that Singapore has been experiencing a 'rising threat of self-radicalization' (Seng, 2009, p. 24) and that a 'good number are self-radicalised via the internet in the first instance' (Lim, 2009, p. 39).

Efforts to integrate and engage various ethnic communities in counter-radicalization efforts, particularly the significance placed on engaging non-Muslims, have also been faced 'with mixed results' (Jerard, 2009, p. 101). There are several reasons for this.

First, we have seen how the Singaporean state traditionally followed a top-down approach to create and forge a Singaporean national identity, the so-called Shared Values Programme. Similar 'contradictions' which plagued the SVP can also be observed in the design and implementation of the preventative, Counter-de-Rad program (Nichol and Sim, 2007, p. 17). For example, Singaporean officials are adamant that 'misconceived' ideology is the only reason behind VEm in Singapore. However, just like the Communist insurgency during the 1950s and 1960s was influenced by internal and external factors, the same is true for JI's VEm. In private, Singaporean officials admit that 'Palestine, Iraq and Afghanistan play a key role in radicalising Muslims' (personal interviews, Singapore, April 2010). Indeed, in more economically advanced countries like Singapore and Malaysia, for example, external factors can be more significant in radicalizing individuals (El-Said and Harrigan, 2013).

Singapore has also traditionally relied on US protection against less friendly neighbours, particularly Indonesia and Malaysia. In recent years, 'Singapore has to rely more and more on the United States [for military protection]' (Porter, 1998). After 9/11, Singapore has come to be seen by many Muslims in the country as part of the 'war on terror', itself viewed by most Muslims as an attack against Islam and Muslims around the world. Singapore's closeness to the United States must have played a key role in radicalizing many in the country. This is clearly reflected in the objects targeted by JI members in 2001: mainly US interests in the country.

Even when 'VEts' were arrested in Singapore in more recent years after 2002, such as Abdul Basheer, for example, who was arrested in early 2007 along with 'three more self-radicalised youths', they were planning to travel to Afghanistan to fight American soldiers there and did not target Singaporean interests (Ibrahim, 2009, p. 43).

We, moreover, know little about JI members, including their 'family background, and … experience in school and at work' (Bin Kader, 2009, p. 128). For example, we don't know what role, if any, 'perceived' discrimination in favour of Chinese played, for instance, in some economic and state sectors in radicalizing JI members. The Singaporean state does not permit interviews with JI members, either inside prison or on ROs. Such an approach would allow us to better understand the causes and triggers of radicalization in Singapore. Only then can we design Counter-de-Rad programs that are absolutely effective and successful.

The government-sponsored Singaporean Counter-de-Rad program follows the Shared Values and all other racial and religious harmony programs implemented in the country since independence. It is also true that the Muslim community, later on, took over the design, implementation and control of most parts of the program so that many today perceive the Singaporean RRP as a bottom-up program (Bin Kader, 2007 and 2009). But the Singaporean state has come to rely almost completely and solely on the Muslim community to counter radical ideology and activism. But the Chinese majority, accustomed to a strong state that mandates and manages everything from the top, has become 'passive', continuing to rely on the state for protection, and have thus failed to engage sufficiently and properly with the Muslim community (Cahyadi et al., 2004; Chin and Vasu, 2007; Shan-Loong, 1999; Nichol and Sim, 2007; Chia, 2011). While the Singaporean state indeed presented the VEt threat as a national problem, the Muslim community was left to manage all aspects of Counter-de-Rad policies and efforts. As noted by several observers, VEm is not the responsibility of one community. Nor can one community alone bring peace and stability (ibid. Also see Bin Kader, 2007 and 2009).

This is not to say that Singapore's Counter-de-Rad efforts have produced no results. On the contrary, the Singaporean government has perhaps gone further than most other countries in producing what amounts to a most integrated, multifaceted, collaborative, bottom-up program managed from the bottom. These efforts have produced other important benefits, some of which the Counter-de-Rad efforts sought. Others came as a by-product of these efforts. One example of both types of benefits is intelligence-gathering.

One can argue that the Singaporean de-radicalization program is a (state security services) intelligence-led program as much as it is a de-radicalization program. In addition to psychological and religious counselling, each detainee is assigned a special case officer, a kind of handler. A case officer is the same official who arrests the detainee and investigates him during the latter's first 30 days in detention under the ISA, and before the RRP starts. All case officers come from a security background and are official employees from the ISD. Officer visits his detainee regularly two to four times a week, depending on each case and on the degree of radicalization of each individual. The aim of the visits is not only to neutralize his radical ideologies and convince him to participate in the RRP, but also to follow up with him during and after detention, with information-gathering being the most important objective sought. Case officers hence develop and maintain a relationship with the detainees on a one-to-one basis. 'The aim is twofold: investigative and mentoring' – investigative in the sense of being focused on intelligence gathering; mentoring in the sense of encouraging the detainees to participate in the RRP program, mentoring them as well as 'providing them with a shoulder to cry on' (all quotations from personal interviews with officials at ISD, Singapore, April 2010). As a result, the relationship becomes strongest between the detainee and his case officer, not between the detainee and his psychologist or religious scholar. This enhances the opportunity of gathering vital information that could prove life-saving and preventative of tragic VEt incidents.

While the state deliberately and consciously sought to gather intelligence from its detainees, such intelligence also came, perhaps unexpectedly, from societal elements. This outcome, which is a common feature of Counter-de-Rad programs viewed in the literature as '*successful*' (El-Said and Harrigan, 2013), is a function of the Singaporean program's ability to improve trust between the Muslim community and secular Singaporean state, and, to a lesser extent, society. As John Harrison of the ICPVTR stated:

> The government sought to involve the community from the very beginning. It was a very smart movement. We are lucky here because there is a high degree of trust between community and government. The community trusts government and vice versa. This is unlike the situation in the West. (Personal interview, Singapore, April 2010)

Tong (2007, p. 18), the former Singaporean Prime Minister, is in accord:

> [Counter-de-Rad] policies ... have over the years contributed to building a foundation of mutual trust and understanding between the communities. Sensitive issues could also be discussed openly because of the trust built up between the government and our Muslim community and between our Muslims and their communities.

Counter-de-Rad efforts carried out extensively by the Muslim community through public forums, seminars, talks, websites and other social events have also played a key role in enhancing general awareness and understanding of the threat of VEm in Singapore. They also served to improve understanding of the Islamic faith in general and hence prevented retaliatory actions by other community members follow-ing the arrest of JI members in 2001, 2002 and 2007. As the Singapore Minister of Law, Shanmugam (2009, p. 8), commented:

> We are very appreciative of the concerted efforts of key members of the community, including religious leaders and organisations, com-munity organisations, youth groups, academics, and individuals, to raise awareness about the virulent terrorist ideology and to clarify any misconceptions about Islam and the position of Muslims on radicalism.

Singaporeans in general also seem to agree with their Minister of Law. As a Singaporean citizen, among the 3,000 attendees of the 2007 forum organized by the Muslim community, commented:

> Before I came here tonight, I thought jihad means fighting for Islam. However, what we observe today is not jihad because from what I see now, victims are children, innocent people, women and those earn-ing a living. (Quoted in Tong, 2007, p. 19)

The upshot of all of these efforts has been to save lives and prevent the occurrence of large-scale, tragic VEt acts. They also empowered and increased the ability of the Muslim community itself to monitor, iden-tify and detect suspicious VEt acts before they took place. According to a high-ranking Singaporean official:

> So far, we have been successful. Often, such success is possible because ordinary citizens step forward to alert the authorities when they see something suspicious or amiss. Singapore's unravelling of the under-ground and secret JI terrorist organisation and its Al Qaeda links in 2001 began months before from a lead given by a member of the pub-lic – a Muslim Singaporean who was concerned about an individual who was preparing to leave to Afghanistan to join Al Qaeda and the Taliban to fight the coalition forces. Ultimately therefore, terrorism is defeated not by Governments but by the people. ... (Seng, 2009, p. 19)

The status of the Muslim scholars and religious leaders has also been improved rather than diminished by their Counter-de-Rad efforts. This outcome is a function of the government's choice to work with and empower competent, credible, moderate and autonomous scholars and religious leaders. Muslim scholars and religious leaders banded together to speak up for and defend their community. In doing so, they turned the Muslim elite into a major stakeholder in the resolution of VEt threat in the country. They (scholars, religious and community leaders) were

> seen as defending Islam against those who dishonour it. ... They were acting as Singaporean Muslim leaders doing their part to tackle security threat faced by all Singaporeans. ... The pursuit of common objectives strengthened the alliance between the Singaporean Government and ethnic and religious communities against a common threat. (Ju-Li, 2009, pp. 74–5)

Conclusion

Since 2002, Singapore has designed and carried out huge and commendable efforts not only to de-radicalize JI members arrested after 2001, but also to counter the appeal of VEt ideology and activism in the country. While these efforts have not eliminated the threat of VEm, they have improved the trustful relationship between the Muslim community and Singaporean state, turned Muslims into key stakeholders in fighting VEm, enhanced intelligence-gathering capabilities and sources, and facilitated a better understanding of Islam and Muslims in Singapore. These are no small achievements and they have been lacking in many other countries attempting to counter a similar threat, both Muslim-majority and Muslim-minority states.

Perhaps one of the most important lessons derived from countering VEt threat in Singapore, a multiracial and multi-religious society, is the official view of VEm as a national threat, rather than a threat posed by one particular community. The state not only engaged with but also empowered Muslim community leaders to play a key role in the entire Counter-de-Rad process. At the same time, the Singaporean state framed VEm as a national threat, faced by and the responsibility of all communities in the country. The absence of a similar approach in other countries has largely undermined their entire Counter-de-Rad efforts by preventing the Muslim community from taking its natural role in such a process. The failure of the British counter-radicalization policies provides a chilling reminder in this context. The UK position with regard to VEt threat was publicized by a statement made by Lord Steven, then security advisor to Gordon Brown: 'Most of all, when will the Muslim community in this country (Britain) accept an absolute, undeniable, total trust: that Islamic terrorism is THEIR problem? They own it. And it is their duty to face it and eradicate it' (quoted in Jerard, 2009, p. 102).

One of the key weaknesses, however, of the Singaporean Counter-de-Rad efforts stems from the state's strength and determination to guide, shape and direct every aspect of Singaporean life. This has turned most Singaporeans to passivity, believing that the state could always protect them no matter what the threat is. The focus on the Muslim community, almost to the exclusion of all others, has also undermined integration of, and engagement with, other communities. This, it could be argued, is probably the most important challenge facing the Singaporean state.

More needs to be done not only with regard to integrating and engaging all communities in Singapore, but also to counter the threat of self-radicalization in the country. For example, the number of radical emails preaching VEm by far exceeds the ones which were built to counter them. Singaporean officials continue to have the view that the 'misconceived' understanding of Islam is the only reason for VEm in the country, thus ignoring other internal and external factors that proved major triggers in even neighbouring countries, let alone in countries in other regions. Such 'contradictions' have, in the past, undermined Singaporean state efforts to create a 'Singaporean Singapore' or a pure Singaporean identity. They might even weaken and undermine the country's entire Counter-de-Rad program.

Singapore needs to pay more attention to, and integrate into its Counter-de-Rad efforts, policies and measures to ameliorate its internally 'perceived' discriminating policies in certain sectors of the state and economy. It also needs to pay more attention to the external triggers of radicalization, just like other countries, including Saudi Arabia, for example, have done. As Angell and Gunaratna (2011, p. 349) noted, although the participation and ownership by the Singaporean Muslim community is an important fundamental step, it is only a 'step in the right direction...requiring a much higher commitment level'. Such issues become more imperative under economic crisis or deteriorating economic conditions, something which Singapore has not experienced, amazingly, since independence.

> It means that we have an opportunity to beat them but we still have to recognize the fact that dangerous groups still exist out there. They are ideologically oriented and remain active, which means that they can still turn things around. (Personal interview with members of International Centre for Political Violence and Terrorism Research at the Singaporean Rajaratnam School of International Studies, Singapore, April 2010)

7
Sudan: De-radicalization and Counter Radicalization in a Radicalizing Environment

Introduction

Sitting at the crucial crossroads of the Arab peninsula, northern Africa and sub-Saharan Africa, Sudan is strategically important. Its stability will have far-reaching consequences not only for the African continent, but also for the United States and Western Europe, as many radical extremists might use Sudan for training, planning and attacking Western targets. The country remains one of the poorest in the Arab world, with a history of volatile narration, including decades of civil war, military coups, religious and ethnic persecutions, and alleged genocide, all of which have claimed hundreds of thousands of lives, displaced millions and torn the country apart economically, politically and ethnically. In the 1990s, Sudan's name became associated with terrorism, training, supporting and 'harbouring' terrorists and terrorist organizations (Waller, 2011). In 2011, Sudan was split into two countries (North and South), both of which remain economically the poorest in their region, unreconciled, unstable, volatile and vulnerable to terrorism, inbound and outbound. Worse, they exist in a region where 'sub-state terrorism is already endemic in Africa' (Arya, 2009).

While the country's name has become synonymous with political instability, terrorism and terrorist organizations, including al-Qaeda (AQ), little attention has been paid to the country's counter terrorism efforts which started in the second half of the 1990s and gained momentum after the 2005 Comprehensive Peace Agreement (CPA). As Waller (2011) noted, 'Sudan made significant progress in limiting the terrorist presence inside its borders' after 2005. As far as we know, no researcher has undertaken a study specifically to shed some light on these efforts, which included measures to restore Sudan's relations with the international community, de-radicalization procedures, counter terrorism measures and post-release efforts to facilitate reintegration of repented individuals back into their society and families. Nor has anybody attempted to provide meaningful evaluation for these efforts, let alone to draw lessons from counter radicalization and de-radicalization (De-rad) measures undertaken in poor, ethnically and politically divided, strategically important, externally influenced, countries like Sudan.

This chapter fills an important gap in the literature. It analyses Sudan's counter terrorism measures in detail as they evolved after the expulsion of Osama bin Laden and his colleagues from Sudan in 1996. It is the first study not only to document Sudan's counter terrorism and De-rad procedures, but also to provide a comprehensive evaluation for the outcome of reforms, the main lessons derived and the main challenges facing them. The chapter proceeds as follows. The next section provides a brief background on Sudan's historical evolution, including the rise and fall of the first national insurgent movement, the Mahdist Movement, during the last years of the 19th century. Countries are prisoners of their own history, and no country is more 'a prisoner of [its] history' than Sudan (Arya, 2009, p. 64). Hence, understanding Sudan's historical political evolution is important for understanding Sudan's political, economic and social challenges today. The third section continues with studying Sudan's historical evolution, but under the Anglo-Egyptian Condominium during 1899–1956, a period which had significant consequences for the country's later and present development. Sections 4 and 5 shed some light on the post-independence political evolution, including the Islamization of the country in the 1990s, the arrival of the AQ leader, Osama bin Laden (OBL) and his colleagues to Sudan in 1992, and international consequences of these developments. Section 6 provides a detailed description of Sudan's counter radicalization and De-rad procedures, while Section 7 evaluates the outcome of these efforts. The final section summarizes and concludes.

Background: Sudan before independence and the rise of the Mehdi Rebellion

Mongaybay (2012) is one of very few sources that documents most of the key developments in Sudan's pre-independence period. Throughout history, Sudan has been divided between two main heritages: the Arab Muslim heritage in the North (Sudan today) and the African, Christian heritage in the South (known as Southern Sudan since 2011). These divisions are based on ethnic, religious and racial differences, and they continue to affect Sudanese political, economic and social developments today. Islam and Arabization spread very gradually in Sudan, taking almost 1,000 years to dominate Sudanese society. It was not before the 16th century that Muslims came to constitute the majority in this country, although the coming of Islam also facilitated the division of the country into Muslim North and Christian South (Mongaybay, 2012).

In 1820 Sudan fell under the direct control of Egypt's Mohammed Ali Pasha, approved by the Turkish Sultan in Istanbul. In 1821 a new government was formed in Sudan, after Ali Pasha's troops defeated, pursued and dispersed the Mamelukes and their followers in Sudan. The new government, which became known as the Turkiyah or Turkish regime, initially proved disastrous to Sudan, and later set the stage for the emergence of the first national rebellion, the Al-Mehdi rebellion, in the late 1880s:

> Soldiers lived off the land and exacted exorbitant taxes from the population. They also destroyed many ancient Meroitic pyramids searching for hidden gold. Furthermore, slave trading increased, causing many of the inhabitants of the fertile Al Jazirah, heartland of Funj, to flee to escape the slave traders. (Mongaybay, 2012)

As its economic situation deteriorated after the 1860s, Egypt's economic difficulties spilled over into Sudan. This meant that Cairo could not only pay less attention, but also afford to transfer fewer resources, to Khartoum, itself suffering from poor economic conditions. The opening of the Suez Canal in the 1860s increased Britain's interest in the region in order to protect its trade and strategic routes to India and the Far East. Khartoum lost direction, the old illegal slave trade was revived and the Sudanese army suffered a lack of equipment and resources. It was within these circumstances that Muhammad Ahmad ibn as Sayyid Abd Allah emerged, determined to expel the Turks from Sudan and restore Islam to its primitive purity (Mongaybay, 2012).

In 1881, Sheikh Ahmad led a rebellion of northern tribes, successfully driving the Egyptians from Sudan. Emboldened by his success, Sheikh Ahmed revealed himself as Al Mahdi al Muntazar ('the awaited guide') sent from God to redeem the faithful and prepare the way for the second coming of the Prophet Isa (Jesus). The Mahdist movement called for return to the *salaf* and for the simplicity of early Islam, abstention from alcohol and tobacco, and the strict seclusion of women. Jihad was soon proclaimed against the Turkiyah by Sheikh Ahmed, who also denounced tax collectors and established a party of his followers, the Ansar. Within a short period of time, the Mahdi managed to attract a large number of followers and to establish an army whose numbers exceeded 60,000 men (Mongaybay, 2012; Arya, 2009, p. 65).

Cairo and London became alert to the increased influence of the Mahdist movement, especially after its advance imperiled communications with Egypt and threatened to cut off military garrisons stationed in and near Khartoum. Attempts to save garrisons and evacuate all foreigners from Sudan ended disastrously. When London eventually decided to send a British-Egyptian army column to Sudan for this purpose on 28 January 1885, the Mahdists had already occupied Khartoum and slaughtered the garrisons which London sought to save. The Mahdists also killed the British governor general, decapitated him, and delivered his head to the Mahdi in his tent. By the end of 1885 the Ansar controlled all of Sudan; only Sawakin, reinforced by Indian army troops, and Wadi Halfa on the northern frontier remained in Anglo-Egyptian hands (Mongaybay, 2012).

The Mahdiyah became known as the first genuine Sudanese nationalist government. Overconfident of his military abilities, the Mahdi maintained that his movement was not simply a religious order that could be accepted or rejected at will, but that it was a universal regime willing and prepared to destroy those who refuse to join and accept its doctrine. Jihad became a *fard ain*, religious duty of every able Muslim, replacing the hajj (pilgrimage to Mecca) as a duty incumbent on the faithful. Zakat (alms-giving) imposed on all citizens became the main source of state revenue.

Sheik Ahmed, however, did not live long enough to see his scheme implemented. Six months after capturing Khartoum he died of typhoid. Internal divisions after his death began undermining the movement, along with ambitious military campaigns. His death ensued in an era of tense regional relations. The successor of the Mahdi, who called himself the Khalifa, the prophet's representative on earth, radicalized the movement further by committing himself to a universal jihad to extend his version of Islam throughout the world. Military campaigns against Ethiopia, Egypt and Eretria took place in 1887, 1889 and 1893. But in 1896, the British and Egyptian allies invaded Sudan and defeated the Mahdist forces in 1898 at the battle of Omdurman, killing more than 11,000 men of the Ansar movement and wounding thousands more. The killing of the Khalifah in November 1899 terminated all organized resistance and subjugated Sudan to the

Anglo-Egyptian Condominium in that year (Mongaybay, 2012; Arya, 2009, p. 65).

Sudan under the Anglo-Egyptian condominium: 1899–1956

Sudan is today facing multiple problems, including a war with the South, civil war in Darfur, serious economic challenges and social disintegration. Jooma (2006, p. 49) states that it is only by understanding the influence of three major narratives that an informed identification of the underlying reasons for the country's multiple difficulties can be appreciated. These are the impact of British colonialism on the creation of Khartoum elites; the rise of Islamism in reaction to elite-driven politics and the eventual manipulation of religious ideology for self-interest; and the rise of a southern-based resistance movement as a response to marginalization by the centre.

Although called the Anglo-Egyptian Condominium, Sudan was in fact 'effectively under the British crown, with Egyptian governance' between 1899 and 1956 (Waller, 2011). The British not only governed Sudan effectively as a colony, but also subjugated the Sudanese to a set of cultures and norms at odds with their own (Waller, 2011).

While in Sudan the British administration initially focused on consolidating its rule in the country as effectively as possible, putting down any rebellions or possible uprisings. It also focused on building a symbol of administration, some state institutions, as well as land, property, tax and criminal and penal codes similar to those implanted in British India. A new Code of Civil Procedures restored the Ottoman law, which separated civil law and sharia, with guidelines provided over the use of sharia and religious courts.

British officers and civilians occupied most high-ranked posts in the administration, with most middle-ranked administrators and officials (including judges) coming from Egypt. The Sudanese had little say in running the affairs of their country and occupied mostly lower-ranked positions in the administration.

Economically the colonial authorities invested little in the development of Sudan. The US Library of Congress (2012a) eloquently summarized the legacy of the British colonial economic policies in Sudan:

Incidental government investment had gone mainly into *ad hoc* projects, such as the construction of cotton gins and oilseed-pressing mills as adjuncts of the irrigation program. A limited amount of rain-fed mechanized farming, similarly on an *ad hoc* basis, had also been developed during World War II. After the war, two development programs – actually lists of proposed investments – were drawn up for the periods 1946–50 and 1951–55. These plans appear to have been a belated effort to broaden the country's economic base in preparation for eventual Sudanese independence. Both programs were seriously hampered by a lack of experienced personnel and materials and had little real impact.

The most damaging and long-lasting influence of the colonial authorities' policies was in the South. Aware of the country's deep ethnic, religious and racial divisions, the British colonial authorities

> exploited ethnic and religious differences as a means to maintain control and they administered the northern and southern provinces separately. The South of Sudan was declared a 'closed area' and was isolated in almost all respects. The essentially Animist and Christian south was held to be more similar to the neighbouring east-African colonies of Kenya, Tanganyika, and Uganda while the predominately Muslim northern Sudan was more similar to Arabic-speaking Egypt. Northerners were prevented from holding positions of power in the south, and trade was discouraged between the two areas. (Arya, 2009, p. 65)

As a result of isolating it completely from the rest of the country, the South remained primitive and backward relative to the North. In addition to a few Arab merchants who controlled the region's limited commercial activities, Arab officials from Khartoum initially controlled the bureaucracy. The colonial government opted then to rule Sudan, both South and North, by indirectly relying on tribal sheikhs and nobles. In the absence of formal social services, Christian missionaries were allowed to prosper in the South and were encouraged to provide social services, including education and operating medical clinics to provide health services to southerners, with government subsidy. In the 1920s, the colonial authorities imposed new restrictions that fomented the South–North divide. Northern Sudanese, for example, were barred from working or entering the South. The British gradually replaced Arab administrators and expelled Arab merchants, thereby severing the South's last economic contacts with the North. The colonial administration also discouraged the spread of Islam, the practice of Arab customs and the wearing of Arab dress. At the same time, the colonial power made efforts to revitalize African customs and tribal life that the slave trade had disrupted. Finally, a 1930 directive stated that blacks in the southern provinces were to be considered a people distinct from northern Muslims and that the region should be prepared for eventual integration with British East Africa (Mongaybay, 2012).

Although Sudanese nationalism began emerging in the 1920s, it gained momentum in the 1940s, particularly during and after the end of the Second World War. Sudanese nationalism was mainly an Arab and Islamic phenomenon arising in, and drawing support from, northern regions and provinces. It was also led by the educated class. They advocated a national government in Khartoum and opposed Britain's policies that prevented the unification of Sudan under an Arab-Islamic regime. Their opposition after 1916, nevertheless, took peaceful means, calling for and relying on such policies as demonstrations and strikes to exert pressure on the colonial administration.

In the 1930s and 1940s, the educated Sudanese revived demands for stronger Sudanese say in their government. In 1942, for example, they organized a quasi-nationalist movement, the Graduates' General Conference, which presented the government with a memorandum that demanded a pledge of self-determination after the end of the Second World War, abolition of the 'closed door' ordinances, an end to the separate curriculum in southern schools, an increase in the number of Sudanese in the civil service, and allowing southerners to seek employment in the North. To allay the fears of the southerners in the South, the nationalists convened in the 1940s at a conference in Juba to assure them that Khartoum would safeguard their political and cultural rights.

London refused the memorandum of the nationalists but agreed to replace its indirect rule in Sudan with a more modern system of local government. It thus established a parliamentary government to administer the unification of North and South in the second half of the 1940s, to replace the advisory executive council which the colonial administration created and staffed in the 1920s to run Sudan.

Weakened by the outcome of the Second World War and subjected to increased Sudanese nationalism, Britain gave in to northern pressure. In 1946 it integrated the South and North together into a single administrative region, without consultation with the southerners. Arabic was made the language of administration in the South and northerners began to hold positions there. Obviously these policies failed to alleviate the problem. After the end of World War II, and to prevent Egypt from gaining total control over Sudan as Britain prepared to leave the colony, London sought to include southerners in a federated government and opened the closed areas (Arya, 2009, p. 65).

In 1956 Sudan gained full independence from Britain. The policies that followed by the nationalist government failed to alleviate the fears of southern leaders that Khartoum's promises to safeguard southern political and cultural rights would be upheld. Several policies implemented by the newly independent state undermined southerners' confidence in such a prospect. Such measures included the nullification of prohibition against Muslim proselytizing in the South and the confirmation of Arabic as the official language of administration. Southerners felt that this latter policy aimed at depriving the few educated English-speaking southerners the opportunity to enter public service. Fearing subjugation by the Muslim North, many in the Christian and animist South formed a guerilla insurgency to combat the new political authority. 'The hostility of southerners toward the northern Arab majority surfaced violently when southern army units mutinied in August 1955 to protest their transfer to garrisons under northern officers. The rebellious troops killed several hundred northerners, including government officials, army officers, and merchants' (Mongaybay, 2012. Also see Arya, 2009, p. 65).

To sum up, violent extremism is not a totally new phenomenon to Sudan. Whether under the Mamelukes, the Turks, the Mahdists or even the British, violent extremism occurred in several phases in pre-independent Sudan. Yet the level and amount committed by state and non-state actors after independence in 1956 is not matched in the history of Sudan. To this we now turn.

Post-independence: civil war, destruction and Islamization

In 1956 Sudan emerged as the first, largest, democratic and independent republic in Africa. It inherited from the colonial power, however, a weak economic foundation, fragile industrial base, poor infrastructure, mostly illiterate and untrained population, and immense animosity between the Arab Muslim northerners of Sudan (the base of the government) and the black Africans of the South, who have mainly Christian or animist beliefs. Common sense suggested that the focus of the newly independent state would be on building the country's weak infrastructure, establishing a strong economic foundation, diversifying the country's narrow economic base and providing health and education to a largely impoverished and illiterate population. Instead, the birth of the Republic of Sudan in 1956 was marred by violence and violent extremism (VEm). As the South anticipated domination by the North following the departure of the British in 1953, southern resentment to northern Muslim Arab domination culminated in a mutiny among southern troops in the British Equatorial Corps and local police in the Equatorial Province of Torit. These troops were angry at what they saw as Khartoum's failure to live up to its promise to Great Britain and create a federal system after the British troops departed Sudan. When Khartoum took a decision to transfer southern troops' garrisons under northern officers in August 1955, southern army units mutinied in protest and killed several hundred northerners, including government officials, army officers and merchants. The Sudanese government reacted quickly and ruthlessly suppressed the revolt. It later executed around 70 southerners for sedition. Khartoum's harsh response not only failed to pacify the South, but gave the Sudanese army a bad reputation as being brutal and an enemy of the South. Worse, some of the mutineers escaped to remote areas and organized resistance to the Arab-dominated government of Sudan. The 1955 mutiny marked the beginning of a long conflict, the first phase of which came to be known as the 'First Sudanese Civil War, also known as Anyanya rebellion or Anyanya I' (Arya, 2009, p. 66).

The conflict with the South has had far more consequences for Sudan. Not only did it shape Sudan's post-independence evolution and history, it also retarded the country's social, institutional and economic development. It also encouraged political instability and led to an endless cycle of weak, ineffective and corrupt military and civilian governments unable to solve the country's social, economic, ethnic and political problems. Sudan, at least until 1989, was ruled by a succession of unstable civilian and military governments which paid more attention to wars, divisions and enriching itself and its cronies than to building a strong Sudanese economy, lifting the Sudanese out of poverty, and developing and prospering the country. One of the most notorious rulers of Sudan was Colonel Jafaar an Nimeiri, 1969–85.

Nimeiri came to power as a result of a military coup supported by the communists and Marxist nationalists. He and the other officers who led the 1969 coup called themselves 'Free Officers' influenced by the Nasserism of Egypt. Nimeiri justified the coup by the inability of the previous civilian government to make important decisions and to solve the country's economic, social and southern problems. He immediately stopped democracy, banned all political parties, purged the government and army of potential opposition and suspended the temporary constitution in place since independence. He also established a Revolutionary Command Council (RCC) to run the country and manned it with his own men. Nimeiri also relied, initially, on communists and Marxist elements for his newly appointed 21 Cabinet members since the administration lacked resources and technical capacity and the communists were the most educated and skilled in the country. At least half of the Cabinet was made up of communists and Marxists who shaped the main policies of the state. A provisional constitution, published in August 1971, described Sudan as a 'socialist democracy' and provided for a presidential form of government to replace the RCC. A plebiscite in September 1971 elected Nimeiri to a six-year term as president (Mongaybay, 2012).

Nimeiri perceived conservative elements, particular the Ansaris and Mahdists, as his arch-enemies and sought to eradicate them. In one incident in the early 1970s, Nimeiri's troops killed more than 3,000 Mahdists and Ansarists. To consolidate his power base in the South, Nimeiri signed a peace agreement in 1972 with southern leaders which temporarily ended the first civil war after independence and made some movement towards federalism.[1] This was followed by a new Constitution, also in 1972, which not only cited Islam as Sudan's official religion, but also acknowledged Christianity as the faith of a large number of Sudanese citizens.

But Nimeiri's schizophrenic rule soon led him to turn against communists and Marxists. Not unlike other Arab regimes, he sought to do this through rapprochement with conservatives and traditionalist Islamists, as well as arresting, exiling and pursuing communists. Nimeiri then established a one-party system, the Sudan Socialist Union (SSU), which assumed control over all other political parties and movements in the country. He also nationalized many businesses, banks and financial institutions, and made statism or massive government intervention in the economy the norm in an attempt to control all aspects of society. As Jooma (2006, p. 50) wrote:

> Jafaar An-Nimeiri came to power through the support of the Communist Party in the 1969 coup, which was heavily influenced by Nasser's Free Officers' Movement in Egypt. Later, however, he moved to institutionalizing Islamic Shariah law and placed more emphasis on pan-Arabism in the face of diminishing support for his rule.

An important development occurred in 1978 which was to change Khartoum's policies towards the South forever: oil was discovered in the South. Nimeiri and successive administrations became reluctant to offer further concessions to the South and, in fact, sought further control over the southern region. In 1979, to consolidate the support of the conservatives behind his policies, Nimeiri appointed Dr Hassan al-Turabi, a founding member of the Sudanese Muslim Brotherhood in 1954, as Justice Minister. Al-Turabi was committed to the Islamization of Sudan and saw the South as an integral part of the country. His four-year tenure as a minister of justice saw a growing Islamic fundamentalist presence in the capital, Khartoum. Nimeiri began violating the peace terms with the South and in 1983 declared all of Sudan an Islamic state. This marked the beginning of what came to be known as the 'Second Sudanese Civil War' which is 'considered by many to be little more than an extension of the first war' (Waller, 2011. Also see Mamdani, 2009, p. 194).

Islamization of Sudan under al-Bashir and al-Turabi

Two years later, in 1985, a military coup deposed Nimeiri and terminated his regime and his one-party system. A transitional military year followed which restored parliamentary elections in 1986. Three major political groups competed in the elections, which represented the main political currents in the country at the time: Umma Party led by Sadiq el-Mahdi, the Democratic Unionist Party and the National Islamic Front (NIF) dominated by the Muslim Brotherhood (MB). The latter emerged as the most powerful Islamic current in the country in the 1980s.

As Owen (1992, pp. 182–3) has shown, the MB in Sudan operated in an arena dominated by two large sectarian Islamic groupings: the Ansar and the Khatmiyya, both with their associated parties that dominated the communalistic politics of the country between periods of military regimes. Dr Hassan al-Turabi artfully used his charisma and leadership skills to promote the ideas and ideology of the MB. In the mid-1970s he established the NIF for that purpose, exploiting a split between Ansaris and Khatmiyyas. He also exploited Nimeiri's reconciliation with the opposition in the 1970s to participate closely with his regime. This allowed him to obtain important posts in the administrative and educational systems, to carve out some positions for his supporters and NIF members, and then to win a substantial number of seats in the 1980 parliamentary elections, thus giving the MB more scope to spread its ideology.

As a result, al-Turabi managed to convince Nimeiri in 1983 to introduce sections of the sharia laws, profiting from the rise of tension with non-Muslims in the South. The NIF soon positioned itself as the main implementer and protector of sharia. Its position was further strengthened as a result of some sharia principles which outlawed interests to the Sudanese banking system and paved the way for the tremendous expansion of Islamic banking that provided the Front with major sources of funds (Owen, 1992, pp. 182–3).

By the mid-1980s, however, NIF's relations with Nimeiri's regime became sour over his refusal to introduce more sharia laws and a conciliatory policy towards the South. In 1985, the NIF participated in a failed coup against Nimeiri, a fact which suggests that al-Turabi and his movement advocated revolutionary, rather than peaceful, change. In addition to the Islamization of Sudan, a unified Sudan under a centralized government in Khartoum, and al-Turabi advocated non-southern-conciliatory tone. The departure of Nimeiri in 1986, as a result of another military coup, served al-Turabi and the NIF well; both had been clearly excluded from Nimeiri's government after the failed military coup in 1985. This change allowed the NIF to participate in the subsequent 1986 elections and to obtain enough seats and a powerful position in the coalition government that was then formed, enabling them to not only to block any possible move towards withdrawing sharia laws, but also to adopt a conciliatory position towards anti-government revolt in the South (Owen, 1992, pp. 182–3).

The NIF was thus able to make maximum use of growing polarization in Sudanese politics which the NIF itself contributed to. It sought to present everything in terms of Islamic sharia/non-Islamic, secular Sudanese or Christian. They came to be seen as protectors of and implementers of sharia, the main guarantor of the unity of Sudan and the main opponent of any policy aimed at granting concessions to non-Muslims in the South. This allowed the NIF to play a powerful role in the new military government that took office in 1989, led by Colonel al-Bashir (Owen, 1992, p. 183). The fact that southern rebels were heavily supported by such countries as Israel and the United States contributed to the NIF's policies and allowed it to present itself as such.

Omar al-Bashir consolidated his position in power by enacting a new government, appointing himself as the chairman of the legislative branch, prime minister, commander of the armed forces and minister of defence. The skilful al-Turabi, by now the ideological leader of NIF, quickly allied himself with al-Bashir. By the end of 1990, al-Turabi and the NIF had sufficient influence to persuade al-Bashir in March 1991 to announce a new version of the sharia law as it related to religiously defined criminal offences. They were not able, however, to persuade al-Bashir to establish a full Islamic state, for which they had been pressing (Owen, 1992, p. 183; Waller, 2011; Arya, 2006). This further aggravated relations with the South and gave al-Bashir a pretext to arrest the nascent democracy restored in 1986. Along with introducing national-level Islamic law, and as relations with the South worsened, al-Bashir also suspended all political parties in 1991 (Dagne, 2006, p. 2; Mamdani, 2009, p. 194; Waller, 2011).

The true colours of the NIF became clearer after the alliance of the movement with al-Bashir in the late 1980s and early 1990s. 'Al-Bashir and al-Turabi were considered to be politically and ideologically aligned. ... During the decade or so of mutual cooperation, President al-Bashir and Dr al-Turabi landscaped the country of Sudan into a hotbed for terrorism and Islamist ideology' (Waller, 2011. Also see Mamdani, 2009). General Bashir and al-Turabi promised to turn Sudan into an Islamic state. Political parties were suspended. The mentor of General al-Bashir

> in this enterprise was Hassan al-Turabi, the founder of the National Islamic Front (NIF) and the head of the Muslim Brotherhood, formally known as the al Ikhwan Al-Moslemoon. They began institutionalising sharia law in the northern part of Sudan. A new Islamic penal code was promulgated in 1991 and more zealous regulations followed in 1996. Turabi also had ambitions to turn Sudan into a hive of pan-Islamic activities. In 1991, he established the Popular Arab and Islamic Conference (PAIC) in Khartoum as a pan-Islamic front to resist America's 'recolonisation' of the Islamic world.

What happened then, Islamization and al-Qaedization of Sudan, is of special significance to the goals and objectives of this chapter. It deserves to be studied specifically in a separate section.

The arrival of Bin Laden and al-Qaedization of Sudan

Following alignment of ideological and political stands in the late 1980s and early 1990s between al-Bashir and al-Turabi, Sudan followed an open-door policy, allowing any Muslim or Islamist who wished to come into the country to enter without a visa. Many were invited personally by the Sudanese government to move into Sudan. This was a time when the Afghan war between the Mujahedeen and Russian forces was drawing to an end; thousands of Mujahedeen were being pursued by the United States and their allies and were thus looking for a refuge. Some Algerian, Tunisian, Egyptian and other Islamic activists returning from Afghanistan were given diplomatic passports. Sudan also began openly supporting the Palestinian Liberation Organization, and later Hamas, against Israel's occupation and human rights violations in the

Occupied Territories, a position that earned Khartoum the wrath of the US government. Sudan even hosted such notorious individuals as Ilich Ramirez Sanchez, better known as Carlos the Jackal, who found shelter in the country before being abducted in August 1994 from Khartoum in a joint French and US intelligence operation by the DST and CIA (Arya, 2009, pp. 67–8).

One of the most distinguished guests hosted by Khartoum was Osama bin Laden (OBL). The Sudanese government not only invited OBL to move to Sudan, but also offered him special privileges and tax exemptions to invest in the country. He divided his time vigorously between business and jihadi activities. According to one source, OBL operated more than 80 businesses and charities while in Sudan (Sandee, 2011). It was also alleged that OBL established an estimated 23 militant training camps and bases of operations whose existence was vehemently denied by the Sudanese government (Sandee, 2011; Waller, 2009).

Arya (2009, p. 68) gave an indication about the size and activities of the businesses and other operations which OBL undertook while in Sudan:

> His [OBL] construction company built a gleaming new highway from Khartoum to Port Sudan. He traded in agricultural commodity exports and invested over US$50 million in Sudan's Al Shamal Islamic Bank. Osama bin Laden's companies and financial enterprises were allowed by the Sudan government to import goods without inspection or payment of taxes. Osama also spent two million dollars to fly Arab *mujahedeen* from Pakistan to Sudan, and built at his own expense 30 training camps in Sudan. It is estimated that over 5,000 *mujahedeen* were trained in these camps by 1994, while they also worked on Osama's construction and agricultural projects on the sidelines.

In addition to inviting OBL, the Sudanese government, suffering from bankruptcy as a result of widespread corruption, increased costs of civil war in the South and collapse of communism in the late 1980s that resulted in reduction of Russian aid to Khartoum, shifted its regional strategy and began forming relations with Iran. By 1991 the two countries had strong economic, political and military ties. According to Waller (2011), Iran began stationing troops in Sudan to train paramilitary, mujahideen and jihadist forces. Sudan, in a very short period of time, 'became viewed as the strategic outpost for the export of Islamic revolution throughout the African continent', with which Arya (2009, p. 67) is in concord. He writes that the relationship between Sudan and

> Iran allowed Turabi to broker a series of meetings between Osama bin Laden and senior leaders of Hezbollah and Iranian intelligence. According to the US indictment of Laden, the Al-Qaeda officials met with an Iranian religious official in Khartoum as part of an overall effort to arrange a tripartite agreement between Al-Qaeda, the NIF and elements of the government of Iran to work together against the US, Israel and other Western countries.

Not surprisingly, the Iranian President described Sudan as 'the vanguard of the Islamic Revolution in the African continent' (Sandee, 2011, p. 67; Waller, 2011). According to the same sources, Tehran also used Sudan as a secure transit point and meeting site for Iranian-based extremist groups.

During the 1990s, therefore, Sudan became a major exporter of international terrorism. Its name was linked to several international terrorist activities and incidents, directly and indirectly, including the first World Trade Center bombing in 1993 and the failed assassination attempt on Egyptian President Hosni Mubarak as he was leaving the African Union Summit meeting in Addis Ababa, Ethiopia in 1995. Allegedly, Sudan's trained al-Qaeda instructors were sent to Somalia and their foot soldiers confronted the Task Force Rangers of the United States in Mogadishu on 3 October 1993 in a grim battle popularly known as Black Hawk Down. Even after OBL was forced to leave Sudan in 1996, the bombings by AQ of American embassies in Kenya and Tanzania, killing 263 people and injuring over 5,000 in August 1998, were also linked to Sudan (BBC News, 1999; Waller, 2011; Sandee, 2011; Shinn, 2009, p. 60).

These activities have had far-reaching consequences for Sudan, its government and its people. In 1993 the Clinton administration listed Sudan as a 'state sponsor of terrorism', followed by a UN Security Council which imposed sanctions on Sudan. Following the 1998 bombings of American embassies in Kenya and Tanzania, President Bill Clinton, in retaliation, ordered a missile strike on the Al Shifa pharmaceutical plant in Khartoum, charging that the site was being used by bin Laden and other terrorists to make VX nerve gas and other chemical weapons (Arya, 2009, p. 68; Waller, 2011).

While Sudan was exporting terrorism in the 1990s, it was receiving a great deal of it as well. The country became both an exporter and importer of violent extremism. With Islamization and al-Qaedization of the country, southern rebellions, supported clandestinely by the Israeli and US governments, led by the opposition National Democratic Alliance (NDA), began intensifying their military activities against Khartoum. They also began operations close to the Eritrean border. A major offensive by the rebels in January 1997 from Eritrea led to them capturing a huge area in the South. Unsettled by these developments, Khartoum retaliated by launching a massive attack against the rebellions (BBC, 1999). Both southern rebels and Sudanese troops committed atrocities, human rights violations and violent extremism (Infoplease, 2012; Mongaybay, 2012; Reeves, 2011). But the burden, thanks to the powerful media resources and commanding propagandist campaign of a superpower that behind the scenes favours one party over the other, fell completely on Khartoum. Only Khartoum was 'accused by international aid agencies of bombing hospitals' and schools in southern towns and villages (BBC, 1999).

By the early years of the 21st century, 'the Second Civil War or Anyanya II', which was led by a rebel leader, John Garang, and started in 1983, cost millions of lives and displaced individuals, as well as billions of wasted dollars to meet the financial needs of the war. According to Dagne, CR-2, the second phase of the civil war, which was simply an extension of the first phase, caused the deaths, either directly or through famine and disease, of an estimated two million Sudanese, and the displacement of more than four million, mostly from the South. 'Regarding the period from 1955 to 2005 as a single war with intermittent ceasefires, the Sudanese conflict is considered the longest-running civil war in history. The half century of fighting claimed more civilian deaths than any war since World War II' (Waller, 2011).

Officially, the civil war ended in 2005, with the signing between Khartoum and the Sudan People's Liberation Movement (SPLM) of the Naivasha Accords, also known as the Comprehensive Peace Agreement (CPA). The CPA incorporated SPLM into the Government of National Unity (GNU) and created a schedule for 2009 national elections and a referendum in 2011. To support the implementation of the CPA, Khartoum was forced to accept a United Nations mission, called UNMIS, which moved into the South in March 2005 (Arya, 2009, p. 66). It is also important to note here that the Bush administration was a significant factor behind the 2005 CPA. As Reeves (2011) wrote: 'The Bush administration ... can rightly claim the CPA as a signature foreign policy achievement. ...' The way the CPA was ramped down and implemented has had, and will have, far-reaching consequences for the security of Sudan and the African region, as we shall see in the final section of this chapter.

As if the war with the South was not destructive enough, another war, now known as 'Sudan's third civil war', erupted in Darfur in 2003–4 (Reeves, 2011). The Darfur conflict has become one of the most contentious, controversial and debatable conflicts in recent times. Like beauty, the cause of the Darfur conflict is in the eyes of the beholder, with US, Israeli and international humanitarian agencies blaming Khartoum and its pro-government militias called the Janjaweed, and more friendly nations taking a more pro-government stand. As Faris (2007) stated, the true causes of the Darfur conflict have 'been profoundly misunderstood'. Some trace the problem 'back to the mid-1980s, before the violence between African and Arab began to simmer' (Faris, 2007). Others trace the root cause of the conflict back to more than one hundred years ago, to the colonial era, when Darfur, formerly an independent sultanate, was integrated into Anglo-Egyptian Sudan in 1922 without consultation with the main stakeholders (Infoplease, 2012; Mongaybay, 2012). Waller (2011) is in accord with this line of argument: 'Darfur, a region in western Sudan, is yet another example of arbitrary national boundaries across ethnic lines. Formerly an independent sultanate, Darfur was integrated into Anglo-Egyptian Sudan in 1922' without any consultation with Darfurians. Some saw the origins of the Darfur conflict to lie behind the nature of the 'evolution of ethnic and religious identities', while others saw 'the breakdown of local administration, the emergence of Arab militia and resistance movements, and regional dimensions to the conflict' as important explanatory factors (de Waal, 2007). Finally, *The European Journal of Development Research* (2005) attributed the conflict to 'regional marginalization', rather than simply 'racial or religious discrimination' as lying behind the January 2004 rebellion in Darfur, which sparked the conflict and led the Sudanese government not only to quell the rebellion, but also to allow pro-government militias, called the Janjaweed, to carry out massacres against black villagers and rebel groups in the region.

Perhaps all of the above-mentioned factors combined contributed to the ongoing Darfur conflict. Two things, however, are important to remember about the Darfur conflict. First, while the war in the South was fought against black Christians and Animists, the Darfur conflict is being fought against black Muslims. This does not support the thesis that the Darfur conflict is caused merely by religious differences. Attempts to solve the conflict based on racial and religious grounds will make a bad situation worse and will have far-reaching consequences for the security of Sudan, the African continent and beyond.[2] Second, and regardless of the true causes of the conflict, Darfur has created the world's worst humanitarian disaster. Since it erupted in 2004 the conflict has claimed the lives of 200,000–300,000 civilians and displaced more than one million (Infoplease, 2012). 'Although violence was the main cause of death during 2004, diseases have been the cause of most deaths since 2005, with displaced populations being the most susceptible' (Degomme and Guha-Sapir, 2010, p. 294). The Darfur conflict requires immediate attention by the international community, one based on true, balanced and impartial understanding of the real causes of the conflict, which has been described as the 'most notorious violence' in the history of Sudan (Waller, 2011), and the 'World's worst ... humanitarian disaster' (Infoplease, 2012). 'Any reduction in humanitarian assistance could lead to worsening mortality rates, as was the case between mid-2006 and mid-2007' (Degomme and Guha-Sapir, 2010, p. 294).

Like the war in the South, the Darfur conflict has also brought disastrous consequences for the Sudanese government and people. The European Union and the United States, for example, have described the killings in Darfur as genocide. This was followed by a UN Security Council resolution, which blamed Khartoum for the atrocities committed in Darfur and strongly criticized its officials, demanding that Sudan stop the Arab militias immediately (Infoplease, 2012). In February 2007, the International Criminal Court at The Hague named two Sudanese high-ranking officials, Ahmad Harun, Sudan's deputy minister for humanitarian affairs, and Ali Kushayb, also known as Ali Abd-al-Rahman, as suspects in the murder, rape and displacement of thousands of civilians in the Darfur region. In May, the Court issued arrest warrants for Haroun and Ali Kosheib, a Janjaweed leader, charging them with mass murder, rape and other crimes. In July 2010 the ICC charged President al-Bashir himself with genocide and issued an arrest warrant against him. It was the first time the court has charged an incumbent head of a state with genocide. Finally, the US government expanded sanctions on Sudan in May 2007, banning 31 Sudanese companies and four individuals from doing business in the United States and banning US firms from doing business in Sudan, with serious consequences for the Sudanese economy (Infoplease, 2012).

It is against this background, one characterized by a prolonged civil war in the South, notorious conflict in the western region (Darfur), financial bankruptcy, economic challenges, high poverty and illiteracy, a weakened and over-stretched administration due to widespread corruption and conflicts in various parts of the country, severe international embargo and high-ranking officials, including the president himself, indicted for war crimes, that Sudan launched some form of de-radicalization efforts, preceded by ad hoc counter-radicalization measures.

International pressure, de-Qaedization, de-radicalization and rehabilitation

Over the past ten years or so, several Islamic currents have come to dominate the Sudanese political system, these are not mutually exclusive and overlap in many areas. There are at least four currents. First is The Sudanese Islamic Movement (ISM), which is an extension of the Muslim Brotherhood Movement and is the largest Islamic movement in Sudan today. The ISM also includes some members of the NIF and the Ruling Party (National Congress Party – NCP – which appropriated Islam from NIF in the late 1990s). To this current should also be added The Sunnah Al-Ansar Group. The National Conference is today an amalgamation of all Islamic currents in Sudan, embracing a large number of all Islamic movements' members, including the above-mentioned movements, as well as traditional Salafi and Sufi movements (see below). It is seen as the general umbrella that incorporates all walks of political life, including Islamist, secular, nationalists, Sufis and traditional Salafists. All of these movements, more or less, are incorporated in the political system, accept the state as the main arbiter of political differences, denounce violence and defend the status quo of the political system.

Second, the Traditional Salafi movement, which is also incorporated in the political system and is part of the National Conference ruling party. Hence they reject violence and accept the state as providing the main space for political manoeuvre and competition between all players in the political game. The movement represents the most common, traditional form of Islam in Sudan.

Third, the Traditional Sufi current. This current focuses on learning and memorizing the Quran, as well as carrying out intensive and extensive prayers on an almost daily basis. They are peaceful, apolitical and do not involve themselves much with politics, unlike almost all the movements mentioned earlier.

Finally is what the Sudanese officials call *al-Salafiyah al-Ilmeyah* (Scientific Salafism). The group is also known as *al takfir walhejra*, which is a minority but represents the most dangerous kind of Islamic currents in Sudan today. The movement believes in organized, clandestine and violent activities. Its members adopt a *takfiri* ideology that excommunicates everyone else. The movement operates clandestinely and finds fertile ground mostly in scientific departments of some universities and colleges. A former member of the movement described it in the following words:

> The *Salafiyeh al-Ilmeyah* consists of those who are calling for the literal interpretation of the Quran and the Sunna. They excommunicate everyone else, including state officials, security personnel, the state, society and even some of their own members. They are chiefly present in universities and particularly in scientific colleges like engineering, medical and technical departments because whoever wants to study humanities, say at Aum Durman University, must memorize at least three parts of the Quran. In the Quranic universities, students have to memorize even ten parts of the Quran, which makes them very knowledgeable in Islam. But this is not required in scientific colleges. Therefore they target scientific colleges because students there are clever and smart but have little understanding of religion, which makes them more vulnerable to radical ideology than those who study Quran very well in Aum Dorman and the Quraanic universities. (Personal interview, Khartoum, January 2012. Also interview with a high-ranking official at the NSID.)

Sudanese officials give two reasons for the emergence of the *takfiri* brand of Salafism in Sudan. The first is external and relates to the imbalanced international relations and justice system, which, they argue, is characterized by double standards practiced by the West towards Muslim causes. Examples include Palestine, South Sudan, Iraq, Afghanistan, Somalia, Chechnya and Bosnia. The second is internal, pertaining to a belief on behalf of *takfiris* that most Muslim rulers are agents serving the interests of Western imperialist states. They see most Muslim rulers as no more than an instrument in the hands of the West through whom Muslim resources are being stolen in return for keeping rulers in power. Weak intellectual ability of youth, severed relationships between them and moderate *fuqaha* and scholars, and reliance on external fatwas issued by incompetent radicals were also deemed as important reasons for youth's deviation from the right path.

It can be argued that Sudan's counterterrorism strategy (CTS) which started more than a decade ago, has been gradual and remains incomplete. The country's CTS can be divided into four main parts: De-Qaedization of Sudan, which includes measures to restore Sudan to the international community (pre-De-rad); De-rad measures, which focused on a small number of detained individuals and involved dialogue with them, studying their social-economic characteristics, and understanding motivation and reasons behind their radicalization; post-release rehabilitation and reintegration measures; and counter radicalization efforts. The following sub-sections shed some light on each of these processes/procedures separately.

De-Qaedization of Sudan

By the mid-1990s, Sudan was increasingly under international and regional pressure to take action against OBL and his colleagues. The country's name had become strongly linked and associated with terrorism, a fact which led the US government to list Sudan as a state sponsor of terrorism and the UN Security Council to impose crippling sanctions on Sudan. Sudan was becoming increasingly isolated internationally and regionally, with pressure from the United States, Egypt and Saudi Arabia in particular causing more hardship and economic suffering for most Sudanese. The pressure on Khartoum increased especially following an assassination attempt against former Egyptian President Hosni Mubarak in Addis Ababa in 1995 and terrorist attacks in Saudi Arabia in 1995–6. Economically, too, Sudan was facing harsh international sanctions, crippling its international trade (trade collapsed in the 1990s), with a high level of public debt as well as a very high level of inflation that suffocated most Sudanese. The country even became bankrupt, no longer able to serve or repay its foreign debt, while the war in the South drained the treasury, absorbing most of the country's resources and increasing the country's foreign debt tremendously. Sudan was in desperate need of financial and technical assistance from the IMF and other international financial institutions, in addition to restoring its international political and trade relations, all of which could be facilitated by the US government. At the same time, the US government was becoming more aggressive towards Sudan and prepared to take action against Khartoum, which it did in 1998 when it ordered a missile strike on the Al Shifa pharmaceutical plant, following the August 1998 al-Qaeda bombings of American embassies in Kenya and Tanzania.

The resulting regional and international pressure on Sudan, as well as economic and financial needs of the country, led Khartoum to take significant measures to limit the presence of violent extremists and terrorists on its soil. It started by expelling OBL and his colleagues from Sudan in 1996, a fact which deeply upset OBL:

OBL was expelled from Sudan in 1996. He was extremely disappointed and criticized the Sudanese government fiercely for expelling him. He was largely disappointed that a government claiming to be Muslim expelled him and let him down. When in Sudan, he had a farm and invested heavily in infrastructure, dams, farms, roads, schools and had a construction company called *al-Hijrah*. After expelling him, the Sudanese government expropriated all of his money, property and investments. He was invited to go to Afghanistan and left millions behind, which the Sudanese government stole and cleaned up. (Interview with Dr Hassan al-Turabi, Al-Jazeerah Channel, 'I knew bin Laden', 29 June 2012)

Since the 1996 expulsion of OBL, 'Sudan made significant progress in limiting the terrorist presence inside its borders, despite contradictory pressures in the government and conflicts within the country' (Waller, 2011). Following OBL's expulsion, relations between al-Turabi and al-Bashir began deteriorating and taking a negative turn. Ever since al-Bashir's military takeover in 1989, it was al-Turabi who had 'been the *de facto* ruler of Sudan, the cleric and political leader who was a major figure in the pan-Arabic Islamic fundamentalist resurgence'. In 1999, al-Bashir ousted al-Turabi and placed him under house arrest, freeing him five years later in 2003. Since then al-Turabi himself toned down his rhetoric and sought rapprochement and reconciliation with the West (Arya, 2009, p. 65. Also see Waller, 2009; Infoplease, 2012).

The Sudanese government has also 'worked to disrupt foreign fighters from using Sudan as a logistics base and transit point *en route* to Iraq' and Afghanistan. Four years after ejecting OBL, Khartoum 'began uprooting al-Qaeda bases in Sudan' and signalled its willingness to cooperate with the international community to counter terrorism in the country, African continent and elsewhere (Bhattacharji, 2008). Bhattacharji (2008) comprehensively summarized Sudan's regional and international counterterrorism efforts in this period:

In 2000, the United States and Sudan entered into a counter-terrorism dialogue, prompting Sudan to close down the Popular Arab and Islamic Conference, which had been functioning as a forum for terrorists. In May 2003, Sudanese authorities raided a suspect terrorist training camp in Kurdufan State, arresting more than a dozen extremists and seizing illegal weapons. Four months later, a Sudanese court convicted a Syrian engineer and two Sudanese nationals of training a group of Saudis, Palestinians, and others to carry out attacks in Iraq, Eritrea, Sudan, and Israel. In August 2004, Sudanese authorities arrested, prosecuted, and convicted Eritreans who had hijacked a Libyan aircraft and forced it to land in Khartoum. Of the twelve major international conventions and protocols against terrorism, Sudan has ratified eleven.[3] Sudan has also worked with neighboring states to combat terrorism in the region. In 2003, Sudan ratified the African Union's Convention on the Prevention and Combating of Terrorism (PDF), and by the end of the year, the Sudanese government had signed additional counter-terrorism agreements with Algeria, Yemen, and Ethiopia. In 2004, Sudan co-hosted a regional workshop with the United Nations Office on Drugs and Crime on terrorism and transnational crime. Sudan has also worked to mediate peace between Uganda and the Lord's Resistance Army, a rebel group that has terrorized civilians in an effort to overthrow the Ugandan government.

The international community, after charging Sudan with harbouring terrorists and sponsoring terrorism, began acknowledging Khartoum's efforts and 'commended Sudan for its counterterrorism practices'. In 2001, for example, the UN Security Council lifted its terrorism-related sanctions against Sudan. In May 2004, the US government removed Sudan 'from a list of countries that were not fully cooperating in U.S. antiterrorism efforts'. After Sudan agreed to the CPA with the South, 'In 2005, the U.S. State Department reported that al-Qaeda elements had not been present in Sudan with the knowledge and consent of the Sudanese government since 2000'. In 2007, 'the U.S. State Department called Sudan a "strong partner in the War on Terror", and praised Sudan for aggressively pursuing terrorist operations that threatened U.S. interests'. By 2007, 'the U.S. State Department reported that, with the exception of Hamas, the Sudanese government did not openly support the presence of terrorists in Sudan' (all quotations from Bhattacharji, 2008).

De-radicalization program

The De-radicalization (De-rad) program started inside detention centres in November 2007 and lasted until December 2008, 13 months. According to Sudanese officials, the motivation behind the De-rad program was 'realization that security measures which are often accompanied with repression and torture are neither the means nor the ideal method to fight extremism and radicalization in society'. 'Soft' measures, including dialogue and good treatment in other Muslim states, they add, have proved their effectiveness in convincing a large number of groups and individuals to repent and steer clear of VEm.

The Sudanese De-rad program is initially an intelligence-led program. Following their arrest, detainees are isolated in individual cells first for 45 days, without trial, without mixing with other inmates and without dialogue. This period is used to extract information from and about the detainees. It is also used as a kind of space given by the authorities to the detainees to allow them to rethink, reconsider and revise their ideology, methods and activities in the hopes that they will repent. The Sudanese law allows arrest without trial for up to six months (one month initially which can be increased to 45 days, three months and then to six months as a maximum period after which the detainee has to be released, unless tried).[4] Most individuals do not stay for six months and spend one to three months in prison at most. Only the most radical elements that refuse to repent and refuse to participate in the De-rad program usually spend up to six months in prison. Dialogue, as part of the De-rad program, starts only after the end of the 45 days, which each detainee spends in his individual cell, after first going through an individual revision process.[5]

Seventy-nine individuals (detainees) participated in the De-rad program, hereafter referred to as participants. The National Security and Intelligence Department (NSID) is fully in charge of the program through its newly established Counter Terrorism Unit (CTU). The NSID and CTU design policies of the program, supervise its implementation and coordinate with other state and non-state institutions involved in the realization of the objectives of the program, particularly the Ministries of Religious Affairs and Education and Civil Society Organizations (CSOs). Three types of individuals qualify for the De-rad program; participants in jihad activities in Afghanistan, Iraq, Somalia and elsewhere; sympathizers with AQ ideology and those sympathizers who went beyond sympathy to provide some kind of service to VEts or would-be VEts. Those who commit/committed a crime or murder are excluded from the program and are sent to court for trial instead.

Sudanese officials, as a result of their intelligence-led approach, have compiled a large set of data and information on the social and demographic characteristics of the 79 participants in the De-rad program. With regard to military activities, for example, four of the 79 participants participated in jihad in Afghanistan, five in Iraq, 34 attempted to travel to Somalia, Afghanistan or Iraq but were arrested in the process, and 36 found jihadi ideology appealing and admired it – had they not been arrested they would have probably been manipulated to join some jihadi activities (Graph 1, Appendix).

Participants have also been classified according to their level of radicalization, and not just by military operations committed or attempted. Group A is made up of the 19 most 'hard-core' elements. They represent the leadership (leaders) of the group who are very radical and *takfireyeen* (excommunicate everyone else); 31 (Group B) were influenced by Group A but were not as radical yet. They do not excommunicate everyone else but joined the group because they do not agree with some or all of the policies of the state and hence became sympathizers with Group A. The final Group C, 29 individuals, were weak believers in AQ ideology and ideas, what officials call 'normal' individuals drawn into the group for various social, economic and family issues (Graph 2. Also see Table 1, which divides detainees according to the leader of their group).

With regard to age group, most participants, as is the case elsewhere, were relatively young. Only seven of the 79 participants were born during the period 1950–60; 12 were born between 1961–70; 23 were born between 1971–80; and 37 were born between 1981–90 (Graph 3).

Only one of the 79 participants had a post-graduate degree. He held a PhD in chemistry and was/became the leader of the group. Thirty-one participants held graduate degrees, while 27 were students, still studying for their first degree at various universities. Seventeen were high school graduates, and the remaining three participants held no formal education but were studying the Quran on their own in *Khalwa*, a traditional form of teaching/learning institution similar to madrasa in Pakistan or *Mahder* in Mauritania where students study through a Sufi tradition or with a Sufi teacher who teaches them free of charge (Graph 4).

With regard to subjects studied by the participants, 34 studied/study humanities (literature, history, geography, economics, etc.), 20 engineering, seven pharmaceuticals, one veterinary science, nine medicine and eight IT. The leadership relies heavily on technical individuals for two reasons. First, their knowledge in explosives and other hardware is very useful. Indeed, many developed such skills while participating in jihad in Afghanistan and Iraq. Second, their religious background is weak, which makes them more vulnerable to manipulative tactics and discourse of radical preachers and VEt groups and individuals. Finally, most participants, 59 out of 79, were single or not married, while only 20 were married.

Several Dialogue Committees, made up of credible, competent, trusted and respected scholars, ulama and scientists from various Islamic currents in the country were organized, including from the main Islamic movements (NIF and Ruling Party and Hizb al-Umma), the Muslim Brotherhood, the Sunnah Al-Ansar Group, the Salafi Brotherhood Group, as well as independent ulama and scholars who specialize in sharia, psychology and sociology from various Sudanese universities and institutions. Each Committee was made up of five to seven individuals ready to carry out dialogue with and debate participants. At least three of each Committee's members are ulama, plus a psychologist, a judge, a sociologist and a retired or working politician in state. The dominance of ulama in the Committees is due to the fact that

> 'According to our experience we found that intellectual treatment is the best way because most of the youth adopt destructive thoughts which can only be countered intellectually'. The inclusion of a working or retired state official is also important because some of the individuals were radicalized as a result of some of their policies, behaviours or acts. 'We also included judges in the committee, high level judges, because some believe that the implementation of Islamic religion in Sudan is wrong and not Islamic. We bring judges in therefore to explain to participants how Islam is being implemented rightly in Sudan'. (all quotations from personal interviews, NSID, Khartoum, December 2011)

Before the dialogue commences, scholars and scientists are provided with full information on each participant, including basic information, ideological beliefs, military operations, the level of radicalization, the results of the investigation team, behaviour of participants inside the detention centre, and other information on family circles.[6] Each participant is also asked to write down on a piece of paper the main political and ideological beliefs which he wants to discuss with the Committee before the dialogue commences. The aim of this exercise is to determine the level of sharia knowledge of each participant, identify the main intellectual points of agreement/disagreement, benefit from these points in the psychological analysis, identify the main misunderstandings that caused the participants to fall into the trap of VEm, keep the dialogue specific to key points and arrange the priorities of the dialogue.

Nine 'misunderstood concepts' were found to dominate the ideas and thinking of participants around which the dialogue program evolved and focused:[7] *al-wala wal bara* ideology (loyalty and excommunication), the Muslim ruler and failure of political elite to defend Islam and Islamic cause (reference was made to secession of the South and conflict in Darfur as examples); the principles of *takfiri* rule in Islam; *al-amer bel-ma'rouf wan-nahe an al-munker* (spreading what Allah called for and preventing what Allah forbade by force); jihad, its ethics, principles and rules and regulations; the position of non-Muslims and their property in Muslim countries; the application of sharia law in Islamic states; interaction with the international community and presence of international peace forces in Sudan; fatwa and who qualifies for its issuance; excommunicating police, security forces, government and political elite; and Sufi methods.

Dialogue then proceeded mainly on an individual level. At least two sessions were attended by each participant, with each session lasting for approximately two hours. At the end of each session, each participant was given a file in order to write his notes and provide feedback on the nature of the dialogue, sessions and main misunderstandings before the dialogue started, developments of these misunderstandings after the dialogue took place, observations about the mechanisms and operations of the dialogue committee, and main intellectual and scientific needs of the participants. This process serves as an evaluative measure carried out at the end of each dialogue, during which participants' responses, opinions and receptivity are evaluated, and participants' preference and suitability for individual or group dialogue are determined.

Individual dialogue in most cases has been deemed more effective in the debate because the participant can talk about whatever subject they want freely without being intimated by other participants who might be more radical or more intelligent. This approach also encourages bonds to be built between participants and committee members more easily, and hence encourages participants to open up and be more frank with committee members.

Although not as integrated as is the case in the Saudi De-rad program, for example, families have also been lightly incorporated into the Sudanese dialogue program. During dialogue, some families were allowed to attend the process and in some cases they were allowed to even participate in it. Mainly fathers attend the dialogue process. Those who are married can have *khalwa shariaysh* (conjugal right). Inside the prison, participants are treated kindly and their families are allowed to visit them after the 45-day investigative period is over.

'Torture makes things worse and makes participants more radical. These guys are prepared to die anyway hence torturing them will only encourage them to do so'. (personal interview with a high-ranking officer at the CTU, Khartoum, January 2012)

Post dialogue *tawfiq* (facilitation or coordination) procedures

Sudan's re-integration procedures are rather weak, but present and worth considering. Efforts have been made to facilitate the re-integration of participants in the dialogue program in their society and with their families after their release. These efforts depend on the needs and financial position of each participant. Generally participants are encouraged to go back to education, either to complete their uncompleted degrees or pursue higher education. Those with educational needs have their fees, or part of them, paid for by the Ministry of Education (ME), which coordinates with NSID to return participates back to education and facilitates their admission to universities and other educational institutions. Those without jobs and who are in need of employment are assisted by NSID in finding new jobs. The most influential (radical) elements among participants in particular are encouraged and supported in pursuing higher education, with the ME lending needy ones financial assistance to pay for tuition fees. As mentioned earlier, each payment and assistance depends on the needs of the participants and their financial position, but the financial assistance is not as large as that given by the Saudi government to beneficiaries from the Saudi De-rad program, for example. Some participants are obviously better off than others and therefore they require less financial support and more of other types of assistance, like a job or admission to a university.

In addition to assisting participants in their educational needs, the Sudanese government also provides some funding to pay for educational fees of children of patricians. The aim of this procedure is to prevent drop-out of participants' children from schools, to secure their future through better education, and to avoid turning them into haters of the state, or creating a new generation of violent extremists who might seek revenge upon the state in later stages for their plights and the plights of their parents. Again, this procedure is coordinated with the ME.

For those who are not able to find a job, the Sudanese government provides some participants with small-scale finance to establish a project, such as producing and selling dairy, livestock, producing olives and olive oil in small grinders. Project financing of such types are given mostly, but not solely, to leaders and the most radical elements of the group for two reasons. First, this group in particular faces more difficulties in finding jobs than other released participants since many businesses would be concerned about employing well-known radicals and violent extremists in many societies. Second, providing income-generating projects to radicals might create an incentive for them to become more committed, learn new businesses and civil skills, including participation, toleration and cooperation. 'We felt that this approach could be more effective in helping these guys repent' (personal interview with officials in CTU at the NSID, Khartoum, January 2012).

As shown earlier, a large number of the participants are single or not married. Marriage is believed to help participants settle down and become more engaged and concerned with family affairs instead of jihad and VEm. Married individuals are more likely to think about the future of their family and children and to seek a job to provide for their family needs of food, drink, shelter and education. Therefore, single participants have also been supported financially in getting married, particularly those with a poor economic background.

Finally, after release, each participant is allocated a 'handler', a security officer who becomes his friend and a friend of the family. The handler's main task is to solve all problems faced by the released participant in society, from financial, to employment, to education and confusion over some ideological issues. The released participant is given the mobile and direct number of his handler, and is encouraged to call him whenever the need arises to do so.

Counterterrorism procedures

Counterterrorism efforts focus on countering radical, violent extremist ideologies at societal level and outside detention centres. Unlike De-rad procedures that seek to de-radicalize individuals who have already become radicalized, counter radicalization aims at either preventing the emergence of violent extremist ideology and activism in society as a whole, countering such ideology and activism in certain areas or regions that incubate them, or both. Counter measures also include efforts to face and undermine the negative and dangerous consequences of radical ideology and activism in the country, including in particular in areas where such ideologies fester.

In Sudan, counter procedures were selective, focusing mainly and overwhelmingly on areas or regions that fester and incubate violent extremist thoughts and activities. Such efforts are coordinated with two key semi-autonomous institutions: *Muntada al-Nahda wal-tawasl al-Hadari* (the Renaissance and Continuation of Civilizations Forum) and International Centre for Dawa Studies (ICDS).

International Centre for Dawa Studies (ICDS)

ICDS[8] was established at the end of 2008. It was founded and continues to be supported by the state, although it is now increasingly trying to rely more on society for its needs, including financial, logistical, furniture, food packages and so forth. It also relies in its scholarly activities on scholars, scientists, professors and ulama from society, particularly from various universities and educational centres in Sudan. Judges, retired or still working, are also invited to participate in scholarly activities of the centre because some radicals believe that the application of law by the state is non-Islamic and judges can deal with this particular issue more effectively. Because the centre deals with and relies on societal elements for most parts of its activities, and because it is increasing its dependence on society for its financial and other needs, the centre is seen as semi-autonomous, 'societal in the eyes of most Sudanese' (personal interview with the Head of ICDS, Khartoum, January 2012).

ICDS organizes various types of activities that aim at countering radical extremist ideology in various parts of the country. The focus is mainly on areas where such an ideology festers and grows. The centre is thus selective in areas where it operates. A strong coordination exists between the centre and NSID. The NSID informs the centre about incubator areas and regions and the centre acts by organizing activities in such areas:

> There is strong coordination between security forces and us. The security forces first collect information about the presence of individuals in certain areas or areas that incubate radical ideology. They then pass this information on to us. Then we act by targeting that region, mosque, area or even individuals embracing radical ideology and imams spreading such ideologies. (Personal interview with the Head of ICDS, Khartoum, January 2012)

The activities of the centre evolve around two types of program; one takes more of a public form while the second is tailored towards certain individuals. The former is organized in the shape of Educational Weeks (*Isboo' thagafi*), and typically consists of *halaqat dirasiyah* (study circles), lectures, seminars, and workshops held mostly in mosques but also in universities, accommodation halls, public halls and areas and institutions in regions deemed as incubators of radical thought. These activities, which last for one week, seek to immunize youth from violent extremist ideology and activism, and to counter radical ideology preached by radical imams, some political leaders, or ideologues. The main clients of the centre are individuals and groups who have embraced or are about to embrace a radical ideology, have not yet committed any violent extremist activity, and are present in regions, areas or institutions deemed by security officers as incubators of radical thought.

The centre currently runs around 20 educational weeks every year and around 30 *halaqa dirasiyeh* every week, with a plan to increase this number to 300 every week. Scholars, ulama and scientists who participate in delivering the material in the *halaqat*, lectures and seminars are paid nominal fees by the centre for their efforts, mainly to cover the costs of their travelling. 'Involving ulama, judges, scholars and other scientists in our activities allows us to activate their role in society, particularly in mosques, and to bridge the gap between youth and them' (personal interview with the Head of the Centre, Khartoum, January 2012).

The centre is aided by some other state institutions (such as the Ministry of Health – MH, for example), which sometimes participate with the centre in organizing a seminar, a lecture or workshop. Subjects discussed vary from HIV patients in a Muslim society,[9] which was delivered in collaboration with the MH, to the discussion of more religiously oriented subjects such as the unity of *ahal al-qebala* (the Unity of the People of various schools of thoughts) to prevent differences between different schools of thoughts such as *Maliki, Hanbali, Shafi'* and *Hanafi*. Other subjects include the implementation of sharia in current times, *Al-Hukum Wa al-Tanzeel, fard ain Jihad* (compulsory martyrdom) and voluntary martyrdom,[10] fatwa in Islam, *al-Hakemiyah* or *Imamah* (ruler and the rule), *al Nahi an al-munkar wal amer Bel-Marouf,* the role of the state in Islam, and jihad outside one's home or country. Targeted groups and institutions vary from mosques whose imams are radical and are seeking to spread radical ideology, to schools, universities and public halls where VEt ideologies fester. As the Head of the Centre explained:

> Our main role is to direct them [vulnerable groups and individuals] to the original and agreed-upon sources of Islam. This is because the ideology which the participants depart from is wrong. They rely on some sources which they cannot trace. They don't even know the names of their sources. The main problem is that they cling to contentious issues which require good knowledge in Islam. We therefore rely on and choose specialists in each subject being discussed when organizing our activities. (Personal interview, Khartoum, January 2012)

In other words, 'the Centre starts where the prison ends. Our role is to provide support in terms of whatever questions radicals might have (personal interview with an ulama of the Centre, Khartoum, January 2012).

The second type of program offered by the Centre targets individuals vulnerable to violent extremist ideas. These are members of society who either turn to the Centre voluntarily for intellectual assistance, or the Centre sometimes targets them, following a tip from security officers, and invites them to attend a dialogue or a debate session with the ulama, or any other activity run by the Centre. So far, and until January 2012, 40 individuals resorted to or were contacted by the Centre for assistance. Those 40 are different from the first group of 79 that were debated inside the detention facility, all of which have by now been released:

> The 40 individuals we assisted were arrested for various minor offences, such as joining a radical group, developing a radical ideology, providing logistics to extremist groups or individuals, preparing for something violent, but they have not yet committed anything. In other words, we can talk about Group A and Group B. Group A is the group which was debated in the prison. This is Group B, which is debated outside prisons.

Some of the participants are very religious and believe in what are they doing vehemently. Others are 'complementary' and join because their friends asked them to do so and because they did not want to let their inviters down. This is obvious because their level of *faker* (intellectuality) differs largely. Some are not knowledgeable at all with regard to religious issues. 'None of the 40 who resorted to us is a specialist in Islam or studied Islam. They do not even know the basic *fagh* books. This means that individuals who have tendencies to become religious but lack religious knowledge are most vulnerable. It is this type of individual we target most in our activities' (personal interview with the Head of ICDS, Khartoum, January 2012).

Renaissance and Continuation of Civilizations Forum (RCCF)[11]

The RCCF was established in 2010, almost two years after the establishment of the ICDS in 2008. Like ICDS, the RCCF was also funded and founded by the state. The mission of the RCCF is larger than the ICDS, which functions mainly at national and local levels. The RCCF is both more nationally and internationally oriented in its activities and objectives. According to its basic law, the RCCF:

> is concerned with Islamic thinking...disciplined middle ground approach...positive interaction between various civilizations...and seeks to spread the comprehensive message of Islam from its divine source with its ethical content and global extension...[it also] seeks to spread the message of the RCCF through connectivity and continuation with Islamic and non-Islamic thinkers inside and outside Sudan, and building bridges of cooperation and complementarities

with them to serve the best interest of all humanity through expos-
ing and presenting Islamic facts, clarifying religion through the right
understanding of Islam, and to correct wrong concepts about Islam.
(Renaissance Forum, 2011, pp. 3, 5, 6)

The activities of the RCCF focus on three key components: research and
studies on Islamic thought; training programs and capacity-building in
poor regions; and lectures, seminars, dialogues, workshops and *nadawat*
that promote *wasatiyeh* (middle ground) and promote true principles of
Islam.

Training programs and capacity-building target different institutions
and individuals involved in countering radical ideology in the country.
For example, in 2011, the RCCF organized nine training programs on
various subjects. Examples of the programs and subjects they focused
on included: Successful Strategy (25-hour training program, attended
by 30 trainees from NSID); Self and Personal Development (25-hour
training program, attended by 60 individuals from youth organizations
from different governorates); The Art of Effective Delivery (20 hours, 30
attendees from Future Organization); and Development of Leadership
Skills (two different programs, 25 hours each, 30 attendees each from
Quran Memorizing Union and Organization for the Care of Immigrant
Students, respectively); The Strategies of Successful Life (25 hours, 76
attendees from the North Khartoum Region); Advanced Training (130
hours, two attendees from the RCCF itself); Preparing Managers and
Design Training Programmes (60 hours, 1 attendee from the RCCF); and
Organization Management to Train Vulnerable Organizations' Staff (25
hours, 30 attendees from Voluntary Students Organization Network).
Not only do institutions and individuals involved in countering radical
ideology qualify for these programs, but also so do vulnerable elements
to radical thought, such as youth from poor regions. The government
subsidizes the cost of all of these programs to encourage participation.

In addition to training programs, the RCCF also organizes lectures and
seminars on various issues related to Islam, the Islamic world and Islamic
thinking. For example, in 2001 the RCCF organized at least eight lectures
on subjects that varied from The Contemporary *Iftaa'* Approach, The
Egyptian Revolution, The Tunisian Revolution and Future Horizons, to
The Prophet's Ways of Social Reform, the Suicide Phenomenon and How to
Deal with Sunnah. These lectures are open to the public, and preceded by
an organized media promotion campaign to promote the event overseen
by the Media Unit of the RCCF. Eminent scholars, not only from Sudan
but also from the Muslim world, are invited to deliver these lectures. For

example, the lectures on the Egyptian and Tunisian revolutions were delivered by Egyptian Mufti Dr Ali Jumaa and the Tunisian head of the Islamic Renaissance Party, Dr Rashid al-Ghanoush, respectively. All lectures and seminars are recorded and documented by the RCCF and later broadcast on TV or radio channels and turned into hard copies distributed to various members of state and society.

The RCCF is also keen to promote cooperation and collaboration between itself and various youth organizations in the country, and also to organize projects that bring benefits to poor regions of the country. Such projects include, for instance, preparing a draft Memorandum of Understanding with National Union for Sudanese Youth, visiting Aum Dorman Project to initiate a Rubbish Recycling System in the area, celebrating the International Environment Day by preparing a Draft Proposal towards Clean Environment in partnership with various civil society organizations and state institutions concerned with the environment.

Publications are also an important aspect of the RCCF's activities. In 2011 alone, the RCCF produced more than 15 publications, ranging from books to small research papers, on such subjects as Religion and Life, The *Hakimeyah* in Islam, Islam and Economic Crisis. They also published all of the Friday sermons delivered by the head of the RCCF, Dr Issam al-Bashir, who is a prominent scholar and ulama in Sudan who delivers Friday sermons in a nearby mosque in Khartoum. The RCCF also has a weekly page which deals with current topics that are arising in Sudanese society, plus a monthly magazine (*al-Nahda*) that publicizes and summarizes the activities of the RCCF. The magazine also discusses in its monthly issue different, important subjects that are widely debated by radicals and their sympathizers, such as *al-Hakimeyah* in Islam, The Path to Hajj, The Prophet's Farewell Speech (and how it called for peaceful coexistence and preventing violence and murdering innocent souls), The Distinguished Leadership, The Confederate with the South, and Islam Is the Religion of All Prophets.[12]

More recently, the RCCF developed its own website (www.nahdaonline.org) which promotes and documents all activities carried out by the RCCF in audio and video formats. Unfortunately, the Internet has not been used to develop websites that counter the radical ideology of radical preachers and groups which use the Internet to spread their violent ways, thoughts and activities.

Outside the RCCF and ICDS, efforts have also been made to counter radical ideology in certain areas and regions where such ideology seems to find fertile ground through other means. Several measures are developed in these targeted regions and areas. They include educational and developmental programs, such as water and health facilities and clinics, schools and *khalawa* (traditional teaching places). In such areas where radical ideology is festering, children of *takfiris* are encouraged by the security authorities to attend state schools, with financial support from the state, in order to prevent them from being influenced by their fathers. This is done in coordination with the Ministry of Education, which is asked to cover these costs. Some radical elements in such regions and areas are also assisted directly by the state in establishing small income-generating projects, such as bakeries, olive and olive oil production. The state believes that, failing to find alternative jobs for them, such an approach creates more discipline and commitment on behalf of the radicals, as well as encouraging participation in society and democratic forums.

In addition the government adopts and supports *qawafal al-duaweeyeh* (missionary activities) that specifically target regions and areas with incubating violent extremist thoughts and ideologies. This program is called 'Targeting Radical Incubators'. In such regions, activities such as lectures and seminars are organized in collaboration with eminent scholars and ulama from Sudanese society. The aim of these activities is to spread the *wasatiyah* (middle ground) ideology and culture, correct misunderstood concepts (such as justifying blood and property of non-Muslims), draw attention to the dangers of *takfiri* ideology and activities, and to create bonds and deepen trust between youth and ulama.

All of the above-mentioned activities have been accompanied by other efforts that aimed at controlling religious institutions in the country. For example, religious institutions, including in particular the traditional *khalwa* institutions, have been brought more under the direct supervision of the ME, and curriculums taught in religious institutions have all been revised. This includes the Islamic Education subject at universities which has been revised to take into consideration the current period, events and circumstances. Some space has also been given to former, repented radical elements to talk about VEt phenomena in Sudanese society in open lectures, Friday sermons and even on TV and newspapers whenever possible. Programmes and shows that stir jihadi feelings among youth have also been restricted on TV and other media outlets, and programs with current and former radical elements have been organized live on TV, along with inviting prominent members of Sudanese religious and political society to deliver public lectures and seminars.

Finally, a medium-term (four-year) program was installed in 2008 to spread the idea of moderation and *wasatiyah* in Sudanese society. The program is being implemented through the Ministry of Religious Affairs and aims to spread the official (correct) version of Islam, which carries the message of peace, moderation and tranquillity. To do this, the subjects of extremism and *takfir* have been liberalized, encouraging society to talk about them in mosques, TV shows and media outlets in a more objective way. To achieve this, the Sudanese government sought to gradually build a partnership between the Ministry of Religious Affairs and *Majma' al Fegeh al-Islami* and the Committee of Sudanese Scholars. It establishes scholarly statutes (*manaber*) in mosques, especially the big ones that attract a large number of worshippers in regions and areas deemed to incubate radical ideology; invites popular scholars and ulama to talk in mosques and religious institutions and revives traditional public and qualitative seminars. It also established a specialized satellite TV network concerned with teaching and broadcasting matters related to sharia, a program which is supervised, run and funded by the Ministry of Religious Affairs in collaboration with the security department.

Gauging Sudan's 'soft' measures

Efforts to evaluate the Sudanese Counter-de-Rad procedures are faced with the usual problems that often plague the evaluation efforts of all Counter-de-Rad programs, including lack of 'data surrounding the efficacy of such initiatives...issues surrounding assessment of their effectiveness and outcomes' and absence of a 'consensus on what constitutes success in reforming a terrorist' (Horgan and Braddock, 2010, pp. 267–8). In most cases researchers seeking to assess the effectiveness of the Sudanese Counter-de-Rad procedures are left at the mercy of the data and information provided by local and national security officials and state institutions which have a motive and tendency to exaggerate the successes of their policies and undermine their failures.

According to Khartoum's top security officers, Sudan's Counter-de-Rad efforts have been 'exceptionally successful'. All 79 formerly detained radicals, they argue, have been released, only six of whom returned to a violent extremist lifestyle. Four of these six returnees participated in the assassination of the American diplomat, Mr Greenfield, in 2008. Of those, two were killed, one by the Sudanese authorities and the second while fighting in Somalia. The remaining two are still at large in Somalia. 'Also, we have been monitoring another five released individuals carefully because we became suspicious of their behaviour, such as calling some terrorists by phone outside the country, or involving themselves in recruitment campaigns' (all quotations from personal interviews with several high-ranking security officers at CTU, Khartoum, January 2012). Whether 6 or 11 receded (7.5 per cent or 13.5 per cent respectively), the recidivism rate has been low and, based on recidivism rate alone, the Sudanese De-rad efforts can be considered successful. The low rates of recidivism in the Sudanese cases are even comparable to those achieved in more resourceful countries, such as Saudi Arabia.

External, international assessment of the Sudanese Counter-de-Rad efforts, on the other hand, particularly by the US government, is less optimistic and tends to undermine the outcome of the Sudanese procedures. For example, a 2008 report by a non-partisan Congressional Research Service stated that, 'while Sudan does not have nuclear or biological weapons, nor does it have ballistic or cruise missiles...Sudan has been developing the capability to produce chemical weapons for many years. In order to do so, Sudan has allegedly obtained help from foreign entities' (quoted in Bhattacharji, 2008). Despite all the overtures which al-Bashir made towards the West since ousting al-Turabi in 1999, 'The US, however, still officially considers Sudan a terrorist state', mainly because Khartoum did not cut off its relations with and end its political support to Hamas[13] and Hezbollah, which Washington labels as 'terrorist organizations' (Infoplease, 2012). The United States, it seems, perceives success or failure of Counter-de-Rad policies in the Middle East and North Africa (MENA) in terms of its special relations with Israel, which is distortionary, in itself radicalizing for many Arab and Muslim youth, and, most importantly, ignores what Horgan and Braddock (2010, p. 267) called 'unanticipated consequence' of Counter-de-Rad policies.

To be sure, it defies belief that only 79 radicals exist/existed in Sudan, a country which allegedly provided hundreds of jihadis to Afghanistan, Iraq, Somalia and other parts of the world. The small number of detained radicals in itself testifies to the narrowness and limited reach of the Sudanese De-rad procedures, which are procedures rather than a program. This has given the impression that 'Although the regime has taken a stand against radical Islamist factions, such groups continue to be tolerated by many in the populace and perhaps some in government' in Sudan (Waller, 2011). Sudan's efforts to detain radicals and prevent them from exporting or importing terrorism is weak, and has been weakened by decades of wars, civil wars and internal divisions and fighting that consumed and sapped the capacity of the state, drained its resources, and overstretched its military, police and security forces. The upshot has been the creation of porous 'borders [which] remain permeable' and attractive to violent extremists seeking safe havens in weak, failed or failing states. 'Even the new country of South Sudan poses a threat of terrorism, having gained an unstable and volatile independence in much the same fashion as its northern neighbor 50 years earlier' (all quotations from Waller, 2011).

Sudan, moreover, has been implementing Counter-de-Rad procedures in an environment that is conducive to violent extremism, both internal and external. Internally, Sudan remains one of the poorest Arab states, with very limited industrial and export base, a high level of poverty, unemployment, corruption and inequities. Agriculture remains the most important sector in the economy, employing 80 per cent of the work force and contributing a third of GDP. Only 7 per cent of the labour force is employed in the narrow industrial sector. 'The Darfur conflict, the aftermath of two decades of civil war in the south, the lack of basic infrastructure in large areas, and a reliance by much of the population on subsistence agriculture ensure much of the population will remain at or below the poverty line for years despite rapid rises in average per capita income' (Central Intelligence Agency, 2012). Sudan today has one of the highest rates of unemployment (18.7 per cent) and number of people living below poverty line (more than 40 per cent) in the Arab world. Borrowing to meet the country's war needs has led to one of the highest levels of public debt (105 per cent of GDP in 2009) in the region, which absorbs a great deal of the public sector resources and deprives the country of badly needed funds for infrastructure, education, health and effective and comprehensive Counter-de-Rad policies. 'Lack of financial resources admittedly is one of the main obstacles faced by our centers' – stated the Al-Nahda Centre and International Centre for Calling Studies, the two chief institutions involved in the counter radicalization procedures in the country (personal interviews with the heads of the al-Nahda, Dr Issam al-Bashir, and International Centre, Dr Ibrahim al-Karori, Khartoum, January 2012).

Despite peace with the South, which led in 2011 to the creation of a new country (The Republic of Southern Sudan – RSS), cross-border provocations and disagreements over their economic resources continue to threaten the fragile peace between the two countries. Less than a year since the implementation of the CPA which created RSS in 2011, the two countries went to war again early this year after continuing to disagree over how to share the region's economic resources, particularly oil and oil dividends. 'Along with conflicts in Somalia and Darfur, the conflict in the south is one of the most radicalising issues in Sudan today. It is no secret that the Bush Administration was significant behind the 2005 CPA' (Reeves, 2011). Despite their important economic element, the NIF government in the 1990s played a key role in portraying the conflicts in the South and Darfur in religious terms. The fact that Israel and the United States have been supporting, from the early days of the 1955 mutiny, southern rebellion movements militarily, financially and politically played into the hands of the NIF government. The upshot has been the revival of the relations between AQ and Sudan following the 205 CPA:

> But in 2006, bin Laden's ties with Sudan resurfaced. After the United Nations proposed to send a peacekeeping force to the war-torn region of Darfur, bin Laden released a tape that told his followers to go to Sudan to fight UN troops. Similar messages were repeated the following year by bin Laden's deputy, Ayman al-Zawahiri, and again by bin Laden himself. The Sudanese government has opposed the presence of non-African UN troops in Darfur, but Sudanese officials have distanced themselves from bin Laden's message. (Bhattacharji, 2008)

In fact, both Israel and the United States have been violating the terms of the 2005 CPA by supplying arms to southern rebels clandestinely (Arya, 2009). Worse, Sudan was promised by successive US administrations that if it takes serious actions against terrorists and terrorism and allows a politically sensitive referendum in the South to go ahead in January 2011 and abides by the results, which it did:

> the United States will move to take the country off its list of state sponsors of terrorism as early as next year [2012]..... In September, the administration presented Sudan with incentives ranging from modest steps like the delivery of agricultural equipment to more sweeping measures, including debt relief, normalized diplomatic relations, the lifting of sanctions and the removal of Sudan from the State Department's list of state sponsors of terrorism, which it has been on since 1993. (Landler, 2010)

Apart from removing Sudan 'from a list of countries considered non-cooperative in the Global War on Terror' and some small support for agricultural projects, the United States has failed to deliver on most of its promises. Crippling 'economic sanctions against Sudan remain' intact and now have become 'linked to the violence in Darfur', perhaps understandably (Landler, 2010). The United States State Department also 'continues to formally designate [Sudan] as a "state sponsor of terrorism"', despite

Khartoum's cooperation with Washington and the international community to fight terrorism in and outside its borders (Bhattacharji, 2008). 'With the exception of Hamas, which the United Nations does not consider a terrorist organization, the government of Sudan no longer supports the presence of extremist elements within the country'. (Waller, 2011)

Radical preachers and politicians have seized the moment and portrayed the conflicts in the South and other parts of the country in terms of a Crusader war against Muslim Sudan, 'Western conspiracies' to prevent the unity of Sudan, to divide and weaken the country in an attempt to exploit its rich and unutilized economic resources. Khartoum's intensive 'lobbying' in Washington 'so it can be removed from the terrorism list' has failed. Many Sudanese, and 'many officials in the ruling party feel that they alienated their Islamic base by cooperating with Washington in areas like Somalia and Iraq without getting anything in return' (all quotations from *Sudan Tribune*, 2011).

Faced with economic and political crises, Khartoum has recently resorted to more 'brutal repression' and austerity (Reeves, 2011). The secession of the South has so far brought more turbulence, radicalism and instability. The new environment in Sudan, both internal and external, is more radicalizing than ever:

> Following the secession of South Sudan, Sudan finds itself in a precarious situation; having given up many of the economic and social centers of gravity in the south, it relies on diplomacy and foreign support more than ever. A newly impoverished base, coupled with an authoritarian regime, provide many factors leading to a violent insurgency. Such an insurgency, together with a strategic location and tolerant population, open doors for the growth of Islamist terrorism on a domestic and especially global level. In the absence of effective, multinational relations, this is precisely what will happen. ... Never has the country been more perilous, and never has it been more fertile with potential. (Waller, 2011)

Conclusion

Sudan's Counter-de-Rad efforts are to be commended. Khartoum has taken serious measures to fight the presence of terrorism in its borders through a variety of 'soft' measures, the aim of which is to win hearts and minds, rather than create a new generation of violent extremists through reliance solely on traditional, military approaches. In fact, Sudan demonstrates that even with little and limited financial resources, poor countries can still do a lot to counter violent extremist ideology and activism locally, nationally and internationally.

We have always argued that the focus on recidivism rate as the main proxy for success of Counter-de-Rad policies is misplaced. These efforts often lead to wider benefits that go beyond recidivism, ignored but significant externalities and 'unintended consequences'. These include improved information, often generated from repented former radicals, that is so vital in saving lives and preventing destruction. They might have also reduced violent extremist incidents in the country. Since the assassination of the American aid worker, Mr Greenfield, in 2008, terrorist incidents have been reported in North Sudan by Scientific Salafist. Cooperation with the international community has also played a key role in preventing attacks and saving lives outside Sudan. The Sudanese Counter-de-Rad procedures have also activated the role of Sudanese scholars and ulama, drew attention to the dangerous consequences of violent extremist ideology and activism, and exposed a destructive version of religion that excommunicates everyone else and seeks to portray the world's problems in a simple 'us versus them' formula.

Al Walid Amir, one of the key high-ranking officers in the CTU, summed up the main benefits of De-rad procedures in Sudan:

> Many former radicals have repented and now accept mixed schools, mixed education, and no longer excommunicate everybody. Many got jobs and returned to their former life. Their views of security forces changed. Now they accept society and cooperation with security forces, and we have deepened our continuation with them after their release. They have also been able to affect other radical individuals and groups not arrested and told them about the good treatment which the state provided to them. They have succeeded in de-radicalizing others. (Personal interview, Khartoum, January 2012)

Unfortunately, Sudan's Counter-de-Rad efforts have been taking place in a rather uniquely radicalizing environment, one, if anything, that is more conducive to VEm. For example, the good treatment inside prisons is not matched by similar optimal treatment outside detention centres. Widespread corruption and impoverished economic base are unlikely to improve the environment. Khartoum is to be condemned for the way it has handled the conflict in Darfur and before in the South. The United States and the international community have the right to take appropriate action to stem genocide and human rights violations, wherever committed, not just in Sudan. But how they choose to do that is important and will perhaps have far-reaching consequences for Sudan's stability and Counter-de-Rad efforts. It is also important to understand and study how the Sudanese themselves perceive external interventions. Many Sudanese today, both officials and civilians, feel let down, if not deceived by, the US successive administrations that continue to support their southern and eastern rivals. Sudan's porous borders are attracting VEts who are exploiting foreign interventions, seeking safe havens and furthering instability. These events, along with economic challenges, poverty, repression and widespread corruption, counter and undermine Counter-de-Rad procedures in the country. Many observers have raised concerns, despite recent leaps in removing terrorism from within, over the presence and return of radicals from Iraq, Somalia, Yemen and Afghanistan, as well as seemingly increased toleration of such groups and individuals by an increasingly impoverished, frustrated and disappointed populace, both in the southern and northern parts of the country. What is clear is that both South and North Sudan will play a principal role in shaping the landscape of Africa over the next decade. This role will be affected not only by developments inside Sudan and the policies of Khartoum and Juba, but also by the role and stand taken by international community to assist both Khartoum and Juba to overcome their differences and economic and political challenges.

Appendix

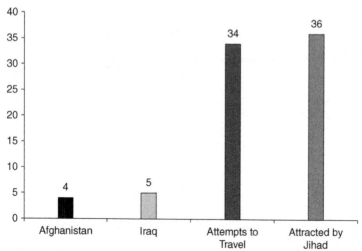

Figure 7.1 Military operations carried out by participants

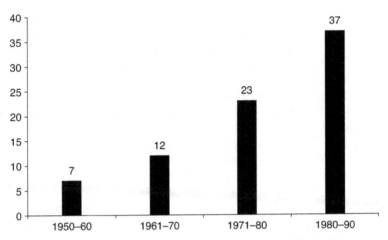

Figure 7.2 Age group of participants in the Sudanese de-radicalization program

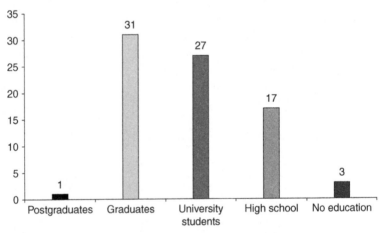

Figure 7.3 The educational level of participants in the Sudanese de-radicalization program

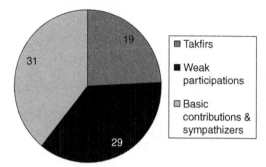

Figure 7.4 The level of radicalization and contribution to jihadi activities of the participants

Table 7.1 Classification of individuals according to groups, ideology, area of operations and targets

Groups	Ideology	Area	Targets
Abu Musab	Excommunicate the state, security forces, some *fugaha* and Sufi methods	The Khartoum *welaya* province	Foreign embassies in Khartoum, foreign individuals, international peace forces, and some high-ranking Sudanese security individuals
Abu Hazem	Not totally an excommunicator group but call for jihad inside Sudan	Greater Darfur province	International Peace Force in Darfur
Abu Fadal	A *takfiri* splinter group from broader Islamic groups. They excommunicate state and society	Outside Islamic states	Call to prepare and be ready for the right time to prepare for the establishment of the caliphate

8
From Militarization to Democratization: The Transformation of Turkey's Counter Terrorism Strategy (CTS)

Introduction

Turkey is both historically and geopolitically one of the most important countries in the region. Not only was its capital regarded as the birth place of one of the most enduring empires (the Ottoman Empire) in the history of the world, but also its geographic location at the intersection between Europe and Asia confers a special geopolitical significance. Throughout history, Turkey became a major centre for trade and migration from and to the region. Turkey, notwithstanding its past religious authority, is also secular as it became the first Islamic state to officially relinquish the Islamic caliphate in the early 1920s and to embark on a process of Westernization, secularization, industrialization and democratization. Such rapid and large transformations have inevitably been associated with a rise in violent extremism (VEm) in the country. To be sure, Turkey has long struggled with the phenomenon of violent extremism whose roots go back to the 1880 first Kurdish rebellion. VEm, however, evolved and endured in Turkey. Today, VEm represents one of the salient features of the Turkish political system, influencing not only the country's social fabric but also its international relations. The Turkish prime minister has recently 'defined terrorism as the biggest obstacle' before the political, economic and democratic development of Turkey (JTW, 2010). Unlike the more usual situation in other countries which face the threat of VEm by one group or set of individuals, Turkey has been facing VEm from groups and individuals with various ideological, political, social, economic and ethnic demands and backgrounds. As Reuters recently (2012) pointed out: 'Kurdish separatists, far left groups, far right groups and Islamist militants, including al-Qaeda, have all carried out bomb attacks in Turkey in the past. (...) So far, VEm has cost Turkey more than '30,000 lives and billions of dollars' (Laciner and Bal, 2011).

As a result of its history of VEm, Turkey has a 'long experience with counter- terrorism' and has become 'a pioneering country in improving and deepening CT efforts' (SECI, 2011, p. 154). Turkey has also recently embarked on a significant reform initiative to counter the appeal of violent extremism and activism in the country. Turkey's counterterrorism strategy (CTS) is multidisciplinary, embracing economic, political, social, religious and human rights laws, as well as societal initiatives. The Turkish CTS is, by far, the most comprehensive counter radicalization process studied in any Muslim-majority state. 'Empirical studies', however, on Turkish CTS 'are very limited' (Sozer and Server, 2011, p. 23) and very little is known about Turkey's new CT initiative that many observers either naively or 'deliberate[ly] attempt to compare [the] Turkish way of fighting terrorism with Israeli method' (Bal, 2010a).

This chapter fills an important gap in the literature by investigating Turkey's recent CTS. It traces the evolution of VEm in Turkey to the late 19th century and sheds light on how the state responded to such challenges and how successful the official response has been in each phase. The chapter also sheds light on the main violent extremist (VEt) groups active in the Turkish political arena today, their political and demographic characteristics, ideological orientations and demands and motivations.

The evolution of VEm in Turkey: a historical perspective

This period is best divided and studied over three main phases, according to the main threats and challenges faced by the central authority: the pre-1923 republican state years; the emergence of the republican state and Kamelist principles between 1923–50 and the post-1950 democratic opening polarization of Turkish politics.

Kurdish uprisings in the pre-1923 republican period

Not only was Turkey the nucleus of the Islamic empire and central to the Islamic caliphate for more than five hundred years, but it was also among only three Middle Eastern states to retain autonomy and to avoid being subjected to European rule after World War I. The other two states were Iran and Saudi Arabia. The presence of foreign troops, therefore, or colonization were not major factors that could lead to the emergence of national rebellious, or radical/violent extremist movements content on fighting foreign occupation and liberating the homeland from the grip of foreign armies, which is an environment often conducive to VEm, as was the case, for example, in Algeria following the French occupation of the country between 1830 and 1960 (El-Said and Harrigan, 2013). Internal and external dynamics, however, still ensured the emergence of opposition, if not rebellious, movements.

In fact the second half of the 19th century experienced the outbreak of more than a 'dozen rebellions' by the Kurdish elements of the Turkish state (Laciner and Bal, 2011). Due to the importance of this issue to later developments in Turkey, and particularly to the evolution of Kurdish VEt movements in their current form, it is important to provide a contextual history on the nature of Kurdish terrorism.

Although an integral part of Turkish society and enjoying full citizenship rights, the origin of Kurds in Turkey is a highly debated and contentious issue. Even today there is no consensus on their origin. Most observers, however, trace their roots to 'strong communities drawn from former inhabitants of both the Balkans and the northern Caucasus' and inhabiting the mountainous areas of northeast Turkey (Halliday, 2005, pp. 61–2). Historically, Islam united all elements of the Empire and created special bonds between the Turks and Kurds. The Kurds saw themselves as Sunni subjects of a fundamentally Islamic empire. The policies of the Ottoman state, based on integration and maintenance of political authority at regional rather than central levels (therefore keeping prestige, political power and influence in the hands of traditional and religious leaders) prevented the emergence of separatist movements in the country. The Kurds therefore did not seek to establish their own state in the areas which they inhabited or mostly congregated in, namely, the northwest (Palmer, 1992).

With the Empire falling behind European rivals, both economically and militarily, the Ottoman state introduced reforms known as *Tanzimat*. As Richards and Waterbury (1996, pp. 40–1) explained:

> The Empire was being threatened by European powers, including in particular the czarist Russia, and needed to modernize, which required a lot of money. European creditors argued that improving stable title to land not only improves productivity, but also taxation and revenue to the sultan. By the mid-19th century a reform program (*Tanzimat*) was introduced and echoed in Iran and Morocco (the *nizam al-jadidi*, new order).

The *Tanzimat* obviously threatened the prestige and position of traditional and religious leaders in three main ways. First, through the imposition of a new taxation system whose revenues would accrue directly to the central authority. Direct taxation, secondly, combined with the development of legal infrastructure for private property, could, and indeed did, lead to the emergence of new propertied interests, or merchant bourgeoisie, more affluent and powerful than traditional leaders. Finally, the *Tanzimat* directly threatened the religious authority and influence of traditional/religious leaders since the *Tanzimat* were more based on and introduced new secular processes and concepts motivated by the desire to Westernize the economy and the military. To accelerate the collapse of the Ottoman Empire, moreover, European powers also began promoting internal divisions, particularly the idea of a separate Kurdish region or state, as will be shown later in what follows.

Out of the dozen or so rebellions Turkey experienced in the second half of the 19th century by the Kurds, the one in 1880 stands out since it is considered as the 'first clear statement of modern Kurdish nationalism' (Laciner and Bal, 2011). The goals and objectives of the rebellion were reflected in a letter from the leader of the rebellion himself, Sheikh Said Ubeydullah, to the British consul at Bashkal in order to convince European powers to come to the aid of the Kurdish cause:

> The Kurdish nation is a nation apart. Its religion is different from that of others, also its laws and custom. The chiefs of Kurdistan, whether they be Turkish or Persian subjects, and the people of Kurdistan, whether Muslim or Christian, are all united and agreed that things cannot proceed as they are with the two governments. It is imperative that the European governments should do something, once they understand the situation. ... We want to take matters into our own hands. We can no longer put up with the oppression. (Quoted in Bulloch and Harvey, 1992, p. 75. Also see Laciner and Bal, 2011).

However, the Kurds did not have a different religion, customs or laws. Nor were some of them actually Christians, as Sheikh Ubeydullah claimed in his letter to the British authorities. Such claims only aimed at attracting European support to the Kurdish cause, which the Kurds received.

The response of the Ottoman Sultan, Abdulhamid II, to the Kurdish uprising deserves attention here, for it presaged the kind of responses seen in countries faced with more contemporary forms of VEm, such as Saudi Arabia, Yemen and Morocco. To stem internal divisions and pre-empt separatist tendencies and spread of VEt ideology and activism, Sultan Abdulhamid II introduced a 'pan-Islamic' strategy that extols Islamic values of unity, tolerance, coexistence and integration. Laciner and Bal (2011) summarized the main elements of this strategy and shed some light on its effectiveness:

> Sultan Abdulhamid II introduced a government policy incorporating the teachings of Islam which became known as 'Pan-Islamism'. With this policy the Sultan was hoping to secure a united empire and, as a considerable majority of the population were members of the Muslim religion, he considered that by extolling the virtues of Islam throughout the empire, this would have a unifying effect. During his time in power (33 years, from 1876 to 1909) this policy proved so effective that despite the crumbling of the Ottoman Empire, the nation remained unified, and from it emerged a new and strong Ottoman nationalism, united by the Muslim faith. It was this policy of unification and the case for nationalism that ultimately defeated the rebellion of Sheikh Ubeydullah, who was unable to secure sufficient Kurdish support. The policies of the Sultan were so effective in creating a nationalistic spirit, which prevailed after his death in 1909, that by the commencement of the First World War in 1914 the Ottoman Empire was able to provide a unified army, incorporating many different people from throughout the Empire, amongst them many Kurds. These were known as the Kurdish Hamidiye Regiments and gave the Sultan total support, fighting alongside other Muslims from the Ottoman Empire. (Also see Bulloch and Harvey, 1992)

Islam played a unifying role in Turkey before the emergence of the Turkish Republic in 1923. When internal divisions emerged, the Turkish Sultan relied on 'pan-Islamism' to maintain the unity of both the Empire and the Turkish state. Hence, Islamic virtues of unity, integration, tolerance, loyalty to the ruler and abhorrence of violent ideologies and activism were promoted to a great effect to maintain the unity of the Islamic nation. This 'pan-Islamic' strategy was buttressed by, and perhaps owes its success to, the other side of the equation, the policy of integration or inclusiveness which Sultan Abdulhamid II simultaneously pursued during his reign in power. The Sultan's integration policy revolved around expanding participation and legitimizing the rule of the central government by giving 'Positions of governmental responsibility...to members of the Kurdish community whose forebears and families had been in conflict with the Empire in the 1880s' (Laciner and Bal, 2011). It was not before the emergence of the Turkish Republic in 1923 and the Kamelist principles in 1925 that Kurdish uprisings returned to the country. Following the 1880 uprising, however, and since the Kurds reside mainly in southeast Turkey, the Kurdish problem came to be known in Turkey as the 'south-east Anatolian issue' or the 'Eastern Question'.

The emergence of the Turkish republic and rise of Kurdish nationalism

Pan-Islamist policy was to be changed after the Young Turks (a group of young, educated, upper-middle-class officers) seized power in 1908 and began to directly challenge the political and legal status of the Caliphate.[1] The tension between Turkish and Kurdish nationalism intensified after 1923, the year in which the new Republic of Turkey was declared and which was preceded by a fierce war of independence against major European powers (France, Italy and Greece).

The leaders of the new republic, headed by Kamel Ataturk, opted for a secular, Westernized state based on Turkish ethnic nationalism and hence initiated several radical Western-inspired steps. To consolidate their grip over politics, the Young Turks, led by Kamel Ataturk, created their own party, the Republican People's Party (RPP) in 1925 that was to dominate the political arena until at least the first multi-party elections in 1950. A one-party system emerged, with membership in the party and national assembly tightly controlled. Although this turned the RPP into a national organization, it represented a departure from the integrative political approach followed by the former Ottoman officials. The RPP's exclusive politics was reflected in the small network of political and economic elite that controlled the party, assembly and the economy (Richards and Waterbury, 1996).

The leaders of the new republic also staged an attack on, and undermined the Ottoman Empire's former 'Pan-Islamic' ideology through their Western-inspired steps which included the following: the abolition of the Caliphate (the nominal leadership of all Muslims in the world held by the Ottoman Sultan since 1517); closure of the religious orders and lodges; granting of full political rights to women (even long before several other European nations); adoption of a new penal code based on the Italian penal code; adoption of Western civil law; complete separation of government and religious affairs; and introduction of a national education system as the uniform standard and adoption of the new Turkish alphabet (derived from the Latin alphabet) (TEUC, 2007).

The termination of the former order was completed in 1931, when Ataturk introduced his five key principles, Kamelism, and later incorporated them into the 1937 constitution. These were: republicanism, nationalism, statism (borrowed from the Ottoman empire and allowing the continuation of state control over the economy and politics), secularism and revolutionarism or reformism (Owen, 1992, p. 27).

Put differently, not only was politics nationalized along Turkish lines (reflected in the elite membership of the RPP), but also a new secular ideology (Kamelism) was introduced to replace the former Ottoman 'pan-Islamist' ideology. Nationalization of politics was also achieved through the Young Turks' homogenization program which sought to 'make Anatolia more homogeneous in order to sustain stability and security' (Laciner and Bal, 2011).

These revolutionary elements of Kamelism and the Western-inspired policies of the Young Turks led to Kurdish insecurities, revived Kurdish nationalism, and increased the tension between the Turks and Kurds. Out of these Kamelist principles, the Kurds were most opposed to two of them: secularism (which threatened not only the political influence of traditional leaders and clerics, but also the former Ottoman's 'pan-Islamist' ideology which unified all Turks), and the new interpretation of nationalism, 'which identified the phenomenon of nationalism as being rooted in ethnic origins rather than in religious ones' (Laciner and Bal, 2011).

While acknowledging internal political dynamics, recognition of external factors must not be neglected as it increased tension between the two groups and encouraged separatist tendencies. This refers to the European powers' desire to further weaken the post–Ottoman Empire state and also to facilitate the control of newly found massive oil reserves in neighbouring areas inhabited by Kurds, particularly in Kirkuk and Mosul. The expectation and potential of economic wealth and political influence did not go unnoticed by many Kurdish leaders, who began to see a new value in a Kurdish autonomous state. It was not surprising therefore that the Treaty of Sèvres, which was signed between the former Ottoman officials and the Allied Forces on 10 August 1920, sought, or allowed for the possibility of, creating an autonomous Kurdish region. Article 62–64 Section III of the Sèvres Treaty stated:[2]

> If within one year from the coming into force of the present treaty the Kurdish people within the areas defined in Art. 62 shall address themselves to the Council of the League of Nations in such a manner as to show that the majority of the population of these areas desires

independence from Turkey...Turkey hereby agrees to execute such a recommendation, and to renounce all rights and title over these areas. ... If and when such renunciation takes place, no objection will be raised by the Principal Allied Powers to the voluntary adhesion to such an independent Kurdish State of the Kurdish inhabiting that part of Kurdistan which hitherto had been included in the Mosul Vilayet. (Quoted in Vanly, 2011, p. 144)

Not surprisingly, the period between 1925 and 1950 experienced 'dozens of public uprisings, particularly in the Kurdish regions, which slowly transformed the public perception of nationalism and the idea of the nation state' (Laciner and Bal, 2011). The Turkish state responded to these revolts by introducing 'the law for the maintenance of order', which was 'used to put down all political activity outside the party [RPP] itself' (Owen, 1992, p. 27).

It is fair to argue here that the idea of a separate Kurdish region had not by then been fomented in the minds of all Kurds. Most of these revolts and uprisings aimed at restoring the former 'pan-Islamist' ideology of the Ottoman's Sultan rather than seeking the creation of an autonomous Kurdish state. The most prominent of these uprisings was the 1925 Kurdish revolt which was triggered by the immediate challenge of the Islamic principles by the new republic. As Owen (1992, p. 27) stated, the Young Turks' challenge of Islamic principles was one of the major factors that led to and marked 'the beginning of the Kurdish and religious revolt of 1925'. One of the key leaders of the 1925 Kurdish rebellion, Sheikh Said, also explained the main reasons behind the revolt as follows: 'I have always thought of Islam that it would be the best suited system for our government to put it into effect and practice. I would never hesitate to declare this' (quoted in Laciner and Bal, 2011). It was not before the emergence of the Turkish and Kurdish left in the 1950s and 1960s, and the emergence of armed Kurdish militias in the 1970s and 1980s, that the idea of a Kurdish autonomous region had been fully fomented and strongly expressed by Kurdish leaders.

The move to democratization and fragmentation of Turkish politics

By the late 1940s the popularity of the RPP, and its obsession with controlling every aspect of the economy and polity began dwindling. The new bourgeoisie or industrial class, created as a result of state policy to diversify the economy and establish a solid industrial sector via heavy government intervention, began demanding more economic freedom.

The introduction of multi-party democracy, albeit cautiously, in 1946 led to the emergence of a new opposition party, the Democratic Party (DP), which further undermined the RPP by attracting some of its members, particularly representatives of the bourgeoisie, as well as new members from the centre-right. The first multi-party democratic elections, which took place in 1950, not only brought the main opposition, DP (established in 1946), into power, but seemed to end the RPP's political monopoly. Distrust and political bickering between the main political parties and actors marred the 1950s. The army, supported by the RPP and bureaucracy, was not willing to give politics up, and wanted to press for closer alliance with the West, including with the United States and Europe, as a way to confront the increasing belligerent mood of the emboldened USSR following the end of World War II. The newly elected DP, on the other hand, remained rightly suspicious of the historic loyalty of the army and bureaucracy to the opposition (RPP). The DP and RPP literally disagreed on every aspect of economic policy. Hence, by 1954 Turkey was becoming more interventionist than ever before in its economic affairs. The government hence pushed strongly for import-substituting industrialization (ISI), a process which started in the early 1920s following the declaration of the republic and characterized by heavy protectionist instruments and inward-looking policies that benefited mainly a large industrialist class that was becoming thirstier and thirstier for freedom.

The DP, moreover, was also opposed to the Kamelist Principles. Increased distrust and suspicion reached its climax in 1960 when the DP, in an attempt to undermine the influence of the RPP, introduced strong measures, including an attempt to establish a committee to investigate allegations that the RPP was engaging in subversive activities. This led the army to stage its first anti-democratic military coup in 1960, to overthrow and ban the DP, and to execute its leader, Adnan Menderes. It also re-imposed the RPP in power (Owen, 1992, p. 125; Richards and Waterbury, 1996; Halliday, 2005).

Lacking coherence and clear objectives, the 1960 coup was used by influential groups of intellectuals and officials to place their own reforms. This included, among others, not only the promulgation of a new, more pro-democracy constitution to replace the 1923 constitution, but also new laws permitting the formation of labour unions and collective bargaining between workers and employers (Owen, 1992, pp. 126–7).

Returning to civilian rule and restoring multi-party elections in 1961 did little to improve the popularity of the RPP or stabilize the political system. The successor of the DP, the Justice Party (JP), for example, won more votes in every election between 1961–71 than the RPP, although it was forced to enter into alliance with the RPP in most cases. The exception was in 1965, when the JP won enough votes to form its own government under the leadership of Suleiman Demirel. The 1960s also began to experience a growing radicalization and militancy of a number of workers and leftist student organizations. Although Turkey is 'not a country…where an organized pro-Soviet mass movement existed…[it still] has a significant communist tradition' (Halliday, 2005, p. 108). The political system was further fragmented by internal divisions and defections. For instance, Suleiman Demirel was not able to maintain unity among members of his party, due in large part to increased militancy in the streets and multiplicity of economic interests caused by the enlarged number of bourgeoisie and their representatives in the party. Competing economic interests also emerged between the large industrial class, the main beneficiary of policies of the state, and the main losers, namely, small artisans, craftsmen and merchant class. This led to defections from the JP and the formation of two new parties by the defectors, National Action Party and Islamist National Order Party, in the mid-1960s (Owen, 1992, p. 126).

In an attempt to stem increased militancy, the government in June 1970 introduced a new law that restricted and regulated the power of labour unions and collective bargaining. Union leaders called for demonstrations against the law which soon turned out to be one of the worst riots in the country's history, with more than 100,000 rioters marching the streets of the capital Istanbul and other large cities, leading the army to intervene in order to quell rioters. Similar unprecedented riots erupted nine months later, when the government attempted to introduce austerity measures in order to reduce fiscal deficit and curb inflation. During the riots, urban guerrillas 'launched a Tupamaro-type campaign of bank robberies and kidnapping', as well as assassinations and destruction of public property (Richards and Waterbury, 1996, p. 270). It was against this background that the army intervened and staged its second coup in 1971.

In a country divided upon itself, the leaders of the 1971 military coup had no coherent economic or political plan. Their intervention was confined to another constitutional modification that further restricted labour unions and collective bargaining. They also agreed on returning the country to a civilian rule as soon as possible, which they did in 1973. But these interventions did little to calm labour, restore stability and instil a government capable of implementing necessary economic reforms.

To start with, neither the JP nor the RPP was able to achieve a clear majority in any of the elections held from 1973 onwards, leaving the option of either forming a minority government or entering into weak coalition with one or more of the smaller parties. Weak coalitions, incapable of implementing austerity and necessary economic reforms, marked the 1970s decade.

To make things worse, not only did a split occur within the RPP itself, over almost everything, including the objectives of the 1971 coup, but the RPP became 'now radicalized' and more overtly socialist under the leadership of Bulent Ecevit (Richards and Waterbury, 1996, p. 301). Ecevit soon began pushing the party into a leftward direction in order to attract new constituencies among working-class and minority groups. The outcome was further polarization of the Turkish political system. While the RPP started to vie for support of radical groups on the left, the National Salvation Party (the successor of the Islamic National Order Party) was vying for support of Turkish rights. Simultaneously, the Justice Party and National Action Party sought the support of the right. 'The stage was set for an increasingly heated ideological confrontation which soon spilled into the streets of towns throughout Turkey' (Owen, 1992, p. 126).

Not surprisingly, political instability remained and labour continued to disrupt the economy even after the 1971 military coup and restoration of multi-party democracy in 1973. In 1977, for example, unions went on strike for eight months. Not only labour unions and workers, but also political organizations themselves became more radical, 'settling accounts with arms', along with 'growing political and labour agitations' (Richards and Waterbury, 1996, p. 270). It was difficult to find a parallel to the Turkish political order in MENA in the 1970s, with the two-party system led by the RPP, now more secular and left-leaning, and the JP, increasingly more pro-business centre-right, polarized and fragmented along ideological lines.

Richards and Waterbury (1996, p. 270), while analysing the main political and economic developments in Turkey in the 1970s, described Turkish violence as more akin to that in Argentina, Italy and Germany of the same period than the kind of violence that emerged in other MENA countries:

> The Turkish political arena underwent a kind of centrifugal process by which radical leftist, fascist, and occasionally Muslim militant groups took up arms and fought among themselves. There appears to be little doubt that fascist groups such as the Grey Wolves were the primary instigators of the troubles. They fought for control of the

university campuses, assassinated both one another and 'marked' political leaders, and used the shantytowns as hideouts. By 1980, twenty to thirty Turks were being killed every day, and the total number of political deaths had reached five thousand.

By the end of the decade the Turkish economy was on the verge of collapsing, thanks to a series of weak coalition governments with political and economic interests too diverse to implement a coherent economic policy. Severe economic crisis, marked by large foreign borrowing, burgeoning fiscal deficit and inflationary pressures undermined the credibility of, and confidence in, the Turkish economy. It was against this economic and political background that the military junta ended the 1970s decade in a similar fashion to its beginning. In 1980, the army thus staged its third, most coherent, and the last coup in 1980.

The re-emergence of the Kurdish challenge in a leftist form

Given the magnitude of the political and economic crisis Turkey was experiencing in the late 1970s, the 1980 military intervention was not unwelcomed by most Turks. There was also a need to sort out the economy, whose public deficit, inflationary pressures and level of foreign debt all reached alarming levels, undermining not only credibility and trust in the economy, but also the welfare of the majority of the Turkish population. Both the public and the army generals, however, saw utility in returning to civilian rule as soon as possible.

Following the 1980 military coup, the military seized control of the government and banned all political parties, which were held responsible for the violence of the 1970s and for deteriorating economic performance as a result of their failure to implement a coherent economic program. Also, militarized trade unions and other radical groups were 'violently suppressed once the military seized direct control of the government in 1980' (Richards and Waterbury, 1996, p. 247).

The second most immediate priority of the army was to restore external and internal balances to the economy. To achieve this, a structural adjustment lending program (SAL), designed in cooperation with the IMF and World Bank, long avoided by a series of weak government coalitions, was signed in January (1980) and soon put in force. In 1983 the army allowed a return to 'controlled democracy', in which the newly established party (Motherland Party – MLP) of Turgut Ozal,[3] a charismatic Western-trained economist turned politician, won majority votes. The MLP dominated politics in the 1980s, winning again in 1987 albeit with less votes than it did in 1983. During Ozal's reign in power, an export-oriented program as part of SAL was put in place and implemented, which successfully transformed the Turkish economy and diversified its export structure. Power of labour unions was destroyed, and political activism of workers also came to an end. Turkey, however, began facing new types of challenges, challenges that were even more overtly militant, VEt and directed at the state itself. The most serious and sustainable challenge came from a Kurdish movement, the Partia Karkare Kurdistan or Kurdish Workers' Party (PKK) which continues to seek the creation of an autonomous Kurdish state or region.

As demonstrated at the beginning of this chapter, Kurdish uprisings and rebellions did not historically, at least overtly, openly or overwhelmingly, seek to establish a separatist Kurdish region. More importantly, Kurdish uprisings almost always took a religious form, seeking to restore the former Ottoman 'Pan-Islamic' policy, which Kurdish leaders believed provided unity and cultural harmony. But in 1984, a Kurdish movement known as the PKK launched a struggle against the Turkish state that continues to endure until the current time (March 2012). The PKK emerged in part out of the Turkish left formation, as a whole, in militant armed actions against the state in the 1970s. As Halliday (2005, pp. 107, 184) wrote: 'The PKK, arising out of the radical student milieu of the 1970s, espoused a Marxist-Leninist ideology and sought to establish a separate Kurdish state'. Turkish observers and academics, like Laciner and Bal (2011) concur that Kurdish socialism initially grew as part of the broader Turkish socialist movements but later in the 1970s. A split occurred between Turkish socialism and Kurdish socialism as the former rejected the latter's nationalistic tendencies, leading to the formation of the PKK. Although the PKK, according to Laciner and Bal, made its first appearance in 1974, it was not before the early 1980s that it openly adopted its VEt methodologies.

The PKK's general and declared objective is to separate parts of Turkey and establish a socialism-based unified independent Kurdistan, covering the territories from four countries where Kurds live: Iran, Iraq, Turkey and Syria. In addition to determining its ideology as Marxism/Leninism, the PKK has also described its methods/strategy to realize its objectives through the adoption of armed struggle, or 'the long term Public war' (SECI, 2011, p. 154).

The PKK was established by Abdullah Ocalan and appeared in its organizational form in 1984, although preparation for its establishment preceded that date by far. Initially, the focus was on setting up the organization's structure, recruitment and training. It follows a typical Marxist-Leninist model of Party/Front/Army. The PKK carried out its first attack in 1984. Its attacks are often carried out by the movement's most violent armed wing, the Public Defence Forces (HPG), which was established in 1986 to complement the Structure-Front Model, and which is positioned in northern Iraq where PKK militants receive training and support in the camps.

The PKK is one of the most adaptable, well-structured and -funded, as well as evolving, terrorist organizations. Being secular, it was one of the first organizations to use women in its VEt operations, including suicide operations. In addition to suicide, PKK's VEt tactics include assassinations; armed attacks and bombings of targets with economic sense such as touristic, in metropolitan cities, and human targets, particularly public officers and personalities opposing them, including Kurds; Molotov-cocktail bombings, arsons, damaging state buildings and vehicles; burning down student dormitories, targeting and killing soldiers and police personnel; carrying out ambushes and raids as well as remote-controlled attacks and explosions targeting security and civilians. Following the democratization process introduced in the early 21st century (see below), the PKK tactics, to give its organization a 'democratic face', expanded to include illegal demonstrations where women and children are put at the forefront to prevent security forces from taking retaliatory action. It also uses children to throw Molotov cocktails at security forces (personal interviews with staff at the Police Academy, Ankara, November 2011. Also see SECI, 2011, pp. 154–7).

The PKK relies heavily on its activities in the EU to fund its operations and structure. Taking advantage of open and democratic institutions in the West, as well as of Kurdish diasporas, the PKK has established several organizations to carry out propaganda, indoctrination and fundraising for the movement under the rubric of 'charity'. Such organizations include the European Kurdish Association Confederation (KON-KURD–1993), Parliament for Kurdish in Exile (SKP-1995), Kurdistan National Congress (KNK-1999), Kurdish Red Crescent and International Kurdish Businessmen Union (KARSAZ-2001). The latter was dissolved due to money-laundering and was replaced with the Cooperative Merchant Union in 2009 (SECI, 2011, p. 158).

The PKK's activities have recently increased tension between Turkey and the EU. According to the European Union's Terrorism Situation and Trend Report (TE-SAT) 2011:

The PKK collects money from its members under the rubric of 'donations and membership fees' in lieu of extortion and illegal taxation.

In addition to organized extortion campaigns, there are indications that the PKK is actively involved in money laundering, illicit drugs and human trafficking, as well as illegal immigration inside and outside the EU (quoted in WINEP, 2011).

These developments have led the Turkish Prime Minister, Recep Tayyip Erdogan, to accuse some EU members of extending 'financial assistance to the terrorist organization PKK ...' (WINEP, 2011). On 12 October 2011, Germany, believed to be the PKK's 'economic centre' and following Erdogan's accusations, reacted immediately by arresting Ali Ihsan K, PKK's chief of North Germany, on charges that he was running the organization's extortion and illegal taxation operations inside Germany[4] (WINEP, 2011).

Although its leader, Abdullah Ocalan, was arrested in 1999, the PKK not only remains operative, but is also the most dangerous terrorist organization operating in Turkey, and there has been little change in its ideology or strategy. So far, 'The PKK terror has cost about 30,000 lives and billions of dollars to Turkey' (Laciner and Bal, 2011). Ironically, and typically for a terrorist organizations, the PKK has killed more of its own people, Kurds, than other races (Bal, Ozeren and Sozer, 2011; SECI, 2011; Bal, 2010b).

Turkey does not only face VEt threat from secular, left-oriented organizations like the PKK.[5] Similar threats also come from right-wing, religiously oriented VEt movements, the most prominent of which are Turkish Hezbollah (TH) and al-Qaeda (AQ).[6] Although the name might imply similarities, 'It is extremely important to clarify that Turkish Hezbollah is completely different from Hezbollah organisation active in Lebanon. There is no connection between the two' (Sozer and Server, 2011, p. 23).

TH and other religiously oriented VEt movements in Turkey emerged in the second half of 1970s and were partly influenced by the Iranian revolution which brought a radical, Shia regime to power in Tehran, and partly by the Egyptian Muslim Brotherhood. TH's declared objective is to overthrow the current regime in Turkey and replace it with a theocratic state or regime based on religious principles and rules in accordance with their interpretation of Islam (personal interview with Alper Sozer, Ankara, November 2011. Also see SECI, 2011, p. 153). Like the PKK, TH has also chosen armed and VEt strategies to bring about their Islamic state. Their tactics include armed attacks, shootings, arsons, cleaver assaults, beating up and throwing acid on women not dressed in an Islamic manner, kidnapping businessmen for ransom, in which torture, interrogation and murder were later discovered, murdering members of parliament, and kidnapping and murdering male/female authors and religious leaders who criticize them and their strategies. In 2001, members of TH assassinated the Diyarbakir police commissioner with five other police officers. TH obtains finances mostly from donations from sympathizers, extortion, fees, sales of magazines and CDs, kidnapping of businessmen for ransom and illegal smuggling of goods (SECI, 2011, p. 160).

Ironically, TH, like the PKK, is made up of overwhelmingly Kurdish members and was initiated in the same region, the southeast.[7] This gave the opportunity for victims of PKK terrorism to join TH, as well as those who oppose the PKK's Marxist/Leninist ideology. Between 1981 and 1991, TH refrained from engaging in any terrorist acts or attacking any target. The focus was on strengthening the structure of the organization and on recruitment. In 1991, however, TH and PKK, which function in the same region but under different ideological basis, launched military attacks and operations against one another, leading to a circle of violence that killed hundreds of militants and civilians. It was not before 1995, moreover, that TH began targeting and attacking Turkish security forces, who began pursuing them in the southeast, pushing frontline leaders out of the region to Mardin and Tarsus first then to Istanbul (Sozer and Server, 2011, pp. 23–4). Until 2003, 696 and 434 people were killed and injured, respectively, as a result of attacks launched by TH (SECI, 2011, p. 160).

TH was dealt a heavy blow on 17 January 2000 when an operation by Turkish security led to the killing of the movement's leader and arrest of two of his top lieutenants. More importantly 'in this operation, a rich digital archive was also seized and about twenty thousand pages were recovered. The seizer of the archive made the networks, structure and operation of Turkish Hezbollah crystal clear for the police' (Sozer and Server, 2011, p. 24). Their safe house was raided and top leaders were arrested, although a few fled to Europe and tried to regroup there. More than 3,000 members of TH were arrested by the police in 2000 (personal interview with Sozer, Ankara, November 2011). TH was thus devastated and almost vanished, although in 2001 they assassinated the chief of the Diyarbakir police department.

Members of the Turkish security forces believe that TH has been following a tactical rather than a strategic shift: they are simply regrouping and recruiting and 'it is only a matter of time before they strike again' (personal interview with several members of the Turkish police, Police Academy, Ankara, November 2011). There are two other indications usually taken by Turkish police to suggest that TH is not completely terminated and that its members might resume VEm in the near future. First is the fact that TH's website still carries violence-prone symbols and messages. Second, former top leaders of TH, like the former commander of the movement's armed wing, who were recently released as a result of changes in criminal procedure, seem to still remain radical. After their release, they stated that they do not regret what they did (Sozer and Server, 2011, p. 24).

In addition to the TH, AQ also emerged in Turkey. Turkish AQ (TAQ) has few links to the mother AQ organization in Afghanistan, although it also seeks to overthrow the regime violently and replace it with an Islamic caliphate. The primary target of TAQ is foreign interests (America and its allies) in Turkey, as well as Islamic countries believed to be collaborating with the West against Muslim interests. Members of TAQ, like members of AQ in other Muslim-majority states, were also found to have served and become indoctrinated in Afghanistan. The largest attack carried out by TAQ occurred in November 2003, when four suicide attacks were carried out in Istanbul against HSCB Bank, the British consulate and two Jewish synagogues which killed 61 people – among them 4 suicide bombers – and injuring 647 others. Although the TAQ's influence had been undermined when the organization was dismantled (with its members arrested or fled) following the 2003 attack, a suspected member of AQ allegedly planning to attack an Israeli cruise ship in Antalya was arrested in the southeastern city of Diyarbakir in 2005 (personal interviews with several members of Turkish police, Police Academy, Ankara, November 2011. Also see SECI, 2011, p. 162).

The PKK, TH and TAQ, respectively, are the most dangerous VEt organizations operating in Turkey today, although they are by no means the only ones. Others, less influential and less known to the outside world include, for example, DHKP/C, another organization with a left-wing Marxist ideology. Like the PKK, DHKP/C also aims to overthrow the current system and replace it with a system based on Marxist-Leninist ideology. Unlike the PKK, DHKP/C does not seek to separate parts of Turkey and create a separate, autonomous state or region for its members or followers. The DHKP/C was also undermined following operations by Turkish security forces against TH in 2000 and TAQ in 2003, causing many members to flee the country. Recently, DHKP/C tried to transfer their members back from Europe to Turkey, which might reflect some attempts to reactivate the organization and its actions in the country (SECI, 2011, p. 154).

Turkey's new CT strategy: from militarization to democratization

Until at least the early 1990s, Turkey treated VEm as a security problem and therefore followed a traditional, hard-line military approach to the phenomenon of VEm. This was particularly the case after the 1980 military coup where the generals not only violently suppressed all trade unions and collective bargaining, but also took a 'decision to seek a military solution to the Kurdish problem' (Richards and Waterbury, 1996, p. 248). However, an important shift in the countering violent extremism (CVEm) strategy occurred in the early 1990s, and gained momentum in the early 21st century. Two intertwined factors, one internal and one external, contributed to this shift. First, the traditional military approach to CVEm not only failed, but made things worse. As argued earlier, Turkey lost more than 35,000 lives to VEm, and most of these losses occurred in the 1990s. In the early 1990s, Turkey was losing on average 5,000 lives annually to VEm. Major Yayla, from the TNP, stated in testimony in the US House of Representatives (2006, pp. 22–3) that Turkey had to make significant changes in its CTS and that 'These changes were made because of increased terrorist threats' caused by implementing a purely military approach. He added that such a shift was necessary 'Due to the effects of different terrorist campaigns over the years', which cost Turkey to lose 'over 35,000 people to terrorism since 1960' SECI (2011, p. 168) and concurred that: 'Turkey has realised that relying solely on security measures does not produce a sustainable solution to the threat of terrorism', hence 'Turkey has gone through a paradigm shift in its counter terrorism strategy' (SECI, 2011, p. 168).

The decision to seek a military solution to the phenomenon of VEm, moreover, fuelled government spending, generated large budgetary deficits and began undermining the economic reforms which Turgut Ozal had started in the early 1980s. Writing in the second half of the 1990s, Richards and Waterbury (1996, pp. 248, 337) suggested that 'Kurdish policy now costs Turkey some US\$ 500 million per year; the total cost is estimated at US\$8 billion', with a former Turkish PM, Tansu Ciller, publicly admitting that 'her country was spending 5% of GDP annually on its war against PKK'. Owen (1992, p. 215) went further to argue that 'The political and sectarian violence', made worse by the decision to seek a military solution to the Kurdish problem, 'was degenerating into "civil war"'.

The second factor that led to a paradigm shift in Turkey's countering violent extremism (CVEm) strategy was the desire to join the EU, a key Turkish wish since the end of World War II.[8] Although Turkey first applied for an associate membership in the EEC in September 1959 and four years later (in September 1963) signed an Association Agreement (known as the Ankara Agreement) aimed at bringing Turkey into a Customs Union with the EEC, relations between Turkey and the EU stagnated. The cause of stagnation was threefold: the 1980 military coup; Turkish authorities' decision to take a military approach to the Kurdish problem; and the Turkish government's strong intervention in economic affairs. These issues became major sticking points in negotiations with the EU, whose membership requires not only establishing a free-market economy, but also adherence to EU legal standards of liberal democracy and human rights. Rule by generals, repression of labour and ruthless suppression of Kurdish organizations were not compatible with entry into the EU. The emergence of 'a national consensus of the sort that the country should join the EU' in the late 1980s and early 1990s, in addition to huge economic costs of the military approach, were responsible for bringing a shift in Turkey's CTS (Richards and Waterbury, 1996, p. 301). One can also argue that, perhaps as a result of the factors mentioned above, that Turkish politics matured in the 1990s, and that as a result of this 'maturity' a shift in favour of a 'softer' approach to the phenomenon of VEm occurred at the expense of a pure military solution that kept the generals' leverage over Turkish politics strong (Halliday, 2005, p. 62).

The first signs of the new approach came on 12 April 1991, when a new Counter Terrorism Law (No. 3713) was enacted and became the cornerstone of CVEm in Turkey. The new CT law not only defined terrorism, terrorist organization and terrorist activity, but also entrusted the entire process of CVEm to the Ministry of Interior and its law enforcement agencies, particularly the Turkish National Police (TNP). The TNP is the largest law enforcement institution in Turkey today and it has been charged with the responsibility of implementing the entire new CT strategy. The TNP operates in or within the municipal boundaries (urban areas), along with the Gendarmerie and Coast Guard. The former is a paramilitary organization that provides security outside urban areas and small towns and villages, while the latter is in charge of coast security[9] (SECI, 2011, p. 165).

To emphasize the point, the responsibility of CVEm was taken away from the army and given to the TNP. This was commensurate with the new rationale prevalent among Turkish official circles, which came to see VEm as a crime, rather than a security threat, and which could be dealt with better by the police than by the army. Major Ahmet

Yayla explained the new rationale behind this shift (US House of Representatives, 2006, p. 21):

> The Turkish Police considers terrorism as a crime problem, which the police can handle...the police are able to address terrorism without disrupting communities. As a result, there is not a backlash by the community against the police, which comes back as a support of the community in the fight against terrorism.

Before discussing the key components of the Turkish CTS, it is important to draw attention to some of the key changes that took place within the TNP in order to enable its cadre to effectively counter violent extremism in the country.

The new approach to CVEm is best described as 'preventative', aimed at taking precautionary measures to prevent possible terrorist attacks. To facilitate the TNP's new responsibilities, two main departments were created that deal directly with VEm around the country: the Anti-Terrorism Department (ATD) and the Intelligence Department (ID), both of which are located in the headquarters of TNP. The ATD and the ID are also supported by satellite anti-terrorism divisions and intelligence divisions established within all of the city and township police departments. While the satellite divisions deal with more immediate threats at a local level, the central departments function at the national level and coordinate, facilitate and provide assistance to the satellite units. One of the most innovative aspects of this cooperation is the level, quality, speed and quantity of intelligence data–gathering.

Local satellite units receive information from their localities and then input or feed this information to a special software package (called POL-NET) developed by experts in the Department of Information Technology (DIT) established in 1982 in collaboration with officers in the field so that the software is developed appropriately to suit the needs and objectives of the officers in the field. When received, the central units analyse this information and make it available to all relevant ATDs, units and personnel (either in the headquarters or cities). The central divisions thus act as an archive and database epicentre in general efforts against CVEm. The upshot has been the establishment of:

> One of the largest closed computer network systems for the TNP, which is an organizational intranet with around 15,000 computers and over 30,000 users in every location where the TNP has jurisdiction including TNP Headquarters, city police departments, police

stations, airports, border gates, and other places where the TNP has infrastructures around the country. Currently, this network is one of the largest Microsoft-based networks in the world (US House of Representatives, 2006, p. 22).

By making the new POL-NET package available to all relevant anti-terrorism institutions and personnel, the TNP ATDs were able to make significant appropriate information available, to share data as soon as needed and to obtain information as fast as possible. It also improved coordination among different Turkish ATDs and units, as well as tremendously improving the TNP effectiveness in CVEm, not only directly, but also indirectly, as we shall see later in what follows.

In addition to POL-NET, ATDs' and units' work is facilitated not only by an internal phone system that connects all AT offices around the country, but also by an internal email system, countrywide radio system, as well as connecting all of the TNP officers together through a GSM phone system which can be used to call any TNP official 24 hours a day free of charge (US House of Representatives, 2006, p. 28).

The police force is the first and most important face of the state. Police forces are the first to see, and be seen by, citizens and even potential VEts while carrying out their duties and responsibilities. They are the ones who halt and oversee crime in the country, including terrorism, whenever and wherever it happens. The way they deal with such problems, therefore, can make a big difference, particularly in terms of societal image of, and response to, police intervention and initiatives. The key therefore lies not only in disrupting crime and VEm, but also in disrupting them without disrupting community life or creating a backlash from the community against the police. This ensures that the community supports police and security officers whenever needed and particularly in the fight against VEm.

In fact, one of the most important objectives of VEt organizations and groups is to create animosity, hostility and even hatred between governments and their societies so that societies will not only turn away, but also turn against their governments. Rather than facilitating and supporting security forces in carrying out their AT responsibilities, societies and communities, if antagonized, could impede and undermine such a process. In some cases, societies and communities can even support criminals and VEts by providing logistical, financial, intelligence and other forms of support that makes it much harder for security forces to carry out their responsibilities of securing the country against threat of VEt attacks.

Countries with weak developmental capacities (unable to manage sustainable growth rates, improve equality, create jobs for their youth and manage relations with their minorities) are often vulnerable and susceptible to antagonistic state–society relations. So are countries with weak political capacity ('falling' or 'failed' states not capable of providing their citizens with security or defending their borders) (El-Said and Harrigan, 2013). But countries with a poor human rights record, and those that fail to uphold the rule of law and resort to torture as an investigative technique are equally vulnerable to alienating their societies and communities (El-Said and Harrigan, 2013).Turkey in the 1980s and early 1990s was no exception. As Major Ahmet Yayla stated (quoted in US House of Representatives, 2006, p. 30):

> One of the main reasons of joining terrorist organizations according to the surveys of the terrorists[10] during their interrogations, was the assumption that the TNP did not consider the international rules of human rights for the suspects in their custody and did not obey the rule of law when it came to the terrorist suspects. In fact, many terrorist suspects were made to believe by their organizations that they would be killed or seriously harmed after they were arrested or they would be detained for months. ... Furthermore, the TNP realized that once a terrorist suspect was arrested, that suspect's relatives and friends became easy recruitment targets for the terrorist organizations.

It is not surprising therefore that 'The most important counter terrorism strategies of Turkey are transparency and zero tolerance to human rights violations' (SECI, 2011, p. 16). The strongest reflection of Turkey's new CTS is the country's 'Democratization Process' initiated in the very early years of the 21st century in preparation for the prospect of negotiations in the Copenhagen Summit of 2002 before picking up and being rejuvenated with unprecedented rigor in 2004 by the Islamically oriented Turkish Justice and Development Party (JDP) which won a landslide victory in the 2002 elections and which continues to dominate Turkish politics until the time of this writing (March 2012). The 'Democratization Process' adopts a holistic approach to the phenomenon of VEm, including political, cultural, social and economic dimensions.

The political dimension: winning hearts and minds

The entire political aspect of the 'Democratization Process' is based on the new philosophy of 'winning hearts and minds' of the segments of the population most vulnerable to VEt ideology and activism among Turks and Kurds alike. It also seeks to win the support of Turkish communities in the fight against VEts. To this end, a number of real laws, translated into unprecedented constitutional reforms, took place between October 2001 and 2005. One of the most important and relevant reforms to the goals of this chapter is the legal banning of torture as an investigative technique, the acquisition of information under duress, the shortening of pre-trial detention periods, the limitation of the death penalty to times of war and terrorist crimes, changes that made the prohibition and dissolution of political parties more difficult, and expansion of the freedom of association and strengthening of civil authority in the National Security Council.[11] Significant changes in the area of gender equality, protection of children and vulnerable persons were also made after a new Civil Code entered into force on 1 January 2002. Following the Copenhagen Summit of European Council in December 2002, three harmonization packages that aimed at translating the preceding constitutional amendments into action by harmonizing them with the EU standards and regulations were introduced. Further reforms, particularly in the field of human rights and protection of minorities, freedom of expression and freedom of association were also made. The most notable of these were the easing of restrictions on broadcasting and the right to learn 'different languages and dialects (Petricusic and Erkan, 2010, pp. 142–4; Gros, et al., 2004, pp. 17–18; Yildiz and Goktepe, 2011). More significant amendments clearly establishing civilian primacy, reforming of the judiciary and extending guarantees for the freedom of the press were also approved by the Parliament (Yildiz and Goktepe, 2011).

As a result of these reforms, and compared with previous decades, the Kurds have been one of the major beneficiaries, in terms of increased prosperity, democratization and institutionalization and harmonization of laws. One of the most visible outcomes of reforms is the setting up of Kurdish departments in Turkish universities with the right to learn and teach the Kurdish language, permitting the establishment of Kurdish radio and TV channels broadcasting in Kurdish language, the right to vote freely and establish Kurdish parties, allowing election campaigns to be conducted in the Kurdish language, with the Ministry of Culture allocating a special budget to spend on developing various Kurdish cultural activities (Bal, 2011a and 2011b). Indeed, at least two political parties, the AKP and BDP, are today associated with the Kurdish interests in the Turkish parliament and for whom most of the Kurdish people vote (Bal, 2011a and 2011b).

The social and cultural dimension

The core of the new 'soft' Turkish CTS is that radicalization is a 'process' that 'can only be challenged through reversing the process' via a more proactive engagement with the community (Yildiz and Goktepe, 2011, p. 4). This approach, otherwise known as 'community policing' assumes greater accountability for the police, a greater role for the community in collaborative problem-solving and a greater concern for civil rights and liberties.

Community policing (CP) is a relatively new approach in Turkey, whose implementation goes back to around the year 2008. It was designed by the TNP and implemented in collaboration with local representatives, clan leaders, village elders, imams, teachers and psychologists. According to Ozeren and Cinoglue (quoted in Yildiz and Goktepe (2011, p. 83), and as part of the new CP philosophy, the TNP carry out four types of social projects/visits.

The first of these projects/visits reflects the new philosophy of TNP, rather than a project/visit per se: a philosophy of 'winning hearts and minds'. It is based on the fact that terrorist organizations in Turkey exploit and make full use of propaganda about bad treatment of security officers, including the use of excessive force against rioters, employing illegal means during interrogations and even torture, and showing disrespectful behaviour to the people of the area. The TNP therefore seeks to correct and change these images not only by changing its old practices of detainment, but also by providing a better treatment for members of various communities, including members of VEt organizations. Rather than relying on abusing and miscomputing the detainees to get information about other members of VEt organizations, POL-NET enables the police to focus more on its effective intelligence-gathering and surveillance instruments instead.

Second, visits to villages, public places and opinion leaders. Most of these visits take place during social events, such as funerals, marriages, offering of condolences, Ramadan and other social rituals. The idea behind these visits is to make the public aware of the dangerous consequences of VEt ideology and activism. People who are followed and trusted by the youth (opinion leaders), like, for example, religious and clan leaders, are visited by police chiefs in their houses and in person. Sometimes a special dinner is organized for opinion leaders during Ramadan, in addition to organizing dinners in every district for the districts' opinion leaders. The latter is often hosted by the governor of the district and chief of police, during which participants are informed about all the projects run by police and about all the new changes that have occurred in laws and regulations (Yildiz and Goktepe, 2011, pp. 89–90).

A police chief, often accompanied by a local governor and the village's imam, also uses such social events (funeral, marriage, Ramadan ceremonies, etc.) to spread the true virtues of Islam, including tolerance, coexistence and forgiveness (personal interviews with officers in Turkish Police Academy, and Dr Sabit Simsek, Head of Interfaith and Intercultural Relations Department, The Presidency of Religious Affairs, Ankara, November 2011).

Third, visits to homes. These take two forms. The first type of visit is to the homes of families who are not themselves engaged in VEt activities but seem to sympathize with VEt organizations and ideology and therefore support them in different ways, including, for example, promoting their ideology, ideas and arguments. The main aim of these visits is to demonstrate to the families that they are not ignored or forgotten by the state or its officials, and to explain to them the dangerous consequences of VEm and the new rules and regulations, including improvements in human rights. They also seek to develop communication with the public and families who sympathize with VEm. Such visits can last up to three hours, and, consistent with the Turkish culture, always take place in the house of the targeted family as it is seen as 'honourable' to be visited by a high-ranking state official (Yildiz and Goktepe, 2011, p. 86).

The second type of visit targets families whose children are showing radical tendencies or who are about to join a VEt organization and, if the situation is not reversed, they will be arrested and imprisoned. VEt organizations in Turkey, as elsewhere, target young individuals in their areas. The TNP relies on its strong data and intelligence-gathering capacity to identify the families of children targeted by VEt organizations and groups. The aim of these visits is to convince the families to talk to their children and persuade them to steer away from VEt organizations and groups. Especially targeted are families who do not have sufficient information about their children, the organizations they join and activities they conduct. Knowing more about their children will lead most families to intervene to prevent their children from committing illegal acts or joining VEt organizations and groups, particularly when presented with facts (Yildiz and Goktepe, 2011, p. 87).

The final type of visit is to families of student leaders who organize riots or demonstrations, and visits to *'Deger Aile'* (Value Family). The former type of family visits occur because such leaders usually have a large following and, if persuaded, their parents can prevent them from participating in demonstrations/riots, throwing stones or even Molotov cocktails which will lead to their imprisonment. The *'Deger Aile'* (Value Family) visits target families whose sons or relatives have already joined a VEt organization or group but have not committed any crime yet. Here families are informed about the activities of their children, their rights and opportunities available for them to leave such groups and organizations behind. Most importantly, the new 'Law of Homecoming and Repentant', which provides members of VEt organizations and groups who did not commit crimes with an exit strategy,[12] is also explained to the families during these visits (Yildiz and Goktepe, 2011, p. 87).

Not all families with children recruited or about to be recruited by VEt organizations and groups are visited. 'Some families are radical themselves and sympathize and support VEt ideologies and activism. There is no point visiting such families because they are radical themselves, need de-radicalization first and visiting them will bear no fruit' (personal interviews with members of Turkish Police Academy and Dr Sabit Simsek of The Presidency of Religious Affairs, Ankara, November 2011).

During all types of visits to the homes of various families, the police officer is often accompanied by an imam, mayor and a psychologist. While the police officer explains to the families the dangerous consequences of VEt ideology and activism, the imam explains and clarifies to the families the legal and moral position of Islam with regard to VEm in general. 'The psychologist is needed in case the family has some psychological issues, therefore we bring the psychologist in order to deal with any kind of psychological problems that might arise during visits to family' (personal interview with Dr M. Alper Sozer of Turkish Police Academy, Ankara, November 2011).

Finally, a cultural and social program has also been designed and implemented by the TNP. The program specifically targets children at schools and colleges because they are the main target of the Turkish VEt groups and organizations.[13] Activities involved in such a program include taking children to watch a movie at the theatre, organizing city tours to historical places, organizing a small show for children in a police department or centre, often including lunch for them, and arranging visits for children to the house of the police chief in the district. This cultural and social program is usually implemented in areas most vulnerable to crime and VEm. The aim of the cultural and social program is to make first contact with children and therefore to reach them before VEt groups do. Also, and more importantly, the cultural and social program seeks 'to spread the message [of peace] to different arrays of the public' and to change the image of the 'police formerly known for their rudeness and ruthlessness' (Yildiz and Goktepe, 2011, p. 88). Again, police officers, depending on the size of the activity, are often accompanied in each cultural/social activity by imams, teachers, village managers and public leaders. The most important example of a cultural program is the Mardin Project in Mardin city, which has so far reached and led to the participation of literally half of all of the 70,000 Mardin students by July 2011, that is, 35,000. In one of its activities, and in addition to students, more than 100 village managers and approximately 1,000 teachers and several public leaders and citizens took part (ibid.).

The economic dimension

The economic performance of Turkey under the JDP has been exceptional and unprecedented to say the least. The country's massive fiscal deficit on the eve of the 2002 elections has been turned into a large surplus of US$1.2 billion by the end of 2011. Between 2000 and 2009, Turkey achieved an annual growth rate of 4.9 per cent, rising to 8.8 per cent in 2011, the highest growth rate achieved inside the EU. Not only did unemployment decline to around 9 per cent in 2011, but inflation also recorded its lowest level since 1970. Finally, Turkey has also been able to improve equity in the country, thanks to 'achieving [both] sustained and equitable economic growth, [while] avoiding costly financial crises' that characterized the 1970s and 1980s (Onis, 2005, p. 2; World Bank, 2011; Today's Zaman, 2011). As a result of these developments, the Turkish economy moved to the position of 'the 15th largest economy in the world and the 6th largest in Europe, [and] the largest in the Middle East' (*The Journal of Turkish Weekly*, 2010).

The impressive Turkish economic performance under the JDP has been achieved by, contrary to general expectations, displaying a strong commitment to the basic principles of fiscal stabilization and structural reforms embodied in the IMF and World Bank structural adjustment program, with a single-minded commitment to fiscal discipline in particular:

> This commitment made a sharp contrast with the experience of the Turkish economy since the late 1980s during which serious fiscal instability has been associated with a major domestic and external debt burden and successive financial crises. ... In addition, the

government has been able to continue with key institutional reforms such as banking sector regulation ... the JDP government has been making a concerted effort for the first time to deal with the pervasive problem of corruption that has been a major negative feature of the Turkish economy during the neo-liberal era. The problem has been attacked through an improvement of the legal system as well as by taking legal action against key businessmen and politicians who are accused of having been involved in corruption during the recent era. (Onis, 2005, pp. 1, 11)

There is also another rationale behind the motivation to improve economic performance in Turkey:

It is also very important to go after the causes of terrorism so that the repeat cycle of the terrorists can be interrupted. If the terrorists lose their justification, they are not going to be able to recruit more people. And by this we can diminish the threat coming from the terrorist organizations. (US House of Representatives, 2006, p. 22)

A study by TNP has shown that unemployment, and by extension a pessimistic future outlook and potential, is a key determinant of membership in VEt organizations like the TH (Sozer and Server, 2011). A regional project, aimed at improving the living standards, particularly in the Eastern province which hosts the two most dangerous VEt organizations in the country, the PKK and TH, has been implemented since 2008. Examples of such projects include the Social Support Programme (SODES),[14] the Project of Supporting Infrastructure of Villages (KOYDES), Multipurpose Social Centre (CATOM), Dicle Development Agency and Firat Development Agency. These projects have been organized and implemented in order to eliminate the underlying social and economic problems exploited by VEt groups and organizations to recruit disgruntled and discontented young individuals. Since the massive economic and social changes Turkey experienced after 1950 led to the relative neglect or rural economy and associated rural–urban migration, such projects also aim to overcome social problems stemming from migration and rapid urbanization (SECI, 2011, p. 166).

In addition to macroeconomic structural reforms and regional policies and initiatives, the Turkish government also installed measures to support repentant, former VEt individuals and facilitate their reintegration into their families and society. Individuals that seek to leave VEm behind and rejoin society are supported in various ways. If they were unemployed, their names are given to specialized employment agencies to assist them in finding new jobs. If they need money, they are referred to a regional fund which provides support to needy and poor families. If the families of incarcerated individuals have no one else to support them, they are also referred to the same regional fund for support. For example, if the incarcerated individual is the main breadwinner and his wife asks for support in joining an IT or sewing course in order to maintain a sustainable income in the future, she is supported in doing so. If the children of the incarcerated VEt need educational support and/or maintenance and food, their needs are met. 'We do this because we want to reach the children and families of VEts before the terrorists reach them and recruit them for their cause before us' (personal interview with Alper Sozer, Turkish Police Academy, Ankara, November 2011). The funding for such support, moreover, comes from charity, which feeds every regional fund[15] and therefore bears little financial cost to the state (personal interview with Dr Sabit Simsek, GD of External Relations, Head of Interfaith and Intercultural Relations Department, The Presidency of Religious Affairs, Ankara, November 2011).

Finally, another key innovation of the Turkish new CT paradigm is a law that compensates losers from destruction and damages caused by terrorism, either by terrorists themselves or security forces while carrying out their CT duties, that is, The Law on Compensation for Terrorism and Counter Terrorism Losses, Law No. 5233 (SECI, 2011, p. 164). The aim of the law is to prevent alienation of communities affected negatively by terrorism or anti-terrorism operations, to avoid turning local communities against the state and its security forces, and to motivate community members to collaborate with the state by showing them that the state cares not only about them but also about their property.

The implications of the new Turkish soft CTS

Nobody claims that the new Turkish 'soft' paradigm has eliminated terrorism in the country. As one Turkish police officer stated: 'We made mistakes for more than 15 years; it will take another 15 years to correct the situation' (personal interview, Turkish Police Academy, Ankara, November 2011). In fact, since October 2011 Turkey has experienced at least two major attacks by a group of PKK members, the first in Southeastern Turkey (October 2011) which killed and injured several Turkish soldiers, policemen and civilians, including a child, and the second (January 2012) in Istanbul when several shops and buildings were attacked in the capital, leading to the arrest of 17 PKK members (Nato International, 2011).

There is no question, however, that not only did the incidence of terrorism decline rather noticeably in Turkey since peaking in the 1990s, but also the total number of fatalities. Academics, scholars and practitioners alike have tended to consider the incidents of terrorism, fatalities per attack and recidivism rates as the main proxies for success of 'soft' counter radicalization and de-radicalization programs (Horgan and Braddock, 2010). While important, these proxies are not problem-free indexes to evaluate the effectiveness of such programs. Increased and enhanced security apparatus and repression by a strong government, say like China, for example, could rapidly reduce the terrorism incidents, at least in the short to medium term. Increased surveillance and constant monitoring of released former VEt individuals can equally reduce the incentive to return to a former life of VE (El-Said and Harrigan, 2013). What has received less attention in the literature, nevertheless, are the other spillovers and positive externalities emerging from the implementation of 'soft' measures to countering VEm.

In the case of Turkey, one of the most significant spillovers is the professionalization of Turkish police, increasing their knowledge about the process of radicalization and enabling them to deal with radicalization in a way that does not lead to a societal or community backlash to police efforts and initiatives. Indeed, professionalization of security apparatus becomes all the more important especially in multi-ethnic states faced by VEt threat as Major Yayla stated:

> One of the first experiences of the police officers in the field was realizing how little they knew about the terrorist organizations they were investigating. In fact, they rarely received specialized training regarding terrorism or investigation techniques of terrorist incidents. Another dilemma was the fact that most of the terrorists had some college education or were college graduates. This posed difficulties especially during interrogation when a mind game between the interrogators and terrorists would take place. (Quoted in US House of Representatives, 2006, p. 21)

To overcome these difficulties, a long-term educational and training plan was put in place to enable TNP officers to perform their duties more effectively and to ensure a better future for TNP. One important reform here was to increase the number of police colleges (equivalent to vocational high schools) from one to five:

> Graduates of the police colleges attend the national Police Academy, which basically provides a bachelor's degree similar to a degree obtained from the universities' criminal justice departments in the U.S. The graduates of the national Police Academy became mid-level managers of the TNP. This initial step proved to be very successful and effective because the schools became more specialized and selective. (ibid., 21)

To ensure that members of TNP involved in AT operations understand the new principles of human rights and rights of minorities, several control mechanisms were enacted to make sure that these principles are implemented. These included improvement through amendments in the administration affairs as well as in training programs, such as the CT Services Basic Training Course which requires all AT officers and personnel to participate in a seminar on human rights. Another Human Rights Course has been organized since 2003 to notify CT personal about the current developments on human rights. Training also takes place at the Faculty of Security Sciences, Police Vocational High Schools and Police Vocational Training Centres, where areas related to terrorism are taught through courses entitled Terrorism and State Security, both of which are being taught inside the Turkish National Police Academy (TNPA). They provide in-depth discussions, seminars and lectures on areas related to terrorism and human rights. A special graduate program, International Terrorism and Transnational Crime, has also been created at the Institute of Security Sciences of the Turkish National Police academy for the same objective of enhancing AT training, knowledge of the new rules of engagement and the latest methods of countering VEm (SECI, 2011, pp. 166–8).

It is no secret that not only is generating information costly, time-consuming and a difficult process, but sharing it, even within the same unit or department is especially difficult, often due to the lack of bonds and trust between and among members of the same department. This is a problem prevalent in developed as much as in developing countries. One of the major spillovers of the extensive and intensive educational and training reform in Turkey tailored to CVEm, in addition to professionalizing and enhancing the knowledge and skills of TNP, has been the creation of special bonds between and among graduates. These bonds not only facilitated data-gathering and -collection, but also the process of sharing it:

> More importantly, police colleges were highly successful in establishing bonds between their students. Almost all of the students became brothers or buddies for life and supported each other through their tenure in the following years. This bond helped eradicate reluctance in sharing the proper information in the following years. College graduates easily and willingly, in fact without being asked, shared information with their co-workers and other police officers in different cities or in the headquarters for the success of the TNP simply because their friends were in charge of those departments and they wanted to help them in their duties so that they would be more successful in providing safety to their citizens. This bond and friendship between the mid-level leadership and later the high-level leadership of the TNP has been one of the biggest secrets behind its success. Finally, even the terrorists who had been arrested under the old system admitted that it was more difficult to influence or maneuver the new interrogators. (Quoted in US House of Representatives, 2006, p. 21)

The bonds created between members of TNP, in addition to the establishment of the POL-NET, led to doing away with the old, basic and less effectual system known as the 'Captain's notes'. The latter refers to the bureau captain who wrote notes regarding terrorists down on his notebook and kept the information for himself because his job and success relied on it. The captain thus had little motive to share his information with other members of TNP or institutions. Worse, once the captain is transferred to another position or retires, this information becomes of little use. POL-NET and the bonds of friendship created among TNP also facilitated the process of tracking terrorists as they moved from one city to another, hence enhancing the effectiveness of TNP in CVE tremendously (personal interviews with members of the Turkish Police Academy, Ankara, November 2011, and US House of Representatives, 206, p. 23).

The new, 'soft' face of the security forces, the professionalization of its members, and the new culture of human rights respect practiced by security forces TNP has had, particularly in the face of continued terrorist attacks that kill more Kurds than Turks, many other significant spillovers. One such spillover relates to the new developments within the Kurdish communities themselves. The PKK seems to be losing a great deal of Kurdish support. Many Kurds have already moved away from supporting the PKK and even Kurdish parties in the Turkish Parliament and have lent their support and votes to the centre parties, particularly the Islamically oriented AKP party which sees Islam, to a large extent, as the main bond and culture that unites all Turkish citizens. It is not surprising therefore that Kurds, in the last two elections, for example, voted more for centre parties, even in Kurdish regions, than they did for Kurdish ones. As Bal (2011b) wrote:

> most of the gains for the Kurds have been obtained through the efforts of the parties of the center, it becomes even more obvious why these parties pick up the votes of a large majority of the Kurds. In large measure they are being represented by parties like the Motherland Party and the Justice and Development Party (AKP). In Turkish political history those Kurds voting for the mainstream parties, however large a proportion they are, may have the lead but they are denounced all the same in certain circles for not being 'real' Kurds. There are even some analysts who write that those Kurds who belong to the mainstream parties are just a 'bloc' of voters suffering from faulty awareness.

The new reforms which have been carried out by the Turkish authorities to CVEm, including the 'democratization process' and community policing in particular, have also improved state–society relations, and the societal image of, and collaboration with, TNP. More local representatives, clan leaders, village elders, imams, teachers, physiologists and psychologists have been joining the CP program in reaching out to their communities and collaborating with the TNP. There is strong evidence which suggests that, as a result of family visits, 'We see that these visits have reduced recruitment of terrorist organisations' (Yildiz and Goktepe, 2011, p. 83).

Probably one of the most important outcomes of reforms is its impact inside the prison environment itself. Improving conditions inside incarceration centres, illegalizing and terminating torture as an investigative technique, treating members of VEt groups and organizations with respect, as well as welfare provisions to needy families of both detainees and released individuals, not only changed the repressive image of TP, but also led to significant gathering of life-saving intelligence. Excerpts from interviews carried out with members of TH and PKK, both inside and outside incarceration centres, are not only full of emotional responses, but also reflect on how simple treatment changed individuals inside the world of VEm (ibid., pp. 84–5). As a detained member of TH, following his knowledge that TP provided needed food, water and gasoline to his family and children in a bitterly cold winter, reacted:

> Did you buy that gasoline for my house?...My brother, I always saw you as Kafirs and even did not look at your faces. Now you are caring about my kid and buying gasoline to stop his crying. How different you are than we have in our minds. Now I will give the details of murders committed by myself. I will also give you all the secrets of the Turkish Hizbullah. (Quoted in Yildiz and Goktepe, 2011, p. 85)

Finally, it goes without saying that the government's 'strong commitment to the goal of EU membership and the associated reform agenda, both on the economic and democratization fronts, helped to inspire confidence among domestic and foreign investors, and this has been one of the key reasons behind the unprecedented economic success of Turkey since the early 21st century' (Onis, 2005, p. 2). Economic prosperity and strengthening the state's developmental capacity has done a great deal to undermine the general conditions conducive to radicalization and extremism that lead to terrorism.

Conclusion

Very few Muslim-majority states have gone as far as Turkey has and undergone the kind of paradigm shift that Turkey experienced in recent years in its attempt to counter the phenomenon of VEm. No question both internal and external factors contributed to such an outcome.

The Turkish experience with CVEm provides several important lessons, with significant policy implications.

First, pure military approaches to the phenomenon of VEm not only don't work, but can also make things worse in terms of increased terrorism incidences and fatalities, as well as accompanied financial costs and general confidence in the economic environment.

Second, a change in official mentality and attitude towards CVEm is necessary for the success of both initiating and sustaining reforms. Unless there is a strong political will behind reforms, the latter might prove half-hearted and unsustainable.

Third, it is wrong to view the effectiveness of 'soft' measures to counter VEm and de-radicalize VEt groups and individuals in the prism of terrorism incidents, fatalities and/or recidivism. Important as these indexes are, they oversimplify the complex issues involved, wrongly presume that countering VEm is a short-term process and largely ignore other benefits that often emerge from implementing such measures. Most prominent among these benefits is the improvement in state-society relations, the image of the state's security forces and ensuing societal collaboration which is vital for successful counter-de-radicalization processes. Another indirect but still significant benefit is improvement in access to vital information related to security and activities of radical and other extremists groups. This, in the case of Turkey, has been a function of improved technical and administrative capacities of national police units involved in AT responsibilities, increased collaboration of detained or potential VEt groups and individuals with security forces (itself caused by improvement in human rights rules, regulations and practices), or both.

Fourth, the experience of Turkey with the process of 'Europeanization' of its rules and regulations suggests that superpowers can play a key role in effecting a change in national policies of developing countries aspiring to join or enhance access to economic, financial or political gains from developed regions and states. Unfortunately, and although several rich countries did enact external policies that aim at encouraging developing countries, particularly those in the Middle East and North Africa, to democratize, improve human rights rules, regulations and practices, and revitalize civil society and local communities, little has been achieved in practice, either in terms of real pressure exerted by the rich countries or in terms of reforms occurring in reality (El-Said and Harrigan, 2011; 2013).

Finally, despite reforms, Turkey could still do more, particularly with regard to de-radicalization inside prisons. For example, there is no dialogue program inside incarceration centres. Such programs proved significant in changing the misled ideas of individuals joining VEt groups and organizations. The Turkish prison chaplain system provides an 'imam only if an incarcerated individual asks for one in order to discuss a specific subject, such as the hajj, prayer, prophet, and so forth but I really have no idea why we do not have a dialogue program like Saudi Arabia, for example' (personal interview with Dr Sabit Simsek, The Presidency of Religious Affairs, Ankara, November 2011).

There is no one size fits all and no silver bullet for an immediate termination of VEt threat. Such a process is country-, culture- and context-specific. It should also be looked upon as a long-term process and part and parcel of a larger package of reform aimed at improving not only the political, but also social and economic environments, as well as state–society relations. This is perhaps the most important lesson derived from the Turkish experience with countering violent extremism.

9
Concluding Remarks

This book analysed the counter radicalization and de-radicalization policies designed and implemented by five United Nations Member States, three of which are Muslim-majority states (Mauritania, Turkey and Sudan) and two Muslim-minority, Western states (Australia and Singapore). All of these countries have one thing in common: at some point over the past decade, they all suffered from the threat of VEm. Some continue to do so more than others. All of them have introduced processes, measures and policies to deal with this threat. They differ however in their resources, population size and demographic mix, level of development, geographical locations, history, legal systems, culture, belief systems and values, and time of implementing Counter-de-Rad policies. They are, in other words, countries that faced a similar threat and designed what are *perceived* to be similar policies which the literature lumps together as counter radicalization and de-radicalization (Counter-de-Rad) policies, but which have different outcomes. Studying such a mix of countries offers one of the most effective ways to derive lessons regarding the conditions conducive to success/failure of these policies, identifying best practices, and even moving forward with the current impasse regarding how best to evaluate and assess Counter-de-Rad policies, as later analysis will demonstrate. A few points are in order here.

First, while most of the processes and measures generally called Counter-de-Rad programs seem similar on the surface, in reality they differ in many important ways. For example, they vary in the way they are being designed and implemented, their components, the agencies charged with their design and implementation, the response and role of civil society, the level and sources of threat, the resources available to them, the role of families, the role of religious dialogue and rehabilitation, the role of incentives offered, and the conditions under which they are being implemented. Despite these significant differences, they are all still described, rather inaccurately, by policymakers, practitioners and even some academics as Counter-de-Rad programs. There remains no agreement on what constitutes a Counter-de-Rad program and what distinguishes such programs from other policies, or even standard prison management practices.

Indeed, and secondly, some of the so-called de-radicalization programs studied in this book and elsewhere do not really amount to a de-radicalization program and do not go beyond a general improvement in prison management and environment. Most of these policies do not really differ from the kind of policies and practices that are already present in several other well-managed prisons, particularly in Western countries that seek to rehabilitate other criminals, gangs and drug addicts. For example, the special 'Shock Incarceration Treatment' program introduced in four main prisons in New York in the late 1980s, long before the so called de-radicalization programs even became popular, includes key components similar to the kind of policies one observes in what is today referred to, for better or worse, as a de-radicalization program that seeks to de-radicalize and/or disengage violent extremists. In fact, New York's 'Shock Incarceration Treatment' program is far more coherent, articulate and comprehensive. It is also better planned, designed and executed, with built-in evaluation and measurement criteria, something that most, if not all, Counter-de-Rad programs lack.

To shed more light on this issue, let's compare some of the components of New York's 'Shock Incarceration Treatment' program with a standard de-radicalization program. The former includes strong chaplaincy, vocational training, psychological support and counselling, community involvement, a 'daily regimen of drill, ceremony, physical training, work and academic education', as well as a post-release or 'after-shock' program to facilitate integration of released inmates back into society (all quotations in Clark, Aziz and MacKenzie, 1994, p. 2). Compare this with what Gunaratna (2009, pp. 148–52) describes as the standard or 'Working Model' of a de-radicalization program 'that involves fixing the terrorist's religious misconceptions, supporting him/her psychologically and offering reintegration into society' through 'Religious Reh abilitation ... Psychological rehabilitation ... Social Rehabilitation ... [and] Vocational Rehabilitation'. The extent, breadth and thoroughness of the former program compared to the latter are obvious.

Even outside the prison walls, programs such as community policing, community involvement, community networking, 'community services ... family members [involvement] ... Family counselling...Employment opportunities' and post-release or 'after-shock' programs, so popular today in counter radicalization programs, are not new inventions (Clark et al., 1994, pp. 4–7). Certainly they were not originally introduced to counter violent extremists, although they have become an integral part of counter radicalization programs since the beginning of this century. Bjorgo and Horgan (2009) have also shown how many of these elements were used in the 1970s and 1980s to provide an 'exit' strategy and de-radicalize and/or disengage right-wing extremists in Europe, like the Red Brigades and the Red Army.

Why then are these programs still called counter radicalization and de-radicalization programs? What distinguishes them from other programs designed to rehabilitate and integrate other criminals? Or right-wing extremists? What is so special about them? It seems that the only exception about Counter-de-Rad programs is their focus today on 'Muslim terrorists', either groups or individuals. Gunaratna (2009, pp. 148, 163) was blatant, while developing his standard 'working model', when he stated that Counter-de-Rad programs focus on 'Muslim terrorists'. It is a model, in other words, that locates 'Islam' at the root of the problem 'as [a] religion [that] has been misused and abused'.

Of course, there are several problems with this line of argument. First, and as alluded to earlier, many of these programs were originally designed to counter VEm by non-Muslim violent extremists, including Christians, Jews, Hindus, the right wing, Tamil Tigers, Basques and others. VEm is not confined to any particular group or individual. Second, not all Counter-de-Rad programs have actually included religious rehabilitation policies (Algeria, Kuwait and Turkey are clear examples). Even Saudi Arabia has long moved away from the narrow focus on religious rehabilitation to inject a more secular focus in the popular Saudi de-radicalization policies: through education, including political education, vocational training, painting, physical education and social and economic programs to facilitate reintegration of detainees. Malaysia, Singapore and Indonesia, to mention but a few other examples, have followed suit. This suggests that the role of religion in causing radicalization has been largely exaggerated and misunderstood. Finally, the use of terminology such as counter radicalization and de-radicalization to simply prescribe rehabilitation and reintegration of 'Muslim radicals' or 'terrorists' only adds to the lexicon impasse many authors have warned against (see Alex Schmid, 2013). More alarmingly, such a practice leads to labelling and stigmatization of many Muslim communities and even detainees, which several Dutch academics in particular have recently argued very strongly against, and which makes it even more difficult to stem community radicalization and facilitate reintegration of released Muslim detainees, both key objectives of Counter-de-Rad policies (see Veldhuis and Kessels, 2013 and Veldhuis, 2012).

Third, the statements 'there is no one size fits all', 'there is no one model for all countries' and 'there is no silver bullet' that can end VEm overnight appear in almost every study of Counter-de-Rad policies. Yet one observes similar policies being prescribed to different countries facing VEm and seeking assistance in designing and implementing CVE strategies. Many countries have wrongly sought to implant or imitate the Saudi model. The International Centre for Political Violence and Terrorism Research in Singapore, headed by Dr Rohan Gunaratna is attempting to position itself as an advisor to other countries facing VEt threats. However, it is notorious for describing and implementing 'working models' that 'look up towards Saudi Arabia' and are patterned almost identically after the Saudi model (Gunaratna, 2009, p. 163). The experiences of the five countries studied in this book, and another eight studied in phase one of this project (see El-Said and Harrigan, 2013) suggest that there are alternative, and sometimes even more successful, models than the Saudi model itself. The key lies in designing programs which are consistent with and derived from each country's political, legal, cultural, historical and social capital tradition.

Each country can develop and implement successful and effective CVE policies if they so wish. Regardless of the type of country involved (Muslim-majority or -minority state), and whether we call them prison management practices, rehabilitation or Counter-de-Rad programs, such policies and programs can work to achieve several goals and objectives. In a world characterized by increased openness, multi-ethnicity and cultural diversity, CVE programs are today multifaceted, although they need to be derived from within and be consistent with, and not necessarily in contradiction to, the legal, cultural and belief systems of each country. Policymakers and practitioners need to think global, act global, national and local while designing and implementing Counter-de-Rad policies. Importing and implanting programs as they are from other countries is counterproductive. Each country has its own specificities, and each country can draw on its rich traditions and social capital to develop effective and suitable CVE policies to its environment. In secular, Western democracies in particular, the Muslim community holds the key to success. Their experience and knowledge of Western and Muslim culture, history and customs enables them to overcome the problem of 'foreignness', lack of 'religious authority' and credentials, and thus enables them to develop programs suitable for Western environments. Singapore, a secular and Muslim-minority state, provides a powerful example on how best to win the hearts and minds of its Muslim and other ethnic communities and to lead them to own the entire Counter-de-Rad process. In Muslim-majority states, the role of civil society is also paramount.

This book confirms several of the key findings that emerged in phase one of this project and which were published in 2013 (El-Said and Harrigan). States with strong developmental capacity, strong political capacity and which enjoy an active and dynamic civil society are not only at lower risk of VEm, but are also better positioned and equipped to deal with it whenever it arises than countries characterized by weak developmental capacity, political capacity and hostile and thwarted civil society. In two countries, Singapore and Turkey, improving the economic conditions of all citizens was seen as a key component of a larger strategy that sought to challenge the appeal of radical ideology by focusing on conditions conducive to radicalization and extremism that lead to terrorism in the first place. Both states have also relied heavily on their dynamic civil society and communities to challenge the appeal of radicalization and extremism in their respective societies. Finally, the Singaporean and Turkish states possess strong political capacity not only to defend their borders and territories, but also to defend and secure their societies, citizens and institutions against any potential threat. Not surprisingly, Singapore and Turkey emerge, in our opinion, as the most successful reformers among the five countries studied in this book.

The remaining three countries (Australia, Mauritania and Sudan) have shown less concerted and coherent efforts than Singapore and Turkey in their CVE efforts. Australia's de-radicalization program, for example, remains a pilot project implemented only in Victoria. While the country has introduced several counter radicalization measures, the Australian Muslim Society remains suspicious of these policies and less collaborative. Mauritania and Sudan's experiences suggest that much can be done even with limited resources available. But they also expose the limits of de-radicalization without proper counter radicalization policies, and the limits of de-radicalization in environments that remain conducive to radicalization and extremism that lead to terrorism in the first place.

Notably, several factors can lead to radicalization and extremism that lead to terrorism. Internal contradictions seem more powerful for conducing VEm in countries like Mauritania and Turkey. In Mauritania, the state manufactured VEm for political reasons under the Ould Taya regime. In Turkey, the largest threat of VEm came from a separatist movement seeking autonomy from the state in regions largely inhabited by Kurds, notably in the southeast. Economic and political disparities, as well as the old military-dominated regime's repressive approaches to the Kurdish problem, aggravated the threat.

In Western democracies like Australia, both internal but perhaps more so external factors seem to be important in radicalizing Muslim communities there. Participation in and support for the 'war on terror', including the occupation of Muslim Iraq and Afghanistan, open support for the state of Israel by the Howard government, active involvement in and support for partition of some Muslim states (like Sudan, Indonesia, Iraq), and support for the US's seemingly unfair policies in the Arab world have created passive conditions conducive to and exploited by radicals to mobilize, recruit and incite against Western democracies. Economic, educational and labour market disadvantages, as well as stigmatization and labelling of the Muslim community by the media and the state's official language combined to turn passive conditions into environments conducive to radical ideology and acts. Regime change under such radicalizing circumstances, whether in Muslim-majority or Muslim-minority states, provides an important opportunity to induce reforms in search of winning the 'hearts and minds' of the most vulnerable members of society. Not only in Australia, but also in Mauritania and Turkey, regime change triggered sustainable CVE measures. This was not the case in Sudan and Singapore, although the latter produced one of the most successful and coherent Counter-de-Rad policies studied in this book. Political will and conviction are therefore key ingredients for successful Counter-de-Rad policies. Not surprisingly, Singapore and Turkey have topped other countries in this area too, reflecting the strongest political commitment and official support behind reforms. This came directly from the countries' highest official authorities, the top leadership.

Finally, there is the issue of assessment and evaluation of Counter-de-Rad programs. There are theoretical and practical issues involved in evaluating these programs. Theoretically, the entire Counter-de-Rad 'Process [is] in Need of Clarity', as the above discussion has already suggested (Horgan, 2008, p. 1). Counter-de-Rad, as a concept, not only currently means different things to different people, but also lacks a theoretical 'framework for guiding the development of such future initiatives' and facilitating the process of 'draw[ing] lessons from existing programs (effective or otherwise)' (Horgan and Braddock, 2010, p. 269). Empirically speaking, long time periods must first elapse before it is possible to evaluate Counter-de-Rad policies effectively. Many such policies remain in their infancy. Second, access to data in such a politically sensitive and highly monopolized area by the state and its officials is not an easy task. State officials have an interest in exaggerating the impact of their policies and understating the failures. Accessing former violent extremist detainees free from government intervention, monitoring and surveillance is not possible in most circumstances. Evaluating such programs in war-zone countries where such programs have been implemented, like Iraq and Afghanistan, has also proved problematic, not least from a security and safety point of view.

Not surprisingly, we are still faced with a major problem: the 'Counterterrorism Initiative [remains] in Need of Evaluation' (Horgan, 2008, p. 1). A more recent report by the Center on Global Counterterrorism Cooperation summarized the problem eloquently in the following words:

> In the field of counterterrorism generally, the measurement of outcomes and impacts is inherently difficult. Despite the massive investment of resources in this field, especially in the post-9/11 period, few states and multilateral organizations have elaborated robust and succinct methodologies to evaluate their counterterrorism measures per se. Likewise, the academic literature on the effectiveness of counterterrorism generally remains in its infancy. (Romaniuk and Chowdhury, 2012, p. 8)

The literature has so far relied heavily on, or rather been obsessed with, two key quantitative indicators through which Counter-de-Rad programs have been evaluated: recidivism and incident rates (ibid. Also see Schmid, 2013 and Horgan and Braddock, 2010). Recidivism refers to the number of released detainees that fail to leave terrorism behind and return to VEm after their release. It is often used to evaluate the effectiveness of de-radicalization programs. Incident rates, on the other hand, are more often used to evaluate the success of counter radicalization measures and refer to the number of terrorist acts or events in one year, month or other period compared to previous periods.

While they can be indicative, both recidivism and incident rates are problematic, and neither can encapsulate the full impact of Counter-de-Rad programs. More importantly, improvements or reduction in both rates can be caused by external factors (inside and outside a country) that have nothing to do with these programs. For example, increase in security forces, improvement in monitoring technology, intensification of repressive policies, and enhanced national, regional and global cooperation can reduce both recidivism and incident rates. On the contrary, temporary improvement in these quantitative indicators might hide deepening hostilities, further exclusions and even sharpening radicalization of certain groups and elements. The eruption of uprisings in the Arab world provides useful lessons here. Countries that implemented, some *arguably* successfully, Counter or de-Rad programs, such as Libya, Egypt, Sudan and Yemen, have experienced some of the worst violence in the region. Most have also experienced a return to VEm and terrorism too, both by newly radicalized individuals and formerly assumed de-radicalized/disengaged groups. The Arab Spring, it is worth noting, was preceded by heavy intensification of, and increase in, authoritarianism, repression and anti-terrorism laws that heavily empowered security personnel at the expense of human rights in the region.

There is a need to expand our methodology, approach and the indicators of success/failure when attempting to evaluate Counter-de-Rad policies. We need to move away from the narrow definition of success and failure that is based on narrow quantitative indicators (recidivism/incident rates) into more equally important, observable and measurable indicators that capture the wider impact of Counter-de-Rad policies, including externalities and spillover effects. Here we can borrow a great deal from the criminology literature which has developed more advanced indicators on how best to evaluate programs inside and outside the prison walls (Clark et al., 1994).

Lacking training and skills in Islam and the Islamic faith, most state officials, particularly in the West, misinterpret conversion and 'confuse conversion with radicalization. ... Conversion is not the same as radicalisation, and good counter-radicalisation policies – whether in or outside prison – never fail to distinguish between the two' (ICSR, 2010, pp. 27, 36). Hamm (2009) argues that conversion to any faith, including to Islam, is not a bad thing and that becoming more religious can have a positive impact on inmates, making them better and more law-abiding individuals. Conversion and religion structure an inmate's daily life and create a new daily balance between eating, learning and citing the Quran, keeping healthy by working out and staying away from drugs, alcohol and crime, doing more charitable deeds and helping other inmates.

The implication of the above observation is that prisons characterized by strong chaplaincies and religious and spiritual programs enjoy less violence and more stability (Hamm, 2009). Hamm also argues that improving the prison environment and conditions (building new and less crowded facilities, improving quality and quantity of food provision, using state-of-the-art monitoring and surveillance technology, preventing smuggling and contraband inside the prison, reducing corruption, increasing the number of security personnel vis à vis inmates, introducing effective educational and vocational training programs, and improving human rights inside prisons) can also have a similar effect of largely reducing violence and crime rates inside detention centres, enhancing security and even facilitating de-radicalization of detainees. Successful de-radicalization programs should also be judged on similar and other criteria. Our case studies show clearly that de-radicalization programs, when properly designed and implemented, have also had a similar impact of reducing violence inside the prison walls, improving relations among inmates and between them and detention staff. They have also improved security and facilitated de-radicalization and reintegration of former detainees. Other similar spillovers can also be observed from our case studies.

In Turkey, counter radicalization policies have led to the introduction of very advanced terrorism studies programs, rigorous training for security personnel and detention centre staff, and produced one of the most advanced and largest security-related dataset systems in the world. It has also played an important role in changing the former repressive face of the Turkish police and security forces. Similar effects can be observed in Australia. There, counter radicalization and community policing has begun to revive the once-vibrant relationship between the Muslim community and Australian police. It is also leading to a more societal collaboration in the fight against terror and to the generation of vital, life-saving information from members of the Muslim community itself regarding potential violent extremists and acts. Counter radicalization policies are also increasingly improving state–community relationships in Australia and elsewhere, as well as triggering one of the largest research projects seen in our five case studies. This project has greatly advanced knowledge of causes of radicalization in the country, of grievances of various communities and of socio-economic characteristics of individuals vulnerable to, and already involved in, VEm. In Singapore, Counter-de-Rad policies brought various Singaporean communities together, turned cultural diversity into an asset and supported the government's key policy of fostering a sense of nationhood in Singapore. In Saudi Arabia, the government's de-radicalization program improved the reputation of the once strongly feared Interior Ministry and turned it into a protector of the nation (Taylor, 2010).

Moreover, Counter-de-Rad polices save a lot of public money, both directly and indirectly. First of all, 'wining hearts and minds' is less costly than waging wars. Since most Counter-de-Rad programs involve incentives, including early release, amnesties, and parole systems, they reduce prison crowding, free up space for additional inmates, reduce expenditure for care and custody, and *might* therefore make important savings in capital construction costs (i.e., building one instead of two or three new prisons) (Clark et al., 1994). In Singapore the Muslim community provided most of the capital required to look after the detainees and their families. In Muslim-majority states too, families are playing the most important role in facilitating the reintegration of their former detainees back into society and the labour market.

Counter-de-Rad programs, of course, still cost money and require more capital. For example, they might require the building of a new facility, increasing the number of detention officials, intensifying supervision (inside and outside detention centres), additional costs involved with the training of more staff and increasing reliance on the latest monitoring and surveillance technology. There are also costs associated with coordinating with teachers, imams, psychologists and families of the detainees. According to the Saudi officials, these costs reach around US$10–12 million annually, excluding the capital cost of constructing new facilities. Although not trivial, these costs remain much lower than waging wars, organizing raids and attacks and, most importantly, creating hatred and ending up radicalizing many more groups and individuals than those who can and have been de-radicalized/disengaged.

Finally, Counter-de-Rad can, and in many cases has, improved the human rights record in many reforming countries. This is a significant outcome, particularly in undemocratic and authoritarian Arab states, where increased repression, discrimination and social exclusion have been cited as among key factors behind the current, ongoing uprisings in the region.

The above-mentioned outcomes and spillovers are not small achievements, but are often neglected in the literature on terrorism. More research on how such externalities and spillovers can be achieved, expanded and maximized can go a long way towards developing broader approaches and indicators to evaluate the effectiveness of Counter-de-Rad programs. They can expand our definition of success/failure, help us to look at these programs more broadly and search for ways to link them with the general objectives of government policies, including social harmony, bridging gaps between cultural diversity and improving state–society–community relations.

Finally, terrorism is a crime like all other crimes. It is not a new phenomenon, nor is its practice confined to one group belonging to one religion, ideology, culture or belief system. Groups and individuals belonging to all backgrounds have practiced VEm. VEm, however, in any society is the business of a small minority of fringe groups and individuals taking matters into their own hands and becoming radical enough to commit acts of terrorism. Nobody is born a terrorist. Terrorism is a process, not an event. This implies that the process can be reversed, if the conditions conducive for success are present. The hope is that this project has assisted in advancing understanding of this process and how best to reverse it.

Notes

1 Introduction

1. Personal interview with a Pakistani Brigadier Major who serves in the Swat Valley, at a conference in Germany which was held under Chatham House rules of confidentiality, August 2012.

2 Counter-de-Rad: Setting the Framework

1. To view the full report, see Counter-Terrorism Implementation Task Force First Report of the Working Group on Radicalization and Extremism that Lead to Terrorism: Inventory of State Programs, http://www.un.org/terrorism/pdfs/ radicalization.pdf.
2. Personal interview with Sheikh Ahmed Ould Daoud, who is a *fageh* and head of one of the Mahadir in Nouakchott, August 2011.
3. Personal interviews in Kuwait, April 2012.
4. This information is taken from a personal interview with Dr Mansour al-Qarni, head of the *Monasaha* (Advice) program in Prince Naif Rehabilitation Centre, The Hague, 8 December, 2011.

3 Radicalization in a Western Context

1. The Australian government allied its Vietnam policy with that of the United States and supported the South against the communist North during the Vietnamese war of 1971–5. The defeat of the South created a refugee crisis and the Australian government was very sympathetic to southern Vietnamese refugees, whom it had supported during the war.
2. Through 'the right of all Australians to equality of treatment and opportunity, and the removal of barriers of race, ethnicity, culture, religion, language, gender or place of birth'.
3. The 'cultural identity' element of Australian multiculturalism emphasized 'the right of all Australians, within carefully defined limits, to express and share their individual cultural heritage, including their language and religion'.
4. This to be achieved through 'economic efficiency', which emphasized 'the need to maintain, develop and utilize effectively the skills and talents of all Australians, regardless of background'.
5. Since the study focused on ethnic minorities, it included minorities from such backgrounds as Tongan, Indigenous Australian, Lebanese, Vietnamese, Somalian, Sudanese, Indian, Chinese, New Zealander, Pacific Islander, Korean and Filipino, with a small sample of 'Anglo' youth acting as a control. Ninety-five per cent of those young men and women surveyed were first- or second-generation immigrants from a non-Anglo background.

6. British-born Jack Roche was a member of the Australian branch of JI. In 2000 he travelled to Afghanistan to fight with the Taliban, and while there he was allegedly also asked by senior al-Qaeda leaders to conduct reconnaissance for attacks to take place during the 2000 Sydney Olympics.

7. In fact, the *Tampa* fiasco went further to expose the double standard of Howard's government, which, as we shall see in what follows, justified Australia's intervention in Afghanistan and his country's support for the United States's 'war on terror' on the premise that the 'Taliban regime in Afghanistan [w]as barbaric and an enemy of civilisation', and that it was in the interest of all Afghanis to rid the country of this barbaric regime. On the other hand, Howard's government was extravagant in 'simultaneously demonising' Afghanis who sailed into Australian waters to claim refugee status. The question the prime minister asked the electorate was 'Do we really want people like this in Australia'? (Schrato and Webb, 2003, p. 92).

8. The ANZUS or ANZUS Treaty is a security treaty which binds Australia and New Zealand and, separately, Australia and the United States to cooperate on defence matters in the Pacific Ocean area only. After 9/11, however, the treaty has been expanded and is understood to relate to attacks and defence matters worldwide.

9. In fact, Sheridan was explaining not only illegal and criminal activities taking place in areas inhabited by minorities in Sydney, but also the rise in VEt activities in Australia during the first decade of the 21st century.

10. According to Lentini (2010) Operation Pendennis is Australia's largest and longest terrorism investigation to date. The task force was comprised of members of Victoria Police, Australian Federal Police (hereafter AFP), the Australian Security Intelligence Organization (hereafter ASIO) and New South Wales Police, who kept a group of men in Melbourne and Sydney who were preparing to conduct a terrorist attack against undisclosed targets in Australia, presumably Victoria, under surveillance from 2004–late 2005. On 8 November 2005 representatives of these agencies launched a series of raids across Victoria and New South Wales. Initially they arrested ten men in Melbourne and nine in Sydney. Throughout 2006 they arrested and charged three additional men in Victoria with crimes associated with terrorist-related activities. By May 2010, juries in Victoria and New South Wales either handed down guilty verdicts or the courts received guilty pleas from the nine men arrested in New South Wales and nine of the 13 men arrested in Victoria, with the jury having acquitted four.

11. According to Harris-Hogan (2012a and 2012b) and Zammit (2012), 33 individuals have been prosecuted for alleged terrorism offences motivated by jihadist ideology in Australia.

12. The source of this information is a personal interview with John Flockton, Clinical Director, Senior Specialist (Forensic) Psychologist High Risk Management Correctional Centre Goulburn Corrective Services NSW Australia, Sydney, November, 2012.

13. In the United Kingdom, for example, 38 per cent of VEts are unmarried and are mostly unmarried in the European Union).

14. As Dr Gaetano (Joe) Ilardi, Senior Sergeant, Counterterrorism Coordination Unit, State Emergencies and Security Department, Victoria Police, stated:

'Most or the largest part of Muslims live in Melbourne and Sydney. Most terrorists exist in these two states too. Half of the neo-jihadi arrested were born in Australia, the rest out the country. The majority are Lebanese, but the head of the group is an Algerian. Most have not completed their education. Only the Algerian leader who has a university degree in engineering. Most were radicalized by the Algerian leader, who initially started preaching to them in the mosque but then excluded them and took them away from the mosque and started radicalizing them there. Most have not even completed school and occupied yellow-collar jobs, like an electrician, taxi driver, etc.' (personal interview, Melbourne, November 2012).

15. Harris-Hogan (2012a) supports this claim: 'It is worth noting that jihadist activity in Australia has almost exclusively contained individuals located in either Melbourne or Sydney'.

16. Being refugees themselves, Lebanese Muslim Australians 'are significantly worse off than Christians. ... There are several reasons for this discrepancy. First, Lebanese Muslims had a lower starting point, as they were already disadvantaged in Lebanon relative to Christians, a legacy of the French colonial system. Second, their immigration was more recent than Lebanese Christian immigration, in large part because they were less likely to be accepted under the White Australia Policy. Third, the majority of Lebanese Muslim immigration representing all of the official Lebanese Muslim sects (Sunni, Shia, Druze and Allawi) occurred during the civil war, making them more likely to have been war refugees. Finally, by settling earlier Lebanese Christians had better established family and social networks available to them for support. As a result of these influences, Lebanese-Australian Muslims are in a worse condition today compared to both other Australian Muslims and Lebanese-Australians' (GTReC, 2014, 6–7).

17. The personal factor, however, might vary from a mundane one (such as failure to get funding for a club or even failure to obtain a bank loan) to the more serious of undergoing personal torture, trauma, or witnessing the torture of a friend or relative, or even the murder of a relative or friend by police force or an occupying power (El-Said and Barrett, 2012a).

18. In fact, a large number dropped out of schools. Not surprisingly, 'VEm in Australia happens at "the margins", among a small number of young individuals with no good jobs, hardly any education, and often spending the night roaming the streets with their friends from one neighbourhood to another' (personal interview with a female Muslim community activist, Sydney, November 2012). As Harris-Hogan (2012a) noted: 'Every case of jihadist terrorism seen in Australia has been a case of individuals on the fringe of their community breaking away from established institutions and forming their own small, socially isolated groups'.

4 Counter Radicalization and De-radicalization in Western Democracies

1. For full details of the project, see Monash University's website at: http://arts. monash.edu.au/radicalisation/about-the-project/index.php. All quotations are taken from the same website.

2.   Australia has a complicated federal system, established on 1 January 1901, which adheres closely to the original model of the United States. The Australian Federation System provides a high degree of autonomy for the government institutions of the federation and the states, a division of power between these organizations, and a judicial authority to determine whether either level of government has exceeded its powers. The Federation of Australia was the process by which the six separate British self-governing colonies of New South Wales, Queensland, South Australia, Tasmania, Victoria and Western Australia formed one nation. They kept the systems of government that they had developed as separate colonies but also would have a federal government that was responsible for matters concerning the whole nation.

3.   This is the most high-security incarceration centre in the capital; it was built in 2001. It currently hosts 29 high-security inmates, not all of whom are convicted of terrorism-related charges. Out of the 29 inmates in Goulburn Super Max, only 11 are convicted of terrorism-related charges. The rest are mostly convicted of murder, and one, a serial killer, convicted of seven murders. Goulburn's maximum capacity is 75 individuals, although it currently holds only 29. The highest number of inmates it has held since its creation was 40 (personal interviews with Goulburn's high-ranking officers, NSW, November 2012).

4.   Very similar challenges were observed in Victoria.

5.   A similar assessment takes place in Victoria.

6.   Similar facilities exist in Victoria where access to clinics and other medical support is readily available. This also includes psychological or clinical services available to major offenders within prison.

7.   The same applies to Victoria prison, more or less. The only difference is the recent, modest religious rehabilitation scheme introduced in Victoria since 2010, which is a pilot scheme more than anything else.

8.   A similar process of attempting to influence other inmates by violent extremist detainees has also been observed in Victoria.

9.   Every Australian state has an Imam Council plus a federal-level council. They choose the mufti. The mufti is inserted by the 12 most recognized Imams who make up the Islamic Council.

10. The parole system is an important 'buffer' system that can and should be used by the Australian authorities to encourage participation in the de-radicalization program. Basically the Australian court and judicial system often sentences offenders to a maximum and a minimum period. After the completion of the minimum period, detainees can be released but they stay on parole until their maximum sentence is completed. If their good behaviour continues, they will be fully released after the end of the maximum period. While on parole, detainees are subject to strict conditions that they have to meet. This includes regular reporting to police station (once or twice a week); informing about any changes related to their accommodations, phone numbers or workplace; their passports are often confiscated and kept with the authorities until they are completely released. They also require permission for any political or social activities they seek to organize or participate in. Any breach for these conditions means they are back to detention centre to spend the rest of the period there. Otherwise, and if their good behaviour

continues, they stay out of the prison for the rest of their maximum sentence. While on parole they are allowed to work and seek employment. As Dr Ilardi stated, 'Our only buffer is the parole period. But once the maximum sentence period is over, we have no choice but to release them, so we lose this buffer after the end of the maximum period' (personal interview, Melbourne, November 2012).

5 Mauritania: From Toleration to Violent Islam

1. Mauritania is the Roman name for Africans before the Islamic conquest, although its roots are Berber (*Atmur-itnagh* or *Tumortana*, which means 'our land'). (For more details, see Ould Muhammad, 1999, and Ould al-Salim, 2008, 83).
2. Mauritania was known in the past as the Changuet Country. It was the name given to Mauritania as well as neighbouring countries whose inhabitants spoke the Arabic dialect, which was known as *al-Hassaneya*. In Arabic-speaking countries, therefore, the Mauritanians were referred to as *Changueteyeen* and sometimes *al-Chanaketah*. (For more details, see Ould al-Salim, 2010, pp. 117–18; Ould al-Salim, 2008).
3. In addition to Changuet Country, Mauritania was also known as "*Belad al-Mulathameen*" (the country of people with scarves). This was mainly because its Senhaja people of Berber origin used to wear scarves that wrapped and covered all of their faces and heads and kept only their eyes exposed to protect them from the sand of the desert. The Mulathameen are the ancestors of the Senhajeyeen who lived in the area from ancient timesu, and who are traced back to the Garamantes tribes (see later analysis in the same section). (For more details, see Ould al-Salim, 2008, pp. 11 and 15).
4. The word Sahel is a French distortion of the Arabic word Sa-hell, which means large space of land; it extends from the Mauritanian Atlantic coast on the west to Chad on the east (Ould al-Salim 2008, p. 148).
5. Mauritania is bound on the west by the Atlantic, north by Morocco, northeast by Algeria, southeast by Mali, and south by Senegal.
6. Berbers of the Sahara traditionally are mainly of two types: the Senhajah and the Zenatah. The Senhajah people were mainly nomads, relying on raising cattle and livestock for livelihood. The Zenatah were themselves of two groups, one nomad and the other settlers. Both the Senhajahs and the Zenatahs embraced Islam at different times, particularly from the 2nd Islamic *hijri* century (12th Christian century) onwards. However, their Islam was not deepened until the Murabiteen Empire was established and consolidated (see above analysis). The Tawarik (or Tawariq) people belonged to the Senhajahs. The latter were a group of Tamazight (Berber) from very old generations and whose ancestors are traced back to the Garamantes and other tribes; spread among them are Arab groups such as the Ansar al-Andaloseyeen (the supporters of the Andalusians), Shorafa and other Arab tribes. They all mixed and lived together, sometimes as a result of internal wars, famines, droughts, trade and immigration. This was especially the case in the Mauritanian space. (For more details, see Ould al-Salim, 2008, 2010, p. 7).

7. According to Ould al-Salim (2008, p. 15), the Berbers (mainly the Mauriis, Numiddans, Getlules, Pharusians and Garamantes), as well as the Ethiopians, were the first (or among the first) to inhabit this area, along with some Arab tribes. The Garamantes in particular, who are of Berber origin, are believed to be among the oldest inhabitants of the area. They were known for carts pulled by bulls and horses, which was seen as revolutionary in the history of the Sahel. They were the only people able to cross the desert south for trade and hunting. The so-called Tawarq people that exist in some parts of the Sahara today are traced back to them. Their immigration to the area, mainly from North Africa, is traced back 300 years before Christ. Because the local inhabitants (Africans) were of a darker colour, the Romans, who entered West Africa in 46 BC before their empire collapsed in the 5th century, called Africans Maures, from the Greek adjective *mauros*, meaning dark or black. 'It is from Mauros and the Latin term Marues that the word Moor is derived, since the inhabitants of Africa were black, the Romans and later the Europeans called them Moors. It is not coincident that the land inhabited by the Moors was called Mauritania and Morocco, meaning "Land of the Blacks"' (Clark, 2011).

8. Arguably, 'the *Maraboutoun* state was the most important Islamic state known in the Sahara', and it extended from the Atlantic coast in the west to Tad-Mali, the Niger jungles in the south, to Morocco and Andalusia in the North (Ould al-Salim, 2008, p. 10).

9. According to the authorities, the Arab Mauritanians represent 70% of the total population, but the non-Arab Mauritanians question this figure. (Personal interviews with Mauritanian officials and civilians, Nouakchott, August 2011. Also see Ould Sheikhana, 2009.)

10. The *al-Zawaya*, sometimes referred to as students, remain today the second most important class in social hierarchy. Traditionally they are members of peaceful tribes with scientific and religious orientations and knowledge. They take care of such social and political roles as the *imammah*, judiciary, teaching and hajj (pilgrimage).

11. *Al-Lahmah* is the third most important social class in Mauritanian society. The word comes from the Arabic *Istelham* (unity or solidarity). *Al-Lahmah* is one of the groups that were historically defeated by new powers.

12. *Al-Sunaa'* refers to crafts people and those who do handiwork such as welding and moulding. They come from different backgrounds and roots.

13. *Al-Zafafoon* is a group of people that specializes in music playing and singing. Historically this career was seen as *ayb* (shame) by Mauritanian society, and the *Maraboutoun* fought this class bitterly.

14. *Al-Harateen* is an old class in Mauritanian society with dark or black skin. They were slaves of the Berbers and later of the Arab ruling elite, and became known in Mauritanian society as *al-Harateen* or the *autagaa'* (freed) class. The origin of this concept is *ahradan* (freed twice). Historically they were referred to as *al-khalasi*, meaning from a Berber father and black mother. Their ancestors can be traced to Africa, including Ethiopia. In the past they inhabited the *wasat* (centre) but more so the northern oasis, where Berbers mixed with black Africans.

15. It is important to note here that although this outcome is a function of significant historical, social and political events, it continues to prevail and shape Mauritanian society today.

16. Ould Tah is a very respected Mauritanian scholar and alam, a former minister of Islamic Affairs and the current Head of The Mauritanian Ulama Union (Rabitat Ulama Mauritania).
17. In fact, France decided in 1899 to name the country Western Mauritania for geopolitical reasons, arguably 'to test the country's skills in running and managing the vacuum'. The real objective was to monitor the central area which suffered from a central vacuum and which was located between France's colonies in North and West Africa (Ould Ibrahim, 2010).
18. The crisis in France in the late 1950s necessitated a new constitution, which coincided with the Fifth French Republic in 1958. The new constitution provided nominal independence to Mauritania and was adopted by Mauritanians in a generally very contentious referendum in 1958. The IRM was thus proclaimed in October 1959. New developments in North Africa and nationalist fever that hit the continent at the time led to a change in Territorial Assembly into Constituent Assembly and immediately started work to initiate a new constitution, which was unanimously adopted by the members of the Assembly and replaced the French Constitution. On 28 November, Mauritania declared independence. (For more details, see US Library of Congress, 2011).
19. The new (1959) constitution proclaimed Islam the official religion of the state, and, somewhat paradoxically, granted freedom of religion at the same time. Despite the inherent contradictions in the constitution, the government sought with acceptable success to balance the demands of the two. (For more details, see the US Library of Congress, 1990).
20. The Mauritanian political elite from the very beginning was fragmented and divided. Some called for closer links with Morocco, some for closer links with Africa, while a third opted for closer links with the colonial power, France. This fragmentation was reflected by political parties. The Mauritanian Entente and Babana Party called for closer links with Morocco. To counterbalance the pro-Moroccan sympathies of many Maures, southern minority groups formed a regional party, the Gorgol Democratic Bloc, committed to the prevention of a Maghribi union and to the maintenance of close ties with black African countries. Following the defeat of the Mauritanian Entente Party at the hands of the progressive Union Party in the 1956 elections, the leaders of Entente, Babana and several of his followers, fled to Morocco. There Babana became head of the National Council of Mauritanian Resistance, supporting Morocco's claims to Mauritania, and, by extension, Mauritania's claims to independence. Amid this fragmentation and political instability, Daddah, with the strong support of France, called for unity among all factions. At the Congress of Aleg in May 1958, the Mauritanian Regroupment Party was formed in a merger of the Mauritanian Progressive Union, elements of the Mauritanian Entente and the Gorgol Democratic Bloc. This party was headed by Daddah as secretary general and Sidi el Moktar as president. Its platform called for Mauritania to join the French Community (francophone Africa) and to reject both Morocco's claim to Mauritania and a 1957 French proposal to unite Mauritania with francophone Saharan states in the joint French-dominated Common Saharan States Organization (US Library of Congress, 1990).
21. According to some sources, the aim was to attack French soldiers only and that they did not expect to find Mauritanian soldiers in the club. They also

added that the fatalities among French soldiers would have been much larger had Mauritanian soldiers not been there and that the attackers panicked when they saw Mauritanian soldiers in the club, leading to on-the-spot, ad hoc adjustment for their plan, resulting infewer fatalities than would have been the case. (For more details, see Ould Sheikhana, 2009, pp. 92–116).

22. These were: Al-Sharif Amali, Al-Shiekh Ould al-Fadal and Aswedat.

23. The head of the Hurmah Group, Ahmad Ould Hurmah, was also sentenced to death in absentia.

24. It is important to remember here that most Mauritanians in general, and defectors in particular, did not espouse violent methods and that among defectors to Morocco only a small group, the Hurmah Group, espoused violent activities. The rest and the majority espoused peaceful means. (For more details, see US Library of Congress, 1990 and 2011; Ould Sheikhana, 2009).

25. Morocco was becoming increasingly dissatisfied with Ould Daddah's policies in the Sahara, leading King Hassan II to support the leaders of the military coup. The African Union, particularly Senegal and Mali, were also becoming increasingly dissatisfied with what they saw as Ould Daddah's closeness to the French authorities. Even the latter increasingly saw Ould Daddah's policies as unpredictable and destabilizing. (For more details, see Ould al-Salim, 1997 and 2010; Ould Sheikhana, 2009; Choplin, 2008).

26. We devote a special section on the country's economic policies later.

27. This has also been the experience of all MENA countries without exception, including the experience of such countries as Turkey, Iran and Israel (Richards and Waterbury, 1996).

28. The human cost of the war was also very high. The war, which lasted for three years and eight months, resulted in more than 3,000 deaths, another 3,000 casualties and led to the arrest of more than 1,000 from both sides (Ould Sidi Muhammad, 2003, p. 298. Also see Ould Sheikhana, 2009, pp. 240–4).

29. The Sahara war upset Algeria, a traditional ally, tremendously. It interpreted the unexpected war as a Mauritanian–Moroccan conspiracy against Algeria. Most West African countries, including in particular Senegal, also began resisting Ould Daddah's closeness to the Arab world, describing Mauritania as a Trojan Horse that is 'leaking Nasserism' and Arabism to West Africa in order to weaken the African roots of Mauritania. Even France began suspecting Ould Daddah's Arab rapprochement, as well as improving relations with China after 1965, which the French saw as a threat to France's traditional influence and interests in West Africa. These policies had a large, negative impact on the county's trade and economic conditions. (For more details, see Ould Sidi Muhammad, 2003; Ould Sheikhana, 2009, pp. 240–4).

30. Although Mauritanians of African origin question these statistics, Ould Daddah and other state officials maintain that 'Mauritania has an overwhelming Arab majority but has minorities from African roots' (quoted in Ould Sheikhana, 2009, p. 120).

31. Gross domestic product (GDP) reflects the value of all final goods and services produced within a nation in a given year. A nation's GDP at purchasing power parity (PPP) exchange rates is the sum value of all goods and services produced in the country valued at prices prevailing in the United States. This is the measure most economists prefer when looking at per capita welfare

and when comparing living conditions or use of resources across countries (CIA World Factbook, 2010).

32. It is important to note here that Islamists did not really have direct or forceful influence over the president or his prime minister. But given the fact that the old regime of Ould Daddah antagonized members of Hizb al-Nahddah, and given the increasing influence of Nasserites and Arab nationalists in the country, the new regime of Ould Haidallah moved closer in gaining the support of Islamists in order to undermine Nasserites and nationalists.

33. As the ICG (2005, p. iii) stated, 'The Mauritanian Islamist movement has assumed various forms: charitable associations, missionary organisations (the Jema'at al-Da'wa wa'l-Tabligh being the most firmly established) and a nebulous set of political groupings whose ideology draws from Wahhabism, the Muslim Brotherhood and thinkers such as the Tunisian Rachid Ghannouchi or the Sudanese Hassan al-Tourabi'.

34. Although some attacks did take place before this period, the problem, particularly in the porous Sahel region, was the presence of not just terrorists, but also smugglers, drug traffickers, weapons dealers and pirates. These various groups learned how to collaborate with, and rely on one another in what is referred to in the Sahel region as 'the Capitalism of Terrorism' (Ould Ibrahim, 2010). It was therefore difficult to distinguish between attacks launched by smugglers and pirates and attacks launched by terrorists. The 1999 attack on participants in the Dakar automobile race by a group of smugglers is a case in point.

35. TTSTI provided $500 million to countries most willing to collaborate with the US government in this initiative. These are: Morocco, Algeria, Niger, Mauritania, Chad, Senegal, Nigeria and Mali (Al Jazeera Network, 2011a).

36. TSCTI builds upon the Pan Sahel initiative and was started in June 2005, just two months before Ould Taya was toppled in a military coup in August, with Exercise Flintlock. Pan Sahara followed a perceived threat of Islamist extremists in the Sahel, particularly al-Qaeda and GSPC, while TSCTI followed increased terrorist attacks by al-Qaeda and its affiliates in the region. (For more information, see Global Security, 2011; Archer and Popovic, 2007).

37. If anything, these initiatives ended up radicalizing more Mauritanians not only because they were seen as a Western endorsement to Ould Taya and his repressive policies, but also as part of what many Mauritanians and Muslims around the world perceived as a Western war against Islam (Ould Ibrahim, 2010; ICG, 2005 and 2006).

38. Ould Tah (a well-respected and recognized Mauritanian scholar, a former Minister of Religious Affairs and a member of the Committee of Ulama which participated in the debates inside prison): 'Listening to the prisoners in the first phase of the process allowed us to divide them into two types: those influenced by some national identities and personalities, and the second type, which is ideological, who believe in jihad and violence. Debate did not work with the latter group' (personal interview with Ould Tah, Nouakchott, August, 2011).

39. Four individuals of this group, classified as the most 'dangerous' among the group, were sentenced to life in imprisonment, including Khadim Ould Semane, Sidi Ould Sidna, Ould Chebarnou and Ould Ibrahim, while one, Didi Ould Bezeid, was sentenced to 12 years for his involvement in the killing of an America aid worker, Christopher Leggett, almost three years ago. The rest

took lighter sentences and some of them 'will be released' soon. Interestingly and almost three years since the first batch of repented radicals were released, the '10-prison group asked Mauritanian President Mohamed Ould Abdel Aziz to pardon them on Eid al-Fitr [August 2012]....The group also appealed to scholars who took part in the last dialogue that led to the release of prisoners who made ideological revisions.' They stated that they 'have already renounced al-Qaeda ideology' and asked the scholars to deliver on their promise of releasing 'all of those who renounce al-Qaeda terrorist ideology'. The 10-Prisoner Group also raised two important points that face not only imprisoned radicals thinking about repentance, but also security officials studying their behaviour. As Didi Ould Bezeid, one of the Salafists who signed the statement, put it: 'the prisoners accused of belonging to al-Qaeda have two bitter options: if they kept silent, it would be said that their silence is a sign of acceptance of prison, and if they spoke and denied the accusations, it would be said that they want to be released to return to al-Qaeda hideouts' (all quotations from Magharebia, 2011. Mauritanian salafists renounce al-Qaeda, seek release, August 17. http://www.magharebia.com/cocoon/awi/xhtml1/en_GB/features/awi/features/2012/08/17/feature-02). Studying and finding solutions to the 'two bitter options' to encourage repentance inside detention centres should now acquire more attention from security officers and researchers.

6   Singapore: Crisis of Identity, Shared Values And Religious Rehabilitation

1. Out of the 15 persons arrested in 2001, 13 were members of the radical regional group JI, while the remaining two were released in January 2002 on Restriction Orders. Out of the 21 arrested in 2002, 19 were JI members. The first group 'were targeting mainly American interests in Singapore, while the second group were planning to target strategic Singaporean interests such as our water pipelines' (Tong, p. 15).
2. When in 1963 Singapore joined the Federation with Malaysia, not only were its relations with Malaysia marked by suspicion, distrust and disagreements, but Indonesia adopted a policy of confrontation against the formation of Malaysia Federation and prohibited trade of goods involving Indonesia within the region. 'This affected Singapore greatly since Indonesia had been the island's second largest trading partner' (Cahyadi et al. 2004, pp. 2, 30). It was not before 1966 that trade between Singapore and Indonesia was resumed.
3. In 1947 strikes took place frequently, with more than 300 major communist-inspired strikes by almost 70,000 workers in that year alone. These are the consequences of labour grievances caused by economic difficulties, rice shortage and rising cost of living neglected or overlooked by the colonial government. For more details, see Goh, 2008; Europe-Solidaire, 2012; Library of Congress, 2012; *New York Times*, 1990; Thinkquest, 2012.
4. Riots broke out in retaliation to the new Chief Minister Lim Yew Hock's decision to close down Singapore Chinese Middle School Students' Union (SCMSSU) due to its Communist activities. Four student leaders from Chinese High School and Chung Cheng High School were also arrested, and

142 students were expelled for their involvement in Communist activities. Riots by students and workers broke out in many parts of the city. (For more details, see Goh, 2008).

5. S. Rajaratnam served as Minister for Culture (1959), Minister for Foreign Affairs (1965), Minister of Labour (1968–71) and second Deputy Prime Minister (1973). He was appointed Senior Minister in 1988 after he retired from active politics. He is also known as a strong believer in multiracial Singapore. In 1966, with the 1964 race riots fresh in his mind, he wrote the National Pledge containing the words, 'One united people, regardless of race, language or religion'. He is recognized and recognizes himself as the theoretician and ideologue of the People's Action Party (PAP), which has dominated Singaporean politics since 1959, in his own words, 'the ideas man', 'a public relations man…who projects the PAP image' (for more details, see Knowledge.net. Singapore: The Singapore Social History Source. http://www.viweb.freehosting.net/SRajaratnam.htm. Retrieved on 26 April 2012).

6. As Mr Chia, a former Communist leader who was arrested in 1963 and spent more than 22 years in prison, stated: 'At the same time, the Vietnam War was raging and Mr Chia says he was among the peace campaigners calling for an end to the heavy American bombing of Indo-China. "We wanted peace. If the war escalated, it probably would have spilled over to the rest of the region." He insists to this day he was a peace campaigner, not an insurgent for the Vietnamese communists or Red China' (quoted in Porter, 1998).

7. MUIS is the main authority responsible for the Islamic affairs in Singapore. It was established in the mid-1960s to promote Muslims' integration and preserve a multiracial, multi-religious society in Singapore. MUIS is under the supervision of the Ministry of Community, Youth and Sports.

8. Individuals placed under ROs include two types. First are those who were detained, charged with a terrorist act and already spent their time in prison but remain, or the authorities continue to view them as, a threat to society after their release. Second are those who are classified as sympathizers or no strong evidence found against them but the authorities remain certain of their complacency or involvement in such activities (personal interviews with officials at the Ministry of Interior, Singapore, April 2010).

9. In fact, Singapore's minister mentor, Lee Kuan Yew, advises other countries in the region to introduce a Singaporean-style ISA. For example, he believes that 'Indonesia's ability to fight terrorism has been hampered by the lack of a Singapore-Style Internal Security Act', stating that 'the Indonesians are saying we do not have the ISC, we can't do anything. They wait for the bomb to go off, then they investigate the crime and they capture the people who did the crime and they prosecute them. And then there is the next bomb and the next bomb' (quoted in Bin Ali, 2007, p. 117).

7 Sudan: De-radicalization and Counter Radicalization in a Radicalizing Environment

1. The civil war between southern and northern Sudan claimed over half a million lives and lasted, officially, until 1972 – although conflict and social strife continued despite the ceasefire (Dagne, CRS-2 from Waller, 2011).

2. As Faris (2007) noted: 'The distinction between "Arab" and "African" in Darfur is defined more by lifestyle than any physical difference: Arabs are generally herders, Africans typically farmers. The two groups are not racially distinct.'

3. These also include the Nuclear Non-Proliferation Treaty and the Comprehensive Test Ban Treaty, the Chemical Weapons and Biological Weapons Conventions (both signed in 1999), the International Convention for the Suppression of Terrorist Bombing (PDF), signed in 2000.

4. 'If we feel that six months is not enough, we can release them for one day only then re-arrest them for another six months if we feel that they are still a threat to society. Yes, we know that we are only fooling the law but better to do this than cause a tragedy in the country' (personal interview with a high-ranking official in the Security and Intelligence Department, Khartoum, December 2011).

5. After the end of the first 45 days in detention, participants are divided into groups of four maximum, based on their level of radicalization, activities committed or attempted, and ideological and educational backgrounds.

6. The authorities prepared a file for each participant, which included every possible piece of information on each participant. The file was then provided to each committee concerned with carrying out dialogue with particular participants.

7. Abdulhay Al-Yosuf, who is one of the scholars who participated in the dialogue program and whose son was one of the participants himself, later wrote a book about the dialogue experience. In the book he identifies 48 'misunderstood concepts' by VEts in Sudan, including by the participants in the dialogue program and their followers in the country. Indeed, a large number of these concepts evolved around secession of the South, presence of international peace forces, Darfur conflict and jihad in other Muslim states. Other misunderstood concepts evolved around the following issues: democracy, Islamic ruler, sharia law, *alwala wa-albara, al-amer bel-ma'rouf wa al-nahe an almunker,* fatwa, treatment of non-Muslims in Muslim states, international agreements between Muslim and non-Muslim states, martyrdom operations, jihad in Afghanistan and Iraq, handing some Arab Mujahedeen to their governments (rendition policy), participation of southern movement in power. (For more details, see Al-Yusuf Abdulhay (2010), *Dialogue with a Youth,* Khartoum: Sudan Press Limited).

8. Information on the Centre is obtained from a lecture specifically prepared for the author by staff of the Centre, as well as from an interview with the aforementioned staff, several scholars and ulama involved in delivering the activities of the Centre, and the head of the centre himself, Dr Ibrahim Al-Karori (Khartoum, 2–10 January 2012).

9. An attempt is made here to explain the causes and consequences of HIV virus and to alleviate social stigma against HIV patients in society.

10. As one active scholar involved in delivering the activities of the Centre stated: 'They confuse jihad *a dafa'* (push) with jihad *al-talab* (demand). In Islam jihad *al-diffa* (defence) is *fard ayn* (compulsory). If the ruler called for it, all Muslims must comply. Jihad *a-talab,* on the other hand, is voluntary, called for by individual Muslims, but even this requires permission from the ruler and *walay al-amer* (person responsible for individual who decided

to respond to this type of jihad). When they understand these points, they repent because they now realize that doing jihad wrongly is a sin' (personal interview, Khartoum, January, 2012).

11. All information on the *Muntada* is derived from personal interviews with the head of the *Muntada*, other staff members (Khartoum, January 2012) and Renaissance and Civil Continuation Forum, *Qutoof Daniyeh* (Hanging Leafs), *Muntada*, 2011.

12. See *Al-Nahda* Magazine, Nos. 10, 12, 13, 14 and 15, The RCCF, 2012.

13. Of course the United Nations and all Arab regimes do not classify Hamas as a terrorist organization, and most Arab regimes, and people, do not treat Hezbollah in the same fashion.

8 From Militarization to Democratization: The Transformation of Turkey's Counter Terrorism Strategy (CTS)

1. The year 1908 witnessed the establishment of the first Kurdish organization (Taali ve Terakki Kurdistan or Recovery and Progress of Kurdistan) whose main activists came from a group of Kurds working in high posts in the Ottoman administration. (For more information see Laciner and Bal, 2011.)

2. However, the nationalist movement, led by Mustafa Kemal Pasha, rejected the settlement and, in a series of successful campaigns, asserted Turkish independence and led to a new agreement in 1923, the Treaty of Lausanne. The latter defined the boundaries and independence of the new Turkish State (Halliday, 2005, p. 62).

3. In 1987, Ozal's government organized a referendum, which returned all former politicians and put an end to the ten-year banishment imposed under the 1982 constitution. Ozal was also skilful in developing a de facto division of labour where his party oversaw the economy while the army oversaw domestic security. His MLP brought politicians from all backgrounds and a variety of religious, nationalists and regional groups. He was seen as being responsible for a Turkish economic miracle, and was elected as president of Turkey in 1989. (For more details, see Owen, 1992, p. 154; Richards and Waterbury, 1996; and Halliday, 2005.)

4. Also, the US government, in May 2008 and April 2011, froze several accounts in the United States belonging to leaders of the PKK due to indications of involvement in drug trafficking, migrant smuggling, human trafficking, commodity, fuel and cigarette smuggling.

5. The PKK is formally 'recognised as a terrorist organisation by the US, the members of the EU, Iraq, Iran, Syria and New Zealand' (Bilgi, 2011, p. 11).

6. Other religiously-oriented organizations include Hizbultahriri (Hizbuttahri) and Islamic Movement (Islami Hareket). TH remains the most dangerous and organized among all religiously oriented organizations in Turkey. (For more details, see Bal, Ozeren and Sozer, 2011, p. 24.)

7. According to Sozer and Server (2011), TH emerged mainly in 'Bookstores which became meeting points for people like Huseyin Velioglu who led the Ilim branch of TH, and Fidan Gungor, who led the Menzil branch of TH'.

8. As soon as World War II ended, Turkey started to move away from its previous somewhat neutral stance towards alliance with the West. Halliday (2005,

p. 107) gave at least two reasons for this shift. First, Turkey anticipated that historic rivalry with Russia would resurface. As Russia was clearly emerging from World War II victory, Turkey anticipated that the more powerful Russia would also be in a more and threatening mood, demanding concessions and other strategic concessions similar to the ones it was demanding from Eastern Europe. Second was the desire to make up with the Allies and access economic advantages.

9. A division of labour hence emerged in Turkey between main security agencies. TNP has jurisdiction over 80 per cent of the population in Turkey, including the cities, towns, townships, greater rural communities, border gates, highways, airports and other stations, while the Gendarmerie has jurisdiction over 15 per cent of the population in the rural countryside and in villages. The main job of the Turkish Military, on the other hand, is to defend the borders of the country and also to deal with the terrorists on the borders of Turkey and in very remote rural areas close to the borders, especially in the southern part of Turkey (US House of Representatives, 2006, pp. 22–3).

10. A study in Turkey based on interviews with PKK and TH members showed that 25 per cent of interviewees reported the influence of enforcement practices on their decision to join the organization (91 per cent of interviewees were interviewed in prisons). The study concluded that 'being subjected to brutality (42 per cent) and viewing law enforcement practices as unreasonable (65 per cent) were reported at high levels, leading to a significant relationship to exist between brutality and law enforcement's influence and reliance on militaristic tactics in an individual's decision to join a terrorist organization' (Yildiz and Goktepe, 2011, p. 80).

11. Major Yayla further elaborated on these reforms by stating that: 'Turkey adopted new and clearer regulations and policies in regard to handling terrorist suspects. First of all, the detention procedures were changed. The duration of detention was shortened to a maximum of four days. Very strict guidelines were adopted as detention rules in order to ensure that no improper behaviours existed against the detainees (US House of Representatives, 206, p. 30).

12. In order to provide an exit strategy for the would-be terrorists, the Turkish authorities also issued a new law, The Law on Reintegration to Society No. 4959, which provides amnesty to members of VE organizations and groups who did not commit any crimes and also facilitate their reintegration into society (SECI, 2011, p. 164).

13. A study by TNP on members of VE organizations in Turkey showed that the average age of members is 14–24 years (Sozer and Server, 2011).

14. SODES is probably the largest of these projects. It is a grant program operated by the state Planning Organization in the Prime Ministry. In this grant, NGOs, public and civil organizations and people can apply to implement projects in three areas: creating jobs; organizing culture, art and sport activities; and organizing social projects. SODES began in 2008. Since then, it has delivered more than US$249 million to various deprived cities. The majority of these projects focus on children and youth (Yildiz and Goktepe, 2011, pp. 82–3).

15. Every region in Turkey has a fund topped up from various charities, including zakat (Muslim tax) which Muslims are obliged to pay to the

poor and needy. A large number of rich Turks prefer to give money to the regional fund and let the latter distribute it to the poor. The money of funds must only be spent within its own region and cannot be transferred to other regions (personal interview, Dr Sabit Simsek, Head of Interfaith and Intercultural Relations Department, The Presidency of Religious Affairs, Ankara, November 2011).

Bibliography

African News24 (2010) 'Mauritania Kidnapping: 7 Charged', 15 March 2010, http://www.news24.com/Africa/News/Mauritania-kidnapping-7-charged-20100315#.

Age, The (2012) 'Man Charged after Vic Terror Raids', http://www.theage.com. au/ action/printArticle?id=3632127, 13 September 2012.

Agius, T. (2012) 'Epigenetics and Migration – Considerations Based on the Incidence of Psychosis in South Asians in Luton, England', *US National Library of Medicine, National Institutes of Health*, http://www.ncbi.nlm.nih. gov/pubmed?term=Tahira%20A %5BAuthor %5D&cauthor=true&cauthor_ uid=22945222.

Al Jazeera Network (2011a) 'Mauritania's Goals in Its Struggle against Al-Qaeda', Al Jazeera Centre for Studies, http://www.aljazeera.net/mritems/streams/2011 /7/26/1_1076198_1.51.pdf, 25 July 2011.

——(2011b) 'Sahara Nations to Set Up Desert Patrol Force – Mali, Mauritania, Niger and Algeria will set up to 75,000 soldiers to secure their shared territory', http://english.aljazeera.net/news/africa/2011/05/201152102915797956. html, 21 May 2011.

——Network (2011c) 'Hasad al Youm (Today's Harvest)', 11 August 2011.

Al-Sirag (2010) http://www.essirage.net/index.php/news-and-reports/790–2010 –11–17–11–13–32, 17 November 2010.

Angell, A. and Gunaratna, R. (2011) *Terrorist Rehabilitation: The U.S. Experience in Iraq* (Boca Raton: CRC Press).

Arab News (2011) 'Treatment of Prisoners of War in Islam', http://www.arab-news.com/node/401802, 22 December 2011.

Archer, T. and Popovic, T. (2007) 'The Trans-Saharan Counter-Terrorism Initiative: The US War on Terrorism in Northwest Africa', UPI (The Finnish Institute of International Affairs, Paper Series No. 16, Finland).

Arya, S. (2009) 'Sudan – Conflicts, Terror, and Oil', in *Journal of Defence Studies*, 3, 4, October, pp. 64–78.

Ashour, O. (2009) *The De-Radicalization of Jihadists: Transforming Armed Islamist Movements* (London: Routledge).

——(2012) 'Libya's Defeated Islamists', in *Jordan Times*, http://jordantimes.com/ print.html, 19 July 2012.

Asia Times (2003) 'Mahathir is Right: Jews Do Rule the World', http://www. atimes.com/atimes/Front_Page/EJ28Aa02.html, 28 October 2003.

Assakina (2011) 'Former Al-Qaeda Prisoners Complain About the Mauritanian Government', http://www.assakina.com/news/news2/8804. html#ixzz1SgTBAKLa, 19 July 2011.

Attran, S. (2006) 'The Moral Logic and Growth of Suicide Terrorism', *The Washington Quarterly* 29, 2, 127–47, http://jeannicod.ccsd.cnrs.fr/docs/00/05/99/38/PDF/ TWQ06spring_atran.pdf.

Australian, The (2005) 'Australia: New Checks on Terror Trainer', N. O'Brien, http:// www.freerepublic.com/focus/f-news/1522587/posts, 15 November 2005.

Australian Government (2013) 'National Agenda for a Multicultural Australia: What is multiculturalism?' http://www.immi.gov.au/media/publications/ multicultural/ agenda/agenda89/whatismu.htm.

Australian Jewish News, The (AJN) (2011) 'Howard Urges Gillard to Support Israel in UN', http://www.jewishnews.net.au/howard-urges-gillard-to-support-israel-in-un/20213, 11 April 2011.

Australian Politics, November 10, 2001, http://australianpolitics.com/ elections/2001/ .

Bal, I. (2010a) 'Is PKK Turkey's Hamas?', *Journal of Turkish Weekly*, http://www.turkishweekly.net/columnist/3333/is-pkk-turkey-39-s-hamas.html., 6 May 2010.

——(2010b) 'The PKK as the Problem of Kurds', International Strategic Research Organisation, Ankara, http://www.usak.org.tr/EN/makale.asp?id=2397, 18 October 2010.

——(2011a) 'Why Become a Terrorist?' *Journal of Turkish Weekly*, http://www.turkishweekly.net/columnist/3481/why-become-a-terrorist.html, 15 July 2011.

—— (2011b) 'Could Kurdish Movement Read June 12 Elections?' *Journal of Turkish Weekly*, http://www.turkishweekly.net/columnist/3505/could-kurdish-movements-read-june-12-elections.html, 25 August 2011.

Bal, I., Ozeren, S. and Sozer, M. (eds) (2011) *Multi-Faceted Approach to Radicalisation in Terrorist Organisations*, NATO Science for Peace and Security Series, Human and Social Dynamic, Vol. 87, Amsterdam: IOS Press.

Berger, P. and Hsiao, M. (1988) *In Search of an East Asian Development Model* (New Brunswick: Transaction Publishers).

Bhattacharji, P. (2008) 'State Sponsors: Sudan, Council on Foreign Relations', http://www.cfr.org/sudan/state-sponsors-sudan/p9367#, 2 April 2008.

Bhui, K., Dinos, S. and Jones, E. (2012a) 'Psychological Process and Pathways to Radicalization', in *Bioterrorism & Biodefense*, 10.4172/2157–2526.S5–003, pp. 1–5.

—— Hicks, M., Lashley, M. and Jones, E. (2012b) 'A Public Health Approach to Understanding and Preventing Violent Radicalization', *BMC Medicine*, 10, p. 16.

Bilgi, S. (2011) 'Revising the Terrorist vs. Guerilla Debate on PKK via Ach Software: Known Answers, Unknown Methods', in I. Bal, S. Ozeren and M. Sozer (eds), *Multi-Faceted Approach to Radicalisation in Terrorist Organisations*, NATO Science for Peace and Security Series E: Human and Social Dynamic, Vol.87 (Amsterdam: IOS Press), pp. 11–21.

Bin Ali, M. (2007) 'Coping with the Threat of Jemmah Islamiyah – The Singapore Experience', in A.H. Bin Kader (ed.), *Fighting Terrorism: The Singapore Perspective* (Singapore: Taman Bacaan, Pemuda Pemudi Melayu Singapura), pp. 108–18.

Bin Kader, A.H. (ed.) (2007) *Fighting Terrorism: The Singapore Perspective* (Singapore: Taman Bacaan, Pemuda of Living Space Pemudi Melayu Singapore).

—— (ed.) (2009) *Countering Radicalism: The Next Generation and Challenges Ahead* (Singapore: Taman Bacaan, Pemuda of Living Space Pemudi Melayu) pp. 18–22.

Birk, A. (2009) *Incredible Dialogues: Religious Dialogue as a Means of Encountering Terrorism in Yemen* (King's College, London: ICSR).

Bjorgo, T. and Horgan, J. (2009) *Leaving Terrorism Behind: Individual and Collective Disengagement* (London: Routledge).

Boland, S. (2000) 'Liberal *Herald* Backs Labor's Attacks on Migrants', in *Green Left*, http://www.greenleft.org.au/node/20714, 26 January 2000.

Boucek, C. (2008) 'Saudi Arabia's 'Soft' Counterterrorism Strategy: Prevention, Rehabilitation and Aftercare', *Carnegie Endowment for International Peace*, Number 97, September.

Brandon, J. (2009) *Unlocking al-Qaeda: Islamist Extremism in British Prisons*. (London: Quilliam Foundation).

British Broadcasting Corporation (BBC) News (1999) 'World: Analysis Sudan: A Political and Military History', http://news.bbc.co.uk/2/hi/africa/84927.stm, 21 February 1999.

——(2011) 'State Multiculturalism Has Failed, says David Cameron', http://www.bbc.co.uk/news/uk-politics-12371994?print=true, 5 February 2011.

Brown, M., Feneley, R. and Maley, J. (2010) 'Terrorists Made in Australia', http://www.smh.com.au/nsw/terrorists-made-in-australia-20100219-olzf.html, 20 February 2010.

Bulloch, J. and Harvey, M. (1992) *No Friends but the Mountains: The Tragic History of the Kurds* (New York: Oxford University Press).

Cahyadi, G., Kursten, B., Weiss, M. and Yang, G. (2004) 'Global Urban Development: Singapore Metropolitan Economic Strategy Report: Singapore's Economic Transformation, June', Global Urban Development, Prague, Czech Republic, http://www.globalurban.org/GUD%20Singapore%20MES%20Report.pdf

Center on Global Counterterrorism Cooperation (2012) 'Colloquium on Measuring Effectiveness in Counterterrorism Programming', February 9–10, Ottawa, Canada.

Central Intelligence Agency (CIA) (2010) 'World Factbook: Mauritania', http://www.cia.gov/library/publications/the-world-factbook/fields/2004.html

—— (2012) 'World Factbook', https://www.cia.gov/library/publications/the-world-factbook/geos/su.html, last reviewed on 10 August 2012.

Chew, V. (2009) 'Public Housing in Singapore', National Library Board Singapore, http://infopedia.nl.sg/articles/SIP_1585_2009-10-26.html

Chia, Y.T. (2011) 'The Elusive Goal of Nation Building: Asian/Confucian Values and Citizenship Education in Singapore During the 1980s', *British Journal of Educational Studies*, 59, 4, pp. 383–402.

Chin, Y. and Vasu, N. (2007) 'The Ties That Bind and Blind: A Report on Inter-racial and Inter-religious Relations in Singapore', Centre of Excellence for National Study, S. Rajaratnam School of International Studies, Nanyang Technological University, http://www.rsis.edu.sg/publications/reports/RSIS%20Social%20resilience%20report.pdf

Choplin, A. (2008) 'Mauritania: Between Islamism and Terrorism', Issue 370, http://www.pambazuka.org/en/category/features/48058/print, 13 May 2008.

Chothia, F. (2013) 'Profile: Who are Nigeria's Ansaru Islamists?' in BBC News, http://www.bbc.co.uk/news/world-africa-2151076?print=true., 11 March 2013.

Clammer, J. (1998) *Race and State in Independent Singapore, 1965–1990: The Cultural Politics of Pluralism in a Multiethnic Society* (Aldershot, UK and Brookfield, VT: Ashgate).

Claridge, D. (1996) 'State Terrorism? Applying a Definitional Model', *Terrorism and Political Violence*, 8, 3, pp. 47–63.

Clark, C., Aziz, D. and MacKenzie, D. (1994) 'Shock Incarceration in New York: Focus on Treatment', U.S. Department of Justice, Office of Justice Programs, National Institute of Justice, http://www.ncjrs.gov/pdffiles/shockny.pdf

Clark, Y. (2011) *Moors and Arabs*, memo, found at: www.africawithin.com/moors/moors_and_arabs.htm.

CNN News (2010) 'Top Militant Sentenced to Death in Mauritania', http://edition.cnn.com/2010/WORLD/africa/10/20/mauritania.court.case/index.html?eref=edition_africa&utm_source=feedburner&utm_medium=feed&utm_campaign=Feed:+rss/edition_africa+(RSS:+Africa).

Collins, J., Noble, G., Poynting, S. and Tabar, P. (2000) *Kebabs, Kids, Cops and Crime: Youth, Ethnicity and Crime* (Pluto Press: Sydney).

Collins, J., Reid, C., Fabiansson, C. and Healey, L. (2007). Final Report 'Tapping the Pulse of Youth in Cosmopolitan South-Western and Western Sydney', *A Research Project Funded by the Department of Immigration and Citizenship*, http://www.immi.gov.au/media/ publications/multicultural/pdf_doc/tapping-pulse-youth.pdf.

Coolsaet, R. and Struye de Swielande, T. (2008) 'Epilogue: Zeitgeist and (De-Radicalisation', in R. Coolsaet (ed.), *Jihadi Terrorism and Radicalization Challenge in Europe* (Burlington: Ashgate), pp. 155–83.

Curran, K. (2006) 'Why God is Often Found Behind Bars: Prison Conversions and the Crisis of Self-narrative', *Research in Human Development* 3, 2&3, pp. 153–8.

Cuthbertson, I.M. (2004) 'Prisons and the Education of Terrorists', *World Policy Journal*, 21, 3, pp. 15–22.

Dagne, T. (2006) *Sudan: Humanitarian Crisis, Peace Talks, Terrorism, and U.S. Polic*, (Washington: Library of Congress, Congressional Research Service). PDF file.

DeAngelis, T. (2009) *Understanding Terrorism*, 40, 10, p. 60.http://www.alnaddy.com/search/?q=.+DeAngelis+%282009%29+Understanding+Terrorism%2C+Vol+40%2C+No&r=625.

Degomme, O. and Guha-Sapir, D. (2010) 'Patterns of Mortality Rates in Darfur Conflict', *The Lancet*, 375, 9711, pp. 294–300, http://www.thelancet.com/journals/lancet/article/PIIS0140–6736(09)61967-X/fulltext.

Department of Immigration and Citizenship (2013). 'Fact Sheet 6 – Australia's Multicultural Policy', Australian Government, http://www.immi.gov.au/media/fact-sheets/06australias-multicultural-policy.htm

De Waal, A. (ed.) (2007) 'War in Darfur and the Search for Peace' (Cambridge, MA: Harvard University Press).

Dodd, V. (2009) 'Government Anti-Terrorism Strategy 'Spies' on Innocent', in *The Guardian*, 16 October 2009.

Economist, The (2008) 'Mauritania: A Bad Example? Africa's Reaction to the Continent's Latest Coup is Being Carefully Watched', http://www.economist.com/node/11921925/print., 14 August 2008.

El-Said, H. (2013) 'Deradicalising Radicals', in *The Concordian*, 4, 1, pp. 10–18, http://www.marshallcenter.org/mcpublicweb/en/component/content/article/70-cat-col-pubs-per-concordiam/1124-art-pubs-per-concordiam-volume-4-1-en.html? directory=116.

—— (2013a). 'Clemency, Civil Accord and Reconciliation: The Evolution of Algeria's Deradicalisation Process', in H. El-Said and J. Harrigan (eds), *Deradicalising Violent Extremists: Counter Radicalisation and Deradicalisation Programmes and Their Impact in Muslim-Majority States* (London: Routledge), pp. 14–41.

—— (2013b) 'Yemen's Passive Approach towards Countering Terrorism', in H. El-Said and J. Harrigan (eds), *Deradicalising Violent Extremists: Counter Radicalisation and Deradicalisation Programmes and Their Impact in Muslim-Majority States* (London: Routledge), pp. 227–53.

—— (2013c) 'Counter Radicalisation Without Deradicalisation: The Case of Morocco', in H. El-Said and J. Harrigan (eds), *Deradicalising Violent Extremists: Counter Radicalisation and Deradicalisation Programmes and Their Impact in Muslim-Majority States* (London: Routledge), pp. 161–85.

El-Said, H. and Barrett, R. (2011) 'Radicalisation and Extremism that Lead to Violent Extremism in the Arab World', in J. Harrigan and H. El-Said (eds), *Globalisation, Democratisation and Radicalisation in the Arab World* (London: Palgrave MacMillan), pp. 199–236.

—— (2012a) 'Saudi Arabia: The Master of Deradicalisation', in H. El-Said and J. Harrigan (eds), *Deradicalising Violent Extremists: Counter-Radicalisation and Deradicalisation Programmes and Their Impact in Muslim-Majority States* (London: Routledge), pp. 194–227.

El-Said, H. and Harrigan, J. (2011) *Globalisation, Democratisation and Radicalisation in the Arab World* (London: Palgrave Macmillan).

—— (2013) *Deradicalising Violent Extremists: Counter-Radicalisation and Deradicalisation Programmes and Their Impact in Muslim-Majority States* (London: Routledge).

Emirates News24/7 (2011) 'Soldiers Wounded in Mauritania Blast', http://www.emirates247.com/news/world/soldiers-wounded-in-mauritania-blast-2011 –02–02–1.350499?ot=ot.PrintPageLayout, 2 February 2011.

Esposito, J. (2010) 'Why Do Media Commentators Get It So Wrong on Islam? And What Is the Cost?' http://www.huffingtonpost.com/john-l-esposito/media-commentators-and-is_b_795825.html, 13 December 2010.

Europe-Solidaire (2012) 'A Summary of Malaysia–Singapore History', http://www.europe-solidaire.org/spip.php?article7878. Retrieved 29 January 2012.

European Journal of Development Research (2005) 'Causes of Conflict in Sudan: Testing the Black Book', 17, 3, http://www.tandfonline.com/doi/abs/10.1080/09578810500209254.

Faris, S. (2007) 'The Real Roots of Darfur', *Atlantic Monthly*, April 2007, http://www.theatlantic.com/doc/200704/darfur-climate. Viewed on 9 August 2012.

Fertey, V. (2009) 'Abdel Aziz Wins Mauritania Poll; Rivals Cry Foul', in Reuters, http://www.reuters.com/article/2009/07/19/us-mauritania-election-idUSTRE 56119Q20090719?feedType=RSS&feedName=worldNews+pageNumber=2&virtualBrandChannel=0, 19 July 2009.

George, C. (2000) 'Neglected Nationhood: Singapore Without Singaporeans?', in C. George (ed.), *Singapore: The Air-Conditioned Nation: Essays on the Politics of Comfort and Control, 1990–2000* (Singapore: Landmark Books).

Githen-Mazer, I. and Lambart, R. (2010) 'Why Conventional Wisdom on Radicalisation Fails: The Persistence of a Failed Discourse', in *International Affairs*, 86, 4, pp. 889–901.

Global Security (2011) 'Trans-Saharan Counterterrorism Initiative (TSCTI)', http://www.globalsecurity.org/military/ops/tscti.htm.

Global Terrorism Research Centre (GTReC) (2014). 'The Unseen Terrorist Connection: Exploring Jihadist Links between Lebanon and Australia', in

Terrorism and Political Violence, Monash University, Caulfield, Australia, http://mc.manuscriptcentral.com/ftpv.

Goh, S. (2008) 'Compare and Contrast the Communist Activities in Singapore During the 1940s with Those in the 1950s', http://voices.yahoo.com/compare-contrast-communist-activities-singapore-2031679.html, 15 October 2008.

Gros, D., Dervis, K., Emerson, M. and Ulgen, S. (2004) 'The European Transformation of Modern Turkey', Centre for European Policy Studies, Brussels/Economics and Foreign Policy Forum, Istanbul, http://www.ceps.be, 13.

Grosscup, B. (2006) *Strategic Terror: The Politics and Ethics of Aerial Bombardment* (London: Zed Books Ltd).

Gunaratna, R. (2007) 'Ideology in Terrorism and Counter Terrorism: Lessons from Combating AQ and Al-Jamaah Al Islamiyah in Southeast Asia', in A.H. Bin Kader (ed.), *Fighting Terrorism: The Singapore Perspective* (Singapore: Taman Bacaan, Pemuda Pemudi Melayu Singapura), pp. 56–94.

—— (2009) 'The Battlefield of the Mind: Rehabilitating Muslim Terrorists', UNISCI Discussion Papers, No. 21 (October), SSN 1696–2206.

Halliday, F. (2005) *The Middle East in International Relations: Power, Politics and Ideology* (Cambridge: Cambridge University Press).

Hamm, M.S. (2007) *Terrorist Recruitment in American Correctional Institutions: An Exploratory Study of Non-Traditional Faith Groups Final Report* (Washington, DC: US Department of Justice).

—— (2009) 'Prison Islam in the Age of Sacred Terror', *The British Journal of Criminology*, 49, 5, pp. 667–85, http://papers.ssrn.com/sol3/papers.cfm?abstract_id=1458826.

Hannah, G., Clutterbuck, L. and Rubin, J. (2008) *Radicalization or Rehabilitation: Understanding the Challenge of Extremist and Radicalized Prisoners* (Cambridge: RAND Corporation).

Harmony Centre (2010) *Harmony Centre Introduction* (Singapore: An-Nahdhah Mosque).

Harrigan, J. and El-Said, H. (2011) (eds) *Globalization, Democratization and Radicalization in the Arab World* (London: Palgrave Macmillan).

Harris-Hogan, S. (2012a) 'Domestic Terror Raids: A Timely Reminder of a Persistent Threat', The Global Terrorism Research Centre, Monash University, http://theconversation.edu.au/ domestic-terror-raids-a-timely-reminder-of-a-persistent-threat-9556, 14 September 2012.

——(2012b) 'The Importance of Family: The Key to Understanding the Evolution of Neojihadism in Australia; Islam and Christian–Muslim Relations', The Global Terrorism Research Centre, Monash University, Caulfield, Australia.

Hassan, M.F. (2007) 'The Roles of Religious Rehabilitation in Singapore', in A.H. Bin Kader (ed.), *Fighting Terrorism: The Singapore Perspective* (Singapore: Taman Bacaan, Pemuda Pemudi Melayu Singapura), pp. 149–60.

Henderson, G. (2012) 'Multiculturalism Still Has a Long Road to Travel to Reach All', in *Sydney Morning Herald*, http://www.smh.com.au/action/printArticle?id=3642351, 18 September 2012.

Hill, M. and Lian, K.F. (1995) *The Politics of Nation Building and Citizenship in Singapore* (London and New York: Routledge).

Hoffman, P. (2004) 'Human Rights and Terrorism', in *Human Rights Quarterly*, 26, 4, pp. 932–55, http://muse.jhu.edu/login?auth=0&type=summary&url=/journals/human_rights _quarterly/v026/26.4hoffman.pdf, November 2004.

Horgan, J. (2008) 'Deradicalization or Disengagement?', in *Perspectives on Terrorism*, 4, 2, http://www.terrorismanalysts.com/pt/index.php/pot/article/view/32/html.

Horgan, J. and Braddock, K. (2010) 'Rehabilitating the Terrorists? Challenges in Assessing the Effectiveness of De-radicalization Programs', *Terrorism and Political Violence* 22, 267–91, http://www.start.umd.edu/sites/default/files/files/publications/Derad.pdf

Hussain, Z. (2009) 'New-Look Mosques Take on Varied Roles', in A.H. Bin Kader (ed.), *Countering Radicalism: The Next Generation and Challenges Ahead* (Singapore: Taman Bacaan Pemuda of Living Space Pemudi Melayu Singapore), pp. 113–15.

Ibrahim, M.F. (2009) 'A Resilient Community with Our Nation's Shared Values as the First Line of Defence against Any Form of Terror Threats', in A.H. Bin Kader (ed.), *Countering Radicalism: The Next Generation and Challenges Ahead* (Singapore: Taman Bacaan Pemuda Pemudi Melayu Singapura), pp. 42–6.

Infoplease (2012) 'Sudan', http://www.infoplease.com/ipa/A0107996.html?pageno=7, 31 May 2012.

Innes, M. (ed.) (2007) *Denial of Sanctuary: Understanding Terrorist Safe Havens* (Westport, CT: Praeger).

International Centre for the Study of Radicalisation and Political Violence (ICSR) (2010) 'Prisons and Terrorism: Radicalisation and De-radicalisation in 15 Countries' (London: King's College), http://icsr.info/wp-content/uploads/2012/10/1277699166Prisonsand TerrorismRadicalisationand Deradicalisationin15Countries.pdf.

International Crisis Group (ICG) (2005) *Islamism in North Africa IV: The Islamist Challenge in Mauritania: Threat or Scapegoat?* Brussels, http://www.crisisgroup.org/en/regions/middle-east-north-africa/north-africa/041-islamism-in-north-africa-4-the -islamist-challenge-in-mauritania.aspx, 11 May 2005.

—— (2006) *Political Transition in Mauritania Results and Prospects*, Executive Summary, No. 53, http://www.crisisgroup.org/en/regions/middle-east-north-africa/north-africa/053-political-transition-in-mauritania-results -and-prospects.aspx, 24 April 2006.

International Food Agency (IFAD) (2002) *Enabling the Rural Poor to Overcome Poverty in Sudan*, http://www.alnaddy.com/search/?q=poverty+in+sudan%2C +IFAD&r=625.

International Institute for Counter-Terrorism (IICT) (2011) *Retracting – Using Ideological Means for Purposes of Deradicalisation*, IDC Herzliya, ICT's Jihadi Websites Monitoring Group, January 2011.

International Peace Institute (IPI) (2010) *A New Approach? Deradicalization Programs and Counterterrorism* (New York: IPI).

Jacobson, M. (2010) *Learning From Dropouts*, Washington Institute, http://www.alnaddy.com/search/?q=Michael+Jacobson+%282010%29.+Learning+from+Dropouts%2C+in+ForeignPolicy.com%2C+February+1.&r=625, 1 February 2010.

Jakarta Post (2009) 'Deradicalization Works', 21 August 2009.

Jarvis, L. (2009) 'The Spaces and Faces of Critical Terrorism Studies'; the final version of this paper has been published in Security Dialogue, 40, 1, pp. 5–27, URL: http://sdi.sagepub.com/content/40/1.toc, February 2009.

Jerard, J. (2009) 'Future Challenges in Fighting Radicalism: Roles of Non-Muslims in Community Engagement Efforts in Singapore', in A.H. Bin Kader (ed.),

Countering Radicalism: The Next Generation and Challenges Ahead (Singapore: Taman Bacaan Pemuda of Living Space Pemudi Melayu Singapura), pp. 94–5.

Jooma, M.B. (2006) 'Sudan: The Crisis of Cohesion'? African Security Review, Institute for Security Studies, 15, 3, pp. 48–51. http://www.iss.co.za/pgcontent.php?UID=19607.

Journal of International Business Studies (JIBS) (2010) 'Terrorism and International Business', 41.

Journal of Turkish Weekly, The (JTW) (2010) 'Future of Turkish-Israeli Relations: What Next?' http://ww.turkishweekly.net/print.asp?typ+2&id=400.

Ju-Li, H. (2009) 'Countering Radicalisation in Singapore: Commonalities and Discourse', in A.H. Bin Kader (ed.), *Countering Radicalism: The Next Generation and Challenges Ahead* (Singapore: Taman Bacaan Pemuda of Living Space Pemudi Melayu Singapore) pp. 69–78.

Kabir, N. (2006) 'Depiction of Muslims in Selected Australian Media, Free Speech or Taking Sides', *M/C Journal*, 9, 4. http://journal.media-culture.org.au/0609/l-kabir.php, online edition, September 2006.

Karabell, Z. (2007) *People of the Book* (London: John Murray).

Koleth, E. (2010) 'Multiculturalism: A Review of Australian Policy Statements and Recent Debates in Australia and Overseas', Parliament of Australia, Social Policy Section, Research Paper no. 6 2010–11. C:\Users\99900609\Desktop\Australia\Multiculturalism_Australia_ Parliament.mht, 8 October 2010.

Krueger, A.B. and Maleckova, J. (2002) 'Does Poverty Cause Terrorism'? *The New Republic*, pp. 27–33, 24 June 2002.

—— (2003) 'Education, Poverty, and Terrorism: Is There a Causal Connection?' *Journal of Economic Perspectives*, 17, 4, pp. 119–44.

Kundnani, A. and Patel, F. (2011) 'Counter-Radicalization Lessons From the United Kingdom', Brennan Centre for Justice, http://www.brennancenter.org/analysis/counter-radicalization-lessons-united-kingdom, 28 July 2011.

Kurlantzick, J. (2008) 'Fighting Terrorism with Terrorists', *Los Angeles Times*, http://www.carnegieendowment.org/publications/index.cfm?fa=view&id=19823&prog=zgp&proj=zusr, 6 January 2008.

Laciner, S. and Bal, I. (2011) 'The Ideological and Historical Roots of Kurdish Movements in Turkey: Ethnicity Demography, Politics', *The Journal of Turkish Weekly*, http://www.turkishweekly.net/print.asp?type=2&id=15, 15 November 2011.

Lake, E. (2007) '1,500 Qaeda Members Freed After Counselling', in *Daily News*, http://www.alnaddy.com/search/?q=E.+Lake+%282007%29+%E2%80%981%2C500+Qaeda+Members+Freed+After+Counselling%E2%80%99%2C+in+New+York+Sun%2C&r=625.

Landler, M. (2010) 'US Revises Offer to Take Sudan Off Terror List', The New York Times, http://www.nytimes.com/2010/11/08/world/africa/08sudan.html?_r=1&pagewanted=print, 7 November 2010.

Leitch Lepoer, B. (1989) *Singapore, Shonan: Light of the South*, Library of Congress Country Studies. Washington, D.C.: Government Printing Office, http://lcweb2.loc.gov/cgi-bin/query/r?frd/cstdy:@field(DOCID+sg0027). Retrieved 25 April 2012.

Lentini, P. (2008) 'Review Essay: Understanding and Combating Terrorism: Definitions, Origins and Strategies', *Australian Journal of Political Science*, 43, 1, March 2008, 133–40.

——(2010) 'If They Know Who Put the Sugar It Means They Know Everything: Understanding Terrorist Activity Using Operation Pendennis Wiretap (Listening Device and Telephone Intercept) Transcripts', Global Terrorism Research Centre, Monash University, May 2011. http://www.arts.monash.edu.au/radicalisation/conferences-and-events/conference-2010/ – downloads/know-sugar-know-everything-pl.pdf

Li, Q. and Schaub, D. (2004) 'Economic Globalization and Transnational Terrorism: A Pooled Time-Series Analysis', *The Journal of Conflict Resolution*, 48, 2, 230–59.

Lim, B.H. (1994) 'Family Values', Speech at the Opening of the NTUC Seminar on Family Values. 19 November 1994. Online. Singapore. Available at: http://www.gov.sg/mita/speech/speeches/v18n6011.htm. Retrieved on 30 April 2012.

——(2009) 'Mainstream Religious Website: A Viable Weapon Against the Spread of Extremist Religious Ideologies in the Internet Age', in A.H. Bin Kader (ed.), *Countering Radicalism: The Next Generation and Challenges Ahead* (Singapore: Taman Bacaan, Pemuda Pemudi Melayu Singapura), pp. 38–41.

Lubeck, P.M. (1998) 'Islamist Response to Globalization: Cultural Conflict in Egypt, Algeria, and Malaysia', in B. Crawford and R. Lipschutz (eds), *The Myth of Ethnic Conflict, Economics and Cultural Violence* (Berkeley: IIS/IAS University of California Press), pp. 293–319.

Lyons, J. (2009) *The House of Wisdom: How the Arabs Transformed Western Civilization* (New York: Bloomsbury Press).

Magharebia (2011). 'A Growing Youth Protest Movement in Mauritania is Challenging the Status Quo', http://www.magharebia.com/cocoon/awi/xhtml1/en_GB/features/awi/features/2011/03/10/feature-02, 3 March 2011.

Mamdani, M. (2009) *Saviors and Survivors: Darfur, Politics, and the War on Terror* (New York: Pantheon Books).

Manne, R. (2006) 'Little America: How John Howard Has Changed Australia', in *The Monthly Essays*, http://www.themonthly.com.au/how-john-howard-has-changed-australia-little-america-robert-manne-184, March 2006.

Maruna, S., Wilson, L. and Claridge, D. (1996) 'State Terrorism? Applying a Definitional Model', *Terrorism and Political Violence*, Volume 8, Issue 3, 47–63.

Middle East Online (2011) 'Mauritanian Leader Dismisses Youth Calls for Protests', http://www.middle-east-online.com/english/?id=46559, 6–8 June 2011.

Miliband, D. (2009) 'War on Terror Was Wrong', *The Guardian*, 15 January 2009.

Ministry of Education (2011) 'Racial Harmony Day Celebrations 2011: HOME: Joint Hopes, Shared Memories', Singaporean Government, http://www.moe.gov.sg/media/press/2011/07/racial-harmony-day-celebration.php, 21 July 2011.

Mohamed, A. (2009) 'Understanding Al-Wala' Wal Bara', in A.H. Bin Kader (ed.), *Countering Radicalism: The Next Generation and Challenges Ahead* (Singapore: Taman Bacaan, Pemuda Pemudi Melayu Singapura), pp. 79–90.

Mongabay (2012) 'Sudan – History', Mongabay.com. http://www.mongabay.com/reference/country_studies/sudan/HISTORY.html, viewed on 31 May 2012.

Musa, M.A. (2007) 'Singaporean Muslim Identity: Tolerant, Adaptive and Progressive Yet Keeping to the Faith', in A.H. Bin Kader (ed.), *Fighting Terrorism: The Singapore Perspective* (Singapore: Taman Bacaan, Pemuda Pemudi Melayu Singapura), pp. 35–9.

Nahid, K. (2006) 'Depiction of Muslims in Selected Australian Media: Free Speech or Taking Sides', 9, 4, September 2006, http://journal.media-culture.org.au/0609/1-kabir.php, online edition.

Nation, The (2013) 'US Air Force Now Hiding Data on Drone Strikes', http://www.nation.com.pk/pakistan-news-newspaper-daily-english-online/national/11-Mar-2013/us-air-force-now-hiding-data-on-drone-strikes, 11 March 2013.

National Heritage Board (2011) The Malays, http://yesterday.sg/discover-more/communities-festivals/communities/the-malays/, retrieved 25 April 2012.

National Library Singapore (2011) 'Social Cohesion and Harmony: Case Study of Singapore', http://libguides.nl.sg/content.php?pid=109756&sid=827175, 14 June 2011.

National Security Preparedness Group (NSPG) (2011) 'Preventing Violent Radicalization in America', http://bipartisanpolicy.org/sites/default/files/NSPG.pdf

Nato International (2011) 'NATO Secretary General Condemns Terrorist Attacks in Turkey', http://www.nato.int/cps/en/SID-128495787CBDDBBB/natolive/news_79664.htm, 19 October 2011.

New York Times, The (1990) 'Headliners; Retiring, Semi'. 2 December 1990, http://query.nytimes.com/gst/fullpage.html?res=9DOCE4DD123DF931A35751C1A9 66958260. Retrieved 29 April 2012.

Nichol, R. and Sim, J.-Y. (2007) 'Singaporean Citizenship, National Education and Social Studies: Control, Constraints, Contradictions and Possibilities', *Citizenship Teaching and Learning*, 3, 1, pp. 17–31.

Neumann, P. (2011) 'Preventing Violent Radicalization in America', National Security Preparedness Group, Bipartisan Policy Centre.

New South Wales Police (2006) 'Cronulla Riots: Review of the Police Response, New South Wales Police, Strike Force Neil', 1 4. http://www.abc.net.au/media-watch/transcripts/ep38cronulla1.pdf.

Onis, Z. (2005) 'The Political Economy of Turkey's Justice and Development Party', Social Science Research Network, Working Paper Series No. 34, http://papers.ssrn.com/sol3/papers.cfm?abstract_id=659463.

Ould Abduallah, D. (1999) *al-Thagafah wa al-Fikir fi Belad Chanquet* (Education and Thought in Chanquet Country) (Nouakchott: University of Nouakchott, The Historical and Studies Laboratory).

Ould al-Salim, H.A. (1997) 'Ba'd Mugqawemat al-Fada' al-Thagafah al-Chanqueti: Madkahl Lidirasta Ishkaliyat al-Majal wal Haweya fi Muritania belams' (Some Potentials of the Changueti Cultural Space: Introduction to the Study of the Space and Identity of Mauritania Yesterday), *Al-Mustagbal Al-Arabi* (Arab Future), 19, 216.

—— (2008) *Al-Mujtama' al-Ahli al-Muritani: Mudun al-Qarnafals 1591–1898* (The Mauritanian Civil Society: The Cities of Carnivals 1591–1898) (Beirut: Centre for Studies of Arabic Unity).

—— (2010) *Islam wa al Thaghafa al-Arabeya fi al-Shara al-Kubra* (Islam and the Arabic Culture in the Sahara) (Beirut: Dar al-Kutob Al-Ilmiyah).

Ould Daoud, A. (2011) 'Mauritania's Experience', a paper submitted to a conference on First Workshop on Upstream Prevention and Downstream Disengagement, Rehabilitation and Reintegration, UNICRI, Lucca, 24–25 May 2011.

Ould Ibrahim, M.A. (2010) 'Al Qaeda in Mauritania: Analytical Study', in *Assakina*, http://www.assakina.com/center/parties/5754.html, 27 November 2010.

Ould Muhammad, M. (1999) 'Besadad Tasmeyat Moritania' (The Process of Naming Mauritania), Faculty of Adaab Publications, No. 6.

Ould Sheikhana, S. (2009) *Muritania al-Mu'aserah: Shahadat wa Wawatha'aq* (Contemporary Mauritania: Testimonies and Documents) (Nouakchott: Dar al-Fikir).

Ould Sidi Muhammad, M.A. (2003). 'State and Society in Mauritania', a PhD Dissertation, University of Baghdad, Faculty of Political Science.

Owen, R. (1992) *State, Power and Politics in the Making of the Modern Middle East* (London: Routledge).

Palmer, A. (1992) *Decline and Fall of the Ottoman Empire* (London: Evans and Company).

Pape, R. (2003) 'The Strategic Logic of Suicide Terrorism', *American Political Science Review*, 97, pp. 341–61.

—— (2005). *Dying to Win: The Strategic Logic of Suicide Terrorism* (New York: Random House).

Pedahzur, A. (ed.) (2006) *Root Causes of Suicide Terrorism: The Globalization of Martyrdom* (London: Routledge).

Peraino, K. (2009) 'Article: The Reeducation of Abu Jandal', in *Newsweek*, 29 May 2009, http://www.alnaddy.com/search/?q=newsweek+magazine&r=625.

Petricusic, A. and Erkan, E. (2010) 'Constitutional Challenges Ahead of the EU Accession: Analysis of the Croatian and Turkish Constitutional Provisions that Require Harmonization with the Acquis Communautaire', *Uluslararasi Hukuk ve Politika Cilt* 6, 22, pp.133–52.

Porges, M. and Stern, J. (2010) 'Getting Deradicalization Right', in *Foreign Affairs*, http://www.foreignaffairs.com/print/66340, May/June 2010, pp. 1–2.

Porter, B. (1998) 'Singapore's Gentle Revolutionary', in *South China Morning Post*, http://www.singapore-window.org/81130sc.html, 30 November 1998.

Prieur, L. (2011) 'Al Qaeda Suspects Killed in Mauritania Car Blast', in Reuters, http://www.reuters.com/article/2011/02/02/us-mauritania-blast-idUS-TRE7110XE20110202, 2 February 2011.

Primoratz, I. (2002) 'State Terrorism', in T. Coady and M. O'Keefe (eds), *Terrorism and Justice: Moral Arguments in a Threatened World* (Melbourne: Melbourne University Press).

RAND Corporation, The (2006) 'Waging the War of Ideas', http://www.rand.org/content/dam/rand/pubs/reprints/2006/RAND_RP1218.pdf

Reeves, E. (2011) 'The History of Sudan's Third Civil War', in *Sudan Tribune*, http://www.sudantribune.com/The-History-of-Sudan-s-Third-Civil,40958, 11 December 2011.

ReliefWeb Report (2009), http://reliefweb.int/sites/reliefweb.int/files/reliefweb_pdf/node-324270.pdf, 13 September 2009.

Reuters (2011) 'Mauritanian Aircraft Attack Al-Qaeda Positions in Mali', http://www.france24.com/en/print.5258512?print=now, 20 October 2011.

——(2012) 'Bomb Injures 15 Police Near Turkey Ruling Party HQ', http://www.reuters.com/article/2012/03/01us-turkey-explosion-idUSTRE8200EI20120301, 1 March 2012.

Richards, A. and Waterbury, J. (1996) *A Political Economy of the Middle East*, 2nd edn (Oxford: Westview Press).

Romaniuk, P. and Chowdhury Fink, N. (2012) *From Input to Impact: Evaluating Terrorism Prevention Programs* (Washington: Center on Global Counterterrorism

Cooperation), http://www.globalct.org/wpcontent/uploads/2012/10/CGCC_
EvaluatingTerrorismPrevention.pdf012.

Sageman, M. (2004) *Understanding Terror Networks* (Philadelphia: University of Pennsylvania Press).

——(2008) *Leaderless Jihad* (Philadelphia: University of Pennsylvania Press).

——(2010) *Leaderless Jihad: Terror Networks in the Twenty First Century* (Philadelphia: University of Pennsylvania Press).

Said, E. (1997) *Covering Islam: How the Media and the Experts Determine How We See the Rest of the World* (London: Vintage).

Sand, N., Gerdzt, M. and Khaw, D. (2012) 'Mental Health-Related Risk Factors For Violence: Using the Evidence to Guide Mental Health Triage Decision Making', *J Psychiatr Ment Health*, 8, 690–701 http://www.ncbi.nlm.nih.gov/pubmed?term=Sands%20N%5BAuthor %5D&cauthor=true&cauthor_uid=23094288, 19 October 2012.

Sandee, R. (2011) 'Islamism, Jihadism and Terrorism in Sudan', Speech to American Enterprise Institute for Public Policy Research, 2007. Web 18 June 2011.

Schmid, A. (2000) 'Towards Joint Political Strategies for De-legitimising the Use of Terrorism', Proceedings of the International Conference on Countering Terrorism Through Enhanced International Cooperation (Courmayeur Mont Blanc, Italy, 22–24 September 2013), pp. 261–2.

—— (2013) 'Radicalisation, Deradicalisation, Counter Radicalisation: A Conceptual Discussion and Literature Review', ICCT Research Paper, http://www.icct.nl/download/file/ICCT-Schmid-Radicalisation-De-Radicalisation-Counter-Radicalisation-March-2013.pdf.

Schrato, T. and Webb, J. (2003) *Understanding Globalisation* (London: SAGE Publications).

Seng, W.K. (2005) 'The Role of Community and Faith Leaders', in A.H. Bin Kader (ed.), *Countering Radicalism: The Next Generation and Challenges Ahead* (Singapore: Taman Bacaan Pemuda Pemudi Melayu Singapura).

—— (2009) 'Debunking Radical Ideology', in A.H. Bin Kader (ed.), *Countering Radicalism: The Next Generation and Challenges Ahead* (Singapore: Taman Bacaan Pemuda Pemudi Melayu Singapura), pp. 23–30.

Shan-Loong, M.L. (1999) 'Shared Values and Their Role in Singapore's Evolving Ideological Framework', in *TRIPODE*, http://marklsl.tripod.com/Writings/values.html, 26 March 1999.

Shanmugam, K. (2009) 'Forward', in A.H. Bin Kader (ed.), *Countering Radicalism: The Next Generation and Challenges Ahead* (Singapore: Taman Bacaan Pemuda Pemudi Melayu Singapura), p. 8.

Sheridan, G. (2011) 'How I Lost Faith in Multiculturalism', in *The Australian*, http://www.theaustralian.com.au/national-affairs/how-i-lost-faith-in-multiculturalism/story-fn59niix-1226031793805, 2 April 2011.

Shinn, D.H. (2009) 'Implications of Terrorism and Counterterrorism in the Horn of Africa', in Sthlm Policy Group (ed.), *Faith, Citizenship, Democracy and Peace in the Horn of Africa* (Lund, Sweden: Lund University) pp. 55–63.

Singaporean Government (1991). White paper on Shared Values. Singapore. https://www.academia.edu/1740666/White_paper_on_shared_values_1991

Soufan Group, The (2013) 'Try to Make Me Go to Rehab: True Power in the Fight Against Violent Extremism', http://soufangroup.com/briefs/details/?Article_Id=529, 3 April 2013.

Southeast European Cooperative Initiative Centre (SECI) (2011) 'Counterterrorism Experience of SECI Member Countries', Anti Terrorism Task Force, Southeast European Cooperative Initiative Centre, Bucharest.

Sozer, M. and M. Server (2011) 'Violent Extremism in Terrorist Organizations: The Case of Turkish Hezbullah', in B. Ihsan, S. Ozeren and M. Sozer (eds) *Multi-Faceted Approach to Radicalisation in Terrorist Organisations*, edited by NATO Science for Peace and Security Series E: Human and Social Dynamic, Vol. 87 (Amsterdam: IOS Press), pp. 23–31.

Speckhard, Anne & Akhmedova, Khapta (2006) 'The New Chechen Jihad: Militant Wahhabism as a Radical Movement and a Source of Suicide Terrorism in Post-War Chechen Society', *Democracy & Security*, 2, pp. 1–53.

Sproat, P.A. (1997) 'An Investigation of the Concept of State Terrorism', a Ph.D. Thesis, Department of Politics, University of Newcastle upon Tyne. http://theses.ncl.ac.uk/dspace/ bitstream/10443/435/1/Sproat97.pdf.

Stern, J. (2010) 'Mind Over Martyr', *Foreign Affairs*, 89, 1, pp. 95–108.

Sudan Tribune (2011) 'Sudan Remains on Terrorism List Despite US Promises', Washington, http://www.sudantribune.com/Sudan-remains-on-terrorism-list,39878, 18 August 2011.

Suder, G. (2004b) 'The Complexity of the Geopolitics Dimension in Risk Assessment for International Business', in G. Suder (ed.), *Terrorism and the International Business Environment* (The Security Business Nexus) (Cheltenham, UK: Edward Elgar), 68–82.

Tahiri, H. (2013) *Community and Radicalization: An Examination of Perceptions, Ideas, Beliefs and Solutions Throughout Australia* (Melbourne: Victoria University).

Taylor, P. (2010) 'Yemen al-Qaeda Link to Guantanamo Bay Prison', *BBC News*, 13 January, http://news.bbc.co.uk/l/hi/programmes/newsnight/8454804.stm.

The European Union Center at the University of Illinois at Urbana-Champaign, Turkey and the European Union (TEUC) (2007) 'A Curriculum Unit on Turkish-EU Relations for Secondary Education, Summer 2007'.

ThinkQuest (2012) 'Communism', http://library.thinkquest.org/12405/19.html. Retrieved 25 April 2012.

Today's Zaman (2011) 'Turkey Embraces Batch of Good News with Budget Surplus, Lower Unemployment', http://www.todayszaman.com/newsDetail_openPrintPage.action?newsId=256877,15 November 2011.

Tong, G.C. (2007) 'After Amman: United to Defeat Terrorism', in A.H. Bin Kader (ed.), *Fighting Terrorism: The Singapore Perspective* (Singapore: Taman Bacaan Pemuda Pemudi Melayu Singapura), pp. 11–20.

—— (2009) 'A National Response Against Terrorism', in A.H. Bin Kader (ed.), *Countering Radicalism: The Next Generation and Challenges Ahead* (Singapore: Taman Bacaan Pemuda Pemudi Melayu Singapura), pp. 15–22.

Trager, E. (2013) 'Egypt's Muslim Brotherhood Set to Prevail Despite Policy Failures', *PolicyWatch* 2049, The Washington Institute, http://www.washingtoninstitute.org/policy-analysis/view/egypts-muslim-brotherhood-set-to-prevail-despite-policy-failures#.UUwFjpmWC4E.mailto, 19 March 2013.

Turner, J. (2010) 'From Cottage Industry to International Organisation: The Evolution of Salafi-Jihadism and the Emergence of the Al Qaeda Ideology', in *Terrorism and Political Violence*, 22, 4, pp. 541–58.

United Nations (2009) *Arab Human Development Report* (New York: United Nations).

United States House of Representatives (2006) 'Police as First Preventers: Local Strategies in the War on Terror', Hearing before the Subcommittee on Prevention of Nuclear and Biological Attack of the Committee on Homeland Security, 109th Congress, 2nd Session, 21 September 2006, Serial No. 105–109. http://bulk.resource.org/gpo.gov/hearings/109h35627.txt.

United States Library of Congress (1990) 'A Country Study: Mauritania, Federal Research Division', http://lcweb2.loc.gov/frd/cs/mrtoc.html.

—— (2011) 'Country Studies: Mauritania', http://www.countrystudies.us/Mauritania/16.htm.

—— (2012a) 'Sudan: Economic Development', http://countrystudies.us/sudan/54.htm.

——(2012b) 'Country Studies: Singapore: World War II', http://countrystudies.us/singapore/8.html. Retrieved 25 April 2012.

Vanley, I.C. (2011) 'The Kurds in Syria and Iraq', in P.G. Kreyenbrook and S. Sperl (eds), *The Kurds: A Contemporary Overview* (London: Routledge).

Vasil, R. (1995) *Asianising Singapore: The PAP's Management of Ethnicity* (Singapore: Heinemann Asia).

Veldhuis, T. (2012) 'Designing Rehabilitation and Reintegration Programmes for Violent Extremist Offenders: A Realist Approach', *ICCT Research Paper*, http://www.icct.nl/download/file/ICCT-Veldhuis-Designing-Rehabilitation-Reintegration-Programme-March-2012.pdf.

Veldhuis, T. and Kessels, E. (2013) 'Thinking before Leaping: The Need for More and Structural Data Analysis in Detention and Rehabilitation of Extremist Offenders', The Hague, bICCT Research Paper, ICCT, http://www.icct.nl/download/file/Veldhuis-Kessels-Thinking-before-Leaping-February-2013.pdf, February 2013.

—— (2013) 'Asking the Right Questions to Optimize Detention and Rehabilitation Policies for Violent Extremist Offenders', *Canadian Diversity*, 9, 4, pp. 33–7.

Vercammen, P., Pearson, M. and Botelho, G. (2013) 'Police: 3 Dead After Ex-cop Vows "War" on Other Police, Their Families', CNN, http://www.cnn.com/2013/02/07/us/lapd-attacks/index.html, 7 February 2013.

Vidino, L. (2010) 'Countering Radicalization in America: Lessons from Europe', United States Institute of Peace, http://www.usip.org/files/resources/SR262%20-%20Countering_ Radicalization_in_America.pdf.

Vidino, L. and Brandon, J. (2012) 'Countering Radicalization in Europe', ICSR, http://icsr.info/wp-content/uploads/2012/12/ICSR-Report-Countering-Radicalization-in-Europe.pdf.

Wade, R. (1990) *Governing the Market: Economic Theory and the Role of Government in East Asian Industrialization* (Princeton: Princeton University Press).

Waller, J. (2011) 'The Terrorist Climate of Sudan: Forecasting Effects of the Southern Secession', in *Small Wars Journal*, http://smallwarsjournal.co/node/11416.

Washington Institute for Near Eastern Policy, The (WINEP) (2011) 'The US Interest in Addressing Germany's PKK Problem', Policy Watch #1887, http://www.washingtoninstitute.org/print.php?template=C05&CID=3438, 28 December 2011.

Weisburd, D., Feucht, T., Hakimi, I., Mock, I.L. and Perry, S. (eds) (2011) *To Protect and Serve: Policing in an Age of Terrorism* (London: Springer, pp. 81–99).

Wikipedia (2012) Singapore, http://en.wikipedia.org/wiki/Singapore, 23 April 2012.

World Analysis (2008) 'Mauritania: Al-Qaeda Unable to Establish Islamic Caliphate in Nouakchott', http://worldanalysis.net/postnuke/html/index. php?name=News&catid =79% topic=5&allstories=1., 31 May 2008.

——(2011) 'AQIM: Al-Qaeda Attacks Mauritania Army Base', http://worldanalysis.net/modules/news/article.php?storyid=1881, 7 June 2011.

World Bank (2011a) 'World Development Indicators' (Washington, DC: World Bank, July 2011).

——(2011b) 'World Bank Development Report' (Washington, DC: World Bank, 2011).

Worth, R., Mazzetti, M. and Shane, S. (2013) 'Drone Strikes' Risks to Get Rare Moment in the Public Eye', in *The New York Times*, http://www.nytimes. com/2013/02/06/   world/middleeast/with-brennan-pick-a-light-on-drone-strikes-hazards.html? pagewanted=all&_r=0&pagewanted=print, 5 February 2013.

Yildiz, S. and Goktepe, F. (2011) 'The Role of Social Projects in Preventing Radicalisation in Terrorist Organisations', in B. Ihsan, O. Suleyman and M. Sozer (eds), *Multi-Faceted Approach to Radicalisation in Terrorist Organisations*, NATO Science for Peace and Security Series E: Human and Social Dynamic, Vol. 87 (Amsterdam: IOS Press), pp. 77–96.

Zammit, A. (2010) 'Who Becomes a Jihadist in Australia?' Researcher, Global Terrorism Research Centre, Monash University, http://arts.monash.edu.au/ radicalisation/conferences-and-events/conference-2010/ – downloads/who-jihadist-australia-az.pdfparative analysis.

——(2012) 'The Holsworthy Barracks Plot: A Case Study of an Al-Shabab Support Network in Australia', Combating Terrorism Centre at West Point, http:// www.ctc.usma.edu/   posts/the-holsworthy-barracks-plot-a-case-study-of-an-al-shabab-support-network-in-australia, 21 June 2012.

Zelin, A. (2013) 'Tunisia's Post-Revolution Blues', in *The Washington Institute*, Also available in Foreign Affairs, http://www.washingtoninstitute.org/ policy-analysis/view/tunisias-post-revolution-blues#.UUwB_FdxaMA.mailto, 6 March 2013.

Zwartz, B. (2012) 'Local Muslim Leaders Condemn Violence', in *The Age*, http:// www.theage.com.au/action/printArticle?id=3642521, 18 September 2012.

Index

9/11 attacks, 1, 266*n*8
    counterterrorism, 260
    home-grown events following, 54
    image of Muslims and Islam after,
        62–3
    mosque attacks, 62
    radicalization, 9, 24
    Singapore after, 168
    US-led initiatives after, 120–1
    World Trade Center, 2
AAM (*Ansar Allah al-Murabiteen*), 118
Abdulhamid II (Sultan), 221–2
ACG (Interagency–After Care Group),
    Singapore, 162–3
aerial bombardment, drone attacks,
    3–4, 25–6, 48
Afghanistan
    military operations, 215
    occupation of, 44, 259
    war on terror, 1–2, 119
Ali Pasha, Mohammed, 176
AlMoustakbal Association, 30, 130–2
al-Qaeda, 96
    Ansar radical fighters, 1
    Australia, 60–1
    drone attacks against, 26
    impact of media, 64
    Mauritania, 96, 113, 116, 118–21,
        126, 132–4, 136, 274*n*39
    Post-release environment, 40, 134
    Singapore, 138, 144, 154
    Sudan, 174, 186–92, 194–6
    Turkey, 219, 232, 234
    Yemen, 17
Anglo-Egyptian Condominium
    (1899–1956), Sudan, 175, 177,
    178–81, 190
Ankara Agreement, 236
Ansaru Islam, 1, 2, 17
ANZUS Treaty, 61, 266*n*8
AQMI (Islamic Land of North
    America), 118, 120
Arab Spring, 1, 16, 135, 261

Assimilation, Australia, 55–6
Association Agreement, Turkey, 236
Ataturk, Kamel, 223, 224
Australia, 1, 6, 11, 53–5, 74–5, 259
    assimilation, 55–6
    counter radicalization measures,
        88–91
    de-radicalization efforts, 80–7
    domestic violence, 34, 70, 75
    evaluation of efforts, 91–5
    family rehabilitation, 37, 83
    federal system, 268*n*2
    Gouleburn high-security prison, 38,
        40, 82–7, 92, 268*n*3
    Howard changing foreign policy,
        60–6
    immigration policy, 55–60
    improvisation/discretionary
        program, 39–40
    Lebanese link, 66–74
    multiculturalism, 53, 55–60
    neo-jihadists, 18, 34, 36, 38, 54–5,
        66, 68–70, 77–8, 83, 93
    Operation Neath, 38, 54, 65, 67,
        78–9, 81, 95
    Operation Pendennis, 38, 54, 65–7,
        78–9, 88, 95, 266*n*10
    participation and support of war on
        terror, 259, 266*n*7
    political system, 42
    post-care/release program, 40
    psychological rehabilitation, 34–5
    religious rehabilitation, 29, 31, 83
    response to emergence of violent
        extremism (VEm), 76–80
    social rehabilitation, 36, 37
Australian Federal Police (AFP), 95,
    266*n*10
Australian Sunni Lebanese
    community, 18, 23, 36, 55–8,
    65–7, 69, 71–4, 77, 90, 265*n*5,
    267*n*14, 267*n*16
al-Bashir, Issam, 207, 211

al-Bashir, Omar, 184–6, 191, 195, 210

Berbers, Mauritania, 99, 103, 269*n*6,
    270*n*14, 270*n*7
bin Laden, Osama, 2, 96, 175, 195
    arrival of, 186–92
    statements by, 65
    Sudan, 175, 186–8, 195, 212
Boko Haram, Nigeria, 2, 17
Boucek, Christopher, 13, 33
Buddhists, 8, 28, 64, 72, 149
Bush (George W.) administration, 25,
    61, 189, 212

Caliphate, 154, 158, 217, 218, 219, 223
Carr, Bob, 59
CDCs (Community Development
    Councils), 150
Changuet Country, 0Mauritania, 98,
    269*n*2–3
Christianity, 8, 63, 148, 183
Citizenship Law 1959, Singapore, 158
civil society
    Mauritania, 103, 128–33
    role of imams, 129–30
    source of soft power, 22–3
civil war, 17, 48
    Lebanon, 56
    Mauritania, 99, 103
    Sudan, 174, 178, 181–4, 187,
        189–91, 210–11, 275*n*1
    Turkey, 235
Clinton administration, 188
Common Sahara Regional
    Organization, 104, 271*n*20
Commonwealth Government
    Counter-Terrorism White Paper
    (2010), 94
Communism, Singapore, 140–4,
    274–5*n*4
Community Outreach Program
    (COR), 88
Community Partnership Program, 90
community policing (CP), 49, 59, 74,
    241, 250, 255, 262
Constitution
    Australia, 57
    Mauritania, 105, 114, 271*n*18
    Singapore, 154
    Sudan, 182–3

Turkey, 224, 226, 240, 277*n*3
Copenhagen Summit of European
    Council, 239, 240
counter-de-rad programs, 5–7, 13–14,
    49–52, 254–8
    assessment and evaluation, 259–60,
        263
    civil society as source of soft power,
        22–3
    conditions conducive to success/
        failure of, 14–17
    development and terrorism, 17–18
    education, 31–3
    evaluating impact and
        effectiveness, 91–5
    family rehabilitation, 37–9
    improvisation/discretionary
        program, 39–40
    international framework for
        countering violent extremism
        (IFCVE), 41–8
    literature, 260–1
    macroeconomic and political
        factors, 17–18
    micro-components of successful,
        26–33
    post-care/release, 40–1
    prison radicalization, 19–22
    psychological rehabilitation, 34–5
    research methodology, 11–12
    role of global environment, 23–6
    Singapore, 166–73
    social rehabilitation, 36–7
    vocational training, 31–3
counter-radicalization, 3, 10
    Australian measures, 88–91
    role of civil society in Mauritania,
        128–33
counterterrorism strategy (CTS)
    economic dimension of Turkey's,
        244–6
    political dimension of Turkey's,
        239–40
    social and cultural dimension of
        Turkey's, 241–4
    Sudan, 193, 202
    Turkey, 219, 235–9, 241, 246–51
CPA (Comprehensive Peace
    Agreement), 174, 189, 196, 211–12
Cronula Riots 2005, 59

cultural identity, Australia, 265*n*3

Darfur, civil war, 178, 190–1, 199,
   211–12, 214, 217, 276*n*2, 276*n*7
de-Qaedization, Sudan, 194–6
de-radicalization, 3, 255–8
   Australia's efforts, 80–7
   definition, 10–11
   Jemaah Islamiyah (JI) members,
      154–66
   Mauritania, 120–8
   role of inducements in, 127–8
   Sudan, 192–209, 196–200
DI (Darul Islam), 154
discretionary program, counter-
   de-rad, 39–40
domestic violence, Australia, 34, 70, 75
DP (Democratic Party), Turkey, 226, 227
drone attacks, 3–4, 25–6, 48

economics
   terrorism and repression in
      Mauritania, 108–13
   Turkish performance, 244–6
empowering communities, counter-
   de-rad programs, 45–6
Erdogan, Recep Tayyip, 232
Esposito, John, 63, 89

family rehabilitation, counter-de rad
   programs, 37–9, 83
First World War, 219, 222
Foreign and Trade Policy White Paper
   (1997), 53
Fraser, Malcolm, 56, 69

al-Gaddafi, Muammar, 15, 16
Garang, John, 189
GDP (gross domestic product)
   Mauritania, 113, 272*n*31
   Singapore, 147
   Sudan, 211
   Turkey, 235
global environment, role in counter
   radicalization, 23–6
global war on terror, 121, 133, 212, *see
   also* war on terror
Golose, Petrus, 13, 27
Gouleburn high-security prison,
   Australia, 38, 40, 82–7, 92, 268*n*3

Grosscup, Beau, 25
GSPC (Salafi Group for Preaching and
   Fighting), 118, 273*n*36
GTReC (Global Terrorism Research
   Centre), 6, 18, 67
Guantánamo Bay, 33, 37

Haledon Street Festival, 90
Harrison, John, 170
HC (Harmony Center), 164–5
HDB (Housing and Development
   Board), 150, 163
hearts and minds, winning, 4, 11,
   20, 45, 156, 213, 239–41, 258–9,
   263
Hizb Al-Nahda (Renaissance Party),
   114–15, 273*n*32
Howard, John, 55, 60–6, 67, 80

ICDS (International Centre for *Dawa*
   Studies), 30, 202–5, 207
identity crisis, Singapore, 144–9
IFCVE (international framework for
   countering violent extremism),
   41–8, 50–1
   assessment and evaluation, 46–8, 49
   empowered communities, 45–6
   lack of peace, 44
   state strength, 41–4
Imam Council, 90, 268*n*9
imams, role in countering radical
   ideology, 129–130
IMF (International Monetary Fund),
   194, 229, 244
immigration policy, Australia, 55–60
improvisation program, counter-
   de-rad, 39–40
Internet, 64, 74, 91, 132, 136, 164, 167,
   207
IPI (International Peace Institute), 13
Iraq, 1, 24, 26, 54, 89, 96, 121, 168,
   193, 213, 230
   invasion/occupation of, 4, 17, 44,
      61–2, 66, 74, 119, 133, 259–60
   jihadi activities, 195, 197, 198, 210
   military operations, 64, 65, 215
IRM (Islamic Republic of Mauritania),
   105, 271*n*18
ISA (Internal Security Act), 138, 163,
   167, 169

ISD (Internal Security Department),
Singapore, 166–7, 169, 170
Islamic Council of Victoria (ICV), 80–1
Islamic fundamentalism, rise in
Singapore, 149–53
Islamic ideology, 75, 159, 223
Islamic Jihad (IJ), 14–16
Islamic Salvation Army (Algerian),
11, 15
Islamic Salvation Front, 15
Islamization, Sudan, 184–6
ISM (Sudanese Islamic Movement), 192

JDP (Justice and Development Party),
Turkey, 239, 244, 245
Jews, 8, 28, 64, 72, 82, 256
JHA (*Jamaat al-Hal Wal Agid*), 101,
102, 103
JI (Jemaah Islamiyah), 35, 60, 138,
154–63
jihadi activities, level of radicalization,
217
JO (al-Jihad Organization), 14–16
JP (Justice Party), Turkey, 227, 228

Karabell, Zachary, 28
Karzai, Hamid, 3
Kruglanski, Arie, 47
Kurdish nationalism, Turkey, 223–225
Kurdish rebellion, Turkey, 218,
219–223, 225
Kurdish Workers' Party (PKK), 230–4,
245–7, 249–50, 277n4–5, 278n10

Lebanese Concession Act, 56
Lebanese link, Australia, 66–74
Lecture and Open Discussion Forum
(LoD), 29, 89
Lee Hsein Long, 164
Lee Kuan Yew, 145, 162, 275n9
Lentini, Peter, 66, 266n10
Liaison Communities (LC), 88, 90
Liberal Party (Australia), 56
Libya, assassination of Stevens, 1
Libyan Islamic Fighting Group (LIFG),
15, 16

MA (*AlMoustakbal* Association), 30,
130–2

macroeconomic factors, counter-
de-rad programs, 17–18
mahadir, countering radical ideology,
29, 30, 129–31
mahdir, 29, 30
Mahdist Movement, 175–7, 181,
183
Malaysia, 44, 45, 87
Maraboutoun Empire, 98–100, 102,
270n13, 270n8
Mauritania, 6, 11, 12, 96–7
civil war, 99, 103
from counter-terrorism to
de-radicalization, 120–8
historical background, 98–104
improvisation/discretionary
program, 39
link between terrorism, economics
and political repression, 108–13
nation building, 104–8
political elite, 271n20
political independence, 104–8
programs refuting violent
ideology, 45
regional war against al-Qaeda, 136
religious rehabilitation, 29–30
rise of Islamic current, 113–16
rise of violent radical ideology, 97
role of civil society in counter
radicalization, 103, 128–33
role of inducements in, 127–8
al-Shabab, 114
social rehabilitation, 36
'soft' measures, 133–7
state-manufactured terrorism,
117–20
violent extremism (VEm), 104–8
Mauritanian Regroupment Party, 105,
271n20
media bias, radicalization, 64, 72
Mehdi rebellion, Sudan, 175–176
MENA (Middle East and North Africa),
210, 228, 252, 272n27
Middle East, 20, 51, 61, 62, 219, 244
and North Africa, 210, 228, 252,
272n27
Miliband, David, 3
MLP (Motherland Party), Turkey, 229,
250, 277n3

Mohammad, Mahathir, 44
Monash University, Global Terrorism
  Research Centre, 6, 18, 67
Moral Education Programme, 148
moral outrage, 24, 44
MRA (Ministry of Religious Affairs),
  Mauritania, 123–4
Mubarak, Hosni, 16, 188, 194
Muhammad, Prophet, 9, 28, 63, 99
MUIS (Islamic Religious Council in
  Singapore), 29, 36, 158, 164–6,
  275*n*7
multiculturalism, Australia, 53, 55–60,
  265*n*3
Muntada al-Nahda wal-tawasl al-Hadarl
  (Renaissance and Continuation
  of Civilization Forum), 30, 202,
  277*n*11
Muslim Brotherhood, 129, 184, 186,
  192, 198, 232, 273*n*33
Muslim-majority states, 4–7, 13, 27,
  41, 87, 125, 140, 162, 219, 234,
  251, 254, 258, 263
Muslim Malays, 140, 155, 166
Muslim-minority states, 6–7, 27, 38,
  41, 55, 139, 172, 258–9
Muslims, suspect communities, 23, 43

National Action Party, 227, 228
National Education Programme, 149
nation building
  Australian multiculturalism, 56
  Mauritania, 104–8
  Singapore, 149
Neath, Operation, 38, 54, 65, 67,
  78–9, 81, 95
neo-jihadists, Australian, 18, 34, 36,
  38, 54–5, 66, 68–70, 77–8, 83, 93
NIF (National Islamic Front), 184–6,
  188, 192, 198, 212
Nigeria, 2, 17, 273*n*35
Nimeiri, Jafaar an, 182–4, 185
NSID (National Security and
  Intelligence Department), 193,
  197, 199, 201, 203, 206
Nuemann, Peter, 9

Ocalan, Abdullah, 230, 232
Omar, Mullah, 15, 96

Operation Neath, 38, 54, 65, 67, 78–9,
  81, 95
Operation Pendennis, 38, 54, 65–7,
  78–9, 88, 95, 266*n*10
organized terrorism, rehabilitating
  radicals, 1–5
Ottoman Empire, Turkey, 218, 220–5,
  230, 277*n*1
Ottoman law, Sudan, 178
Ould Abdel Aziz, Mohamed, 113, 117,
  121, 123, 133, 135–6, 274*n*39
Ould Daddah, Mokhtar, 105–6,
  108–15, 272*n*25, 272*n*29–30,
  273*n*32
Ould Haidalla, Mohamed Khouna,
  113–14, 117, 273*n*32
Ould Hurmah, Ahmad, 107–8,
  272*n*23
Ould Taya, Maaouya, 29, 113–14,
  117–21, 123, 128–31, 133, 259,
  273*n*36
Ould Vall, Ely (Mohamed), 121–4,
  132–3, 135
Ozal, Turgut, 229, 230, 235, 277*n*3

PAIC (Popular Arab and Islamic
  Conference), 186
Pakistan, 1–3, 6, 11, 15, 17, 25–6, 96,
  187, 198
pan-Islamic ideology, 186, 222, 222–4,
  225, 230
Pendennis, Operation, 38, 54, 65–7,
  78–9, 88, 95, 266*n*10
PERGAS (The Singapore Institute
  Scholars and Religious Teachers
  Association), 158
PIRA (Provisional Irish Republican
  Army), 19
PKK (Partia Karkare Kurdistan),
  230–4, 245–7, 249–50, 277*n*4–5,
  278*n*10
Polisario Front, 111, 114
political independence, Mauritania,
  104–8
politics, counter-de-rad programs,
  17–18
POL-NET software, 237, 238, 241, 249
Post-care/release program, counter-
  de-rad, 40–1

prison radicalization, 19–22, 81–2, 84,
86–8
counter-de-rad programs, 19–22,
255–6
dialogue with radical prisoners,
134–6
Goulburn high-security, 38, 40,
82–7, 92, 268n3
role of inducements in
Mauritanian, 127–8
psychological rehabilitation,
counter-de rad programs, 34–5
Public Housing Policy (PHP),
Singapore, 153

Quran, 28, 31, 100, 118, 132, 159,
193, 198, 261
Quranic schools, 30, 118, 131, 192
Quran Memorizing Union, 206

Racial Harmony Day, Singapore, 150
radical Islamism, 116, 159, 210
radicalization, 6–7
jihadi activities, 217
media impact on, 64, 72
prisoners, 19–22, 81–2, 84, 86–8
treating as process, 7
radicals, rehabilitating, 1–5
RCC (Revolutionary Command
Council), 182, 183
RCCF (Renaissance and Continuation
of Civilizations Forum), 30, 202,
205–9, 277n11
rehabilitation
counter-de-rad programs, 27–31
radicals, 1–5
Sudan, 192–209
Religious Knowledge Programme,
Singapore, 148–9, 152
religious rehabilitation, counter-
de-rad programs, 27–31, 83, 87
repression, 42, 50–1, 77, 118, 120
Arab Spring, 261
de-radicalization program, 196
political, 133
Sudan, 213, 215
terrorism, economics and political,
in Mauritania, 108–13
Turkey, 236, 247

research methodology, 11–12
Rice, Condoleezza, 61
Roche, Jack, 60, 266n6
RPP (Republican People's Party),
Turkey, 223–8
RRG (Religious Rehabilitation Group),
158–62
RRP (Religious Rehabilitation
Program), 29, 159, 161, 163, 167,
169–70
RSS (Republic of Southern Sudan), 211

Said, Edward, 63
salafism, 2, 192, 193
Salafists, 1–2, 17, 71, 99–100, 128,
192, 198–9
Saudia Arabia
education and vocational training,
33
psychological rehabilitation, 34–5
religious rehabilitation, 27
social rehabilitation, 36
Saudi Arabia, 87
de-radicalization program, 44
improvisation/discretionary
program, 39
post-care/release program, 40–1
programs refuting violent ideology,
45
religious rehabilitation, 27
social rehabilitation, 36–7
Scientific Salafism (*al-Salafiyah
al-Ilmeyah*), 192, 193, 214
SCLG (Social Community Liaison
Group), 90
SCMSSU (Singapore Chinese Middle
School Students' Union), 274–5n4
Second World War, *see* World War II
al-Shabab
Mauritania, 114
Somalia, 2, 17, 67
Shared Value Programme (SVP),
Singapore, 149–52, 168–9
Singapore, 6, 11, 138–9, 172–3
Communist threat, 140–4
crisis of identity, 144–9
evolution of state, 140–4
failure of shared values, 149–53
family rehabilitation, 39

impact of counter-de-rad efforts, 166–72, 262–3
racial tension, chaos and insecurity, 140–4
religious rehabilitation, 29
rise of Islamic fundamentalism, 149–53
social rehabilitation, 36
White Paper, 149, 151
Social Programme, Singapore, 161–2
social rehabilitation, counter-de rad programs, 36–7
SODES (Social Support Programme), Turkey, 245, 278n14
soft measures
Australia, 76, 80, 92, 94
civil society as soft power source, 22–3
Counter-de-Rad programs, 13–14
Mauritania, 121, 133–7
Sudan's, 196, 209–13
Turkey, 246–51
Somalia, 2, 17, 25–6, 54, 67, 96, 188, 193, 197, 209–11, 213, 215
Soufan Group, 21, 22
Sozer, M. Alper, 243, 246
Sproat, Peter, 24
SSU (Sudan Socialist Union), 183
START (Study of Terrorism and Responses to Terrorism), 47
Stern, Jessica, 18
Stevens, Christopher, 1
Strategic Terror (Grosscup), 25
Sudan, 6, 11, 12, 174–5, 213–15
al-Qaedization of, 186–92
Anglo-Egyptian Condominium (1899–1956), 178–81
background, 175–8
before independence, 175–8
civil war, 174, 178, 181–4, 187, 189–91, 210–11, 275n1
counterterrorism procedures, 202, 261
de-Qaedization, 194–6
de-radicalization, 216
de-radicalization program, 196–200
educational level of participants in de-radicalization, 216
gauging 'soft' measures, 209–13

improvisation/discretionary program, 39
International Centre for Dawa Studies (ICDS), 202–5
Islamization under al-Bashir and al-Turabi, 184–6
al-Medhi rebellion, 175–6
Osama bin Laden, 186–8, 195, 212
participant age in de-radicalization, 216
post dialogue *tawfiq* procedures, 200–202
post-independence, 181–6
programs refuting violent ideology, 45
religious rehabilitation, 30–1
Renaissance and Continuation of Civilizations Forum (RCCF), 205–9
social rehabilitation, 36
suicide terrorism, 24–6
Sunnah Al-Ansar Group, 192, 198
suspect communities, Muslims, 23, 43
Syria, 1, 17, 42, 55, 89, 91, 195, 230, 277n5

takfir (excommunication), 131, 192–3, 199, 208–9, 217
Taliban, Afghanistan and Pakistan, 1–2
Tamil Tigers, 51, 256
Tampa (Norwegian cargo ship), 61, 266n7
Tanzimat (Ottoman reforms), Turkey, 220–1
tawfiq (facilitation or coordination), 200–202
terrorism
definitions and terminologies, 7–11
political, in Mauritania, 108–13
problem in Mauritania, 122–7
state-manufactured, in Mauritania, 117–20
suicide, 24–6
TNP (Turkish National Police), 235–9, 241–3, 245, 247, 248, 249, 250, 278n13, 278n9
TSCTI (Trans–Sahara Counter Terrorism Initiative), 120–1, 273n36

al-Turabi, Hassan, 184–6, 188, 195, 210
Turkey, 6, 11, 12, 218–19, 25153
  civil war, 235
  counterterrorism strategy (CTS), 235–9, 262
  economic dimension of CTS, 244–6
  emergence of Turkish republic, 223–5
  evolution of violent extremism (VEm) in, 219–29
  fragmentation of Turkish politics, 225–9
  historical background, 219–29
  improvisation/discretionary program, 39
  Kurdish nationalism, 223–5
  Kurdish uprisings in pre-1923 republican period, 219–23
  move to democratization, 225–9
  philosophy for 'winning hearts and minds', 239–40
  re-emergence of Kurdish challenge in leftist form, 229–34
  social and cultural dimension of CTS, 241–4
  social rehabilitation, 36–7
Turkish Hezbollah (TH), 232–4, 251, 277n6

United Nations Member States, Counter-de-Rad programs, 6
United States, drone strikes, 3–4, 25–6, 48

Value Family ('Deger Aile'), 242, 243
Varghese, Peter, 65
Vietnam War, 56, 145, 265n1, 275n6
Violent Extremism (VEm), 76
  Australia's response to emergence of, 76–80

countering Islamic, in Singapore, 154–66
definition, 9–10
evolution of VEm in Turkey, 219–29
Mauritania, 104–8, 133–4
national problem in Singapore, 157
phenomenon of terrorism, 2–3
research methodology, 11–12
vocational training, counter-de-rad programs, 31–3

war on terror, 1, 3–4, 13, 66
  Bush announcement of, 61–2
  collaboration with Western powers, 118
  global, 121, 133, 212
  impact on role of police, 77
  participation and support, 259, 266n7
  Singapore, 168
  Sudan as US partner in, 196
White Paper, Singapore, 149, 151
'winning hearts and minds,' 4, 11, 20, 45, 156, 213, 239–40, 241, 258–9, 263
Wong Kan Seng, 156, 158
Working Group on Radicalization and Extremism, 23, 265n1
World Bank, 111, 147, 229, 244
World War I, 219, 222
World War II, 43, 56, 140, 141, 179, 180, 189, 226, 236, 277–8n8

Yayla, Ahmet, 235, 237, 239, 247, 278n11
Yemen, 1, 3–5, 11, 15–17, 25–6, 31, 33, 40, 42, 144, 160, 196, 215, 221, 261
al-Yosuf, Abdulhay, 276n7

al-Zawahiri, Ayman, 65, 212